CONFORMITY AND CONFLICT

CONFORMITY AND CONFLICT

Readings in cultural anthropology

SIXTH EDITION

Edited by
JAMES P. SPRADLEY
DAVID W. McCURDY

Macalester College

Little, Brown and Company
Boston   Toronto

Library of Congress Cataloging-in-Publication Data

Conformity and conflict.

Includes bibliographical references.
1. Ethnology.   2. Social history.   I. Spradley,
James P.   II. McCurdy, David W.
GN325.C69   1986   306   86–20984
ISBN 0–316–80776–1

Library of Congress Catalog Card No. 86–20984

ISBN 0-316-80776-1

9 8 7 6 5 4 3 2 1

MV

Published simultaneously in Canada
by Little, Brown & Company (Canada) Limited

Printed in the United States of America

To Barbara Spradley and Carolyn McCurdy

Preface

Cultural anthropology has a twofold mission: to understand other cultures and to communicate that understanding. Seventeen years ago, in preparing the first edition of this book, we sought to make communication easier and more enjoyable for teachers and students alike. We focused on the twin themes stated in the title—conformity, or order, and conflict, or change—while organizing selections into sections based on traditional topics. We balanced the coverage of cultures between non-Western and Western (including American) so students could make their own cultural comparisons and see the relation between anthropology and their lives. We searched extensively for scholarly articles written with insight and clarity. Students and teachers in hundreds of colleges and universities responded enthusiastically to our efforts, and a pattern was set that carried through four subsequent editions.

This new sixth edition retains the features of earlier editions: the focus on themes, the coverage of Western cultures, and the combination of professionalism and readability in the selections. As in previous editions, we have revamped topics and added or subtracted selections in response to the suggestions of instructors and students across the country. We have also expanded section introductions to include the definition of basic anthropological concepts and added review questions after each article. A complementary instructor's manual, which offers abstracts of each selection along with true or false and multiple choice questions, is available from the publisher to instructors requesting it on school letterhead.

Many people have made suggestions and contributed toward this edition of *Conformity and Conflict*. In particular we would like to express appreciation to Bradford Gray, Scott Huler, Virginia Shine, Kay Crawford, Susan Dege, Deborah Elliston, Elizabeth Olson, Denee Williams, and the many instructors and students whose suggestions have guided us.

Contents

III   *Language and communication*

Asking for a drink at Brady's bar is a complex speech event composed
of several speech acts and rituals, each used to display verbal skill and
to maintain male values and solidarity.

The frown, the smile, the dilated pupil, the distance at which we
converse, and other forms of nonverbal behavior all serve to convey
meaning in social encounters.

The Tchikrin of Brazil signal their social condition by the length of
their hair, the ornaments they wear, and the colors painted on their
bodies.

The women's veil stands for everything from personal protection to
female honor in Mediterranean societies.

IV   *Kinship and family*

Kin relationships based on the sharing of vital substances expand the
anthropologist's definition of kinship.

Once thought to be a universal rule governing human mating and
marriage, the incest taboo is disappearing in Western society, leading
to possible new forms of the family and kinship ties.

In the past, sororities served to maintain class distinctions by limiting
a college woman's access to males of acceptable rank.

Melanesian political structure, based on the personal influence of a
"big-man," cannot reach the size and complexity of the Polynesian
system that ascribed the right of authority over a large pyramid of
kinship groups to a chief.

Like Papuan big-men, congressmen use "pork" and "kin" (staff) in a
long process to gain power.

A New Guinea Highlander unconsciously treats the anxiety caused by
his wife's continuing illness with increasingly strong magic.

American baseball players employ magical practices as they try to
ensure successful performance.

The celebration of Memorial Day in America symbolizes unity in the
face of the competing interests and values of American subgroups.

The Rarámuri of Mexico have transformed the Christian god, devil,
and Easter to fit their own religious values on balance and harmony.

The introduction of a hatchet-sized steel axe changes Australian
aborigines' authority structure, economic exchange, and view of the
meaning of life itself.

Cargo cults are religious revitalization movements based on the belief
that ancestors will return and bring Western goods, or "cargo," with
them; these cults have swept New Guinea and its adjacent islands in
response to disorientation caused by Western influence.

The world market for cocaine robs Bolivian villages of their men and
causes problems of health, nutrition, transportation, and family.

As *patron* of a Peruvian *hacienda*, Alan Holmberg and a team of
anthropologists from Cornell University restructure the feudal
community into a democratic cooperative.

CONFORMITY AND CONFLICT

I

Culture and the contemporary world

Many students associate cultural anthropology with the study of primitive peoples. They picture the anthropologist as that slightly peculiar person who, dressed in khaki shorts and pith helmet, lives among some exotic tribe in order to record the group's bizarre and not altogether pleasant customs. Like most stereotypes, this one is not completely true but it does reflect anthropology's traditional interest in describing the culture of less complex societies. In the last century, when anthropology became a recognized discipline, its members collected and analyzed the growing numbers of reports on non-Western peoples by missionaries, travelers, and colonial administrators. This tradition continued into the twentieth century, although the collection of data was refined by actual fieldwork. Impressed by the variety of human behavior, anthropologists sought to record these cultures that were vanishing before the onslaught of Western civilization. Such studies continue among remote groups, and reports of this research are regularly found in professional journals.

During recent decades, however, anthropologists have developed wider interests. As primitive groups have been obliterated or assimilated, anthropologists have increasingly studied subcultures within more complex societies. Certainly World War II and the Cold War stimulated this trend. The United States government employed anthropologists to describe societies in whose territories we fought. The Cold War years, marked by competition with the Russians for influence in developing nations, led to studies of peasant life styles and culture change.

Today, however, our position in the world has changed. Americans are less welcome in developing nations. Concurrently, problems in our own country have multiplied and taken the center stage of national concern. It is not surprising that anthropologists have extended their attention to subcultures within our own society.

But what can anthropology contribute to an understanding of American life? After all, other social scientists have been doing research in this country for years. Is there anything special about anthropology? In many ways the answer to this question is no. The various social sciences often share the same interests. Yet, as a result of their intensive cross-culture experience, anthropologists have developed a unique perspective on the nature and the significance of *culture*. This view has emerged from over a century of fieldwork among populations whose behavior was dramatically different from the anthropologists' own. Why, for example, did Iroquois women participate with apparent relish in the gruesome torture of prisoners? How could Bhil tribesmen put chili powder in the eyes of witches, blindfold them, and swing them over a smoky fire by their feet? What possessed Kwakiutl chiefs to destroy their wealth publicly at potlatch ceremonies? Why did Rajput widows cast themselves upon their husbands' funeral pyres? Why did Nagas engage in raids to acquire human heads? In every case, anthropologists were impressed by the fact that this "bizarre" behavior was intentional and meaningful to the participants. Bhils wanted to swing witches; to them it was appropriate. Kwakiutl chiefs made careful investments to increase the wealth they destroyed. These acts were planned; people had a notion of what they were going to do before they did it, and others shared their expectations.

CULTURE

The acquired knowledge that people use to interpret their world and generate social behavior is called *culture*. Culture is not behavior itself, but the knowledge used to construct and understand behavior. It is learned as children grow up in society and discover how their parents, and others around them, interpret the world. In our society we learn to distinguish objects such as cars, windows, houses, children, and food; to recognize attributes like sharp, hot, beautiful, and humid;

to classify and perform different kinds of acts; to evaluate what is good and bad and to judge when an unusual action is appropriate or inappropriate. How often have you heard parents explain something about life to a child? Why do you think children are forever asking why? During socialization children learn a culture, and because they learn it from others, they share it with others, a fact that makes human social existence possible.

✗ Culture is thus the system of knowledge by which people design their own actions and interpret the behavior of others. It tells an American that eating with one's mouth closed is proper, while an Indian knows that to be polite one must chew with one's mouth open. There is nothing preordained about culture categories; they are arbitrary. The same act can have different meanings in various cultures. For example, when adolescent Hindu boys walk holding hands, it signifies friendship, while to Americans the same act may suggest homosexuality. This arbitrariness is particularly important to remember if we are to understand our own complex society. We tend to think that the norms we follow represent the "natural" way human beings do things. Those who behave otherwise are judged morally wrong. This viewpoint is *ethnocentric*, which means that people think their own culture represents the best, or at least the most appropriate, way for human beings to live.

Although in our complex society we share many cultural norms with everyone, each of us belongs to a number of groups possessing exclusive cultural knowledge. We share some categories and plans with family members alone. And our occupational group, ethnic group, voluntary society, and age group each has its distinctive culture. Instead of assuming that another's behavior is reasonable to him, that it is motivated by a different set of cultural norms, we frequently assume that he has intentionally violated accepted conventions. In their attempt to build bridges of understanding across cultural barriers, anthropologists have identified the universality of ethnocentrism many years ago. The study of subcultures in our own society is another attempt to further mutual understanding, as some of the selections in this volume indicate.

How do anthropologists discover and map another culture? Are their methods applicable in the United States? Typically anthropologists live among the people of the society that interests them. They learn the culture by observing, asking questions, and participating in daily activities — a process resembling childhood socialization or enculturation. Obviously, the anthropologist cannot become a child, and must try to learn the norms in a strange group despite his or her foreign appearance and advanced age. Those who study in the United States have followed a similar procedure.

More than anything else, the study of culture separates anthropologists from other social scientists. Other scholars do not ignore culture; they assume their subjects have it, but their main interest is to account for human behavior by plotting correlations among variables. Some social scientists have explained the rise in the American divorce rate as a function of industrialization; this hypothesis can be tested by seeing if higher divorce rates are associated with industrialization and mobility. Anthropologists share a concern for this kind of explanation; for example, many have employed the Human Relations Area Files, a collection of ethnographies describing several hundred societies, as data for testing more general hypotheses. Almost every anthropologist starts with an *ethnography*, the description of a particular culture, and such studies are required to understand the complexity within American society.

As anthropologists have encountered, studied, and compared the world's societies, they have learned more about the concept of culture itself. As we have seen, culture is the knowledge people use to generate behavior, not behavior itself; it is arbitrary, learned, and shared. In addition, culture is adaptive. Human beings cope with their natural and social environment by means of their traditional knowledge. Culture allows for rapid adaptation because it is flexible and permits the invention of new strategies — although change often appears to be painfully slow to those who are in a hurry for it. By the same token, the adaptive nature of culture accounts for the enormous variety of the world's distinct societies.

Culture is a system of interrelated parts. If Americans were to give up automobiles, then other modes of travel, places for courtship, marks of status, and sources of income would have to be found. Culture meets personal needs; through it, people seek security and a sense of control over experience. Indeed, every tradition includes ways to cure the sick, to prepare for the unexpected, and to support the individual. In a complex society with many ways of life in contact with each other, change is persistent. It may be illusion to think that people can control the course of change, or can modify the resulting culture conflict. But if we can understand human cultures — including our own — the illusion may become reality.

CULTURE AND VALUES

It is easy for people to feel that their own way of life is natural and God-given. One's culture is not like a suit of clothing that can be discarded easily or exchanged for each new life style that comes along. It is rather like a security blanket, and though to some it may appear worn and tattered, outmoded and ridiculous, it has great meaning to its owner. Although there are many reasons for this fact, one of the most important is the value-laden nature of what we learn as members of society. Whether it is acquired in a tribal band, a peasant village, or an urban neighborhood, each culture is like a giant iceberg. Beneath the surface of rules, norms, and behavior patterns there is a system of values. Some of these premises are easily stated by members of a society, while others are outside their awareness. Because many difficulties in the modern world involve values, we must examine this concept in some detail.

A value is an arbitrary conception of what is *desirable* in human experience. During socialization all children are exposed to a constant barrage of evaluations — the arbitrary "rating system" of their culture. Nearly everything they learn is labeled in terms of its desirability. The value attached to each bit of information may result from the pain of a hot stove, the look of disapproval from a parent, the smile of appreciation from a teacher, or some specific verbal instruction. When parents tell a child, "You should go to college and get a good education," they are expressing a value. Those who do not conform to society's rating system are identified with derogatory labels or are punished in a more severe way. When a Tlingit Indian says to his nephew, "You should marry your father's sister," he is expressing one of the core values of his culture. When a young couple saves income for future emergencies, they are conforming to the American value that the future is more important than the present. When a tramp urinates in an alley, he is violating the value attached to privacy. All these concepts of what is desirable combine cognitive and affective meanings. Individuals internalize their ideas about right and wrong, good and bad, and invest them with strong feelings.

Why do values constitute an inevitable part of all human experience? That human potential is at odds with the requirements of social life is well known. Behavior within the realm of possibility is often outside the realm of necessity. There are numerous ways to resolve the conflict between what people *can do* by themselves, and what they *must do* as members of society. It is a popular notion that prisons and other correctional institutions are the primary means by which our society enforces conformity, but this is not the case. Socialization may be ineffective for a few who require such drastic action, but for the vast majority in any society, conformity results from the internalization of values. As we learn through imitation, identification, and instruction, values are internalized. They provide security and contribute to a sense of personal and social identity. For this reason, individuals in every society cling tenaciously to the values they have acquired and feel threatened when confronted with others who live according to different conceptions of what is desirable.

CULTURAL RELATIVISM

A misconception about values has been spawned by science and, in particular, by the anthropological doctrine of cultural relativism. Some have maintained that it is possible to separate values from facts, and since science is limited to facts, it is possible to do "value-free" research. By an exercise in mental gymnastics, the very scholars who admit the influence of values in the behavior of others sometimes deny it for themselves. Preferences operate whenever an individual must *select* one action from a multitude of possible courses. Anyone who decides to observe one thing and not another is making that decision on the basis of an implicit or explicit conception of desirability. Science is an activity that makes many value judgments — including which approaches to information gathering are the best. When biologists decide to examine the structure of the DNA molecule using an empirical approach, rather than a mystical, intuitive, or religious one, they are doing so with reference to their sense of what is desirable. Even the decision to study DNA rather than some other substance involves an exercise of values. When doing research on human behavior, the influence of one's values is undeniable. The "objective observer" who is detached from the subject matter, who refrains from allowing values to influence observations, is a myth. This fact does not suggest a retreat from the *quest for objectivity*. It does not mean that social scientists are free to disparage the customs encountered in other societies, or to impose their morals on those being studied. Skilled anthropologists are aware of their own values and then approach other cultures with tolerance and respect. They *identify* rather than *deny* the influence of their own viewpoints. They strive to achieve the ideal of value-free research but realize that it would be naive to assume such a goal possible.

Cultural relativism rests on the premise that it is possible to remain aloof and free from making value judgments. Put simply, this doctrine is based on four interrelated propositions.

1. Each person's value system is a result of his or her experience, i.e., it is learned.
2. The values that individuals learn differ from one society to another because of different learning experiences.

3. Values, therefore, are relative to the society in which they occur.
4. There are no universal values, but we should respect the values of each of the world's cultures.

Cultural relativism has enabled the uninformed to understand what appears to be strange and immoral behavior. Although we may not believe it is good to kill infants, for example, we have found it intelligible in the context of a native Australian band. Although Americans generally believe in the desirability of monogamous marriage (or at least serial monogamy), we have found the practice of polygamy in other societies to be comprehensible when related to their cultures. This view presents numerous difficulties. Does one respect a society that believes it best to murder six million of its members who happen to be Jewish? How do anthropologists respect the values of a head-hunting tribe when their own heads are at stake?

Moreover, all the statements in this doctrine of relativism are either based on implicit values (i.e., empiricism), or they are outright statements of desirability. The belief that it is good to *respect* the ideals of each of the world's cultures is itself a "relative" value. An extreme relativism is based on the philosophy that it is best to "let everyone do his or her own thing." Given unlimited resources and space this might have been possible, but in the modern world this philosophy represents a retreat from the realities facing us. It absolves the believer from the responsibility of finding some way to resolve conflicts among the world's different value systems. What is needed today is not a "live and let live" policy but a commitment to a higher, more inclusive, value system, and this requires changes that are extremely difficult to achieve.

CONFORMITY AND CONFLICT

Every social system is a moral order; shared values act as the mortar binding together the structure of each human community. Rewards and punishments are based on commonly held values; those persons achieving high status do so in terms of cultural rating systems. These values are expressed in symbolic ways — through food, clothing, wealth, language, behavior — all of which carry implicit messages about good and bad. The pervasiveness of values gives each person a sense of belonging, a sense of being a member of a community, the feeling of joining other human beings who share a commitment to the good life. But the moral nature of every culture has two sides — it facilitates adaptation and survival on the one hand, but it often generates conflict and destruction on the other. Let us examine each of these possibilities.

For almost a million years, people have successfully adapted to a variety of terrestrial environments. From the frozen tundra to the steaming jungle, people have built their homes, reared their children, performed their rituals, and buried their dead. In recent years we have escaped the thin layer of atmosphere surrounding the earth to live, if only for a few days, in outer space and beneath the ocean. All these achievements have been possible because of a unique endowment, our capacity for culture. Wherever people wandered, they developed patterns for organizing behavior, using natural resources, relating to others, and creating a meaningful life. A genetic inheritance did not channel behavior into specialized responses but instead provided a reservoir of plasticity that was shaped by values into one of the many ways to be human. Children in every society do not learn the entire range of potential human behavior — they are taught to *conform* to a very limited number of behavior patterns that are appropriate to a particular society. Human survival depends on cultural conformity, which requires that every individual become a specialist, be committed to a few values, and acquire knowledge and skills of a single society.

This very specialization has led to diversity, resulting in a myriad of contrasting cultures. This volume contains only a small sample of the different symbolic worlds created by people in their attempt to cope with the common problems of human existence. We will see how the generosity of the American Christmas spirit stands in contrast to the daily sharing among the Bushmen. Chicago suburbanites and natives of the Brazilian jungle both adorn their bodies with paint, clothing, and rings, but neither can comprehend how the other defines these symbols. All elements of human experience — kinship, marriage, age, race, sexuality, food, warfare — are socially defined and valued. The difficulty of moving from one cultural world to another is immense.

Cultural diversity has fascinated people for centuries. The study of strange and exotic peoples has attracted the curious for many generations. In the isolation of a remote jungle village or South Sea island, anthropologists found a natural laboratory for carrying out research. Their research reports often seemed more like novels than scientific studies and were read by both professionals and laymen; seldom did any reader feel threatened by the strange behavior of far-off "savages."

But isolation rapidly disappeared, sometimes by virtue of the anthropologists' intrusion! Exploration gave way to colonization, trade, and the massive troop movements of modern warfare. Today it is impossible to find groups of people who are isolated from the remainder of the world. Instead we have a conglomeration of cultures within a single nation, and often within a single city. Anthropologists need only walk down the street from the university to encounter those who have learned a culture unlike their own. Individuals with different language styles, sexual practices, religious rituals, and a host of other strange behavior patterns sit in their classrooms or play with their children on the urban playgrounds. Anthropology today is a science concerned with understanding how people can survive in a world where village, hamlet, city, and nation are all *multicultural*. In isolation, each value system was interesting. Crowded into close and intimate contact, these distinct culture patterns often lead to conflict, oppression, and warfare. Barbara Ward has eloquently summed up our situation:

> In the last few decades, mankind has been overcome by the most change in its entire history. Modern science and technology have created so close a network of communication, transport, economic interdependence — and potential nuclear destruction — that planet Earth, on its journey through infinity, has acquired the intimacy, the fellowship, and the vulnerability of a spaceship.[1]

In a sense, our greatest resource for adapting to different environments — the capacity to create different cultures — has become the source of greatest danger. Diversity is required for survival in the ecological niches of earth, but it can be destructive when all people suddenly find themselves in the same niche. Numerous species have become extinct because of their inability to adapt to a changing *natural* environment. Culture was the survival kit that enabled us to meet fluctuating natural conditions with flexibility, but now we are faced with a radically altered *human* environment. Successful adaptation will require changes that fly in the face of thousands of years of cultural specialization. Our ingenuity has been used to develop unique cultures, but thus far we have failed to develop satisfactory patterns and rules for articulating these differences. Can we survive in a world where our neighbors and even our children have different cultures? Can we adapt to the close, intimate fellowship of a spaceship when each group of passengers lives by different values?

TOWARD A MULTICULTURAL SOCIETY

What is required? In the first place, instead of suppressing cultural diversity by stressing assimilation into the mainstream of American life, we must recognize the extent to which our culture is pluralis-

1. Barbara Ward, *Spaceship Earth* (New York: Columbia University Press, 1966), p. vii.

tic. We must accept the fact that groups within our society are committed to disparate and sometimes conflicting values. The second requirement for a truly multicultural society is that we continuously examine the *consequences* of each value system. What is the long-range effect of our commitment to a "gospel of growth?" What are the results of a belief in male superiority? How do our values of privacy affect those without homes? What is the consequence for minority groups when all students are taught to use "standard English"? As we study American culture we must discover the effect of our dominant values on every sector of life. The ideals that have made this country what it is have also been destructive to some citizens. In our efforts to assimilate ethnic groups, we have destroyed their pride and self-identity. In our attempt to offer the advantages of education to American Indians, we have induced them to become failures because our schools are not able to educate for diversity. In order to demonstrate the tolerance built into American values, we have created the "culturally deprived," but the sophistication of labels does not conceal our prejudice. The absence of men in the families of the urban poor is a logical consequence of welfare institutions created from a single value system. The consumer suffers from dangerous products because in our culture productive enterprise is more important than consumer protection. We have only begun to understand some of the consequences of our values, and during the next few decades our survival will demand that the study of values be given top priority.

Finally, the most difficult task for the contemporary world is to induce people to relinquish those values with destructive consequences. This will not be simple, and it probably will not occur without a better understanding of the nature and the function of the world's many value systems. People's capacity to learn has not yet reached its full potential. In every society, children learn to shift from *egocentric* behavior to *ethnocentric* behavior. In deference to desirable community standards, individuals give up those things they desire, and life in a particular society becomes secure and meaningful, with conventional values acting as warp and woof of social interaction.

Can we now learn to shift from *ethnocentric* to *homocentric* behavior? Can we relinquish values desirable from the standpoint of a single community but destructive to the wider world? This change will require a system of ideals greater than the conventions of any localized culture. The change will necessitate a morality that can articulate conflicting value systems and create a climate of tolerance, respect, and cooperation. Only then can we begin to create a culture that will be truly adaptive in today's world.

II

Culture and fieldwork

Culture, as its name suggests, lies at the heart of cultural anthropology. And the concept of culture, along with ethnography, sets anthropology apart from other social and behavioral sciences. Let us look more closely at these concepts.

To understand what anthropologists mean by culture, imagine yourself in a foreign setting, such as a market town in India, forgetting what you might already know about that country. You step off a bus onto a dusty street where you are immediately confronted by strange sights, sounds, and smells. Men dress in Western clothes, but of a different style. Women drape themselves in long shawls that entirely cover their bodies and peer at you through a small gap in this garment as they walk by. Buildings are one- or two-story affairs, open at the front so you can see inside. Near you some people sit on wicker chairs eating strange foods. Most unusual is how people talk. They utter vocalizations unlike any you have ever heard, and you wonder how they can possibly understand each other. But obviously they do since their behavior seems organized and purposeful.

Scenes such as this confronted early explorers, missionaries, and anthropologists, and from their observations an obvious point emerged. People living in various parts of the world looked and behaved in dramatically different ways. And these differences correlated with groups. The people of India had customs different from those of the Papuans; the British did not act and dress like the Iroquois.

Two possible explanations for group differences came to mind. Some argued that group behavior was inherited. Dahomeans of the African Gold Coast, for example, were characterized as particularly "clever and adaptive" by one British colonial official, while, according to the same authority, another African group was "happy-go-lucky and improvident." Usually implied in such statements was the idea that group members were born that way. Such thinking persists to the present and in its least discriminating guise takes the form of racism.

But a second explanation also emerged. Perhaps, rather than a product of inheritance, the behavior characteristic of a group was learned. The way people dressed, what they ate, how they talked — all these could more easily be explained as acquisitions. Thus, a baby born on the African Gold Coast would, if immediately transported to China and raised like other children there, grow up to dress, eat, and talk like a Chinese. Cultural anthropologists focus on the explanation of learned behavior.

The idea of learning, and a need to label the lifestyles associated with particular groups, led to the definition of culture. In 1871, British anthropologist Sir Edward Burnet Tylor argued that, "Culture . . . is that complex whole which includes knowledge, belief, art, law, morals, custom, and any other capabilities and habits acquired by man as a member of society."[1]

The definition we present here places more emphasis on the importance of knowledge than does Tylor's. We will say that *culture is the acquired knowledge that people use to generate behavior and interpret experience.*

Important to this definition is the idea that culture is a kind of knowledge, not behavior. It is in people's heads. It reflects the mental categories they learn from others as they grow up. It helps them *generate* behavior and *interpret* what they experience. At the moment of birth, we lack a culture. We don't yet have a system of beliefs, knowledge, and patterns of customary behavior. But from that moment until we die, each of us participates in a kind of universal schooling that teaches us our native culture. Laughing and smiling are genetic responses, but as infants we soon learn when to smile, when to

1. Edward Burnet Tylor, *Primitive Culture* (New York: Harper Torchbooks, Harper and Row, 1958; originally published by John Murray, London, 1871) p. 1.

laugh, and even how to laugh. We also inherit the potential to cry, but we must learn our cultural rules for when it is appropriate.

As we learn our culture, we acquire a way to interpret experience. For example, we Americans learn that dogs are like little people in furry suits. Dogs live in our houses, eat our food, share our beds. They hold a place in our hearts; their loss causes us to grieve. Indian villagers, on the other hand, view dogs as pests that admittedly are useful for hunting in those few parts of the country where one still can hunt, and as watchdogs. Quiet days in Indian villages are often punctuated by the yelp of a dog that has been threatened or actually hurt by its master or a bystander.

Clearly, it is not the dogs that are different in these two societies. Rather, it is the meaning that dogs have for people that varies. And such meaning is cultural; it is learned as part of growing up in each group.

Ethnography is the process of discovering and describing a particular culture. It involves anthropologists in an intimate and personal activity as they attempt to learn how the members of a particular group see their worlds.

But which groups qualify as culture-bearing units? How does the anthropologist identify the existence of a culture to study? This was not a difficult question when anthropology was a new science. As Tylor's definition notes, culture was the whole way of life of a people. To find it, one sought out distinctive ethnic units, such as Bhil tribals in India or Apaches in the American Southwest. Anything one learned from such people would be part of their culture.

But discrete cultures of this sort are becoming more difficult to find. The world is increasingly divided into large national societies, each subdivided into a myriad of subgroups. Anthropologists are finding it increasingly attractive to study such subgroups, because they form the arena for most of life in complex society. And this is where the concept of the microculture enters the scene.

Microcultures are systems of cultural knowledge characteristic of subgroups within larger societies. Members of a microculture will usually share much of what they know with everyone in the greater society, but will possess a special cultural knowledge that is unique to the subgroup. For example, a college fraternity has a microculture within the context of a university and nation. Its members have special daily routines, jokes, and meanings for events. It is this shared knowledge that makes up their microculture and which can serve as the basis for ethnographic study. More and more, anthropologists are turning to the study of microcultures, using the same ethnographic techniques they employ when they investigate the broader culture of an ethnic or national group.

More than anything else, it is ethnography that is anthropology's unique contribution to social science. Most scientists, including many who view people in social context, approach their research as *detached observers.* As social scientists, they observe the human subjects of their study, categorize what they see, and generate theory to account for their findings. They work from the outside, creating a system of knowledge to account for other people's behavior. Although this is a legitimate and often useful way to conduct research, it is not the main task of ethnography.

Ethnographers seek out the insider's viewpoint. Because culture is the knowledge people use to generate behavior and interpret experience, the ethnographer seeks to understand group members' behavior from the inside, or cultural, perspective. Instead of looking for a *subject* to observe, ethnographers look for an *informant* to teach them the culture. Just as a child learns its native culture from parents and other people in its social environment, the ethnographer learns another culture by inferring folk categories from the observation of behavior and by asking informants what things mean. This point, along with a discussion of culture, is described in James Spradley's article on culture and ethnography in this section.

Anthropologists employ many strategies during field research to understand another culture better. But all strategies and all research ultimately rest on the cooperation of *informants.* An informant is neither a subject in a scientific experiment nor a respondent who answers the investigator's questions. An informant is a teacher who has a special kind of pupil—a professional anthropologist. In this unique relationship a transformation occurs in the anthropologist's understanding of an alien culture. It is the informant who transforms the anthropologist from a tourist into an ethnographer. The informant may be a child who explains how to play hopscotch, a cocktail waitress who teaches the anthropologist to serve drinks and to encourage customers to leave tips, an elderly man who teaches the anthropologist to build an igloo, or a grandmother who explains the intricacies of Zapotec kinship. Almost any individual who has acquired a repertoire of cultural behavior can become an informant.

Ethnography is not as easy to do as you might think. For one thing, we Americans are not taught to be good listeners. We prefer to observe and draw our own conclusions. We like a sense of control in social contexts; passive listening is a sign of weakness in our culture.

But listening and learning from others is at the heart of ethnography, and we must put aside our discomfort with the student role.

It is also not easy for informants to teach us about their cultures. Culture is often *tacit;* it is so regular and routine that it lies below a conscious level. A major ethnographic task is to help informants remember their culture, to make their knowledge part of their *explicit culture.*

But, in some cases, it is necessary to infer cultural knowledge by observing an informant's behavior because the cultural rules governing it cannot be expressed in language. Speaking distances, which vary from one culture to the next, and language sound categories, called phonemes, are good examples of this kind of tacit culture.

Naive realism may also impede ethnography. *Naive realism* is the belief that people everywhere see the world in the same way. It may, for example, lead the unwary ethnographer to assume that beauty is the same for all people everywhere, or, to use our previous example, dogs should mean the same thing in India as they do in the United States. If an ethnographer fails to control his or her own naive realism, inside cultural meanings will surely be overlooked. The article by Laura Bohannan presents an example of naive realism as she describes her attempt to tell the story of *Hamlet* to Tiv elders. So does Richard Lee's description of the meaning of the gift of an ox to !Kung hunters.

Culture shock and ethnocentrism may also stand in the way of ethnographers. *Culture shock* is a state of anxiety that results from cross-cultural misunderstanding. Immersed alone in another society, the ethnographer understands few of the culturally defined rules for behavior and interpretation used by his or her hosts. The result is anxiety about proper action and an inability to interact appropriately in the new context.

Ethnocentrism can be just as much of a liability. *Ethnocentrism* is the belief and feeling that one's own culture is best. It reflects our tendency to judge other people's beliefs and behavior using values of our own native culture. Thus, if we come from a society that abhors painful treatment of animals, we are likely to react with anger when an Indian villager hits a dog with a rock. Our feeling is ethnocentric.

It is impossible to rid ourselves entirely of the cultural values that make us ethnocentric when we do ethnography. But it is important to control our ethnocentric feeling in the field if we are to learn from informants. Informants resent negative judgment.

Finally, the role assigned to ethnographers by informants affects the quality of what can be learned. Ethnography is a personal enterprise, as all the articles in this section illustrate. Unlike survey research using questionnaires or short interviews, ethnography requires prolonged social contact. Informants will assign the ethnographer some kind of role and what that turns out to be will affect research. Richard Kurin illustrates this point nicely in this section as he describes the evolution of his status in a Pakistani village.

KEY TERMS

culture	subject
ethnography	respondent
microculture	naive realism
tacit culture	ethnocentrism
explicit culture	culture shock
informant	detached observer

1

Ethnography and culture

JAMES P. SPRADLEY

Most Americans associate science with detached observation; we learn to observe whatever we wish to understand, introduce our own classification of what is going on, and explain what we see in our own terms. In this selection, James Spradley argues that cultural anthropologists work differently. Ethnography is the work of discovering and describing a particular culture; culture is the learned, shared knowledge that people use to generate behavior and interpret experience. To get at culture, ethnographers must learn the meanings of action and experience from the insider's or informant's point of view. Many of the examples used by Spradley also show the relevance of anthropology to the study of culture in this country.

Ethnographic fieldwork is the hallmark of cultural anthropology. Whether in a jungle village in Peru or on the streets of New York, the anthropologist goes to where people live and "does fieldwork." This means participating in activities, asking questions, eating strange foods, learning a new language, watching ceremonies, taking field-notes, washing clothes, writing letters home, tracing out genealogies, observing play, interviewing informants, and hundreds of other things. This vast range of activities often obscures the nature of the most fundamental task of all fieldwork — doing ethnography.

Ethnography is the work of describing a culture. The central aim of ethnography is to understand another way of life from the native point of view. The goal of ethnography, as Malinowski put it, is "to grasp the native's point of view, his relation to life, to realize *his* vision of *his* world."[1] Fieldwork, then, involves the disciplined study of what the world is like to people who have learned to see, hear, speak, think, and act in ways that are different. Rather than *studying people*, ethnography means *learning from people*. Consider the following illustration.

George Hicks set out, in 1965, to learn about another way of life, that of the mountain people in an Appalachian valley.[2] His goal was to discover their culture, to learn to see the world from their perspective. With his family he moved into Little Laurel Valley, his daughter attended the local school, and his wife became one of the local Girl Scout leaders. Hicks soon discovered that stores and storekeepers were at the center of the valley's communication system, providing the most important social arena for the entire valley. He learned this by watching what other people did, by following their example, and slowly becoming part of the groups that congregated daily in the stores. He writes:

> At least once each day I would visit several stores in the valley, and sit in on the groups of gossiping men or, if the storekeeper happened to be alone, perhaps attempt to clear up puzzling points about kinship obligations. I found these hours, particularly those spent in the presence of the two or three excellent storytellers in the Little Laurel, thoroughly enjoyable. . . . At other times, I helped a number of local men gather corn or hay, build sheds, cut trees, pull and pack galax, and search for rich stands of huckleberries. When I needed aid in, for example, repairing frozen water pipes, it was readily and cheerfully provided.[3]

In order to discover the hidden principles of another way of life, the researcher must become a *student*. Storekeepers and storytellers and local farmers become *teachers*. Instead of studying the "climate," the "flora," and the "fauna" that made up the environment of this Appalachian valley, Hicks tried to discover how these mountain people defined and evaluated trees and galax and huckleberries. He did not attempt to describe social life in terms of what most Americans know about "marriage," "family," and "friendship"; instead he sought to discover how these mountain people identified relatives and friends. He tried to learn the obligations they felt toward kinsmen and dis-

1. Bronislaw Malinowski, *Argonauts of the Western Pacific* (London: Routledge, 1922), 22.

2. George Hicks, *Appalachian Valley* (New York: Holt, Rinehart, and Winston, 1976).

3. Ibid., 3.

cover how they felt about friends. Discovering the *insider's view* is a different species of knowledge from one that rests mainly on the outsider's view, even when the outsider is a trained social scientist.

Consider another example, this time from the perspective of a non-Western ethnographer. Imagine an Eskimo woman setting out to learn the culture of Macalester College. What would she, so well schooled in the rich heritage of Eskimo culture, have to do in order to understand the culture of Macalester College students, faculty, and staff? How would she discover the patterns that made up their lives? How would she avoid imposing Eskimo ideas, categories, and values on everything she saw?

First, and perhaps most difficult, she would have to set aside her belief in *naive realism,* the almost universal belief that all people define the *real* world of objects, events, and living creatures in pretty much the same way. Human languages may differ from one society to the next, but behind the strange words and sentences, all people are talking about the same things. The naive realist assumes that love, snow, marriage, worship, animals, death, food, and hundreds of other things have essentially the same meaning to all human beings. Although few of us would admit to such ethnocentrism, the assumption may unconsciously influence our research. Ethnography starts with a conscious attitude of almost complete ignorance. "I don't know how the people at Macalester College understand their world. That remains to be discovered."

This Eskimo woman would have to begin by learning the language spoken by students, faculty, and staff. She could stroll the campus paths, sit in classes, and attend special events, but only if she consciously tried to see things from the native point of view would she grasp their perspective. She would need to observe and listen to first-year students during their week-long orientation program. She would have to stand in line during registration, listen to students discuss the classes they hoped to get, and visit departments to watch faculty advising students on course selection. She would want to observe secretaries typing, janitors sweeping, and maintenance personnel plowing snow from walks. She would watch the more than 1600 students crowd into the post office area to open their tiny mailboxes, and she would listen to their comments about junk mail and letters from home and no mail at all. She would attend faculty meetings to watch what went on, recording what professors and administrators said and how they behaved. She would sample various courses, attend "keggers" on weekends, read the *Mac Weekly,* and listen by the hour to students discussing things like their "relationships," the "football team," and "work study." She would want to learn the *meanings* of all these things. She would have to listen to the members of this college community, watch what they did, and participate in their activities to learn such meanings.

The essential core of ethnography is this concern with the meaning of actions and events to the people we seek to understand. Some of these meanings are directly expressed in language; many are taken for granted and communicated only indirectly through word and action. But in every society people make constant use of these complex meaning systems to organize their behavior, to understand themselves and others, and to make sense out of the world in which they live. These systems of meaning constitute their culture; ethnography always implies a theory of culture.

Culture

When ethnographers study other cultures, they must deal with three fundamental aspects of human experience: what people do, what people know, and the things people make and use. When each of these are learned and shared by members of some group, we speak of them as *cultural behavior, cultural knowledge,* and *cultural artifacts.* Whenever you do ethnographic fieldwork, you will want to distinguish among these three, although in most situations they are usually mixed together. Let's try to unravel them.

Recently I took a commuter train from a western suburb to downtown Chicago. It was late in the day, and when I boarded the train only a handful of people were scattered about the car. Each was engaged in a common form of *cultural behavior: reading.* Across the aisle a man held the *Chicago Tribune* out in front of him, looking intently at the small print and every now and then turning the pages noisily. In front of him a young woman held a paperback book about twelve inches from her face. I could see her head shift slightly as her eyes moved from the bottom of one page to the top of the next. Near the front of the car a student was reading a large textbook and using a pen to underline words and sentences. Directly in front of me I noticed a man looking at the ticket he had purchased and reading it. It took me an instant to survey this scene and then I settled back, looked out the window, and read a billboard advertisement for a plumbing service proclaiming it would open any plugged drains. All of us were engaged in the same kind of cultural behavior: reading.

This common activity depended on a great many *cultural artifacts,* the things people shape or make from natural resources. I could see artifacts like books and tickets and newspapers and billboards, all of which contained tiny black marks arranged into intricate patterns called "letters." And these tiny artifacts were arranged into larger patterns of words, sentences, and paragraphs. Those of us on that commuter train could read, in part, because of still other artifacts: the bark of trees made into paper; steel made into printing presses; dyes of various colors made into ink; glue used to hold book pages together; large wooden frames to hold billboards. If an ethnographer wanted to understand the full cultural meaning of reading in our society, it would involve a careful study of these and many other cultural artifacts.

Although we can easily see behavior and artifacts, they represent only the thin surface of a deep lake. Beneath the surface, hidden from view, lies a vast reservoir of *cultural knowledge*. Think for a moment what the people on that train needed to know in order to read. First, they had to know the grammatical rules for at least one language. Then they had to learn what the little marks on paper represented. They also had to know the meaning of space and lines and pages. They had learned cultural rules like "move your eyes from left to right, from the top of the page to the bottom." They had to know that a sentence at the bottom of a page continues on the top of the next page. The man reading a newspaper had to know a great deal about columns and the spaces between columns and what headlines mean. All of us needed to know what kinds of messages were intended by whoever wrote what we read. If a person cannot distinguish the importance of a message on a billboard from one that comes in a letter from a spouse or child, problems would develop. I knew how to recognize when other people were reading. We all knew it was impolite to read aloud on a train. We all knew how to feel when reading things like jokes or calamitous news in the paper. Our culture has a large body of shared knowledge that people learn and use to engage in this behavior called *reading* and make proper use of the artifacts connected with it.

Although cultural knowledge is hidden from view, it is of fundamental importance because we all use it constantly to generate behavior and interpret our experience. Cultural knowledge is so important that I will frequently use the broader term *culture* when speaking about it. Indeed, I will define culture as *the acquired knowledge people use to interpret experience and generate behavior.* Let's consider another example to see how people use their culture to interpret experience and do things.

One afternoon in 1973 I came across the following news item in the *Minneapolis Tribune:*

CROWD MISTAKES RESCUE ATTEMPT, ATTACKS POLICE

Nov. 23, 1973. Hartford, Connecticut. Three policemen giving a heart massage and oxygen to a heart attack victim Friday were attacked by a crowd of 75 to 100 persons who apparently did not realize what the policemen were doing.

Other policemen fended off the crowd of mostly Spanish-speaking residents until an ambulance arrived. Police said they tried to explain to the crowd what they were doing, but the crowd apparently thought they were beating the woman.

Despite the policemen's efforts the victim, Evangelica Echevacria, 59, died.

Here we see people using their culture. Members of two different groups observed the same event but their *interpretations* were drastically different. The crowd used their cultural knowledge (a) to interpret the behavior of the policemen as cruel and (b) to act on the woman's behalf to put a stop to what they perceived as brutality. They had acquired the cultural principles for acting and interpreting things in this way through a particular shared experience.

The policemen, on the other hand, used their cultural knowledge (a) to interpret the woman's condition as heart failure and their own behavior as a life-saving effort and (b) to give her cardiac massage and oxygen. They used artifacts like an oxygen mask and an ambulance. Furthermore, they interpreted the actions of the crowd in an entirely different manner from how the crowd saw their own behavior. The two groups of people each had elaborate cultural rules for interpreting their experience and for acting in emergency situations, and the conflict arose, at least in part, because these cultural rules were so different.

We can now diagram this definition of culture and see more clearly the relationships among knowledge, behavior, and artifacts (Figure 1). By identifying cultural knowledge as fundamental, we have merely shifted the emphasis from behavior and artifacts to their *meaning*. The ethnographer observes behavior but goes beyond it to inquire about the meaning of that behavior. The ethnographer sees artifacts and natural objects but goes beyond them to discover what meanings people assign to these objects. The ethnographer observes and records emotional states but goes beyond them to discover the meaning of fear, anxiety, anger, and other feelings.

As represented in Figure I, cultural knowledge exists at two levels of consciousness. *Explicit culture* makes up part of what we know, a level of knowledge people can communicate about with relative ease. When George Hicks asked storekeepers and others in Little

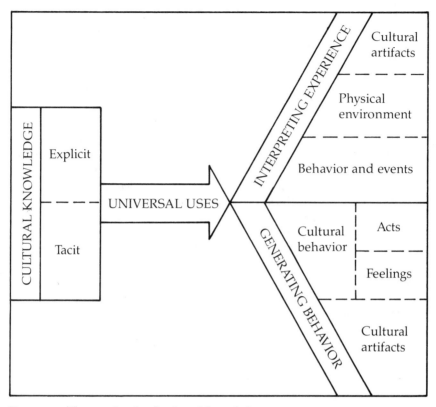

FIGURE I. *The two levels of cultural knowledge*

Laurel Valley about their relatives, he discovered that any adult over fifty could tell him the genealogical connections among large numbers of people. They knew how to trace kin relationships and the cultural rules for appropriate behavior among kinsmen. All of us have acquired large areas of cultural knowledge such as this which we can talk about and make explicit.

At the same time, a large portion of our cultural knowledge remains tacit, outside our awareness. Edward Hall has done much to elucidate the nature of tacit cultural knowledge in his books *The Silent Language* and *The Hidden Dimension*.[4] The way each culture defines space often occurs at the level of tacit knowledge. Hall points out that all of us have acquired thousands of spatial cues about how close to

4. Edward T. Hall, *The Silent Language* (Garden City, N.Y.: Doubleday, 1959); *The Hidden Dimension* (Garden City, N.Y.: Doubleday, 1966).

stand to others, how to arrange furniture, when to touch others, and when to feel cramped inside of a room. Without realizing that our tacit culture is operating, we begin to feel uneasy when someone from another culture stands too close, breathes on us when talking, touches us, or when we find furniture arranged in the center of the room rather than around the edges. Ethnography is the study of both explicit and tacit cultural knowledge; the research strategies discussed in this book are designed to reveal both levels.

The concept of culture as acquired knowledge has much in common with symbolic interactionism, a theory that seeks to explain human behavior in terms of meanings. Symbolic interactionism has its roots in the work of sociologists like Cooley, Mead, and Thomas. Blumer has identified three premises on which this theory rests.

The first premise is that "human beings act toward things on the basis of the meanings that the things have for them."[5] The policemen and the crowd in our earlier example interacted on the basis of the meanings things had for them. The geographic location, the types of people, the police car, the policemen's movements, the sick woman's behavior, and the activities of the onlookers—all were *symbols* with special meanings. People did not act toward the things themselves, but to their meanings.

The second premise underlying symbolic interactionism is that the "meaning of such things is derived from, or arise out of, the social interaction that one has with one's fellows."[6] Culture, as a shared system of meanings, is learned, revised, maintained, and defined in the context of people interacting. The crowd came to share their definitions of police behavior through interacting with one another and through past associations with the police. The police officers acquired the cultural meanings they used through interacting with other officers and members of the community. The culture of each group was inextricably bound up with the social life of their particular communities.

The third premise of symbolic interactionism is that "meanings are handled in, and modified through, an interpretive process used by the person dealing with the things he encounters."[7] Neither the crowd nor the policemen were automatons, driven by their culture to act in the way they did. Rather, they used their cultural knowledge to interpret and evaluate the situation. At any moment, a member of the

5. Herbert Blumer, *Symbolic Interactionism* (Englewood Cliffs, N.J.: Prentice-Hall, 1969), 2.
6. Ibid.
7. Ibid.

crowd might have interpreted the behavior of the policemen in a slightly different way, leading to a different reaction.

We may see this interpretive aspect more clearly if we think of culture as a cognitive map. In the recurrent activities that make up everyday life, we refer to this map. It serves as a guide for acting and for interpreting our experience; it does not compel us to follow a particular course. Like this brief drama between the policemen, a dying woman, and the crowd, much of life is a series of unanticipated social occasions. Although our culture may not include a detailed map for such occasions, it does provide principles for interpreting and responding to them. Rather than a rigid map that people must follow, culture is best thought of as

> a set of principles for creating dramas, for writing script, and of course, for recruiting players and audiences. . . . Culture is not simply a cognitive map that people acquire, in whole or in part, more or less accurately, and then learn to read. People are not just map-readers; they are map-makers. People are cast out into imperfectly charted, continually revised sketch maps. Culture does not provide a cognitive map, but rather a set of principles for map making and navigation. Different cultures are like different schools of navigation to cope with different terrains and seas.[8]

If we take *meaning* seriously, as symbolic interactionists argue we must, it becomes necessary to study meaning carefully. We need a theory of meaning and a specific methodology designed for the investigation of it. This book presents such a theory and methodology.

REVIEW QUESTIONS

1. What is the definition of culture? How is this definition related to the way anthropologists do ethnographic fieldwork?

2. What is the relationship among cultural behavior, cultural artifacts, and cultural knowledge?

3. What is the difference between tacit and explicit culture? How can anthropologists discover these two kinds of culture?

4. What are some examples of naive realism in the way Americans think about people in other societies?

---

8. Charles O. Frake, "Plying Frames Can Be Dangerous: Some Reflections on Methodology in Cognitive Anthropology," *Quarterly Newsletter of the Institute for Comparative Human Development* 3 (1977): 6–7.

2

Eating Christmas in the Kalahari

RICHARD BORSHAY LEE

What happens when an anthropologist living among the bushmen of Africa decides to be generous and to share a large animal with everyone at Christmastime? This compelling account of the misunderstanding and confusion that resulted takes the reader deeper into the nature of culture. Richard Lee carefully traces how the natives perceived his generosity and taught the anthropologist something about his own culture.

The !Kung Bushmen's knowledge of Christmas is thirdhand. The London Missionary Society brought the holiday to the southern Tswana tribes in the early nineteenth century. Later, native catechists spread the idea far and wide among the Bantu-speaking pastoralists, even in the remotest corners of the Kalahari Desert. The Bushmen's idea of the Christmas story, stripped to its essentials, is "praise the birth of white man's god-chief"; what keeps their interest in the holiday high is the Tswana-Herero custom of slaughtering an ox for his Bushmen neighbors as an annual goodwill gesture. Since the 1930's, part of the Bushmen's annual round of activities has included a December congregation at the cattle posts for trading, marriage brokering, and several days of trancedance feasting at which the local Tswana headman is host.

As a social anthropologist working with !Kung Bushmen, I found that the Christmas ox custom suited my purposes. I had come to the Kalahari to study the hunting and gathering subsistence economy of the !Kung, and to accomplish this it was essential not to provide them

Originally published as "A Naturalist at Large: Eating Christmas in the Kalahari." With permission from *Natural History*, Vol. 78, No. 10; Copyright the American Museum of Natural History, 1969.

with food, share my own food, or interfere in any way with their food-gathering activities. While liberal handouts of tobacco and medical supplies were appreciated, they were scarcely adequate to erase the glaring disparity in wealth between the anthropologist, who maintained a two-month inventory of canned goods, and the Bushmen, who rarely had a day's supply of food on hand. My approach, while paying off in terms of data, left me open to frequent accusations of stinginess and hardheartedness. By their lights, I was a miser.

The Christmas ox was to be my way of saying thank you for the cooperation of the past year; and since it was to be our last Christmas in the field, I determined to slaughter the largest, meatiest ox that money could buy, insuring that the feast and trance dance would be a success.

Through December I kept my eyes open at the wells as the cattle were brought down for watering. Several animals were offered, but none had quite the grossness that I had in mind. Then, ten days before the holiday, a Herero friend led an ox of astonishing size and mass up to our camp. It was solid black, stood five feet high at the shoulder, had a five-foot span of horns, and must have weighed 1,200 pounds on the hoof. Food consumption calculations are my specialty, and I quickly figured that bones and viscera aside, there was enough meat — at least four pounds — for every man, woman, and child of the 150 Bushmen in the vicinity of /ai/ai who were expected at the feast.

Having found the right animal at last, I paid the Herero £20 ($56) and asked him to keep the beast with his herd until Christmas day. The next morning word spread among the people that the big solid black one was the ox chosen by /ontah (my Bushman name; it means, roughly, "whitey") for the Christmas feast. That afternoon I received the first delegation. Ben!a, an outspoken sixty-year-old mother of five, came to the point slowly.

"Where were you planning to eat Christmas?"

"Right here at /ai/ai," I replied.

"Alone or with others?"

"I expect to invite all the people to eat Christmas with me."

"Eat what?"

"I have purchased Yehave's black ox, and I am going to slaughter and cook it."

"That's what we were told at the well but refused to believe it until we heard it from yourself."

"Well, it's the black one," I replied expansively, although wondering what she was driving at.

"Oh, no!" Ben!a groaned, turning to her group. "They were

right." Turning back to me she asked, "Do you expect us to eat that bag of bones?"

"Bag of bones!" It's the biggest ox at /ai/ai."

"Big, yes, but old. And thin. Everybody knows there's no meat on that old ox. What did you expect us to eat off it, the horns?"

Everybody chuckled at Ben!a's one-liner as they walked away, but all I could manage was a weak grin.

That evening it was the turn of the young men. They came to sit at our evening fire. /gaugo, about my age, spoke to me man-to-man.

"/ontah, you have always been square with us," he lied. "What has happened to change your heart? That sack of guts and bones of Yehave's will hardly feed one camp, let alone all the Bushmen around /ai/ai." And he proceeded to enumerate the seven camps in the /ai/ai vicinity, family by family. "Perhaps you have forgotten that we are not few, but many. Or are you too blind to tell the difference between a proper cow and an old wreck? That ox is thin to the point of death."

"Look, you guys," I retorted, "that is a beautiful animal, and I'm sure you will eat it with pleasure at Christmas."

"Of course we will eat it; it's food. But it won't fill us up to the point where we will have enough strength to dance. We will eat and go home to bed with stomachs rumbling."

That night as we turned in, I asked my wife, Nancy: "What did you think of the black ox?"

"It looked enormous to me. Why?"

"Well, about eight different people have told me I got gypped; that the ox is nothing but bones."

"What's the angle?" Nancy asked. "Did they have a better one to sell?"

"No, they just said that it was going to be a grim Christmas because there won't be enough meat to go around. Maybe I'll get an independent judge to look at the beast in the morning."

Bright and early, Halingisi, a Tswana cattle owner, appeared at our camp. But before I could ask him to give me his opinion on Yehave's black ox, he gave me the eye signal that indicated a confidential chat. We left the camp and sat down.

"/ontah, I'm suprised at you: you've lived here for three years and still haven't learned anything about cattle."

"But what else can a person do but choose the biggest, strongest animal one can find?" I retorted.

"Look, just because an animal is big doesn't mean that it has plenty of meat on it. The black one was a beauty when it was younger, but now it is thin to the point of death."

"Well I've already bought it. What can I do at this stage?"

"Bought it already? I thought you were just considering it. Well, you'll have to kill it and serve it, I suppose. But don't expect much of a dance to follow."

My spirits dropped rapidly. I could believe that Ben!a and /gaugo just might be putting me on about the black ox, but Halingisi seemed to be an impartial critic. I went around that day feeling as though I had bought a lemon of a used car.

In the afternoon it was Tomazo's turn. Tomazo is a fine hunter, a top trance performer . . . and one of my most reliable informants. He approached the subject of the Christmas cow as part of my continuing Bushman education.

"My friend, the way it is with us Bushmen," he began, "is that we love meat. And even more than that, we love fat. When we hunt we always search for the fat ones, the ones dripping with layers of white fat: fat that turns into a clear, thick oil in the cooking pot, fat that slides down your gullet, fills your stomach and gives you a roaring diarrhea," he rhapsodized.

"So, feeling as we do," he continued, "it gives us pain to be served such a scrawny thing as Yehave's black ox. It is big, yes, and no doubt its giant bones are good for soup, but fat is what we really crave and so we will eat Christmas this year with a heavy heart."

The prospect of a gloomy Christmas now had me worried, so I asked Tomazo what I could do about it.

"Look for a fat one, a young one . . . smaller, but fat. Fat enough to make us //gom ('evacuate the bowels'), then we will be happy."

My suspicions were aroused when Tomazo said that he happened to know of a young, fat, barren cow that the owner was willing to part with. Was Tomazo working on commission, I wondered? But I dispelled this unworthy thought when we approached the Herero owner of the cow in question and found that he had decided not to sell.

The scrawny wreck of a Christmas ox now became the talk of the /ai/ai water hole and was the first news told to the outlying groups as they began to come in from the bush for the feast. What finally convinced me that real trouble might be brewing was the visit from u!au, an old conservative with a reputation for fierceness. His nickname meant spear and referred to an incident thirty years ago in which he had speared a man to death. He had an intense manner; fixing me with his eyes, he said in clipped tones:

"I have only just heard about the black ox today, or else I would have come here earlier. /ontah, do you honestly think you can serve meat like that to people and avoid a fight?" He paused, letting the implications sink in. "I don't mean fight you, /ontah; you are a white man. I mean a fight between Bushmen. There are many fierce ones here, and with such a small quantity of meat to distribute, how can you give everybody a fair share? Someone is sure to accuse another of taking too much or hogging all the choice pieces. Then you will see what happens when some go hungry while others eat."

The possibility of at least a serious argument struck me as all too real. I had witnessed the tension that surrounds the distribution of meat from a kudu or gemsbok kill, and had documented many arguments that sprang up from a real or imagined slight in meat distribution. The owners of a kill may spend up to two hours arranging and rearranging the piles of meat under the gaze of a circle of recipients before handing them out. And I knew that the Christmas feast at /ai/ai would be bringing together groups that had feuded in the past.

Convinced now of the gravity of the situation, I went in earnest to search for a second cow; but all my inquiries failed to turn one up.

The Christmas feast was evidently going to be a disaster, and the incessant complaints about the meagerness of the ox had already taken the fun out of it for me. Moreover, I was getting bored with the wisecracks, and after losing my temper a few times, I resolved to serve the beast anyway. If the meat fell short, the hell with it. In the Bushmen idiom, I announced to all who would listen:

"I am a poor man and blind. If I have chosen one that is too old and too thin, we will eat it anyway and see if there is enough meat there to quiet the rumbling of our stomachs."

On hearing this speech, Ben!a offered me a rare word of comfort. "It's thin," she said philosophically, "but the bones will make a good soup."

At dawn Christmas morning, instinct told me to turn over the butchering and cooking to a friend and take off with Nancy to spend Christmas alone in the bush. But curiosity kept me from retreating. I wanted to see what such a scrawny ox looked like on butchering, and if there *was* going to be a fight, I wanted to catch every word of it. Anthropologists are incurable that way.

The great beast was driven up to our dancing ground, and a shot in the forehead dropped it in its tracks. Then, freshly cut branches were heaped around the fallen carcass to receive the meat. Ten men volunteered to help with the cutting. I asked /gaugo to make the breast bone cut. This cut, which begins the butchering process for most large game, offers easy access for removal of the viscera. But it also allows the hunter to spot-check the amount of fat on an animal. A fat game animal carries a white layer up to an inch thick on the chest, while in a thin one, the knife will quickly cut to bone. All eyes fixed on his hand as /gaugo, dwarfed by the great carcass, knelt to the breast. The first cut opened a pool of solid white in the black skin. The second and third cut widened and deepened the creamy white. Still no bone. It was pure fat; it must have been two inches thick.

"Hey /gau," I burst out, "that ox is loaded with fat. What's this about the ox being too thin to bother eating? Are you out of your mind?"

"Fat?" /gau shot back, "You call that fat? This wreck is thin, sick, dead!" And he broke out laughing. So did everyone else. They rolled on the ground, paralyzed with laughter. Everybody laughed except me; I was thinking.

I ran back to the tent and burst in just as Nancy was getting up. "Hey, the black ox. It's fat as hell! They were kidding about it being too thin to eat. It was a joke or something. A put-on. Everyone is really delighted with it!"

"Some joke," my wife replied. "It was so funny that you were ready to pack up and leave /ai/ai."

If it had indeed been a joke, it had been an extraordinarily convincing one, and tinged, I thought, with more than a touch of malice as many jokes are. Nevertheless, that it was a joke lifted my spirits considerably, and I returned to the butchering site where the shape of the ox was rapidly disappearing under the axes and knives of the butchers. The atmosphere had become festive. Grinning broadly, their arms covered with blood well past the elbow, men packed chunks of meat into the big cast-iron cooking pots, fifty pounds to the load, and muttered and chuckled all the while about the thinness and worthlessness of the animal and /ontah's poor judgment.

We danced and ate that ox two days and two nights; we cooked and distributed fourteen potfuls of meat and no one went home hungry and no fights broke out.

But the "joke" stayed in my mind. I had a growing feeling that something important had happened in my relationship with the Bushmen and that the clue lay in the meaning of the joke. Several days later, when most of the people had dispersed back to the bush camps, I raised the question with Hakekgose, a Tswana man who had grown up among the !Kung, married a !Kung girl, and who probably knew their culture better than any other non-Bushman.

"With us whites," I began, "Christmas is supposed to be the day of friendship and brotherly love. What I can't figure out is why the

Bushmen went to such lengths to criticize and belittle the ox I had bought for the feast. The animal was perfectly good and their jokes and wisecracks practically ruined the holiday for me."

"So it really did bother you," said Hakekgose. "Well, that's the way they always talk. When I take my rifle and go hunting with them, if I miss, they laugh at me for the rest of the day. But even if I hit and bring one down, it's no better. To them, the kill is always too small or too old or too thin; and as we sit down on the kill site to cook and eat the liver, they keep grumbling, even with their mouths full of meat. They say things like, 'Oh, this is awful! What a worthless animal! Whatever made me think that this Tswana rascal could hunt!' "

"Is this the way outsiders are treated?" I asked.

"No, it is their custom; they talk that way to each other too. Go and ask them."

/gaugo had been one of the most enthusiastic in making me feel bad about the merit of the Christmas ox. I sought him out first.

"Why did you tell me the black ox was worthless, when you could see that it was loaded with fat and meat?"

"It is our way," he said smiling. "We always like to fool people about that. Say there is a Bushman who has been hunting. He must not come home and announce like a braggart, 'I have killed a big one in the bush!' He must first sit down in silence until I or someone else comes up to his fire and asks, 'What did you see today?' He replies quietly, 'Ah, I'm no good for hunting. I saw nothing at all [pause] just a little tiny one.' Then I smile to myself," /gaugo continued, "because I know he has killed something big.

"In the morning we make up a party of four or five people to cut up and carry the meat back to the camp. When we arrive at the kill we examine it and cry out, 'You mean to say you have dragged us all the way out here in order to make us cart home your pile of bones? Oh, if I had known it was this thin I wouldn't have come.' Another one pipes up, 'People, to think I gave up a nice day in the shade for this. At home we may be hungry but at least we have nice cool water to drink.' If the horns are big, someone says, 'Did you think that somehow you were going to boil down the horns for soup?'

"To all this you must respond in kind. 'I agree,' you say, 'this one is not worth the effort; let's just cook the liver for strength and leave the rest for the hyenas. It is not too late to hunt today and even a duiker or a steenbok would be better than this mess.'

"Then you set to work nevertheless; butcher the animal, carry the meat back to the camp and everyone eats," /gaugo concluded.

Things were beginning to make sense. Next, I went to Tomazo.

He corroborated /gaugo's story of the obligatory insults over a kill and added a few details of his own.

"But," I asked, "why insult a man after he has gone to all that trouble to track and kill an animal and when he is going to share the meat with you so that your children will have something to eat?"

"Arrogance," was his cryptic answer.

"Arrogance?"

"Yes, when a young man kills much meat he comes to think of himself as a chief or a big man, and he thinks of the rest of us as his servants or inferiors. We can't accept this. We refuse one who boasts, for someday his pride will make him kill somebody. So we always speak of his meat as worthless. This way we cool his heart and make him gentle."

"But why didn't you tell me this before?" I asked Tomazo with some heat.

"Because you never asked me," said Tomazo, echoing the refrain that has come to haunt every field ethnographer.

The pieces now fell into place. I had known for a long time that in situations of social conflict with Bushmen I held all the cards. I was the only source of tobacco in a thousand square miles, and I was not incapable of cutting an individual off for noncooperation. Though my boycott never lasted longer than a few days, it was an indication of my strength. People resented my presence at the water hole, yet simultaneously dreaded my leaving. In short I was a perfect target for the charge of arrogance and for the Bushmen tactic of enforcing humility.

I had been taught an object lesson by the Bushmen; it had come from an unexpected corner and had hurt me in a vulnerable area. For the big black ox was to be the one totally generous, unstinting act of my year at /ai/ai and I was quite unprepared for the reaction I received.

As I read it, their message was this: There are no totally generous acts. All "acts" have an element of calculation. One black ox slaughtered at Christmas does not wipe out a year of careful manipulation of gifts given to serve your own ends. After all, to kill an animal and share the meat with people is really no more than the Bushmen do for each other every day and with far less fanfare.

In the end, I had to admire how the Bushmen had played out the farce—collectively straight-faced to the end. Curiously, the episode reminded me of the *Good Soldier Schweik* and his marvelous encounters with authority. Like Schweik, the Bushmen had retained a thorough-going skepticism of good intentions. Was it this independence of spirit, I wondered, that had kept them culturally viable in the face of genera-tions of contact with more powerful societies, both black and white?

The thought that the Bushmen were alive and well in the Kalahari was strangely comforting. Perhaps, armed with that independence and with their superb knowledge of their environment, they might yet survive the future.

REVIEW QUESTIONS

1. What was the basis of the misunderstanding experienced by Lee when he gave an ox for the Christmas feast held by the !Kung?

2. Construct a model of cross-cultural misunderstanding, using the information presented by Lee in this article.

3. Why do you think the !Kung ridicule and denigrate people who have been successful hunters or who have provided them with a Christmas ox? Why do Americans expect people to be grateful to receive gifts?

3

Shakespeare in the bush

LAURA BOHANNAN

Cultural anthropologists are all concerned with meaning, *with the difficult task of translation from one language to another. In this classic of anthropology, Laura Bohannan shows the difficulty of translating the meaning of* Hamlet *to the Tiv in West Africa. She forcefully demonstrates the way in which different cultures provide distinct and separate worlds of meaning for those who have learned to live by them.*

Just before I left Oxford for the Tiv in West Africa, conversation turned to the season at Stratford. "You Americans," said a friend, "often have difficulty with Shakespeare. He was after all, a very English poet, and one can easily misinterpret the universal by misunderstanding the particular."

I protested that human nature is pretty much the same the whole world over; at least the general plot and motivation of the greater tragedies would always be clear — everywhere — although some details of custom might have to be explained and difficulties of translation might produce other slight changes. To end an argument we could not conclude, my friend gave me a copy of *Hamlet* to study in the African bush: it would, he hoped, lift my mind above its primitive surroundings, and possibly I might, by prolonged meditation, achieve the grace of correct interpretation.

It was my second field trip to that African tribe, and I thought myself ready to live in one of its remote sections — an area difficult to cross even on foot. I eventually settled on the hillock of a very knowledgeable old man, the head of a homestead of some hundred and forty people, all of whom were either his close relatives or their wives and children. Like the other elders of the vicinity, the old man spent most of his time performing ceremonies seldom seen these days in the more accessible parts of the tribe. I was delighted. Soon there would be three months of enforced isolation and leisure, between the harvest that takes place just before the rising of the swamps and the clearing of new farms when the water goes down. Then, I thought, they would have even more time to perform ceremonies and explain them to me.

I was quite mistaken. Most of the ceremonies demanded the presence of elders from several homesteads. As the swamps rose, the old men found it too difficult to walk from one homestead to the next, and the ceremonies gradually ceased. As the swamps rose even higher, all activities but one came to an end. The women brewed beer from maize and millet. Men, women, and children sat on their hillocks and drank it.

People began to drink at dawn. By midmorning the whole homestead was singing, dancing, and drumming. When it rained, people had to sit inside their huts: there they drank and sang or they drank and told stories. In any case, by noon or before, I either had to join the party or retire to my own hut and my books. "One does not discuss serious matters when there is beer. Come, drink with us." Since I lacked their capacity for the thick native beer, I spent more and more time with *Hamlet*. Before the end of the second month, grace descended on me. I was quite sure that *Hamlet* had only one possible interpretation, and that one universally obvious.

Early every morning, in the hope of having some serious talk before the beer party, I used to call on the old man at his reception hut — a circle of posts supporting a thatched roof above a low mud wall to keep out wind and rain. One day I crawled through the low doorway and found most of the men of the homestead sitting huddled in their ragged cloths on stools, low plank beds, and reclining chairs, warming themselves against the chill of the rain around a smoky fire. In the center were three pots of beer. The party had started.

The old man greeted me cordially. "Sit down and drink." I accepted a large calabash full of beer, poured some into a small drinking gourd, and tossed it down. Then I poured some more into the same gourd for the man second in seniority to my host before I handed my calabash over to a young man for further distribution. Important people shouldn't ladle beer themselves.

"It is better like this," the old man said, looking at me approvingly and plucking at the thatch that had caught in my hair. "You should sit and drink with us more often. Your servants tell me that when you are not with us, you sit inside your hut looking at a paper."

The old man was acquainted with four kinds of "papers": tax receipts, bride price receipts, court fee receipts, and letters. The messenger who brought him letters from the chief used them mainly as a badge of office, for he always knew what was in them and told the old man. Personal letters for the few who had relatives in the government or mission stations were kept until someone went to a large market where there was a letter writer and reader. Since my arrival, letters were brought to me to be read. A few men also brought me bride price receipts, privately, with requests to change the figures to a higher sum. I found moral arguments were of no avail, since in-laws are fair game, and the technical hazards of forgery difficult to explain to an illiterate people. I did not wish them to think me silly enough to look at any such papers for days on end, and I hastily explained that my "paper" was one of the "things of long ago" of my country.

"Ah," said the old men. "Tell us."

I protested that I was not a storyteller. Storytelling is a skilled art among them; their standards are high, and the audiences critical — and vocal in their criticism. I protested in vain. This morning they wanted to hear a story while they drank. They threatened to tell me no more stories until I told them one of mine. Finally, the old man promised that no one would criticize my style "for we know you are struggling with our language." "But," put in one of the elders, "you must explain what we do not understand, as we do when we tell you our stories." Realizing that here was my chance to prove *Hamlet* universally intelligible, I agreed.

The old man handed me some more beer to help me on with my storytelling. Men filled their long wooden pipes and knocked coals from the fire to place in the pipe bowls; then, puffing contentedly, they sat back to listen. I began in the proper style, "Not yesterday, not yesterday, but long ago, a thing occurred. One night three men were keeping watch outside the homestead of the great chief, when suddenly they saw the former chief approach them."

"Why was he no longer their chief?"

"He was dead," I explained. "That is why they were troubled and afraid when they saw him."

"Impossible," began one of the elders, handing his pipe on to his neighbor, who interrupted, "Of course it wasn't the dead chief. It was an omen sent by a witch. Go on."

Slightly shaken, I continued. "One of these three was a man who knew things" — the closest translation for scholar, but unfortunately it also meant witch. The second elder looked triumphantly at the first. "So he spoke to the dead chief saying, 'Tell us what we must do so you may rest in your grave,' but the dead chief did not answer. He vanished, and they could see him no more. Then the man who knew things—his name was Horatio—said this event was the affair of the dead chief's son, Hamlet."

There was a general shaking of heads around the circle. "Had the dead chief no living brothers? Or was this son the chief?"

"No," I replied. "That is, he had one living brother who became the chief when the elder brother died."

The old men muttered: such omens were matters for chiefs and elders, not for youngsters; no good could come of being behind a chief's back; clearly Horatio was not a man who knew things.

"Yes, he was," I insisted, shooing a chicken away from my beer. "In our country the son is next to the father. The dead chief's younger brother had become the great chief. He had also married his elder brother's widow only about a month after the funeral."

"He did well," the old man beamed and announced to the others, "I told you that if we knew more about Europeans, we would find they really were very like us. In our country also," he added to me, "the younger brother marries the elder brother's widow and becomes the father of his children. Now, if your uncle, who married your widowed mother, is your father's full brother, then he will be a real father to you. Did Hamlet's father and uncle have one mother?"

His question barely penetrated my mind; I was too upset and thrown too far off balance by having one of the most important elements of *Hamlet* knocked straight out of the picture. Rather uncertainly I said that I thought they had the same mother, but I wasn't sure—the story didn't say. The old man told me severely that these genealogical details made all the difference and that when I got home I must ask the elders about it. He shouted out the door to one of his younger wives to bring his goatskin bag.

Determined to save what I could of the mother motif, I took a deep breath and began again. "The son Hamlet was very sad because his mother had married again so quickly. There was no need for her to do so, and it is our custom for a widow not to go to her next husband until she has mourned for two years."

"Two years is too long," objected the wife, who had appeared with the old man's battered goatskin bag. "Who will hoe your farms for you while you have no husband?"

"Hamlet," I retorted without thinking, "was old enough to hoe his mother's farms himself. There was no need for her to remarry." No one looked convinced. I gave up. "His mother and the great chief told Hamlet not to be sad, for the great chief himself would be a father to Hamlet. Furthermore, Hamlet would be the next chief: therefore he must stay to learn the things of a chief. Hamlet agreed to remain, and all the rest went off to drink beer."

While I paused, perplexed at how to render Hamlet's disgusted soliloquy to an audience convinced that Claudius and Gertrude had behaved in the best possible manner, one of the younger men asked me who had married the other wives of the dead chief.

"He had no other wives," I told him.

"But a chief must have many wives! How else can he brew beer and prepare food for all his guests?"

I said firmly that in our country even chiefs had only one wife, that they had servants to do their work, and that they paid them from tax money.

It was better, they returned, for a chief to have many wives and sons who would help him hoe his farms and feed his people; then everyone loved the chief who gave much and took nothing — taxes were a bad thing.

I agreed with the last comment, but for the rest fell back on their favorite way of fobbing off my questions: "That is the way it is done, so that is how we do it."

I decided to skip the soliloquy. Even if Claudius was here thought quite right to marry his brother's widow, there remained the poison motif, and I knew they would disapprove of fratricide. More hopefully I resumed, "That night Hamlet kept watch with the three who had seen his dead father. The dead chief again appeared, and although the others were afraid, Hamlet followed his dead father off to one side. When they were alone, Hamlet's dead father spoke."

"Omens can't talk!" The old man was emphatic.

"Hamlet's dead father wasn't an omen. Seeing him might have been an omen, but he was not." My audience looked as confused as I sounded. "It *was* Hamlet's dead father. It was a thing we call a 'ghost.' " I had to use the English word, for unlike many of the neighboring tribes, these people didn't believe in the survival after death of any individuating part of the personality.

"What is a 'ghost?' An omen?"

"No, a 'ghost' is someone who is dead but who walks around and can talk, and people can hear him and see him but not touch him."

They objected. "One can touch zombis."

"No, no! It was not a dead body the witches had animated to sacrifice and eat. No one else made Hamlet's dead father walk. He did it himself."

"Dead men can't walk," protested my audience as one man.

I was quite willing to compromise. "A 'ghost' is a dead man's shadow."

But again they objected. "Dead men cast no shadows."

"They do in my country," I snapped.

The old man quelled the babble of disbelief that arose immediately and told me with that insincere, but courteous, agreement one extends to the fancies of the young, ignorant, and superstitious, "No doubt in your country the dead can also walk without being zombis." From the depths of his bag he produced a withered fragment of kola nut, bit off one end to show it wasn't poisoned, and handed me the rest as a peace offering.

"Anyhow," I resumed, "Hamlet's dead father said that his own brother, the one who became chief, had poisoned him. He wanted Hamlet to avenge him. Hamlet believed this in his heart, for he did not like his father's brother." I took another swallow of beer. "In the country of the great chief, living in the same homestead, for it was a very large one, was an important elder who was often with the chief to advise and help him. His name was Polonius. Hamlet was courting his daughter, but her father and her brother . . . [I cast hastily about for some tribal analogy] warned her not to let Hamlet visit her when she was alone on her farm, for he would be a great chief and so could not marry her."

"Why not?" asked the wife, who had settled down on the edge of the old man's chair. He frowned at her for asking stupid questions and growled, "They lived in the same homestead."

"That was not the reason," I informed them. "Polonius was a stranger who lived in the homestead because he helped the chief, not because he was a relative."

"Then why couldn't Hamlet marry her?"

"He could have," I explained, "but Polonius didn't think he would. After all, Hamlet was a man of great importance who ought to marry a chief's daughter, for in his country a man could have only one wife. Polonius was afraid that if Hamlet made love to his daughter, then no one else would give a high price for her."

"That might be true," remarked one of the shrewder elders, "but a chief's son would give his mistress's father enough presents and patronage to more than make up the difference. Polonius sounds like a fool to me."

"Many people think he was," I agreed. "Meanwhile Polonius sent his son Laertes off to Paris to learn the things of that country, for it was the homestead of a very great chief indeed. Because he was afraid that Laertes might waste a lot of money on beer and women and gambling, or get into trouble by fighting, he sent one of his servants to Paris secretly, to spy out what Laertes was doing. One day Hamlet came upon Polonius's daughter Ophelia. He behaved so oddly he frightened her. Indeed" — I was fumbling for words to express the dubious quality of Hamlet's madness — "the chief and many others had also noticed that when Hamlet talked one could understand the words but not what they meant. Many people thought that he had become mad." My audience suddenly became much more attentive. "The great chief wanted to know what was wrong with Hamlet, so he sent for two of Hamlet's age mates [school friends would have taken long explanation] to talk to Hamlet and find out what troubled his heart. Hamlet, seeing that they had been bribed by the chief to betray him, told them nothing. Polonius, however, insisted that Hamlet was mad because he had been forbidden to see Ophelia, whom he loved."

"Why," inquired a bewildered voice, "should anyone bewitch Hamlet on that account?"

"Bewitch him?"

"Yes, only witchcraft can make anyone mad, unless, of course, one sees the beings that lurk in the forest."

I stopped being a storyteller, took out my notebook and demanded to be told more about these two causes of madness. Even while they spoke and I jotted notes, I tried to calculate the effect of this new factor on the plot. Hamlet had not been exposed to the beings that lurk in the forest. Only his relatives in the male line could bewitch him. Barring relatives not mentioned by Shakespeare, it had to be Claudius who was attempting to harm him. And, of course, it was.

For the moment I staved off questions by saying that the great chief also refused to believe that Hamlet was mad for the love of Ophelia and nothing else. "He was sure that something much more important was troubling Hamlet's heart."

"Now Hamlet's age mates," I continued, "had brought with them a famous storyteller. Hamlet decided to have this man tell the chief and all his homestead a story about the man who had poisoned his brother because he desired his brother's wife and wished to be chief himself. Hamlet was sure the great chief could not hear the story without making a sign if he was indeed guilty, and then he would discover whether his dead father had told him the truth."

The old man interrupted, with deep cunning, "Why should a father lie to his son?" he asked.

I hedged: "Hamlet wasn't sure that it really was his dead father." It was impossible to say anything, in that language, about devil-inspired visions.

"You mean," he said, "it actually was an omen, and he knew witches sometimes send false ones. Hamlet was a fool not to go to one skilled in reading omens and divining the truth in the first place. A man-who-sees-the-truth could have told him how his father died, if he really had been poisoned, and if there was witchcraft in it; then Hamlet could have called the elders to settle the matter."

The shrewd elder ventured to disagree. "Because his father's brother was a great chief, one-who-sees-the-truth might therefore have been afraid to tell it. I think it was for that reason that a friend of Hamlet's father — a witch and an elder — sent an omen so his friend's son would know. Was the omen true?"

"Yes," I said, abandoning ghosts and the devil; a witch-sent omen it would have to be. "It was true, for when the storyteller was telling his tale before all the homestead, the great chief rose in fear. Afraid that Hamlet knew his secret he planned to have him killed."

The stage set of the next bit presented some difficulties of translation. I began cautiously. "The great chief told Hamlet's mother to find out from her son what he knew. But because a woman's children are always first in her heart, he had the important elder Polonius hide behind a cloth that hung against the wall of Hamlet's mother's sleeping hut. Hamlet started to scold his mother for what she had done."

There was a shocked murmer from everyone. A man should never scold his mother.

"She called out in fear, and Polonius moved behind the cloth. Shouting, 'A rat!' Hamlet took his machete and slashed through the cloth." I paused for a dramatic effect. "He had killed Polonius!"

The old men looked at each other in supreme disgust. "That Polonius truly was a fool and a man who knew nothing! What child would not know enough to shout, 'It's me!' " With a pang, I remembered that these people are ardent hunters, always armed with bow, arrow, and machete; at the first rustle in the grass an arrow is aimed and ready, and the hunter shouts "Game!" If no human voice answers immediately, the arrow speeds on its way. Like a good hunter Hamlet had shouted, "A rat!"

I rushed in to save Polonius's reputation. "Polonius did speak. Hamlet heard him. But he thought it was the chief and wished to kill him to avenge his father. He had meant to kill him earlier that evening. . . ." I broke down, unable to describe to these pagans, who had no belief in individual afterlife, the difference between dying at one's prayers and dying "unhousell'd, disappointed, unaneled."

This time I had shocked my audience seriously. "For a man to raise his hand against his father's brother and the one who has become his father—that is a terrible thing. The elders ought to let such a man be bewitched."

I nibbled at my kola nut in some perplexity, then pointed out that after all the man had killed Hamlet's father.

"No," pronounced the old man, speaking less to me than to the young men sitting behind the elders. "If your father's brother has killed your father, you must appeal to your father's age mates; *they* may avenge him. No man may use violence against his senior relatives." Another thought struck him. "But if his father's brother had indeed been wicked enough to bewitch Hamlet and make him mad that would be a good story indeed, for it would be his fault that Hamlet, being mad, no longer had any sense and thus was ready to kill his father's brother."

There was a murmer of applause. *Hamlet* was again a good story to them, but it no longer seemed quite the same story to me. As I thought over the coming complications of plot and motive, I lost courage and decided to skim over dangerous ground quickly.

"The great chief," I went on, "was not sorry that Hamlet had killed Polonius. It gave him a reason to send Hamlet away, with his two treacherous age mates, with letters to a chief of a far country, saying that Hamlet should be killed. But Hamlet changed the writing on their papers, so that the chief killed his age mates instead." I encountered a reproachful glare from one of the men whom I had told undetectable forgery was not merely immoral but beyond human skill. I looked the other way.

"Before Hamlet could return. Laertes came back for his father's funeral. The great chief told him Hamlet had killed Polonius. Laertes swore to kill Hamlet because of this, and because his sister Ophelia, hearing her father had been killed by the man she loved, went mad and drowned in the river."

"Have you already forgotten what we told you?" The old man was reproachful. "One cannot take vengeance on a madman; Hamlet killed Polonius in his madness. As for the girl, she not only went mad, she was drowned. Only witches can make people drown. Water itself can't hurt anything. It is merely something one drinks and bathes in."

I began to get cross. "If you don't like the story, I'll stop."

The old man made soothing noises and himself poured me some more beer. "You tell the story well, and we are listening. But it is clear that the elders of your country have never told you what the story really means. No, don't interrupt! We believe you when you say your marriage customs are different, or your clothes and weapons. But people are the same everywhere; therefore, there are always witches and it is we, the elders, who know how witches work. We told you it was the great chief who wished to kill Hamlet, and now your own words have proved us right. Who were Ophelia's male relatives?"

"There were only her father and her brother." Hamlet was clearly out of my hands.

"There must have been many more; this also you must ask of your elders when you get back to your country. From what you tell us, since Polonius was dead, it must have been Laertes who killed Ophelia, although I do not see the reason for it."

We had emptied one pot of beer, and the old men argued the point with slightly tipsy interest. Finally one of them demanded of me, "What did the servent of Polonius say on his return?"

With difficulty I recollected Reynaldo and his mission. "I don't think he did return before Polonius was killed."

"Listen," said the elder, "and I will tell you how it was and how your story will go, then you may tell me if I am right. Polonius knew his son would get into trouble, and so he did. He had many fines to pay for fighting, and debts from gambling. But he had only two ways of getting money quickly. One was to marry off his sister at once, but it is difficult to find a man who will marry a woman desired by the son of a chief. For if the chief's heir commits adultery with your wife, what can you do? Only a fool calls a case against a man who will someday be his judge. Therefore Laertes had to take the second way: he killed his sister by witchcraft, drowning her so he could secretly sell her body to the witches."

I raised an objection. "They found her body and buried it. Indeed Laertes jumped into the grave to see his sister once more — so, you see, the body was truly there. Hamlet, who had just come back, jumped in after him."

"What did I tell you?" The elder appealed to the others. "Laertes was up to no good with his sister's body. Hamlet prevented him, because the chief's heir, like a chief, does not wish any other man to grow rich and powerful. Laertes would be angry, because he would have killed his sister without benefit to himself. In our country he would try to kill Hamlet for that reason. Is this not what happened?"

"More or less," I admitted. "When the great chief found Hamlet was still alive, he encouraged Laertes to try to kill Hamlet and arranged a fight with machetes between them. In the fight both the young men were wounded to death. Hamlet's mother drank the poisoned beer that the chief meant for Hamlet in case he won the fight. When he saw his mother die of poison, Hamlet, dying, managed to kill his father's brother with his machete."

"You see, I was right!" exclaimed the elder.

"That was a very good story," added the old man, "and you told it with very few mistakes. There was just one more error, at the very end. The poison Hamlet's mother drank was obviously meant for the survivor of the fight, whichever it was. If Laertes had won, the great chief would have poisoned him, for no one would know that he arranged Hamlet's death. Then, too, he need not fear Laertes' witchcraft; it takes a strong heart to kill one's only sister by witchcraft.

"Sometime," concluded the old man, gathering his ragged toga about him, "you must tell us some more stories of your country. We, who are elders, will instruct you in their true meaning, so that when you return to your own land your elders will see that you have not been sitting in the bush, but among those who know things and who have taught you wisdom."

REVIEW QUESTIONS

1. In what ways does Bohannan's attempt to tell the story of *Hamlet* to the Tiv illustrate the concept of naive realism?

2. Using Bohannan's experience of telling the story of *Hamlet* to the Tiv and the response of the Tiv elders to her words, illustrate cross-cultural misunderstanding.

3. What are the most important parts of *Hamlet* that the Tiv found it necessary to reinterpret?

4

Acceptance in the field: Doctor, lawyer, Indian chief

RICHARD KURIN

*As we have seen in the previous articles, ethnographic fieldwork
is a personal endeavor. It requires that anthropologists live and work
in foreign communities, interview informants, observe events, join
in activities, and generally insinuate themselves into the rhythm of
daily life. It is no wonder that informants struggle to "place" their
unexpected guests, to give these strange, inquisitive foreigners a
social identity that makes some sense in local terms. In this
article, Richard Kurin traces the history of his identity as it
is defined for him by Pakistani villagers. Initially identified by the
term "Englishman," a name that gives no inside status in the
community, he goes on to become a "teacher," "doctor," "lawyer,"
and, finally, kinsman to his hosts.*

I was full of confidence when — equipped with a scholarly proposal,
blessings from my advisers, and generous research grants — I set out to
study village social structure in the Punjab province of Pakistan. But
after looking for an appropriate fieldwork site for several weeks without success, I began to think that my research project would never get
off the ground. Daily I would seek out villagers aboard my puttering
motor scooter, traversing the dusty dirt roads, footpaths, and irrigation
ditches that crisscross the Punjab. But I couldn't seem to find a village
amenable to study. The major problem was that the villagers I did
approach were baffled by my presence. They could not understand

With permission from *Natural History*, vol. 89, no.11; Copyright the American Museum
of Natural History, 1980.

why anyone would travel ten thousand miles from home to a foreign country in order to live in a poor village, interview illiterate peasants, and then write a book about it. Life, they were sure, was to be lived, not written about. Besides, they thought, what of any importance could they possibly tell me? Committed as I was to ethnographic research, I readily understood their viewpoint. I was a *babu log* — literally, a noble; figuratively, a clerk; and simply, a person of the city. I rode a motor scooter, wore tight-fitting clothing, and spoke Urdu, a language associated with the urban literary elite. Obviously, I did not belong, and the villagers simply did not see me fitting into their society.

The Punjab, a region about the size of Colorado, straddles the northern border of India and Pakistan. Partitioned between the two countries in 1947, the Punjab now consists of a western province, inhabited by Muslims, and an eastern one, populated in the main by Sikhs and Hindus. As its name implies — *punj* meaning "five" and *ab* meaning "rivers" — the region is endowed with plentiful resources to support widespread agriculture and a large rural population. The Punjab has traditionally supplied grains, produce, and dairy products to the peoples of neighboring and considerably more arid states, earning it a reputation as the breadbasket of southern Asia.

Given this predilection for agriculture, Punjabis like to emphasize that they are earthy people, having values they see as consonant with rural life. These values include an appreciation of, and trust in, nature; simplicity and directness of expression; an awareness of the basic drives and desires that motivate men (namely, *zan, zar, zamin* — "women, wealth, land"); a concern with honor and shame as abiding principles of social organization; and for Muslims, a deep faith in Allah and the teachings of his prophet Mohammad.

Besides being known for its fertile soils, life-giving rivers, and superlative agriculturists, the Punjab is also perceived as a zone of transitional culture, a region that has experienced repeated invasions of peoples from western and central Asia into the Indian subcontinent. Over the last four thousand years, numerous groups, among them Scythians, Parthians, Huns, Greeks, Moguls, Persians, Afghans, and Turks, have entered the subcontinent through the Punjab in search of bountiful land, riches, or power. Although Punjabis — notably Rajputs, Sikhs, and Jats — have a reputation for courage and fortitude on the battlefield, their primary, self-professed strength has been their ability to incorporate new, exogenous elements into their society with a minimum of conflict. Punjabis are proud that theirs is a multiethnic society in which diverse groups have been largely unified by a common language and by common customs and traditions.

Given this background, I had not expected much difficulty in locating a village in which to settle and conduct my research. As an anthropologist, I viewed myself as an "earthy" social scientist who, being concerned with basics, would have a good deal in common with rural Punjabis. True, I might be looked on as an invader of a sort; but I was benevolent, and sensing this, villagers were sure to incorporate me into their society with even greater ease than was the case for the would-be conquering armies that had preceded me. Indeed, they would welcome me with open arms.

I was wrong. The villagers whom I approached attributed my desire to live with them either to neurotic delusions or nefarious ulterior motives. Perhaps, so the arguments went, I was really after women, land, or wealth.

On the day I had decided would be my last in search of a village, I was driving along a road when I saw a farmer running through a rice field and waving me down. I stopped and he climbed on the scooter. Figuring I had nothing to lose, I began to explain why I wanted to live in a village. To my surprise and delight, he was very receptive, and after sharing a pomegranate milkshake at a roadside shop, he invited me to his home. His name was Allah Ditta, which means "God given," and I took this as a sign that I had indeed found my village.

"My" village turned out to be a settlement of about fifteen hundred people, mostly of the Nunari *qaum*, or "tribe." The Nunaris engage primarily in agriculture (wheat, rice, sugar cane, and cotton), and most families own small plots of land. Members of the Bhatti tribe constitute the largest minority in the village. Although traditionally a warrior tribe, the Bhattis serve in the main as the village artisans and craftsmen.

On my first day in the village I tried explaining in great detail the purposes of my study to the village elders and clan leaders. Despite my efforts, most of the elders were perplexed about why I wanted to live in their village. As a guest, I was entitled to the hospitality traditionally bestowed by Muslim peoples of Asia, and during the first evening I was assigned a place to stay. But I was an enigma, for guests leave, and I wanted to remain. I was perceived as being strange, for I was both a non-Muslim and a non-Punjabi, a type of person not heretofore encountered by most of the villagers. Although I tried to temper my behavior, there was little I could say or do to dissuade my hosts from the view that I embodied the antithesis of Punjabi values. While I was able to converse in their language, Jatki, a dialect of western Punjabi, I was only able to do so with the ability of a four-year-old. This achievement fell far short of speaking the *t'et'*, or "genuine form," of the villagers. Their idiom is rich with the terminology of agricultural operations and rural life. It is unpretentious, uninflected, and direct, and villagers hold high opinions of those who are good with words, who can speak to a point and be convincing. Needless to say, my infantile babble realized none of these characteristics and evoked no such respect.

Similarly, even though I wore indigenous dress, I was inept at tying my *lungi*, or pant cloth. The fact that my *lungi* occasionally fell off and revealed what was underneath gave my neighbors reason to believe that I indeed had no shame and could not control the passions of my *nafs*, or "libidinous nature."

This image of a doltish, shameless infidel barely capable of caring for himself lasted for the first week of my residence in the village. My inability to distinguish among the five varieties of rice and four varieties of lentil grown in the village illustrated that I knew or cared little about nature and agricultural enterprise. This display of ignorance only served to confirm the general consensus that the mysterious morsels I ate from tin cans labeled "Chef Boy-ar-Dee" were not really food at all. Additionally, I did not oil and henna my hair, shave my armpits, or perform ablutions, thereby convincing some commentators that I was a member of a species of subhuman beings, possessing little in the form of either common or moral sense. That the villagers did not quite grant me the status of a person was reflected by their not according me a proper name. In the Punjab, a person's name is equated with honor and respect and is symbolized by his turban. A man who does not have a name, or whose name is not recognized by his neighbors, is unworthy of respect. For such a man, his turban is said to be either nonexistent or to lie in the dust at the feet of others. To be given a name is to have one's head crowned by a turban, an acknowledgment that one leads a responsible and respectable life. Although I repeatedly introduced myself as "Rashid Karim," a fairly decent Pakistani rendering of Richard Kurin, just about all the villagers insisted on calling me *Angrez* ("Englishman"), thus denying me full personhood and implicitly refusing to grant me the right to wear a turban.

As I began to pick up the vernacular, to question villagers about their clan and kinship structure and trace out relationships between different families, my image began to change. My drawings of kinship diagrams and preliminary census mappings were looked upon not only with wonder but also suspicion. My neighbors now began to think there might be a method to my madness. And so there was. Now I had become a spy. Of course it took a week for people to figure out whom I was supposedly spying for. Located as they were at a crossroads of Asia, at a nexus of conflicting geopolitical interests, they had many possibilities to consider. There was a good deal of disagreement on the issue, with the vast majority maintaining that I was either an American, Russian, or Indian spy. A small, but nonetheless vocal, minority held steadfastly to the belief that I was a Chinese spy. I thought it all rather humorous until one day a group confronted me in the main square in front of the nine-by-nine-foot mud hut that I had rented. The leader spoke up and accused me of spying. The remainder of the group grumbled *jahsus! jahsus!* ("spy! spy!"), and I realized that this ad hoc committee of inquiry had the potential of becoming a mob.

To be sure, the villagers had good reason to be suspicious. For one, the times were tense in Pakistan—a national political crisis gripped the country and the populace had been anxious for months over the uncertainty of elections and effective governmental functions. Second, keenly aware of their history, some of the villagers did not have to go too far to imagine that I was at the vanguard of some invading group that had designs upon their land. Such intrigues, with far greater sophistication, had been played out before by nations seeking to expand their power into the Punjab. That I possessed a gold seal letter (which no one save myself could read) from the University of Chicago to the effect that I was pursuing legitimate studies was not enough to convince the crowd that I was indeed an innocent scholar.

I repeatedly denied the charge, but to no avail. The shouts of *jahsus! jahsus!* prevailed. Confronted with this I had no choice.

"Okay," I said. "I admit it. I am a spy!"

The crowd quieted for my long-awaited confession.

"I am a spy and am here to study this village, so that when my country attacks you we will be prepared. You see, we will not bomb Lahore or Karachi or Islamabad. Why should we waste our bombs on millions of people, on factories, dams, airports, and harbors? No, it is far more advantageous to bomb this strategic small village replete with its mud huts, livestock, Persian wheels, and one light bulb. And when we bomb this village, it is imperative that we know how Allah Ditta is related to Abdullah, and who owns the land near the well, and what your marriage customs are."

Silence hung over the crowd, and then one by one the assemblage began to disperse. My sarcasm had worked. The spy charges were defused. But I was no hero in light of my performance, and so I was once again relegated to the status of a nonperson without an identity in the village.

I remained in limbo for the next week, and although I continued my attempts to collect information about village life, I had my doubts as to whether I would ever be accepted by the villagers. And then, through no effort of my own, there was a breakthrough, this time due to another Allah Ditta, a relative of the village headman and one of my leading accusers during my spying days.

I was sitting on my woven string bed on my porch when Allah Ditta approached, leading his son by the neck. "Oh, *Angrez!*" he yelled, "this worthless son of mine is doing poorly in school. He is supposed to be learning English, but he is failing. He has a good mind, but he's lazy. And his teacher is no help, being more intent upon drinking tea and singing film songs than upon teaching English. Oh son of an Englishman, do you know English?"

"Yes, I know English," I replied, "after all, I am an *Angrez.*"

"Teach him," Allah Ditta blurted out, without any sense of making a tactful request.

And so, I spent the next hour with the boy, reviewing his lessons and correcting his pronunciation and grammar. As I did so, villagers stopped to watch and listen, and by the end of the hour, nearly one hundred people had gathered around, engrossed by this tutoring session. They were stupefied. I was an effective teacher, and I actually seemed to know English. The boy responded well, and the crowd reached a new consensus. I had a brain. And in recognition of this achievement I was given a name — "Ustad Rashid," or Richard the Teacher.

Achieving the status of a teacher was only the beginning of my success. The next morning I awoke to find the village sugar vendor at my door. He had a headache and wanted to know if I could cure him.

"Why do you think I can help you?" I asked.

Bhai Khan answered, "Because you are a *ustad*, you have a great deal of knowledge."

The logic was certainly compelling. If I could teach English, I should be able to cure a headache. I gave him two aspirins.

An hour later, my fame had spread. Bhai Khan had been cured, and he did not hesitate to let others know that it was the *ustad* who had been responsible. By the next day, and in fact for the remainder of my stay, I was to see an average of twenty-five to thirty patients a day. I was asked to cure everything from coughs to colds to typhoid, elephantiasis, and impotency. Upon establishing a flourishing and free medical practice, I received another title, *hakim*, or "physician." I was not yet an anthropologist, but I was on my way.

A few days later I took on yet another role. One of my research interests involved tracing out patterns of land ownership and inheritance. While working on the problem of figuring out who owned what, I was approached by the village watchman. He claimed he had been swindled in a land deal and requested my help. As the accused was not another villager, I agreed to present the watchman's case to the local authorities.

Somehow, my efforts managed to achieve results. The plaintiff's grievance was redressed, and I was given yet another title in the village — *wakil*, or "lawyer." And in the weeks that followed, I was steadily called upon to read, translate, and advise upon various court orders that affected the lives of the villagers.

My roles as a teacher, doctor, and lawyer not only provided me with an identity but also facilitated my integration into the economic structure of the community. As my imputed skills offered my neighbors services not readily available in the village, I was drawn into exchange relationships known as *seipi*. *Seipi* refers to the barter system of goods and services among village farmers, craftsmen, artisans, and other specialists. Every morning Roshan the milkman would deliver fresh milk to my hut. Every other day Hajam Ali the barber would stop by and give me a shave. My next-door neighbor, Nura the cobbler, would repair my sandals when required. Ghulam the horse-cart driver would transport me to town when my motor scooter was in disrepair. The parents of my students would send me sweets and sometimes delicious meals. In return, none of my neighbors asked for direct payment for the specific actions performed. Rather, as they told me, they would call upon me when they had need of my services. And they did. Nura needed cough syrup for his children, the milkman's brother needed a job contact in the city, students wanted to continue their lessons, and so on. Through *seipi* relations, various neighbors gave goods and services to me, and I to them.

Even so, I knew that by Punjabi standards, I could never be truly accepted into the village life because I was not a member of either the Nunari or Bhatti tribe. As the villagers would say, "You never really know who a man is until you know who his grandfather and his ancestors were." And to know a person's grandfather or ancestors properly, you had to be a member of the same or a closely allied tribe.

The Nunari tribe is composed of a number of groups. The nucleus consists of four clans — Naul, Vadel, Saddan, and More — each named for one of the four brothers thought to have originally founded the tribe. Clan members are said to be related by blood ties, also called *pag da sak*, or "ties of the turban." In sharing the turban, members of each clan can share the same blood, the same honor, and the same name. Other clans, unrelated by ties of blood to these four, have become attached to this nucleus through a history of marital relations or of continuous political and economic interdependence. Marital relations, called *gag da sak*, "ties of the skirt," are conceived of as relations in which alienable turbans (skirts) in the form of women are exchanged with other, non-turban-sharing groups. Similarly, ties of political and economical domination and subordination are thought of as relations in which the turban of the client is given to that of the patron. A major part of my research work was concerned with reconstructing how the four brothers formed the Nunari tribe, how additional clans became associated with it, and how clan and tribal identity were defined by nomenclature, codes of honor, and the symbols of sharing and exchanging turbans.

To approach these issues I set out to reconstruct the genealogical relationships within the tribe and between the various clans. I elicited genealogies from many of the villagers and questioned older informants about the history of the Nunari tribe. Most knew only bits and pieces of this history, and after several months of interviews and research, I was directed to the tribal genealogists. These people, usually not Nunaris themselves, perform the service of memorizing and then orally relating the history of the tribe and the relationships among its members. The genealogist in the village was an aged and arthritic man named Hedayat, who in his later years was engaged in teaching the Nunari genealogy to his son, who would then carry out the traditional and hereditary duties of his position.

The villagers claimed that Hedayat knew every generation of the Nunari from the present to the founding brothers and even beyond. So I invited Hedayat to my hut and explained my purpose.

"Do you know Allah Ditta son of Rohm?" I asked.

"Yes, of course," he replied.

"Who was Rohm's father?" I continued.

"Shahadat Mohammad," he answered.

"And his father?"

"Hamid."

"And his?"

"Chigatah," he snapped without hesitation.

I was now quite excited, for no one else in the village had been able to recall an ancester of this generation. My estimate was that Chigatah had been born sometime between 1850 and 1870. But Hedayat went on.

"Chigatah's father was Kamal. And Kamal's father was Nanak. And Nanak's father was Sikhu. And before him was Dargai, and before him Maiy. And before him was Siddiq. And Siddiq's father was Nur. And Nur's Asmat. And Asmat was of Channa. And Channa of Nau. And Nau of Bhatta. And Bhatt was the son of Koduk."

Hedayat had now recounted sixteen generations of lineal ascendants related through the turban. Koduk was probably born in the sixteenth century. But still Hedayat continued.

"Sigun was the father of Koduk. And Man the father of Sigun. And before Man was his father Maneswar. And Maneswar's father was the founder of the clan, Naul."

This then was a line of the Naul clan of the Nunari tribe, ascending twenty-one generations from the present descendants (Allah Ditta's sons) to the founder, one of four brothers who lived perhaps in the fifteenth century. I asked Hedayat to recite genealogies of the other Nunari clans, and he did, with some blanks here and there, ending with Vadel, More, and Saddan, the other three brothers who formed the tribal nucleus. I then asked the obvious question, "Hedayat, who was the father of these four brothers? Who is the founding ancestor of the Nunari tribe?"

"The father of these brothers was not a Muslim. He was an Indian *rajput* [chief]. The tribe actually begins with the conversion of the four brothers," Hedayat explained.

"Well, then," I replied, "who was this Indian chief?"

"He was a famous and noble chief who fought against the Moguls. His name was Raja Kurin, who lived in a massive fort in Kurinnagar, about twenty-seven miles from Delhi."

"What!" I asked, both startled and unsure of what I had heard. "Raja Kurin is the father of the brothers who make up—"

"But his name! It's the same as mine," I stammered. "Hedayat, my name is Richard Kurin. What a coincidence! Here I am living with your tribe thousands of miles from my home and it turns out that I have the same name as the founder of the tribe! Do you think I might be related to Raja Kurin and the Nunaris?"

Hedayat looked at me, but only for an instant. Redoing his turban, he tilted his head skyward, smiled, and asked, "What is the name of your father?"

I had come a long way. I now had a name that could be recognized and respected, and as I answered Hedayat, I knew that I had finally and irrevocably fit into "my" village. Whether by fortuitous circumstance or by careful manipulation, my neighbors had found a way to take an invading city person intent on studying their life and transform him into one of their own, a full person entitled to wear a turban for participating in, and being identified with, that life. As has gone on for centuries in the region, once again the new and exogenous had been recast into something Punjabi.

Epilogue: There is no positive evidence linking the Nunaris to a historical Raja Kurin, although there are several famous personages identified by that name (also transcribed as Karan and Kurran). Estimated from the genealogy recited by Hedayat, the founding of the tribe by the four brothers appears to have occurred sometime between 440 and 640 years ago, depending on the interval assumed for each generation. On that basis, the most likely candidate for Nunari progenitor (actual or imputed) is Raja Karan, ruler of Anhilvara (Gujerat), who was defeated by the Khilji Ala-ud-Din in 1297 and again in 1307. Although this is slightly earlier than suggested by the genealogical data, such genealogies are often telescoped or otherwise unreliable.

Nevertheless, several aspects of Hedayat's account make this association doubtful. First, Hedayat clearly identifies Raja Kurin's conquerors as Moguls, whereas the Gujerati Raja Karan was defeated by the Khiljis. Second, Hedayat places the Nunari ancestor's kingdom only twenty-seven miles from Delhi. The Gujerati Raja Karan ruled several kingdoms, none closer than several hundred miles to Delhi.

Other circumstances, however, offer support for this identification of the Nunari ancestor. According to Hedayat, Raja Kurin's father was named Kam Deo. Although the historical figure was the son of Serung Deo, the use of "Deo," a popular title for the rajas of the Vaghela and Solonki dynasties, does seem to place the Nunari founder in the context of medieval Gujerat. Furthermore, Hedayat clearly identifies the saint (*pir*) said to have initiated the conversion of the Nunaris to Islam. This saint, Mukhdum-i-Jehaniyan, was a contemporary of the historical Raja Karan.

Also of interest, but as yet unexplained, is that several other groups living in Nunari settlement areas specifically claim to be descended from Raja Karan of Gujerat, who is said to have migrated northward into the Punjab after his defeat. Controverting this theory, the available evidence indicates that Raja Karan fled, not toward the Punjab, but rather southward to the Deccan, and that his patriline ended with him. It is his daughter Deval Devi who is remembered: she is the celebrated heroine of "Ashiqa," a famous Urdu poem written by Amir Khusrau in 1316. She was married to Khizr Khan, the son of Karan's conqueror; nothing is known of her progeny.

REVIEW QUESTIONS

1. An anthropologist's informants usually identify him or her in ways that fit their own culture. What social identities did Kurin acquire as his stay in a Pakistani village progressed?

2. Using Kurin's experience as a guide, how do you think the way informants identify the anthropologist affects the quality of field-work?

3. Most ethnographers initially find it difficult to conduct fieldwork because they are strangers who take much but give little. How did Kurin deal with this problem, and how do you think it benefited and impaired his field research?

III

Language and communication

Culture is a system of symbols that allows us to represent and communicate our experience. We are surrounded by symbols — the flag, a new automobile, a diamond ring, billboard pictures, and, of course, spoken words.

A *symbol* is anything that we can perceive with our senses that stands for something else. Almost anything we experience can come to have symbolic meaning. Every symbol has a referent that it calls to our attention. The term *mother-in-law* refers to a certain kind of relative, the mother of a person's spouse. When we communicate with symbols, we call attention not only to the referent but also to numerous connotations of the symbol. In our culture, *mother-in-law* connotes a stereotype of a person who is difficult to get along with, who meddles in the affairs of her married daughter or son, and who is to be avoided. Human beings have the capacity to assign meaning to anything they experience in an arbitrary fashion. This fact gives rise to limitless possibilities for communication.

Symbols greatly simplify the task of communication. Once we learn that a word like *barn*, for example, stands for a certain type of building, we can communicate about a whole range of specific buildings that fit into the category. And we can communicate about barns in their absence; we can even invent flying barns and dream about barns. Symbols make it possible to communicate the immense variety of human experience, whether past or present, tangible or intangible, good or bad.

Many channels are available to human beings for symbolic communication — sound, sight, touch, and smell. Language, our most highly developed communication system, uses the channel of sound (or for some deaf people, sight). *Language* is a system of cultural knowledge used to generate and interpret speech. It is a feature of every culture and a distinctive characteristic of the human animal. *Speech* refers to the behavior that produces vocal sounds. Our distinction between language and speech is like the one made for culture and behavior. Language is part of culture, the system of knowledge that generates behavior. Speech is the behavior generated and interpreted by language.

Every language is composed of three subsystems for dealing with vocal symbols: phonology, grammar, and semantics. Let's look briefly at each of these.

Phonology consists of the categories and rules for forming vocal symbols. It is concerned not directly with meaning but with the formation and recognition of the vocal sounds to which we assign meaning. For example, if you utter the word *bat,* you have followed a special set of rules for producing and ordering sound categories characteristic of the English language.

A basic element defined by phonological rules for every language is the phoneme. *Phonemes* are the minimal categories of speech sounds that serve to keep utterances apart. For example, speakers of English know that the words *bat, cat, mat, hat, nat,* and *fat* are different utterances because they hear the sounds /b/, /c/, /m/, /h/, /n/, and /f/ as different categories of sounds. In English each of these is a phoneme. Our language contains a limited number of phonemes from which we construct all our vocal symbols.

Phonemes are arbitrarily constructed, however. Each phoneme actually classifies slightly different sounds as though they were the same. Different languages may divide up the same range of speech sounds into different sound categories. For example, speakers of English treat the sound /t/ as a single phoneme. Hindi speakers take the same general range and divide it into four phonemes: /t/, /tʰ/, /T/, and /Tʰ/. (The lowercase *t*'s are made with the tongue against the front teeth, while uppercase *t*'s are made by touching the tongue to the roof of the mouth further back than would be normal for an English speaker. The *h* indicates a puff of air, called aspiration, associated with the *t* sound.) Americans are likely to miss important distinctions among Hindi words because they hear these four different phonemes as a single one. Hindi speakers, on the other hand, tend to hear more than one sound category as they listen to English speakers pronounce *t*'s. The situation is reversed for /w/ and /v/. We treat these as two phonemes, whereas Hindi speakers hear them as one. For them, the English words *wine* and *vine* are the same.

Phonology also includes rules for ordering different sounds. Even when we try to talk nonsense, we usually create words that follow English phonological rules. It would be unlikely, for example, for us ever to begin a word with the phoneme /ng/ usually written in English as "ing." It must come at the end or in the middle of words.

Grammar is the second subsystem of language. *Grammar* refers to the categories and rules for combining vocal symbols. No grammar contains rules for combining every word or element of meaning in the language. If this were the case, grammars would be so unwieldy that no one could learn all the rules in a lifetime. Every grammar deals with *categories* of symbols, such as the ones we call nouns and verbs. Once you know the rules covering a particular category, you can use it in the appropriate order.

Morphemes are the categories in any language that carry meaning. They are minimal units of meaning that cannot be subdivided. Morphemes occur in more complex patterns than you may think. The term *bats*, for example, is actually two morphemes, /bat/ meaning a flying mammal and /s/ meaning plural. Even more confusing, two different morphemes may have the same sound shape. /Bat/ can refer to a wooden club used in baseball as well as a flying mammal.

The third subsystem of every language is semantics. *Semantics* refers to the categories and rules for relating vocal symbols to their referents. Like the rules of grammar, semantic rules are simple instructions to combine things; they instruct us to combine words with what they refer to. A symbol can be said to *refer* because it focuses our attention and makes us take account of something. For example, /bat/ refers to a family of flying mammals, as we have already noted.

Language regularly occurs in a social context, and to understand its use fully, it is important to recognize its relation to sociolinguistic rules. *Sociolinguistic rules* combine meaningful utterances with social situations into appropriate messages. The first article in this section, by James Spradley and Brenda Mann, illustrates the importance of sociolinguistic rules in the context of a college bar. The authors show how it would be impossible to understand talk in the bar by just using phonological, grammatical, and semantic rules alone. One also has to discover the social situations for speaking, ways of speaking, and the motivations of the talkers.

Although language is the most important human vehicle for communication, almost anything we can sense may represent a symbol that conveys meaning. The way we sit, how we use our eyes, how we dress, the car we own, the number of bathrooms in our house—all these things carry symbolic meaning. We learn what they mean as we acquire our culture. Indeed, a major reason we feel so uncomfortable when we enter a group with a strange culture is our inability to decode our hosts' symbolic world. The articles by Edward and Mildred Hall, Terence Turner, and Elizabeth and Robert Fernea discuss the importance of nonlinguistic symbols and illustrate how anthropologists approach the discovery and interpretation of these basic carriers of meaning.

Key terms

symbol	grammar
language	morpheme
speech	semantics
phonology	sociolinguistic rules
phoneme	nonlinguistic symbols

5

Ethnolinguistics:
How to ask for a drink at Brady's

JAMES P. SPRADLEY and
BRENDA J. MANN

Human languages must contain the linguistic *rules for producing meaningful utterances. But there is more to speaking than the linguistic elements — phonemes, morphemes, and grammar — that permit us to transmit direct meaning. Utterances also take place in social contexts, and these exert a subtle effect on how people talk. Every culture contains* sociolinguistic *rules that define appropriate utterances. In this selection, James Spradley and Brenda Mann analyze the way customers at a college bar use their language not only meaningfully, but appropriately. They show that a single speech event, called* asking *for a drink, is much more complicated than it appears. It consists of several speech acts and takes on ritual forms, such as "dominance displays," "ritual reversals," "reciprocal exchanges," "drinking exchanges," "drinking contests," and "asking for the wrong drink." These rituals function to display a male customer's verbal skills and to intensify male values and the sense of belonging to the male society found in this particular bar.*

Brady's Bar is obviously a place to drink. Every night a crowd of college-age men and women visit the bar for this purpose. But even a casual observer could not miss the fact that Brady's is also a place to *talk*. Drinking and talking are inseparable. The lonely drinker who sits in silence is either drawn into conversation or leaves the bar. Everyone feels the anxious insecurity of such a person, seemingly alone in the crowd at Brady's.

James P. Spradley and Brenda J. Mann, pp. 120–143 (in edited form) from *The Cocktail Waitress: Women's Work in a Man's World.* Copyright © 1975 John Wiley and Sons, Inc. Reprinted with permission of Random House, Inc.

It is also believed that drinking affects the way people talk, lubricating the social interchange. If liquor flows each night in Brady's like a stream from behind the bar, talking, laughing, joking, and dozens of simultaneous conversations cascade like a torrent from every corner of the bar. Early in our research we became aware that our ethnography would have to include an investigation of this speech behavior.

The importance of drinking and talking has also been observed by anthropologists in other societies. Take, for example, the Subanun of the Philippine Islands, studied by Charles Frake. Deep in the tropical rain forests of Zamboanga Peninsula on the island of Mindanao, these people live in small family groups, practicing swidden agriculture. Social ties outside the family are maintained by networks to kin and neighbors rather than through some larger formal organization. Social encounters beyond the family occur on frequent festive occasions that always include "beer" drinking. Unlike Brady's Bar with separate glasses for each person, the Subanun place fermented mash in a single, large Chinese jar and drink from this common container by using a long bamboo straw. A drinking group gathers around the jar, water is poured over the mash, and each person in turn sucks beer from the bottom of the jar. As the water passes through the mash it is transformed into a potent alcoholic beverage. There are elaborate rules for these drinking sessions that govern such activities as competitive drinking, opposite-sexed partners drinking together under the cover of a blanket, and games where drinking is done in chugalug fashion. But the drinking is secondary to the talking on these occasions and what Frake has said about the Subanun might easily apply to Brady's Bar:

> The Subanun expression for drinking talk, . . . "talk from the straw," suggests an image of the drinking straw as a channel not only of the drink but also of drinking talk. The two activities, drinking and talking, are closely interrelated in that how one talks bears on how much one drinks and the converse is, quite obviously, also true. . . . Especially for an adult male, one's role in the society at large, insofar as it is subject to manipulation, depends to a considerable extent on one's verbal performance during drinking encounters.[1]

We will examine the verbal performances of those who participate in the social life at Brady's. We focus on a single speech event, *asking for a drink,* and the social function of this event. This is intended as a partial ethnography of speaking, a description of the cultural rules for using speech at Brady's Bar.

1. Charles O. Frake, "How to Ask for a Drink in Subanun," *American Anthropologist* 66 pt. 2 (1964): 128–129.

THE ETHNOGRAPHY OF SPEAKING

"What would a stranger have to know to act appropriately as a cocktail waitress and to interpret behavior from her perspective?" An ethnography of speaking asks this question in reference to the way people talk. It goes beyond the usual linguistic study that analyzes speech in abstraction from its usage. Instead of describing linguistic rules that generate *meaningful* utterances, we sought to discover the sociolinguistic rules that generate *appropriate* utterances. This approach is extremely important because people at Brady's are not interested in merely saying things that make sense; they seek instead to say things that reveal to others their skill in verbal performances. Indeed, this often requires that a person utter nonsense, at least so it seems to the outsider.

In order to discover the rules for using speech, we began by recording what people said to one another, noting whenever possible the gestures, tone of voice, setting, and other features of the verbal interaction. Then we examined these samples of speech usage for recurrent patterns and went back to listen for more instances. At first we sought to identify the major speech events that were typical of the bar. A speech event refers to activities that are directly governed by rules for speaking. On any evening the waitress participates in many different speech events. For example, Denise enters the bar shortly after 6:30 in the evening and almost her first act is to exchange some form of *greeting* with the bartender, the day employees who are present, and any regulars she recognizes. At the bar she *asks for a drink,* saying to John, "I'd like a gin gimlet." This particular speech event takes many forms and is one that Denise will hear repeatedly from customers throughout the evening. She will also label this speech event *taking an order.* John refuses her request, fixes a Coke instead, and replies "You know you can't have a drink now, you start work in thirty minutes."

The evening begins slowly so Denise stands at her station talking to a regular customer. They are participating in a speech event called a *conversation.* As more customers arrive, Denise will say, "Hi, Bill," "Good to see you, George. Where have you been lately?" "Hi, how are things at the 'U' these days?" and other things to *greet* people as they walk in. She will *give orders* to the bartender, *answer the phone,* make an *announcement* about last call, and possibly get into an *argument* with one table when she tries to get them to leave on time. Like the other waitresses, Denise has learned the cultural rules in this bar for identifying particular speech events and participating in the verbal exchanges they involve. She has acquired the rules for greeting people, for arguing, and for giving orders, rules that define the appropriate ways to speak in such events.

It wouldn't take long for a stranger to see that *asking for a drink* is probably the most frequent speech event that occurs in the bar. But, although it is an important activity, it appears to be a rather simple act. A stranger would only have to know the name of one drink, say Pabst Beer, and any simple English utterance that expresses a desire in order to appropriately ask for a drink. The waitress approaches the table, asks, "What would you like?" and a customer can simply say, "I'll have a Pabst." And once a person knows all the names for the other beverages it is possible to use this sentence to ask for any drink the bartenders can provide. A stranger might even go out of the bar thinking that asking for a drink is a rather trivial kind of speech behavior. That was certainly our impression during the first few weeks of fieldwork.

But as time went on we discovered that this speech event is performed in dozens of different ways. The people who come to Brady's have elaborated on a routine event, creating alternative ways for its execution. The well-socialized individual knows the rules for selecting among these alternatives and for manipulating them to his own advantage. Asking for a drink thus becomes a kind of stage on which the customer can perform for the waitress and also the audience of other customers. A newcomer to the bar is frequently inept at these verbal performances, and one can observe regulars and employees smiling at one another or even laughing at some ill-timed and poorly performed effort at asking for a drink. Our goal was not to predict what people would say when they asked for a drink but to specify the alternative ways they could ask for a drink, the rules for selecting one or another alternative, and the social function of these ways of talking. We especially wanted to know how the waitress would interpret the alternatives she encountered in the course of her work. At the heart of the diverse ways to ask for a drink was a large set of speech acts, and it was largely through observing the way people manipulated these different acts that we discovered how to ask for a drink in Brady's Bar.

Speech acts

In order to describe the way people *use* speech we begin with the speech act as the minimal unit for analysis. In every society people use language to accomplish purposes: to insult, to gather information, to persuade, to greet others, to curse, to communicate, etc. An act of speaking to accomplish such purposes can be a single word, a sentence, a paragraph, or even an entire book. A speech act refers to the way any utterance, whether short or long, is used and the rules for this use.

Our informants at Brady's Bar recognized many different categories of speech acts. They not only identified them for us but would frequently refer to one or another speech act during conversations in the bar. For example, at the end of a typically long evening the employees and a few real regulars are sitting around the bar talking about the events of the night. "Those guys in the upper section tonight were really obnoxious," recalls Sue. "They started off *giving me shit* about the way I took their orders and then all night long they kept *calling* my name. After last call they kept *hustling* me and when I finally came right out and said no, they really *slammed* me." The other waitress, Sandy, talks of the seven Annies who were sitting at one of her tables: "They kept *asking* me to tell them what went into drinks and they were drinking Brandy Alexanders, Singapore Slings, Brandy Manhattans, and Peapickers. Then they kept *muttering* their orders all evening so I could hardly hear and *bickering* over the prices and *bitching* about the noise — it was really awful."

Giving shit, calling, hustling, slamming, asking, muttering, bickering, and *bitching* are all ways to talk; they are speech acts used at Brady's Bar. There are at least thirty-five such named speech acts that our informants recognized and these form a folk taxonomy shown in Figure I. . . .

RITUALS OF MASCULINITY

Probably the most important outcome of the various ways to ask for a drink at Brady's Bar is related to the way they symbolize the values of *masculinity* that lie at the heart of bar culture. During our observations of the way male customers asked for drinks, it became clear that these performances had a ritual quality about them. Goffman has identified the nature of this ceremonial or ritual quality in social interaction:

> To the degree that a performance highlights the common official values of the society in which it occurs, we may look upon it, in the manner of Durkheim and Radcliffe-Brown, as a ceremony — as an expressive rejuvenation and reaffirmation of the moral values of the community.[2]

In a sense, the routine performances of asking for a drink at Brady's Bar have been transformed into rituals that express important male

2. Erving Goffman, *The Presentation of Self in Everyday Life* (Garden City, N.Y.: Doubleday, 1959), 35.

FIGURE I. *Some speech acts used in Brady's Bar*

WAYS TO TALK AT BRADY'S BAR	Slamming
	Talking
	Telling
	Giving shit
	Asking
	Begging
	Begging off
	Gossiping
	Joking
	Teasing
	Muttering
	Ordering
	Swearing
	Sweet talking
	Pressuring
	Arguing
	Bantering
	Lying
	Bitching
	P.R.ing
	Babbling
	Harping
	Crying over a beer
	Hustling
	Introducing
	Flirting
	Daring
	Bickering
	Apologizing
	Calling
	Greeting
	Bullshitting
	Hassling
	Admitting
	Giving orders

values. Customers and other members of this community seldom view these speech events as rituals, but nevertheless they function in this manner. These ritual performances reinforce masculine virtues and symbolize full membership in the male world of Brady's Bar.

Furthermore, these rituals take on an added meaning when we consider that the ongoing social life at Brady's often obscures the presence of a deep structural conflict. It stems from the fact that the bar functions both as a *business* and as a *men's ceremonial center* where masculine values are reaffirmed. The conflict between these two features of the bar is partially mediated by a set of speech acts that customers employ to ask for drinks. We need to examine this structural conflict briefly.

On the one hand, the bar is a business establishment that is organized to sell drinks for a profit. It has no membership dues, no initiation rituals, no rules except legal age that restrict certain classes of people from buying drinks. Any adult can open the doors, walk into the bar, and order any drink in the house. The only requirement for drinking is payment of the usual fees. As a business establishment Brady's Bar has an air of efficiency, casualness, and impersonality. There is no readily apparent organization except the division between employees and customers. Even the spatial arrangement can be seen purely in economic terms with the bar and tables arranged for the efficient distribution of drinks. It is possible for an individual to stop in for a drink without ever suspecting that the bar is much different from a restaurant, a bank, or department store except for the menu, small services rendered, or items sold. At one level, then, Brady's is primarily a place of business.

On the other hand, Brady's Bar is a *men's ceremonial center*. As we have seen in earlier chapters, there is a formal social structure that ascribes to men the places of high status. The spatial patterns in the bar reflect the values of a male-oriented culture, with certain places having an almost sacred atmosphere. The language patterns also serve to reaffirm male values, providing an important symbol of membership in the informal men's association. Even the division of labor that appears to be a strict business function reflects the subordinate position of women in the bar as well as the wider society. At another level, then, Brady's Bar is primarily a place where men can come to play out exaggerated masculine roles, acting out their fantasies of sexual prowess, and reaffirming their own male identities.

The essence of the *ceremonial function is to reaffirm the official values of manhood in our culture.* But this is difficult to do when women enter almost every night to drink and talk. Some even select the same drinks as men and all have the right to sit at the bar itself. Strangers visit

Brady's frequently for a quick drink, never entering into the social and ceremonial life of the bar. Students tend to be a transient group that results in a constant turnover of customers. Relationships among people in the bar are frequently impersonal and businesslike. All of this works counter to the ceremonial function that requires some common public expression of the moral values on which masculine identities are constructed. It requires some way to highlight the virtues of strength, toughness, aggressiveness, and dominance over females. Most important, it requires some corporate group of males staging the ritual performances together. It is possible that these ceremonial functions could be carried out by restricting membership to men in a formal way as done by athletic clubs or men's associations in certain New Guinea societies. Some "male only" bars still employ this device. The moral values of masculinity could be reaffirmed by aggressive physical activity from which women are excluded as is done in competitive football from Little League teams for boys to the National Football League. But Brady's managers do not even allow the escalation of the rare fights that do occur but halt them before they hardly begin. Drinks at Brady's could be restricted to men alone or special uniforms and ceremonial regalia could be created to symbolize their corporate unity and importance. But Brady's has none of these. Instead, *male values are reaffirmed by the use of elaborate patterns of language.* It is not so much *what* people say but *how* they speak that serves to mediate between the business and ceremonial functions of the bar.

Language is used to symbolize status and masculinity in public displays. Equally important, customers use speech performances to create a sense of corporate belonging, a feeling of full membership in the men's association that constitutes the hub of this society. Asking for a drink becomes not only a display of an individual's masculinity but a membership ritual announcing to those present that the speaker *belongs*; he is a man who has ties with other men, a male who is at home in a truly male world. Such rituals occur during *dominance displays, ritual reversals, reciprocal exchanges, drinking contests,* and *asking for the wrong drink.* We shall consider each of these in turn.

DOMINANCE DISPLAYS

One frequent way that men ask for a drink is not to ask for a drink at all. In the situation where it is appropriate to ask for a drink, they ask instead for the waitress. This may be done in the form of *teasing, hustling, hassling* or some other speech act. But, whatever the form, it serves as a ritual in which masculine values are symbolized for the people at Brady's. Consider the following example of hassling.

Sandy is working the upper section. She walks up to the corner table where there is a group of five she has never seen before: four guys and a girl who are loud and boisterous. She steps up to the table and asks, "Are you ready to order now?" One of the males grabs her by the waist and jerks her towards him. "I already know what I want, I'll take you," he says as he smiles innocently up at her. Sandy removes his hand and steps back from the table. She takes the orders from the others at the table and then turns back to the first man. He reaches over and pulls her towards him, prolonging the ritual of asking for a drink with a question, "What's good here, do you know?" Sandy patiently removes his hand for the second time, "If you haven't decided yet what you want to drink, I can come back in a few minutes." "Oh, please, don't leave me!" He grabs her by the leg this time, the only part of her he can reach and inquires, "What's your name, honey? Are you new here? I don't think I've seen you before? What nights do you work?" The others at the table begin to smile and chuckle, making the situation worse; Sandy knows that several nearby customers are also watching the encounter. Finally, in desperation she heads for the bar and he calls out, "I'll have a Screwdriver."

Back at her station, she gives the bartender the order and tells Mike, a regular sitting by her station, about the *obnoxo* in the upper section. Mike listens and puts his arm protectively around her, "Look, just make them come down to the bar if they want to order. If they give you any more shit tell me and I'll take care of them." The order is ready and Sandy balances her tray as she heads back to the waiting customers, planning to stand on the opposite side of the table in hopes of avoiding a repeat performance.

This kind of performance is not exceptional. For the waitress it is a recurrent feature of each night's work. The details vary from customer to customer but the basic features remain constant. She approaches a table where, instead of asking for a drink, a customer seizes upon the brief encounter to display his manly skills. "Where have you been all my life?" asks one. "Sit down and talk to us," says another. "Have I ever told you that I love you?" "Haven't I seen you someplace before?" "Wouldn't you like to sit on my lap?" And often the verbal requests are punctuated with attempts to invade the personal space of the waitress. One customer asks for his drink in a low, muffled voice, requiring the waitress to move closer or bend down so she can hear. Another grabs her as she starts to leave. Some pinch, grab a wrist, pat, or securely retain the waitress with an arm around her waist. Except for the regular customer whom she knows well, these direct attempts at physical contact are obvious violations of the usual rules governing interaction between men and women. Indeed, their value seems to lie in this fact, as if to say that here is a real man, one who can act out his aggressive fantasies.

Thus Brady's Bar provides male customers with a stage where they can perform; it offers an audience to appreciate their displays of manliness. Furthermore, this ritual setting gives a special legitimacy to expressing one's masculinity. Asking for a drink becomes an occasion to act out fantasies that would be unthinkable in the classroom, on the street, and even perhaps when alone with a female. But here, in the protective safety of the bar, a customer can demonstrate to others that he has acquired the masculine attributes so important in our culture.

But the masculinity rituals would not be effective without the cooperation of the waitress. She has learned to respond demurely to taunts, invitations, and physical invasions of her personal space. She smiles, laughs, patiently removes hands, ignores the questions, and moves coyly out of reach. It is precisely these qualities of her response that complement the performance of male customers. When she meets a particularly aggressive and obnoxious customer she may complain to bartenders or regulars, providing these men with their opportunity to demonstrate another aspect of manliness — the protector role. But the cultural expectations are clear; *she should remain dependent and passive.* As waitresses move•back and forth between the bar and their tables, they also move between these two kinds of encounters — warding off the tough, aggressive males, and leaning on the strong, protective males.

Although the waitresses know it is important to keep their place during these encounters, it is also clear they *could* act otherwise in dealing with aggressive customers. Like the bartenders, they might refuse to allow customers to act in offensive ways. They could become aggressive themselves, "tough broads" who brusquely reprimand customers and have them removed from the bar. On occasion they all have acted in this way towards a customer, something it would be *possible* to do with relative frequency. For example, one night Joyce was making her way to the table in the corner of the upper section and she had a tray load of expensive cocktails. Doug, a regular, stepped out in front of her, blocking the path. "C'mon, Doug. Don't make me spill these drinks." He was drunk. "I'll move if you give me a kiss," he replied. "Not now, Doug. I have to get these drinks to that table. Now *please* move!" Doug stood his ground, refusing to budge an inch. "If you don't move, Doug, I'm gonna kick you in the shins, and I mean it!" Doug didn't move, but instead, beer in one hand, he reached out to put the other arm around Joyce. That was all it took. Joyce gave him a good hard kick in the shins, and then, to her surprise, Doug kicked her back! Joyce glared at him and he finally let her through to the table. She felt both angry and proud as she carried the tray of ten heavy drinks to the table. Most of the frozen daiquiris were melting and the Bacardis had spilled over the tops of glasses. But for one brief moment an encounter with an aggressive male had been changed into a relationship in which she felt on equal footing. But in the process she had destroyed the ritual quality of Doug's attempt to demonstrate his manliness.

RITUAL REVERSALS

The ritual quality of asking for a drink does not always have a serious tone. Waitresses and customers often work together to create humorous scenes for the audiences around them, using speech acts like *bantering, joking,* and *teasing,* in ways that appear to be serious. These performances are particularly effective in symbolizing masculine values when they call attention to subtle possibilities that some individual is *not* acting like a woman or man. Two examples may serve to illuminate this complex use of language in asking for a drink. The first one humorously suggests that the waitress is sexually aggressive in the way reserved for men. The second implies that a male customer is less than a man because of homosexual tendencies.

Recall an earlier example when Sue waited on a Cougar regular who came to Brady's with three friends. When she approached their table they were engrossed in conversation and to get their attention she placed her hand on one customer's shoulder. He turned to see who it was and then said loudly in mock anger, "Don't you touch me!" Sue jumped back, pretending to be affected by his response. "I'm sorry. Do you want another beer?" He smiled. "No, thanks, a little later." She continued on her circular path around the section. A few minutes later she was back in the area and as she passed the same table the customer reached out and grabbed her by the waist. "Watch the hands," she said. "I'll have another Pabst now," the regular said. She brought him the beer. "That was fast!" he commented as she set the bottle down. "I'm a fast girl," was her response. "Oh, you mean with the beer?" To which she answered, as she collected the money and turned to leave, "What did you think I meant?" In this encounter, first the customer and then the waitress *jokingly* suggest that she may be a sexually aggressive female, thereby underscoring the important cultural value of actually being a passive female.

During the course of our research, a popular song included in the juke box selections at the bar had to do with a football player called Bruiser LaRue, an implied homosexual. Playing this song or making loud requests for someone to play it, provided abundant opportunities for treating homosexuality in a humorous manner. One such opportunity involved asking for a drink. Holly notices two regulars come in the door and because it is crowded they end up along the wall at the back of the lower section where she has just taken an order for another round. Because of the crowd and noise, neither bartender sees these well-known regulars or has a chance to greet them. Holly already knows their drinks so does not need to wait for their orders, but one of them says with a smile, "I'll have a Pink Lady, tell him it's for Bruiser LaRue." At the bar when Holly passes the message on, the bartender immediately scans her section to see who this "Bruiser LaRue" might be. Smiles and laughter are quickly exchanged across the noisy bar, and the ritual is complete. If either bartender or customer were to admit even the possibility of being homosexual or accuse another male of such behavior, it would be a serious violation of cultural norms. By joking about it in the presence of a waitress, they uphold the dominant masculine values, saying, in effect, "We are so manly we can even joke about being effeminate." In a similar fashion, it is not uncommon for a waitress to approach a table of male customers who have just sat down and one will say, "My friend here wants a Pink Lady," or "Bill wants a Gold Cadillac." The waitress smiles, the customers poke one another, smile, laugh, and add other comments. The incongruity of "a man like one of us" having a "female drink" has provided a brief ritual reversal of the sacred values. Because it occurs in a humorous context, no one is threatened and all settle down to a night of drinking, comfortable in their sense of manhood.

RECIPROCAL EXCHANGES

There are several contexts in which customers order drinks for other people with an expectation of reciprocity. Buying in rounds is the most frequent kind of exchange and occurs with almost every group of men who stay for any length of time in the bar. A typical sequence goes something like this. Six men take their places at a table and begin with separate orders: a scotch and soda, two Buds, a Lowenbrau, a Brandy Manhattan, and a whiskey tonic. The waitress brings the drinks, arranged in order on her tray, and places each one down for the respective customer. Fred, who is sitting in the corner where the waitress stands announces, "I'll get this one," and hands her a $10 bill. He has assumed the temporary responsibility to ask for drinks desired by anyone at the table. Half an hour later the waitress checks the table: "How're you doin' here?" Fred shakes his head that they aren't quite ready, and the others keep right on talking. But the question has signaled the group to prepare to order soon. The next time the waitress approaches their table, Bill, sitting next to Fred, looks up and says, "Another round." The responsibility for asking has now shifted to him and he orders for everyone. In this case he might check individually or act on a knowledge of his friends' drinking habits. When the drinks arrive he pays for the second round. Soon another member of the group will take over, and before the evening ends each of the six customers will have taken one or more turns. It is not uncommon for the composition of a table to change, adding new drinkers, losing some to other tables, expanding and contracting with the ebb and flow of people, creating ever widening circles of reciprocal exchange.

These exchanges did not seem unusual to us until we discovered that female customers almost never order or pay in rounds. Those who do are usually waitresses from other bars; they know that this practice eases the work-load for the cocktail waitress, both in taking orders and making change. Why then do men almost always order in rounds, asking for drinks in this reciprocal fashion? When we observed the other ways that men typically make work difficult for waitresses it seems improbable that ordering in rounds was intended to assist the cocktail waitresses. Whatever the reason for this practice, it is a continual reminder that *males belong to groups of men in the bar.* The individual nature of asking for a drink is transformed into a shared, social experience. When men request drinks and pay for them in rounds they reaffirm their ties to one another and their common membership in a kind of men's association.

Numerous occasions occur when a single individual will buy for another person or a whole group at another table. The reciprocity in these exchanges may never occur or it can take place at a later date, but the expectation of a return drink underlies the action. In the course of an evening the waitress may have frequent orders of this nature. Two guys and a girl are drinking at a table near the lower waitress station. One of the guys signals the waitress and says, "Would you take a drink to Mark, over there? It's his birthday. Tell him it's from us." Drawing on her recollection of Mark's original order she asks the bartender for a whiskey sour and delivers it to Mark, who hasn't even finished his first drink. Another friend of Mark's sitting nearby sees the extra drink arrive and when he learns it is Mark's birthday, he orders a round for everyone at the table, again in honor of the occasion.

As the bar becomes more crowded, waitresses are often kept running to take drinks to an acquaintance here who was recently engaged, a friend there who got a new job, or someone else a customer hasn't seen for a while. "Take a drink to that guy over there in the red shirt who just came in, a gin and tonic, and tell him Bob sent it," a customer tells the waitress, pointing across the bar. Fighting her way back through the crowd to the bar and then over to the man in the red shirt, the waitress says, "This is from Bob." The surprised and pleased customer looks over the crowd, locates Bob at his table and calls loudly, "Thanks, Bob, I'll talk to you later." Other people notice, look briefly in his direction, and the noisy hum of activity continues at a steady pace.

A regular at the bar motions for Stephanie: "I owe Randy one from last week. Do you know what he's drinking? Whatever it is, send him one from me." Randy is in the other waitress section so Stephanie passes the word on to Joyce and soon Randy has an unrequested drink arrive at his table. He remembers the debt when the waitress identifies the regular; a wave and shouted words of thanks that cannot be heard above the noise complete the transaction. Later the same night customers will ask for other drinks to be delivered at other places. "I want another round for Alan — tell him congratulations on his new job." "I hear Ron got engaged, take him a drink from me."

In these and similar cases, the drink is purchased, not because someone wants a drink, but rather as a symbol of a friendship tie. On many occasions these exchanges are followed by shouting and gestures that serve not only to communicate between friends but to announce to others that the participants are inside members of the bar crowd. Even when the transaction is known only to the buyer, recipient, and waitress, the ritual performance has fulfilled its function. The customers have both demonstrated they are not alone in an impersonal, business establishment. They know people here and are known by others. The very act of establishing social ties in this manner gives these customers an additional reason for being in the bar. Their claim to membership has been announced, acknowledged, and confirmed.

Sometimes reciprocal exchanges are done in a humorous manner, emphasizing certain masculine values as well as reaffirming membership in the men's association. Recall an earlier example when one night a man at the bar called Holly over and said, "I want you to take a drink to the guy over there in the sport coat and tell him Dan said to get fucked." When the message and drink were delivered they brought a return order — a Harvey Wallbanger for Dan and a 75¢ tip for Holly. The message with its overtones of a tough man who could even use obscenity in the presence of a woman was clear. The return order of a Harvey Wallbanger, a drink with sexual connotations, brought smiles to the faces of bartenders, waitress, and customers alike. In addition, the exchange highlighted publicly the social ties between two customers.

Later on that same evening, Holly was asked to take a double vodka tonic to Gene, a regular, who was already quite intoxicated. A friend across the bar had observed Gene's steady drinking all night and increasingly boisterous behavior. Gene was finishing the last drink he would order when the "gift" arrived. "This is from Bill," said Holly with a smile, loud enough for others at the table to hear. Faced with the choice of increasing physical discomfort and a reputation that he wasn't man enough to down another drink, Gene raised the drink in a smilingly reluctant toast and finished off the double vodka tonic.

On a typical evening drinks criss-cross the bar in these ways with considerable frequency. The senders and receivers come to be recognized as full members of the bar society. Even those who do not participate in these rituals themselves gain a secure sense that there is a lot of action at Brady's. They are reassured that this is a place where male customers, in general, and themselves, in particular, truly belong.

DRINKING CONTESTS

Sometimes customers ask for drinks that involve a challenge to another man's ability to drink. In an earlier chapter we mentioned how waitresses become customer's "lucky charms" in these contests. The night is slow and two guys sitting at Joyce's station pass the time by "chugging," a kind of drinking contest. A coin was flipped and first one customer called and then the other. If a call identified the correct side of the coin, the customer who called was not required to down his drink in a single gulp. Each failure to call the coin correctly meant asking for another drink and chugging it down until one or the other contestants called a halt, thereby losing the game.

At times, such contests involve tthe entire bar, as customers become spectators cheering on the early demise of the participants. One evening, several of the Cougars were seated at the bar. It was late and they had been there most of the evening. The bar was noisy, but suddenly became quiet as John ceremoniously placed six empty shot glasses in front of one of the football players. "Okay, Larry, ol' boy, let's see you handle this!" Holly and Sue crowded together into the lower waitress station to get a better look as John slowly filled each shot glass with tequila. People seated at tables stood to get a better view. Someone had dared Larry to drink six straight shots of tequila and he was going to do it. John finished pouring and stepped back, bowing in deference to Larry. "It's all yours," he added. Larry picked up the first glass, toasted his audience, and downed it. Everyone applauded and cheered. He picked up the second, toasted again, and downed it too. Again, the group applauded and so it went until all six glasses were empty. Larry had met the challenge and the game was over. Someone slapped Larry on the back, he reddened and headed for the men's room. Activity returned to normal. The contest was over.

While this was one of the more dramatic contests, similar ones take place frequently at Brady's. Such drinking contests bring males together in a competitive sport, one they are allowed to play inside the bar, but in a way which symbolizes desirable masculine traits—a willingness to compete, strength, endurance, and the ability to imbibe great quantities of strong liquor. It is a contest that places emphasis on *how* one plays the game rather than who wins. Larry may have made a fast retreat to the bathroom, but he *had* played the game, and that is what counted. In addition, those who participated as spectators demonstrated their ties with Larry and others in the bar.

ASKING FOR THE WRONG DRINK

One of the most curious ways that males ask for drinks involves intentional errors in ordering. This kind of asking for a drink appears to involve a combination of two speech acts: *ordering* and *telling*, or giving information. Consider the following example. Two young men enter the bar and take a table next to the wall in the lower section. The waitress approaches their table and places a napkin in front of each one. She waits in silence for their order. One of them looks up at her and says calmly:

"Two double Sloe Screws on the rocks, uhhhh, for Joe and Bill."

The waitress turns quickly, goes to the bar, and in a moment returns with two, tall, dark bottles of Hamm's beer. A stranger might think this interaction strange, and at first this kind of "asking for a drink" seemed out of place, but in time we noted other similarly strange games being played. For example, someone comes in and says, "I'll have a banana daiquiri with Drambuie," or another persons says, "Make mine a double Harvey Wallbanger." As you watch the waitress in these and other situations, you observe that frequently the drinks people ask for are not served. A scotch and soda is given instead of the banana daiquiri, a bourbon and water is served instead of the double Harvey Wallbanger, two Hamm's are delivered instead of two double Sloe Screws on the rocks.

In no case where a person asks for one drink and is given another, at least in situations like the examples noted, does the customer complain that he received the wrong drink. Two factors complicate the situation. First, sometimes people do order "Sloe Screws" or "Harvey Wallbangers" and the waitress brings these drinks. Second, occasionally the bartender mixes the wrong drink or the waitress serves the wrong drink and the customer *does* complain. If we return to our original ethnographic goal, we can now ask, "What does a stranger to Brady's Bar have to know in order to ask for a drink in this manner, or to interpret correctly when someone else asks for a drink in this manner? Furthermore, why does this kind of "asking" go on?

If the stranger were to assume the role of cocktail waitress, she would have to know the following:

1. That the drink requested was not actually desired.
2. That another drink was actually being requested.
3. What that other drink was.

Waitresses do acquire the rules for correctly interpreting these kinds of requests. But what are these rules and how do they operate?

Let's go back to the customer who said, "Two double Sloe Screws on the rocks, uhhhh, for Joe and Bill." In addition to the utterance itself, he also communicates a *metamessage,* a message about the message, that serves to identify the kind of speech act he intends it to be. The meta-message says something like, "Don't take us seriously, we really don't want two double Sloe Screws on the rocks. We aren't *ordering* but only *teasing.*" But how is such a metamessage sent and how does the waitress interpret it correctly? Sometimes this information is sent by the *tone* of a speech act or by accompanying gestures or facial expressions. But when a customer uses these metamessage forms he also signals to others that he is teasing or joking. He may then be seen as a "ham," someone unsophisticated in bar culture. The ideal is to ask for a double Sloe Screw on the rocks or a banana daiquiri with Drambuie in a perfectly serious tone of voice and manner, *sending metamessages in ways that are not obvious* to the surrounding audience. At least three alternatives are open to the sophisticated, well-enculturated customer.

First, he may choose to make a referential mistake that the wait-ress will recognize but other, less sophisticated customers will not. Let's take the order for two double Sloe Screws on the rocks. "On the rocks" is a feature of several drinks at Brady's. It means that liquor will be served only with ice and not the usual additional liquid. Whiskey on the rocks, for example, is whiskey without soda, water, or anything except ice. Vodka on the rocks is vodka and ice, nothing more. If a customer wants to order something "on the rocks," it usually means naming a type of liquor, not a fancy drink containing liquor and other mixtures. For example, if you order a Screwdriver on the rocks (vodka and orange juice), it would mean a Screwdriver without orange juice, the same thing as vodka on the rocks. This order would be quickly recognized by waitresses as a *referential mistake*. It is a name that sounds like a drink, but no one knowledgeable in the ways of the bar would ask for this drink, unless perhaps as a joke. A Sloe Screw is a mixture of sloe gin and orange juice. When the customer said, "Two double Sloe Screws on the rocks," he was talking nonsense. He asked for a drink that doesn't exist at Brady's Bar, but when he made this obvious and intentional error of reference, he also signaled to the waitress that he was *teasing*, not *ordering*. He might have asked for sloe gin on the rocks, in which case the waitress could have brought the two customers each a glass of sloe gin and ice.

A second way to unobtrusively let the waitress know that a named drink is not desired involves the connotations of certain drinks. If they are clearly female drinks such as a Pink Lady or Gold Cadillac, this can signal that the customer doesn't really want them. Both a Sloe Screw and a Harvey Wallbanger have implicit sexual connotations that are widely recognized by the people at Brady's. "A glass full of tequila" carries the connotation of an impending contest and other features of the setting can make it clear that no contest is planned. If a regular wants to tease the waitress, he will not name a scotch and soda or gin and tonic for these ordinary drinks do not have the special connotations that could signal the use of a different speech act.

Finally, customers can signal the intended speech act by combining two or more speech acts. When the customer asked for two double Sloe Screws on the rocks, he added, "for Joe and Bill." He was *telling* the waitress something else, in addition to the apparent order. The waitress can quickly guess that the customers are teasing, but how will she know to bring them bottles of Hamm's beer? If she doesn't recognize the two customers as regulars or know their customary drinks, she can use this additional information to check with bartenders: "What do Joe and Bill over there in the corner usually drink?"

These complicated ways of asking for drinks have many functions for both the customer and waitress. Most important, they clearly demonstrate that the customer has mastered the use of bar language. As an individual learns to use the language of this culture with skill, he also becomes recognized as a regular, one who has gained entrance to the inner circle of this little society. . . .

REVIEW QUESTIONS

1. What do Spradley and Mann mean by "speech events" and "speech acts"? What is the relationship between the two?

2. What are the rituals associated with asking for a drink at Brady's Bar, and what are the functions of each?

3. How does asking for a drink reaffirm male values and male group solidarity at Brady's Bar?

4. What is a metamessage? What are examples of metamessages associated with asking for a drink at Brady's? Can you think of metamessages that you use in verbal performance?

5. How does asking for a drink at Brady's compare with male-oriented TV beer commercials?

6

The sounds of silence

EDWARD T. HALL and
MILDRED REED HALL

*People communicate with more than just words. An important part
of every encounter are the messages we send with our bodies and
faces: the smile, the frown, the slouch of the shoulders, or the tightly
crossed legs are only a few gestures which add another dimension to
our verbal statements. These gestures as well as their social meaning
change from one culture to another. In this article, the Halls describe
and explain the function of nonverbal behavior in social encounters.*

Bob leaves his apartment at 8:15 A.M. and stops at the corner drugstore
for breakfast. Before he can speak, the counterman says, "The usual?"
Bob nods yes. While he savors his Danish, a fat man pushes onto the
adjoining stool and overflows into his space. Bob scowls and the man
pulls himself in as much as he can. Bob has sent two messages without
speaking a syllable.

Henry has an appointment to meet Arthur at 11 o'clock; he arrives at 11:30. Their conversation is friendly, but Arthur retains a
lingering hostility. Henry has unconsciously communicated that he
doesn't think the appointment is very important or that Arthur is a
person who needs to be treated with respect.

George is talking to Charley's wife at a party. Their conversation
is entirely trivial, yet Charley glares at them suspiciously. Their physical proximity and the movements of their eyes reveal that they are
powerfully attracted to each other.

José Ybarra and Sir Edmund Jones are at the same party and it is important for them to establish a cordial relationship for business reasons. Each is trying to be warm and friendly, yet they will part with mutual distrust and their business transaction will probably fall through. José, in Latin fashion, moved closer and closer to Sir Edmund as they spoke, and this movement was miscommunicated as pushiness to Sir Edmund, who kept backing away from this intimacy, and this was miscommunicated to José as coldness. The silent languages of Latin and English cultures are more difficult to learn than their spoken languages.

In each of these cases, we see the subtle power of nonverbal communication. The only language used throughout most of the history of humanity (in evolutionary terms, vocal communication is relatively recent), it is the first form of communication you learn. You use this preverbal language, consciously and unconsciously, every day to tell other people how you feel about yourself and them. This language includes your posture, gestures, facial expressions, costume, the way you walk, even your treatment of time and space and material things. All people communicate on several different levels at the same time but are usually aware of only the verbal dialog and don't realize that they respond to nonverbal messages. But when a person says one thing and really believes something else, the discrepancy between the two can usually be sensed. Nonverbal-communication systems are much less subject to the conscious deception that often occurs in verbal systems. When we find ourselves thinking, "I don't know what it is about him, but he doesn't seem sincere," it's usually this lack of congruity between a person's words and his behavior that makes us anxious and uncomfortable.

Few of us realize how much we all depend on body movement in our conversation or are aware of the hidden rules that govern listening behavior. But we know instantly whether or not the person we're talking to is "tuned in" and we're very sensitive to any breach in listening etiquette. In white middle-class American culture, when someone wants to show he is listening to someone else, he looks either at the other person's face or, specifically, at his eyes, shifting his gaze from one eye to the other.

If you observe a person conversing, you'll notice that he indicates he's listening by nodding his head. He also makes little "Hmm" noises. If he agrees with what's being said, he may give a vigorous nod. To show pleasure or affirmation, he smiles; if he has some reservations, he looks skeptical by raising an eyebrow or pulling down the corners of his mouth. If a participant wants to terminate the conversation, he may start shifting his body position, stretching his legs, crossing or uncrossing them, bobbing his foot or diverting his gaze from the speaker. The more he fidgets, the more the speaker becomes aware that he has lost his audience. As a last measure, the listener may look at his watch to indicate the imminent end of the conversation.

Talking and listening are so intricately intertwined that a person cannot do one without the other. Even when one is alone and talking to oneself, there is part of the brain that speaks while another part listens. In all conversations, the listener is positively or negatively reinforcing the speaker all the time. He may even guide the conversation without knowing it, by laughing or frowning or dismissing the argument with a wave of his hand.

The language of the eyes — another age-old way of exchanging feelings — is both subtle and complex. Not only do men and women use their eyes differently but there are class, generation, regional, ethnic and national cultural differences. Americans often complain about the way foreigners stare at people or hold a glance too long. Most Americans look away from someone who is using his eyes in an unfamiliar way because it makes them self-conscious. If a man looks at another man's wife in a certain way, he's asking for trouble, as indicated earlier. But he might not be ill-mannered or seeking to challenge the husband. He might be a European in this country who hasn't learned our visual mores. Many American women visiting France or Italy are acutely embarrassed because, for the first time in their lives, men really look at them — their eyes, hair, nose, lips, breasts, hips, legs, thighs, knees, ankles, feet, clothes, hairdo, even their walk. These same women, once they have become used to being looked at, often return to the United States and are overcome with the feeling that "No one every really looks at me anymore."

Analyzing the mass of data on the eyes, it is possible to sort out at least three ways in which the eyes are used to communicate: dominance vs. submission, involvement vs. detachment, and positive vs. negative attitude. In addition, there are three levels of consciousness and control, which can be categorized as follows: (1) conscious use of the eyes to communicate, such as the flirting blink and the intimate nose-wrinkling squint; (2) the very extensive category of unconscious but learned behavior governing where the eyes are directed and when (this unwritten set of rules dictates how and under what circumstances the sexes, as well as people of all status categories, look at each other); and (3) the response of the eye itself, which is completely outside both awareness and control — changes in the cast (the sparkle) of the eye and the pupillary reflex.

The eye is unlike any other organ of the body, for it is an extension of the brain. The unconscious pupillary reflex and the cast of the eye have been known by people of Middle Eastern origin for years — although most are unaware of their knowledge. Depending on the context, Arabs and others look either directly at the eyes or deeply *into* the eyes of their interlocutor. We became aware of this in the Middle East several years ago while looking at jewelry. The merchant suddenly started to push a particular bracelet at a customer and said, "You buy this one." What interested us was that the bracelet was not the one that had been consciously selected by the purchaser. But the merchant, watching the pupils of the eyes, knew what the purchaser really wanted to buy. Whether he specifically knew *how* he knew is debatable.

A psychologist at the University of Chicago, Eckhard Hess, was the first to conduct systematic studies of the pupillary reflex. His wife remarked one evening, while watching him reading in bed, that he must be very interested in the text because his pupils were dilated. Following up on this, Hess slipped some pictures of nudes into a stack of photographs that he gave to his male assistant. Not looking at the photographs but watching his assistant's pupils, Hess was able to tell precisely when the assistant came to the nudes. In further experiments, Hess retouched the eyes in a photograph of a woman. In one print, he made the pupils small, in another, large; nothing else was changed. Subjects who were given the photographs found the woman with the dilated pupils much more attractive. Any man who has had the experience of seeing a woman look at him as her pupils widen with reflex speed knows that she's flashing him a message.

The eye-sparkle phenomenon frequently turns up in our interviews of couples in love. It's apparently one of the first reliable clues in the other person that love is genuine. To date, there is no scientific data to explain eye sparkle; no investigation of the pupil, the cornea or even the white sclera of the eye shows how the sparkle originates. Yet we all know it when we see it.

One common situation for most people involves the use of the eyes in the street and in public. Although eye behavior follows a definite set of rules, the rules vary according to the place, the needs and feelings of the people, and their ethnic background. For urban whites, once they're within definite recognition distance (16–32 feet for people with average eyesight), there is mutual avoidance of eye contact — unless they want something specific: a pickup, a handout or information of some kind. In the West and in small towns generally, however, people are much more likely to look at and greet one another, even if they're strangers.

It's permissible to look at people if they're beyond recognition distance; but once inside this sacred zone, you can only steal a glance at strangers. You *must* greet friends, however; to fail to do is insulting. Yet, to stare too fixedly even at them is considered rude and hostile. Of course, all of these rules are variable.

A great many blacks, for example, greet each other in public even if they don't know each other. To blacks, most eye behavior of whites has the effect of giving the impression that they aren't there, but this is due to white avoidance of eye contact with *anyone* in the street.

Another very basic difference between people of different ethnic backgrounds is their sense of territoriality and how they handle space. This is the silent communication, or miscommunication, that caused friction between Mr. Ybarra and Sir Edmund Jones in our earlier example. We know from research that everyone has around himself an invisible bubble of space that contracts and expands depending on several factors: his emotional state, the activity he's performing at the time and his cultural background. This bubble is a kind of mobile territory that he will defend against intrusion. If he is accustomed to close personal distance between himself and others, his bubble will be smaller than that of someone who's accustomed to greater personal distance. People of North European heritage — English, Scandinavian, Swiss and German — tend to avoid contact. Those whose heritage is Italian, French, Spanish, Russian, Latin American or Middle Eastern like close personal contact.

People are very sensitive to any intrusion into their spatial bubble. If someone stands too close to you, your first instinct is to back up. If that's not possible, you lean away and pull yourself in, tensing your muscles. If the intruder doesn't respond to these body signals, you may then try to protect yourself, using a briefcase, umbrella or raincoat. Women — especially when traveling alone — often plant their pocketbook in such a way that no one can get very close to them. As a last resort, you may move to another spot and position yourself behind a desk or a chair that provides screening. Everyone tries to adjust the space around himself in a way that's comfortable for him; most often, he does this unconsciously.

Emotions also have a direct effect on the size of a person's territory. When you're angry or under stress, your bubble expands and you require more space. New York psychiatrist Augustus Kinzel found a difference in what he calls Body-Buffer Zones between violent and nonviolent prison inmates. Dr. Kinzel conducted experiments in which each prisoner was placed in the center of a small room and then Dr. Kinzel slowly walked toward him. Nonviolent prisoners allowed him to come quite close, while prisoners with a history of violent behavior couldn't tolerate his proximity and reacted with some vehemence.

Apparently, people under stress experience other people as looming larger and closer than they actually are. Studies of schizophrenic patients have indicated that they sometimes have a distorted perception of space, and several psychiatrists have reported patients who experience their body boundaries as filling up an entire room. For these patients, anyone who comes into the room is actually inside their body, and such an intrusion may trigger a violent outburst.

Unfortunately, there is little detailed information about normal people who live in highly congested urban areas. We do know, of course, that the noise, pollution, dirt, crowding and confusion of our cities induce feelings of stress in most of us, and stress leads to a need for greater space. The man who's packed into a subway, jostled in the street, crowded into an elevator and forced to work all day in a bull pen or in a small office without auditory or visual privacy is going to be very stressed at the end of his day. He needs places that provide relief from constant overstimulation of his nervous system. Stress from overcrowding is cumulative and people can tolerate more crowding early in the day than later; note the increased bad temper during the evening rush hour as compared with the morning melee. Certainly one factor in people's desire to commute by car is the need for privacy and relief from crowding (except, often, from other cars); it may be the only time of the day when nobody can intrude.

In crowded public places, we tense our muscles and hold ourselves stiff, and thereby communicate to others our desire not to intrude on their space and, above all, not to touch them. We also avoid eye contact, and the total effect is that of someone who has "tuned out." Walking along the street, our bubble expands slightly as we move in a stream of strangers, taking care not to bump into them. In the office, at meetings, in restaurants, our bubble keeps changing as it adjusts to the activity at hand.

Most white middle-class Americans use four main distances in their business and social relations: intimate, personal, social, and public. Each of these distances has a near and a far phase and is accompanied by changes in the volume of the voice. Intimate distance varies from direct physical contact with another person to a distance of six to eighteen inches and is used for our most private activities — caressing another person or making love. At this distance, you are overwhelmed by sensory inputs from the other person — heat from the body, tactile stimulation from the skin, the fragrance of perfume, even the sound of breathing — all of which literally envelop you. Even at the far phase, you're still within easy touching distance. In general, the use of intimate distance in public between adults is frowned on. It's also much too close for strangers, except under conditions of extreme crowding.

In the second zone — personal distance — the close phase is one and a half to two and a half feet; it's at this distance that wives usually stand from their husbands in public. If another woman moves into this zone, the wife will most likely be disturbed. The far phase — two and a half to four feet — is the distance used to "keep someone at arm's length" and is the most common spacing used by people in conversation.

The third zone — social distance — is employed during business transactions or exchanges with a clerk or repairman. People who work together tend to use close social distance — four to seven feet. This is also the distance for conversation at social gatherings. To stand at this distance from someone who is seated has a dominating effect (e.g., teacher to pupil, boss to secretary). The far phase of the third zone — seven to twelve feet — is where people stand when someone says, "Stand back so I can look at you." This distance lends a formal tone to business or social discourse. In an executive office, the desk serves to keep people at this distance.

The fourth zone — public distance — is used by teachers in classrooms or speakers at public gatherings. At its farthest phase — 25 feet and beyond — it is used for important public figures. Violations of this distance can lead to serious complications. During his 1970 U.S. visit, the president of France, Georges Pompidou, was harassed by pickets in Chicago, who were permitted to get within touching distance. Since pickets in France are kept behind barricades a block or more away, the president was outraged by this insult to his person, and President Nixon was obliged to communicate his concern as well as offer his personal apologies.

It is interesting to note how American pitchmen and panhandlers exploit the unwritten, unspoken conventions of eye and distance. Both take advantage of the fact that once explicit eye contact is established, it is rude to look away, because to do so means to brusquely dismiss the other person and his needs. Once having caught the eye of his mark, the panhandler then locks on, not letting go until he moves through the public zone, the social zone, the personal zone and, finally, into the intimate sphere, where people are most vulnerable.

Touch also is an important part of the constant stream of communication that takes place between people. A light touch, a firm touch, a blow, a caress are all communications. In an effort to break down barriers among people, there's been a recent upsurge in group-encounter activities, in which strangers are encouraged to touch one another. In special situations such as these, the rules for not touching are broken with group approval and people gradually lose some of their inhibitions.

Although most people don't realize it, space is perceived and distances are set not by vision alone but with all the senses. Auditory space is perceived with the ears, thermal space with the skin, kinesthetic space with the muscles of the body and olfactory space with the nose. And, once again, it's one's culture that determines how his senses are programmed — which sensory information ranks highest and lowest. The important thing to remember is that culture is very persistent. In this country, we've noted the existence of culture patterns that determine distance between people in the third and fourth generations of some families, despite their prolonged contact with people of very different cultural heritages.

Whenever there is great cultural distance between two people, there are bound to be problems arising from differences in behavior and expectations. An example is the American couple who consulted a psychiatrist about their marital problems. The husband was from New England and had been brought up by reserved parents who taught him to control his emotions and to respect the need for privacy. His wife was from an Italian family and had been brought up in close contact with all the members of her large family, who were extremely warm, volatile, and demonstrative.

When the husband came home after a hard day at the office, dragging his feet, and longing for peace and quiet, his wife would rush to him and smother him. Clasping his hands, rubbing his brow, crooning over his weary head, she never left him alone. But when his wife was upset or anxious about her day, the husband's response was to withdraw completely and leave her alone. No comforting, no affectionate embrace, no attention — just solitude. The woman became convinced her husband didn't love her and, in desperation, she consulted a psychiatrist. Their problem wasn't basically psychological but cultural.

Why has man developed all these different ways of communicating messages without words? One reason is that people don't like to spell out certain kinds of messages. We prefer to find other ways of showing our feelings. This is especially true in relationships as sensitive as courtship. Men don't like to be rejected and most women don't want to turn a man down bluntly. Instead, we work out subtle ways of encouraging or discouraging each other that save face and avoid confrontations.

How a person handles space in dating others is an obvious and very sensitive indicator of how he or she feels about the other person. On a first date, if a woman sits or stands so close to a man that he is acutely conscious of her physical presence—inside the intimate-distance zone—the man usually construes it to mean that she is encouraging him. However, before the man starts moving in on the woman, he should be sure what message she's really sending; otherwise, he risks bruising his ego. What is close to someone of North European background may be neutral or distant to someone of Italian heritage. Also, women sometimes use space as a way of misleading a man and there are few things that put men off more than women who communicate contradictory messages—such as women who cuddle up and then act insulted when a man takes the next step.

How does a woman communicate interest in a man? In addition to such familiar gambits as smiling at him, she may glance shyly at him, blush and then look away. Or she may give him a real come-on look and move in very close when he approaches. She may touch his arm and ask for a light. As she leans forward to light her cigarette, she may brush him lightly, enveloping him in her perfume. She'll probably continue to smile at him and she may use what ethnologists call preening gestures—touching the back of her hair, thrusting her breasts forward, tilting her hips as she stands or crossing her legs if she's seated, perhaps even exposing one thigh or putting a hand on her thigh and stroking it. She may also stroke her wrists as she converses or show the palm of her hand as a way of gaining his attention. Her skin may be unusually flushed or quite pale, her eyes brighter, the pupils larger.

If a man sees a woman whom he wants to attract, he tries to present himself by his posture and stance as someone who is self-assured. He moves briskly and confidently. When he catches the eye of the woman, he may hold her glance a little longer than normal. If he gets an encouraging smile, he'll move in close and engage her in small talk. As they converse, his glance shifts over her face and body. He, too, may make preening gestures—straightening his tie, smoothing his hair, or shooting his cuffs.

How do people learn body language? The same way they learn spoken language—by observing and imitating people around them as they're growing up. Little girls imitate their mothers or an older female. Little boys imitate their fathers or a respected uncle or a character on television. In this way, they learn the gender signals appropriate for their sex. Regional, class, and ethnic patterns of body behavior are also learned in childhood and persist throughout life.

Such patterns of masculine and feminine body behavior vary

widely from one culture to another. In America, for example, women stand with their thighs together. Many walk with their pelvis tipped slightly forward and their upper arms close to their body. When they sit, they cross their legs at the knee or, if they are well past middle age, they may cross their ankles. American men hold their arms away from their body, often swinging them as they walk. They stand with their legs apart (an extreme example is the cowboy, with legs apart and thumbs tucked into his belt). When they sit, they put their feet on the floor with legs apart and, in some parts of the country, they cross their legs by putting one ankle on the other knee.

Leg behavior indicates sex, status, and personality. It also indicates whether or not one is at ease or is showing respect or disrespect for the other person. Young Latin-American males avoid crossing their legs. In their world of *machismo,* the preferred position for young males when with one another (if there is no older dominant male present to whom they must show respect) is to sit on the base of their spine with their leg muscles relaxed and their feet wide apart. Their respect position is like our military equivalent; spine straight, heels and ankles together — almost identical to that displayed by properly brought up young women in New England in the early part of this century.

American women who sit with their legs spread apart in the presence of males are *not* normally signaling a come-on — they are simply (and often unconsciously) sitting like men. Middle-class women in the presence of other women to whom they are very close may on occasion throw themselves down on a soft chair or sofa and let themselves go. This is a signal that nothing serious will be taken up. Males, on the other hand, lean back and prop their legs up on the nearest object.

The way we walk, similarly, indicates status, respect, mood, and ethnic or cultural affiliation. The many variants of the female walk are too well known to go into here, except to say that a man would have to be blind not to be turned on by the way some women walk — a fact that made Mae West rich before scientists ever studied these matters. To white Americans, some French middle-class males walk in a way that is both humorous and suspect. There is a bounce and looseness to the French walk, as though the parts of the body were somehow unrelated. Jacques Tati, the French movie actor, walks this way; so does the great mime, Marcel Marceau.

Blacks and whites in America — with the exception of middle- and upper-middle-class professionals of both groups — move and walk very differently from each other. To the blacks, whites often seem incredibly stiff, almost mechanical in their movements. Black males, on the other hand, have a looseness and coordination that frequently makes whites a little uneasy; it's too different, too integrated, too alive, too male. Norman Mailer has said that squares walk from the shoulders, like bears, but blacks and hippies walk from the hips, like cats.

All over the world, people walk not only in their own characteristic way but have walks that communicate the nature of their involvement with whatever it is they're doing. The purposeful walk of North Europeans is an important component of proper behavior on the job. Any male who has been in the military knows how essential it is to walk properly (which makes for a continuing source of tension between blacks and whites in the Service). The quick shuffle of servants in the Far East in the old days was a show of respect. On the island of Truk, when we last visited, the inhabitants even had a name for the respectful walk that one used when in the presence of a chief or when walking past a chief's house. The term was *sufan*, which meant to be humble and respectful.

The notion that people communicate volumes by their gestures, facial expressions, posture and walk is not new; actors, dancers, writers, and psychiatrist have long been aware of it. Only in recent years, however, have scientists begun to make systematic observations of body motions. Ray L. Birdwhistell of the University of Pennsylvania is one of the pioneers in body-motion research and coined the term kinesics to describe this field. He developed an elaborate notation system to record both facial and body movements, using an approach similar to that of the linguist, who studies the basic elements of speech. Birdwhistell and other kinesicists such as Albert Sheflen, Adam Kendon, and William Condon take movies of people interacting. They run the film over and over again, often at reduced speed for frame-by-frame analysis, so that they can observe even the slightest body movements not perceptible at normal interaction speeds. These movements are then recorded in notebooks for later analysis.

To appreciate the importance of nonverbal-communication systems, consider the unskilled inner-city black looking for a job. His handling of time and space alone is sufficiently different from the white middle-class pattern to create great misunderstandings on both sides. The black is told to appear for a job interview at a certain time. He arrives late. The white interviewer concludes from his tardy arrival that the black is irresponsible and not really interested in the job. What the interviewer doesn't know is that the black time system (often referred to by blacks as C. P. T. — colored people's time) isn't the same as that of whites. In the words of a black student who had been told to make an appointment to see his professor: "Man, you *must* be putting me on. I never had an appointment in my life."

The black job applicant, having arrived late for his interview, may further antagonize the white interviewer by his posture and his eye behavior. Perhaps he slouches and avoids looking at the interviewer; to him, this is playing it cool. To the interviewer, however, he may well look shifty and sound uninterested. The interviewer has failed to notice the actual signs of interest and eagerness in the black's behavior, such as the subtle shift in the quality of the voice — a gentle and tentative excitement — an almost imperceptible change in the cast of the eyes and a relaxing of the jaw muscles.

Moreover, correct reading of black-white behavior is continually complicated by the fact that both groups are comprised of individuals — some of whom try to accommodate and some of whom make it a point of pride *not* to accommodate. At present, this means that many Americans, when thrown into contact with one another, are in the precarious position of not knowing which pattern applies. Once identified and analyzed, nonverbal-communications systems can be taught, like a foreign language. Without this training, we respond to nonverbal communications in terms of our own culture; we read everyone's behavior as if it were our own, and thus we often misunderstand it.

Several years ago in New York City, there was a program for sending children from predominantly black and Puerto Rican low-income neighborhoods to summer school in a white upper-class neighborhood on the East Side. One morning, a group of young black and Puerto Rican boys raced down the street, shouting and screaming and overturning garbage cans on their way to school. A doorman from an apartment building nearby chased them and cornered one of them inside a building. The boy drew a knife and attacked the doorman. This tragedy would not have occurred if the doorman had been familiar with the behavior of boys from low-income neighborhoods, where such antics are routine and socially acceptable and where pursuit would be expected to invite a violent response.

The language of behavior is extremely complex. Most of us are lucky to have under control one subcultural system — the one that reflects our sex, class, generation, and geographic region within the United States. Because of its complexity, efforts to isolate bits of nonverbal communication and generalize from them are in vain; you don't become an instant expert on people's behavior by watching them at cocktail parties. Body language isn't something that's independent of the person, something that can be donned and doffed like a suit of clothes.

Our research and that of our colleagues has shown that, far from being a superficial form of communication that can be consciously manipulated, nonverbal-communication systems are interwoven into the fabric of the personality and, as sociologist Erving Goffman has demonstrated, into society itself. They are the warp and woof of daily interactions with others and they influence how one expresses oneself, how one experiences oneself as a man or a woman.

Nonverbal communications signal to members of your own group what kind of person you are, how you feel about others, how you'll fit into and work in a group, whether you're assured or anxious, the degree to which you feel comfortable with the standards of your own culture, as well as deeply significant feelings about the self, including the state of your own psyche. For most of us, it's difficult to accept the reality of another's behavioral system. And, of course, none of us will ever become fully knowledgeable of the importance of every nonverbal signal. But as long as each of us realizes the power of these signals, this society's diversity can be a source of great strength rather than a further—and subtly powerful—source of division.

REVIEW QUESTIONS

1. What are the ways people communicate with each other nonverbally, according to Edward and Mildred Hall?

2. What are the four culturally learned speaking distances used by Americans?

3. How does the nonverbal communication described by the Halls relate to the concept of tacit culture discussed in the last section?

4. Why is nonverbal communication so likely to be a source of cross-cultural misunderstanding?

7

Cosmetics: The language of bodily adornment

TERENCE S. TURNER

Bodily adornment among the Tchikrin of Brazil includes elaborate painting, earplugs, lip plugs, and various styles of clothing. Terence Turner not only describes these practices, but deciphers their complex code to reveal their meaning. He suggests that body decorations have similar functions in all societies.

Something profound in the nature of man, in his role as a member of a society or culture, seems to be bound up with his universal urge to decorate or transform the surface of his body. We might well ask if the boundaries and appendages of the body carry some universal symbolic significance, and if so, whether their adornment is a way of focusing and expressing this symbolic meaning. In other words, bodily adornment may be a kind of symbolic language. But if it is, how can we decipher its "message"?

The Tchikrin, one of the least-known people of the central Brazilian wilderness (a region virtually unpenetrated by Brazilian settlers), are among the world's most exotic body adorners. Their elaborate body painting, their penis sheaths and earplugs, and their spectacular lip plugs raise the question of the symbolic significance of bodily adornment in a uniquely compelling way.

The Tchikrin are the northernmost group of the large Kayapo tribe, a member of the Ge-speaking linguistic family. Their villages are

Originally published as "Tchikrin: A Central Brazilian Tribe and Its Language of Bodily Adornment." With permission from *Natural History*, vol. 78, no. 8; Copyright the American Museum of Natural History, 1969.

built in a circle around a large central plaza, each house the residence
of an extended family. Throughout their lives the women remain in the
households of their birth. Men, however, leave their maternal houses
at about the age of eight, when they move to the men's house, which
is usually built in the center of the plaza. Only after consummating
their marriages by fathering a child do men move into their wives'
houses.

The pattern of a man's life cycle focuses on his movement from
his maternal household, to the men's house, to his wife's household.
Before, during, and after these moves, he is classified according to
named age grades, each with its distinctive social properties, styles of
body painting and hair cutting, and bodily ornaments. There is a separate and rather different system of age grades for women.

Newborn and nursing infants of both sexes are classified in a
category whose name means "little ones." They are the most elabo-
rately ornamented Tchikrin of any age. A few days after a baby's birth,
its ear lobes — and if it is a boy, its lower lip — are pierced, usually by
its father. Cigar-shaped earplugs of reddened wood are inserted in the
ear lobes and replaced from time to time with larger ones until the
holes in the lobes have become quite large. A narrow dowel or string of
beads is also inserted in a boy's lower lip, but this ornament is not
enlarged until much later in life. At the same time, the mother crochets
cotton bands, reddens them with paint, and fastens them around the
infant's wrists, ankles, and knees. When these grow too tight they are
cut away and replaced with larger ones.

The cast-off arm and leg bands and the discarded sets of earplugs
are saved by the mother in a special pouch, together with the baby's
desiccated umbilical cord. The bands and plugs constitute a sort of
record of the baby's growth — analogous, in a way, to a modern
mother's "baby book." When the baby grows older the father takes its
pouch and hangs it on, or buries it at the root of, a hardwood tree in
the savanna. This gives the child a magical infusion of strength and
well-being, symbolically neutralizing the weakness and vulnerability of
its infancy, for hardwood trees are potent sources of strength, endurance, and health in Kayapo ritual symbolism. The red color of the
earplugs and cotton bands serves much the same symbolic function —
the fostering of growth and strength — for red is associated with
health, energy, and vitality.

Body painting is an outstanding feature of the decoration of both
male and female babies. Mothers, grandmothers, or other kinswomen,
using a stylus made of the center rib of a leaf, draw complex linear
patterns over the entire body of the child. Women also paint each other

in this complex style, but except for rare ceremonial occasions, they are not allowed to paint men and older boys. Since only women use the stylus method, the men paint each other in a rougher, simpler pattern.

When a boy is weaned, learns to talk well, and can walk easily, which usually happens between the ages of three and four, he "graduates" from the age grade of little ones to that of "boys about to enter the men's house." This transition, like most changes from one major age category to the next, is accompanied by changes in bodily adornment and features of grooming such as hair style. The boy is now stripped of his infantile ornaments (earplugs and cotton arm and leg bands) and his hair is cut short. Boys of this age spend little time with their mothers and sisters; they already form a quasi-independent masculine play group, a precursor of the age sets and societies of the men's house. Their semi-independence of their maternal families and passage out of infancy are expressed not only by doffing their infantile ornaments and long hair but also by the infrequency with which their mothers paint them in the time-consuming linear "stylus" fashion. Boys of this age are far more apt to be painted with broad areas or bands of black and red, applied directly with the hand.

At about the age of eight (the Tchikrin do not reckon age by number of years, but by broad criteria of physical size and maturity) a decisive event occurs in a boy's life. In a brief but solemn ceremony, an unrelated man called a "substitute father" comes to the boy's maternal house, where he sits waiting silently with his wailing father and mother. The substitute father leads him out into the plaza and paints his body solid black. He then takes the boy by the hand into the men's house, which becomes his home.

He is now cut off from the world of family and blood relationships. The painting ritual thus marks the end of childhood for the boy and he enters a new age grade called "the painted ones." From this time on the boy will never again (except for rare ceremonial occasions) be painted by a woman. Henceforth, he will be painted only by other men, in the rough hand style or with a stamp made of a fruit rind that is cut in a simple pattern.

At puberty, boys go through a brief ceremony in which they are given penis sheaths to wear. After this they may replace their beaded lip ornaments with small versions of the mature men's lip plugs. They also let their hair grow long again, in the style of adult men and women.

Hair is associated with sexual powers. Long hair connotes full participation in sexually based relationships. However, since infants as well as mature adults have long hair, it is evident that the Kayapo

notion of participation in sexual relations is considerably different and
more complex than our own. For the Kayapo, there are two modes of
sexual participation. One, like our own culture's conception, consists
of the mature individual's active exercise of his sexual powers, above
all in the relationship between husband and wife. The other, for which
our culture has no counterpart, consists of the infant's passive biological (and social) dependence on the family, a dependence founded upon
its parents' procreative sexual relationship. The Kayapo think of an
infant before it is weaned more as an extension of its parents' biological
being than as an independent individual. It is conceived as still participating in the biological communion with its parents that it enjoyed in
the womb. This is understandable in view of the Kayapo notion of
pregnancy — that the fetus grows by nursing inside the mother. Birth,
therefore, does not fundamentally change the relationship between
mother and infant; it merely transfers its locus from inside her body to
outside. The father is also involved in this biological connection, for
while the child is still in the womb, his semen — like the mother's
milk — is thought to nourish the fetus. The birth of the baby termi-
nates this direct physical link with the father, a rupture that renders
the father's relation to his newborn child extremely delicate and
fraught with danger. In order to minimize this danger, for several days
the father abstains from physical exertions or "strong" and "dangerous" acts, such as killing animals, that might otherwise have a deleterious impact on the child's health.

Because weaning marks the end of full physical communion between mother and child, a child's hair is cut at this time. Short hair
symbolizes the attenuation of his direct biological connection with
others, a connection that is restored when the child grows to physical
maturity and is ready to exercise his own sexual powers. The same
principle underlies the custom of cutting the hair as a gesture of
mourning for the death of a spouse, sibling, or child. The effect of such
a kinsman's death is equivalent to weaning, since it suppresses ties,
which the Kayapo conceive as based on an intimate biological bond,
between the person who has died and the survivor.

A distinction is made between hair of the head and hair of the
face and body. Facial hair is customarily plucked as a matter of ordinary grooming of both sexes and all ages. Here again, however, the
sexual significance of hair emerges in one of the more stereotyped
forms of Kayapo love-play — it is considered to impart a special *frisson*
for lovers to pluck a stray eyebrow or eyelash from each other's face
with their teeth.

The Kayapo recognize, in ritual and other ways, the correlation between the development of sexual maturity and the weakening of family ties. They attempt to offset this tendency toward the isolation of the individual from social control by developing alternate forms of communal integration of the individual's developing sexual powers. Public recognition of the individual's steps toward sexual and social maturity is ritually associated with changes in his social status that move him inexorably toward marriage and the founding of his own family.

The penis sheath is the symbolic expression of the social control and regulation of mature male sexual powers. It is bestowed at puberty, and only after the sheath-bestowing ceremony is a youth's hair allowed to grow long again. Sheath and coiffure are thus complementary aspects of the public recognition of the growing boy's biological sexuality and, at the same time, of its integration into the social order.

Penis sheath, lip plug, and long hair symbolize the community's recognition of a boy's physical maturity, but they do not confer on him the right to put his newly recognized powers into practice. He only wins this right by going through the initiation ceremony, which is completely distinct from the penis-sheath rite and centers around the ceremonial "marriage," or betrothal, of the boy. This ritual marriage is not considered binding: it only establishes in principle the boy's ability to have sexual relations and marry any girl he chooses. Going through the initiation ceremony entitles a boy to move up into the age grade of "bachelor youths."

Bachelor youths eventually become engaged in earnest. Engagement, a private arrangement with a girl and her parents, culminates in the girl's pregnancy and the birth of a child. This event marks the climax of the youth's transition from boyhood to mature manhood, and he thereupon passes from the symbolic tutelage of his substitute father, who has presided over the successive stages of the long initiation process. Having founded his own family, he is definitively free of his lingering childhood bonds to his maternal family. He is entitled to move out of the men's house into his wife's house, and simultaneously to graduate to the age grade of mature men, significantly called "fathers." Fathers make up the membership of the men's societies, which meet (but do not reside) in the men's house and conduct the political affairs of the community.

These vital transitions in a man's life are expressed by a final transformation in bodily ornamentation — the replacement of the youth's small lip plug by a saucerlike plate, which may reach a diameter of four inches, or an alternative form, a long cylinder of rock crystal or wood. As an expression of mature manhood, this extraordinary ornament has a complex significance.

One aspect of its symbolism is implicit in the contrast between the lip plug and earplug. Both hearing and speaking have specific social associations for the Kayapo, and these associations relate to each other as complementary passive and active values. Hearing is a passive activity. The word *mari* "hearing" signifies understanding in the passive sense of knowing about something. Hearing in this sense is used in the common idiomatic expression of affirmation of specific relationships. If a man has good relations with his father's side of the family, for example, he says, "I hear them strongly" (*mari taytch*). Speaking, on the other hand, is perhaps the most fundamental social act of self-assertion, and its assertive connotations are highly elaborated and associated with mature masculinity. Flamboyant oratory is one of the major activities of Kayapo men.

The huge lip plugs of the father's age grade are consciously associated with this flamboyant oral assertiveness. The dynamism and oral aggressiveness of adult male public behavior rests on a foundation of sexual assertiveness: graduation to father status depends on a man's actually siring a child. The fulfillment of male sexual powers in paternity and the resulting integration of men in specific family units are, in other words, what earn men the right to aggressive, oral self-assertion in the men's house. The full-size lip plug, in its double character as the badge of paternity and the symbol of mature male oral aggressiveness, precisely embodies this relationship between the phallic and oral components of adult masculinity, and by the same token, of the family and communal levels of men's social relations.

If paternity is the criterion for communal recognition of male maturity, then infants assume a reciprocal importance as the "objective correlatives" of manhood in both its biological and social aspects (phallic power and family membership). Infants, then, are the passive extensions, or corroborations, of the father's sexual powers and social position as *paterfamilias*. The relation of the infant to its father is in fact analogous to that between hearing (in its Kayapo sense of passive affirmation of social relations) and speaking (considered as social self-assertion). The symbolic complementarity of infantile earplug and paternal lip plug neatly expresses this social complementarity, especially when the phallic connotations of the cigar-shaped earplugs are taken into account. The same considerations explain why women do not wear lip plugs and why neither adult men nor women wear earplugs.

In contrast to the man's pattern of life, for the Tchikrin woman there is no dramatic transformation in social relations involved in biological parenthood. The residence rule dictates that women spend their entire life cycle in the households into which they are born. The contrasts between female and male body decoration reflect the differences in social pattern.

Girls, like boys, dispense with their earplugs and have their hair cut upon weaning. They continue, however, to wear crocheted red cotton arm and leg bands — in recognition of their continuing membership in their parental families — until they are judged ready for childbearing.

At about the age of eight — the same age that a boy leaves home to enter the men's house — a girl is initiated into sexual relations under the aegis of a special ceremonial guardian. This event marks her graduation into the age grade of "given ones." In all probability the name indicates (the Kayapo have no explicit explanation for it) that girls of this age grade are considered to be "bestowed" upon the initiated men of the village for sexual purposes. Given ones are expected to take an active and enthusiastic part in communal dances; dancing in groups during communal rituals is, in fact, their chief collective activity.

The rite that recognizes that a girl has reached the stage of potential motherhood bears many resemblances to the boy's ceremony of induction into the men's house, and has the same purpose of formally dissolving the childhood bond to the parental family. In the girls' ceremony, a "substitute mother" paints the girls' thighs, breasts, and upper arms with broad black stripes, and cuts off their arm and leg bands (the symbols of parental ties). Henceforth, they are known as "black-thighed ones," and are considered ready to consummate their courtships with one of their suitors in marriage by giving birth to a child. Only this event differentiates women in a social sense from their parental families, since it enables them to set up distinct families of their own within the household they share with their parents. Independence from the paternal family (established much earlier for boys by their move to the men's house) is the prerequisite for social recognition of their reproductive powers as fully developed, autonomous, and "adult." This recognition, as we have seen, is symbolized for both sexes by long hair. For this reason, a woman is allowed to wear her hair long only upon the birth of her first child.

After attaining black-thighed status, a girl is qualified to join one of the mature women's societies, whose members gather regularly, every few weeks or so, to paint each other. It is interesting that while adult women often use the hand technique of the mature men to paint each other, they may equally well employ the stylus method used by mothers to paint their infants. Men and boys are almost never painted in this style after they leave home for the men's house; the use of it by adult women is another mark of their greater continuity with the social circumstances of childhood.

The typical daily routine of a Tchikrin mother, however, has relatively little place for collective activities. She must nurse her baby and care for her young children. One of the most frequent maternal chores is delousing, which, interestingly enough, conforms to a sexually asymmetrical pattern partially similar to that of body painting. Women delouse children, other women, and men (usually their husbands), but men do not delouse women.

A woman's day usually includes a trip to her garden or perhaps an expedition to gather firewood, normally cut by women. She is likely to return from either heavily burdened. She must cook for her husband and children (each nuclear family within the household gardens and cooks for itself). The Tchikrin, like other members of the Ge linguistic group, lack pottery. They cook by baking bundles of food wrapped in leaves, in a temporary earth "oven" composed of heated stones, leaves, and earth. At the end of the day a woman may get a little time to relax with her husband on the family bed, a mat-covered platform of split logs.

Lip plug, earplugs, penis sheath, hair style, cotton leg and arm bands, and body painting make up a symbolic language that expresses a wide range of information about social status, sex, and age. As a language, however, it does more than merely communicate this information from one individual to another: at a deeper level, it establishes a channel of communication *within* the individual between the social and biological aspects of his personality.

The social and psychological "message" of bodily adornment is coded and transmitted on an even more basic level by the colors used in body painting, and the symbolic associations of the parts of the body to which each color is applied. The colors of Tchikrin body painting are red (made from the seeds of the urucú plant), black (made from the juice of the genipa fruit), and, rarely, white (made from white clay), and these are used in determinate ways. Red is always applied on the extremities of the body — the forearms and hands, lower legs and feet, and the face. Black is always used on the trunk and upper parts of the limbs, as well as for the square cheek patches and borders along the shaved area of the forehead. The black face paintings, executed with painstaking care, are often covered immediately after they are finished with a heavy coat of red, which renders them almost invisible. The explanation for this practice lies in the symbolic values of the colors involved.

Red always connotes energy, health, and "quickness," both in the sense of swiftness and of heightened sensitivity (which the Kayapo conceive of as "quickness" or "lightness" of skin). Black, on the other hand, is associated with transitions between clearly defined states or categories, with "borderline" conditions or regions where normal clear-cut structures of ideas and rules of behavior are "blacked out."

It is interesting that the word for black, *tuk*, also means "dead," and is the adjective used for the zone of land just outside the village, which separates it from the completely wild forest and savanna country. The graveyard and the secluded camps used by groups going through "transitional" rites, such as initiation, are located in this interstitial area. Death itself is conceived of by the Tchikrin as a transitional phase between life and total extinction. The ghosts of the dead live on for one generation in the village of the dead, after which they "die" once more, this time passing into total oblivion.

White, which occurs only in relatively infrequent ceremonial decorations, is associated less with transition than with the pure, "terminal" state of complete transcendence of the normal social world. It is, for example, the color of ghosts. White clay is the food of ghosts, and the villages of the ghosts are always located near outcroppings of white clay or rocks.

Body painting for both ordinary social and ritual occasions seems to be a means of expressing heightened integration and participation in the social order as well as a means of heightening individual biological and psychological powers. Red is applied on the parts of the body most immediately associated with swiftness, agility, and sensory contact with the outside world (feet, hands, and face). This seems logical enough from what we have seen of the symbolic values of the color red. Black is used for the parts of the body most intimately associated with the individual's biological being, his inner self as contrasted with his faculties of relating to the world (the trunk, upper parts of the limbs, and certain areas of the head).

Why should black, which symbolizes the marginal, transitional, or imperfectly integrated aspects of the social order, be thus associated with the individual's presocial (biological) being in those situations where integration into society is being dramatized and reaffirmed?

To answer this question adequately we must start from an understanding of the symbolic significance of the skin in Kayapo culture. The skin, for the Kayapo, is the boundary of the individual on several levels of meaning. In the obvious physical sense, it separates the individual from the external environment, which includes other people. But in a more subtle sense, the skin symbolizes the boundary between two levels of the human personality: the lower level, based on presocial drives emanating from the individual's biological constitution, and the higher level of moral conscience and intellectual consciousness based on cultural principals derived from social sources outside the individual. More simply, this inner, psychological boundary corresponds to the boundary between the physical individual and his society.

The proper balance of relations between the levels of the individual's personality, like proper relations between individuals in society, depends in Kayapo thought on the right sort of communication taking place across these two correlated boundaries. They must be crossed in both directions, for society needs the biological energies of individuals, but it also needs to control them to prevent disruption and chaos. The individual subsists through his biological energies, but he needs the steadying influence of social values, cognitive categories, and moral principles or he will "go berserk" (a recognized condition in Kayapo, known as *aybanh*). Disease, death, the breaking of certain taboos, and going berserk are all conceived as improper forms of eruption of the biological level of existence into the social, orderly level.

The interesting point for our purposes is that all of these "eruptions" are associated with disorders or treatments of the skin: sick people are painted red, dead people either red or black, taboo-breakers get hives or other skin diseases, the skin of berserks becomes alternately overheated and then cold and insensitive, etc. When black, the color associated with transition between the social and asocial worlds, is painted on the skin of the central parts of the body, it expresses the transcendence of the boundary between individual and society and thus reaffirms the mutual integration of the biological individual and the "body social."

It becomes easy to understand, then, why the Tchikrin paint over the black designs of the face with red: They are concerned not so much with esthetic results as with a symbolic statement, in which both colors have complementary "messages" to transmit. The overpainting with red serves to energize, to charge with biological and psychic life-force, the sensory and intelligent part of the person whose socialization has been asserted by the black designs below.

Body painting at this general level of meaning really amounts to the imposition of a second, social "skin" on the naked biological skin of the individual. This second skin of culturally standardized patterns symbolically expresses the "socialization" of the human body — the subordination of the physical aspects of individual existence to common social values and behavior.

It would be misleading to lay too much emphasis on the superficial differences between Tchikrin body adornment and our own culture's elaborate array of clothing and hair styles, makeup, and jewelry. Among the Tchikrin, as among ourselves, the decoration of the surface of the body serves as a symbolic link between the "inner man" and some of his society's most important values.

REVIEW QUESTIONS

1. What meanings do the Tchikrin give red and black body paint, lip plugs, long hair, earplugs, and cotton bands?

2. What does Turner mean when he says body painting and adornment symbolize a kind of "social skin"?

3. How does Turner explain that, on some occasions, the Tchikrin paint their faces black but immediately cover this pigment with a coat of red?

4. What does bodily adornment tell us about basic Tchikrin values, particularly as they concern growth and sex roles?

5. What are some of the forms of bodily adornment in our country and what do they mean?

8

Behind the veil

ELIZABETH W. FERNEA and
ROBERT A. FERNEA

As we have seen from the articles in this section, symbols come in many forms, from speech utterances to speaking distances, from speech acts to the color of body paints. But some symbols carry more meaning than others; they stand for core values that organize society and govern many behaviors. In this article, Elizabeth and Robert Fernea trace the meaning of such a symbol, the veil worn by women in the Middle East. Often viewed by Westerners as a symbol of restriction and inequality of women, for the women who wear it the veil signals honor, personal protection, the sanctity and privacy of the family, wealth and high status, and city life.

Blue jeans have come to mean America all over the world; three-piece wool suits signal businessmen; and in the 1980s pink or green hair says "punk." What do we notice, however, in societies other than our own? Ishi, the last of a "lost" tribe of North American Indians who stumbled into twentieth-century California in 1911, is reported to have said that the truly interesting objects in the white culture were pockets and matches. Rifa'ah Tahtawi, one of the first young Egyptians to be sent to Europe to study in 1826, wrote an account of French society in which he noted that Parisians used many unusual objects of dress, among them something called a belt. Women wore belts, he said, apparently to keep their bosoms erect, and to show off the slimness of their waists and the fullness of their hips. Europeans are still fascinated by the Stetson hats worn by American cowboys; an elderly Dutch lady of our acquaintance recently carried six enormous Stetsons back to the Hague as presents for the male members of her family.

Like languages (Inca, French) or food (tacos, hamburgers) clothing has special meaning for people who wear it that strangers may not understand. But some objects become charged with meaning to other cultures. The veil is one article of clothing used in Middle Eastern societies that stirs strong emotions in the West. "The feminine veil has become a symbol: that of the slavery of one portion of humanity," wrote French ethnologist Germaine Tillion in 1966. A hundred years earlier, Sir Richard Burton, British traveler, explorer, and translator of the *Arabian Nights*, recorded a different view. "Europeans inveigh against this article [the face veil] . . . for its hideousness and jealous concealment of charms made to be admired," he wrote in 1855. "It is, on the contrary, the most coquettish article of women's attire . . . it conceals coarse skins, fleshy noses, wide mouths and vanishing chins, whilst it sets off to best advantage what in these lands is most lustrous and liquid — the eye. Who has not remarked this at a masquerade ball?"

In the present generation, the veil has become a focus of attention for Western writers, both popular and academic, who take a measure of Burton's irony and Tillion's anger to equate modernization of the Middle East with the discarding of the veil and to look at its return in Iran and in a number of Arab countries as a sure sign of retrogression. "Iran's 16 million women have come a long way since their floor-length cotton veil officially was abolished in 1935," an article noted in the 1970s, just before the Shah was toppled. Today, with Ayatollah Khomeini in power, those 16 million Iranian women have put their veils back on again, as if to say that the long way they have come is not in the direction of the West.

The thousands of words written about the appearance and disappearance of the veil and of *purdah* (the seclusion of women) do little to help us understand the Middle East or the cultures that grew out of the same Judeo-Christian roots as our own. The veil and the all-enveloping garments that inevitably accompany it (the *milayah* in Egypt, the *abbayah* in Iraq, the *chadoor* in Iran, the *yashmak* in Turkey, the *burga'* in Afghanistan, and the *djellabah* and the *haik* in North Africa) are only the outward manifestations of cultural practices and meanings that are rooted deep in the history of Mediterranean and Southwest Asian society and are now finding expression once again. Today, with the resurgence of Islam, the veil has become a statement of difference between the Middle East and the Western world, a boundary no easier to cross now than it was during the Crusades or during the nineteenth century, when Western colonial powers ruled the area.

In English, the word *veil* has many definitions, and some of them are religious, just as in the Middle East. In addition to a face cover, the term also means "a piece of material worn over the head and shoulders, a part of a nun's head dress." The Arabic word for veiling and secluding comes from the root word *hajaba*, meaning barrier. A *hijab* is an amulet worn to keep away the evil eye; it also means a diaphragm used to prevent conception. The gatekeeper or doorkeeper who guards the entrance to a government minister's office is a *hijab*, and in a casual conversation a person might say, "I want to be more informal with my friend so-and-so, but she always puts a *hijab* (barrier) between us."

In Islam, the Koranic verse that sanctions a barrier between men and women is called the Sura of the *hijab* (curtain): "Prophet, enjoin your wives, your daughters and the wives of true believers to draw their garments close round them. That is more proper, so that they may be recognized and not molested. Allah is forgiving and merciful." Notice, however, that veils of the first true believers did not conceal but rather announced the religious status of the women who wore them, drawing attention to the fact that they were Muslims and therefore to be treated with respect. The special Islamic dress worn by increasing numbers of modern Muslim women has much the same effect; it also says, "treat me with respect."

Certainly some form of seclusion and of veiling was practiced before the time of Muhammad, at least among the urban elites and ruling families, but it was his followers, the first converts to Islam, who used veiling to signal religious faith. According to historic traditions, the *hijab* was established after the wives of the Prophet Muhammad were insulted by people coming to the mosque in search of the Prophet. Muhammad's wives, they said, had been mistaken for slaves. The custom of the *hijab* was thus established, and in the words of historian Nabia Abbott, "Muhammad's women found themselves, on the one hand, deprived of personal liberty, and on the other hand, raised to a position of honor and dignity." It is true, nonetheless, that the forms and uses of veiling and seclusion have varied greatly in practice over the last thousand years since the time of the Prophet, and millions of Muslim women have never been veiled at all. It is a luxury poorer families cannot afford, since any form of arduous activity, such as working in the fields, makes its use impossible. Thus it is likely that the use of the veil was envied by those who could not afford to do so, for it signaled a style of life which was generally admired. Burton, commenting on the Muslims portrayed in the *Arabian Nights*, says, "The women, who delight in restrictions which tend to their honour, accepted it willingly and still affect it, they do not desire a liberty or rather a license which they have learned to regard as inconsistent with their time-honored notions of feminine decorum and delicacy. They would think very meanly of a husband who permitted them to be exposed, like hetairae, to the public gaze."

The veil bears many messages about its wearers and their society, and many men and women in Middle Eastern communities today would quickly denounce nineteenth century Orientalists like Sir Richard Burton and deny its importance. Nouha al Hejelan, wife of the Saudi Arabian ambassador to London, told Sally Quinn of *The Washington Post*, "If I wanted to take it all off [the *abbayah* and veil], I would have long ago. It wouldn't mean as much to me as it does to you." Basima Bezirgan, a contemporary Iraqi feminist, says, "Compared to the real issues that are involved between men and women in the Middle East today, the veil itself is unimportant." A Moroccan linguist, who buys her clothes in Paris, laughs when asked about the veil. "My mother wears a *djellabah* and a veil. I have never worn them. But so what? I still cannot get divorced as easily as a man, and I am still a member of my family group and responsible to them for everything I do. What is the veil? A piece of cloth." However, early Middle Eastern feminists felt differently. Huda Sharawi, an early Egyptian activist who formed the first Women's Union, removed her veil in public in 1923, a dramatic gesture to demonstrate her dislike of society's attitude toward women and her defiance of the system.

"The seclusion of women has many purposes," states Egyptian anthropologist Nadia Abu Zahra. "It expresses men's status, power, wealth, and manliness. It also helps preserve men's image of virility and masculinity, but men do not admit this; on the contrary they claim that one of the purposes of the veil is to guard women's honor." The veil and *purdah* are symbols of restriction, in men's behavior as well as women's. A respectable woman wearing conservative Islamic dress today on a public street is signaling, "Hands off! Don't touch me or you'll be sorry." Cowboy Jim Sayre of Deadwood, South Dakota, says, "If you deform a cowboy's hat, he'll likely deform you." A man who approaches a veiled woman is asking for similar trouble; not only the woman but also her family is shamed, and serious problems may result. "It is clear," says Egyptian anthropologist Ahmed Abou Zeid, "that honor and shame which are usually attributed to a certain individual or a certain kinship group have in fact a bearing on the total social structure, since most acts involving honor or shame are likely to affect the existing social equilibrium."

Veiling and seclusion almost always can be related to the maintenance of social status. The extreme example of the way the rich could use this practice was found among the wealthy sultans of prerevolutionary Turkey. Stories of their women, kept in harems and guarded by eunuchs, formed the basis for much of the Western folklore concerning the nature of male-female relationships in Middle Eastern society. The forbidden nature of seclusion inflamed the Western imagination, but the Westerners who created erotic fantasies in films and novels would not have been able to enter the sultans' palaces any more than they could have penetrated their harems! It was eroticism plus opulence and luxury, the signs of wealth, that captured the imagination of the Westerner—and still does, as witnessed by the popularity of "Dallas" and "Dynasty."

The meaning associated with veiling or a lack of veiling changes according to locality. Most village women in the Egyptian delta have not veiled, nor have the Berber women of North Africa, but no one criticizes them for this. "In the village, no one veils, because everyone is considered a member of the same large family," explained Aisha Bint Muhammad, a working-class wife of Marrakesh. "But in the city, veiling is *sunnah*, required by our religion." Veiling has generally been found in towns and cities, among all classes, where families feel that it is necessary to distinguish themselves from strangers. Some women, who must work without the veil in factories and hotels, may put such garments on when they go out on holidays or even walk on the streets after work.

Veiling and *purdah* not only indicate status and wealth; they also have some religious sanction and protect women from the world outside the home. *Purdah* delineates private space and distinguishes between the public and private sectors of society, as does the traditional architecture of the area. Older Middle Eastern houses do not have picture windows facing on the street, nor do they have walks leading invitingly to front doors. Family life is hidden away from strangers; behind blank walls may lie courtyards and gardens, refuges from the heat, cold, and bustle of the outside world, the world of nonkin that is not to be trusted. Outsiders are pointedly excluded.

Even within the household, among her close relatives, a traditional Muslim woman may veil before those kinsmen whom she could legally marry. If her maternal or paternal cousins, her brothers-in-law, or her sons-in-law come to call, she covers her head, or perhaps her whole face. To do otherwise, to neglect such acts of respect and modesty, would be considered shameless.

The veil does more than protect its wearers from known and unknown intruders; it can also conceal identity. Behind the anonymity of the veil, women can go about a city unrecognized and uncriticized. Nadia Abu Zahra reports anecdotes of men donning women's veils in order to visit their lovers undetected; women may do the same. The veil is such an effective disguise that Nouri Al-Sa'id, the late prime minister of Iraq, attempted to escape death from revolutionary forces in 1958 by wearing the *abbayah* and veil of a woman; only his shoes gave him away. When houses of prostitution were closed in Baghdad in the early 1950s, the prostitutes donned the same clothing to cruise the streets. Flashing open their outer garments was an advertisement to potential customers.

Political dissidents in many countries have used the veil for their own ends. The women who marched, veiled, through Cairo during the Nationalist demonstrations against the British after World War I were counting on the strength of Western respect for the veil to protect them against British gunfire. At first they were right. Algerian women also used the protection of the veil to carry bombs through French army checkpoints during the Algerian revolution. But when the French discovered the ruse, Algerian women discarded the veil and dressed like Europeans to move about freely.

The multiple meanings and uses of *purdah* and the veil do not fully explain how such practices came to be so deeply embedded in Mediterranean society. However, their origins lie in the asymmetrical relationship between men and women and the resulting attitudes about men's and women's roles. Women, according to Fatma Mernissi, a Moroccan sociologist, are seen by men in Islamic societies as in need of protection because they are unable to control their sexuality and hence are a danger to the social order. In other words, they need to be restrained and controlled so that men do not give way to the impassioned desire they inspire, and society can thus function in an orderly way.

The notion that women present a danger to the social order is scarcely limited to Muslim society. Anthropologist Julian Pitt-Rivers has pointed out that the supervision and seclusion of women was also found in Christian Europe, even though veiling was not usually practiced there. "The idea that women not subjected to male authority are a danger is a fundamental one in the writings of the moralists from the Archpriest of Talavera to Padre Haro, and it is echoed in the modern Andalusian *pueblo*. It is bound up with the fear of ungoverned female sexuality which had been an integral element of European folklore ever since prudent Odysseus lashed himself to the mast to escape the sirens."

Pitt-Rivers is writing about northern Mediterranean communities, which like those of the Middle Eastern societies, have been greatly concerned with family honor and shame rather than with individual guilt. The honor of the Middle Eastern extended family, its ancestors and its descendants, is the highest social value. The misdeeds of the grandparents are indeed visited on their grandchildren, but so also grandparents may be disgraced by grandchildren. Men and women always remain members of their natal families. Marriage is a legal contract, but a fragile one that is often broken; the ties between brother and sister, mother and child, father and child are lifelong and enduring. The larger natal family is the group to which the individual man or woman belongs and to which the individual owes responsibility in exchange for the social and economic security that the family group provides. It is the group that is socially honored — or dishonored — by the behavior of the individual.

Both male honor and female honor are involved in the honor of the family, but each is expressed differently. The honor of a man, *sharaf*, is a public matter, involving bravery, hospitality, and piety. It may be lost, but it may also be regained. The honor of a woman, *'ard*, is a private matter involving only one thing, her sexual chastity. Once believed to be lost, it cannot be regained. If the loss of female honor remains only privately known, a rebuke may be all that takes place. But if the loss of female honor becomes public knowledge, the other members of the family may feel bound to cleanse the family name. In extreme cases, the cleansing may require the death of the offending female member. Although such killings are now criminal offenses in the Middle East, suspended sentences are often given, and the newspapers in Cairo and Baghdad frequently carry sad stories of runaway sisters "gone bad" in the city, and the revenge taken upon them in the name of family honor by their brothers or cousins.

This emphasis on female chastity, many say, originated in the patrilineal society's concern with the paternity of the child and the inheritance that follows the male line. How could the husband know that the child in his wife's womb was his son? He could not know unless his wife was a virgin at marriage. Marriages were arranged by parents, and keeping daughters secluded from men was the best way of seeing that a girl remained a virgin until her wedding night.

Middle Eastern women also look upon seclusion as practical protection. In the Iraqi village where we lived from 1956 to 1958, one of us (Elizabeth) wore the *abbayah* and found that it provided a great deal of protection from prying eyes, dust, heat, and flies. Parisian ladies visiting Istanbul in the sixteenth century were so impressed by the ability of the all-enveloping garment to keep dresses clean of mud and manure and to keep women from being attacked by importuning men that they tried to introduce it into French fashion. Many women have told us that they felt self-conscious, vulnerable, and even naked when they first walked on a public street without the veil and *abbayah* — as if they were making a display of themselves.

The veil, as it has returned in the last decade in a movement away from wearing Western dress, has been called a form of "portable seclusion," allowing women to maintain a modest appearance that indicates respectability and religious piety in the midst of modern Middle Eastern urban life. This new style of dress always includes long skirts, long sleeves, and a head covering (scarf or turban). Some outfits are belted, some are loose, and some include face veils and shapeless robes, as well as gloves so that no skin whatsoever is exposed to the public eye. However, these clothes are seldom black, like the older garments. The women wearing such clothes in Egypt may work in shops or offices or go to college; they are members of the growing middle class.

This new fashion has been described by some scholars as an attempt by men to reassert their Muslim identity and to reestablish their position as heads of families, even though both spouses often must work outside the home. According to this analysis, the presence of the veil is a sign that the males of the household are in control of their women and are more able to assume the responsibilities disturbed or usurped by foreign colonial powers, responsibilities which continue to be threatened by Western politics and materialism. Other scholars argue that it is not men who are choosing the garb today but women themselves, using modest dress as a way of communicating to the rest of the world that though they may work outside their homes, they are nonetheless pious Muslims and respectable women.

The veil is the outward sign of a complex reality. Observers are often deceived by the absence of that sign and fail to see that in Middle Eastern societies (and in many parts of Europe) where the garb no longer exists, basic attitudes are unchanged. Women who have taken off the veil continue to play the old roles within the family, and their chastity remains crucial. A woman's behavior is still the key to the honor and the reputation of her family, no matter what she wears.

In Middle Eastern societies, feminine and masculine continue to be strong poles of identification. This is in marked contrast to Western society, where for more than a generation great equality between men and women has been reflected in the blurring of distinctions between male and female clothing. Western feminists continue to state that biology is not the basis of behavior and therefore should not be the basis for understanding men's and women's roles. But almost all Middle Eastern reformers, whether upper or middle class, intellectuals or clerics, argue from the assumption of a fundamental, a God-given difference, social and psychological as well as physical, between men and women. There are important disagreements between these reformers today about what should be done, however.

Those Muslim reformers still strongly influenced by Western models call for equal access to divorce, child custody, and inheritance; equal opportunities for education and employment; abolition of female circumcision and "crimes of honor"; an end to polygamy; and a law regulating the age of marriage. But of growing importance are reformers of social practice who call for a return to the example set by the Prophet Muhammad and his early followers; they wish to begin by eliminating what they feel to be the licentious practices introduced by Western influence, such as sexual laxity and the consumption of alcohol. To them, change in the laws affecting women should be in strict accord with their view of Islamic law, and women should begin by expressing their modesty and piety by wearing the new forms of veiling in public life. Seclusion may be impossible in modern urban societies, but conservative dress, the new form of veiling, is an option for women that sets the faithful Muslim apart from the corrupt world of the nonbeliever as it was believed to do in the time of the Prophet.

A female English film director, after several months in Morocco, said in an interview, "This business about the veil is nonsense. We all have our veils, between ourselves and other people. The question is what the veils are used for, and by whom." Today the use of the veil continues to trigger Western reaction, for as Islamic dress, it is not only a statement about the honor of the family or the boundary between family and stranger. Just as the changes in the nun's dress in the United States tell us something about the woman who wears it and the society of which she is a part, the various forms of veiling today communicate attitudes and beliefs about politics and religious morality as well as the roles of men and women in the Middle East.

REVIEW QUESTIONS

1. What is the meaning to Westerners of the veil worn by Middle Eastern women? How does this view reflect Western values?

2. List the symbolic meanings of the veil to Middle Eastern women. How do these meanings relate to the Muslim concept of *purdah* and to other important Middle Eastern values?

3. There has been a resurgence of the veil in several Middle Eastern societies over the past few years. How can you explain this change?

4. Using this article as a model, analyze the meaning of some American articles of clothing. How do these relate to core values in this country?

IV

Kinship and family

Social life is essential to human existence. We remain in the company of other people from the day we are born to the time of our death. People teach us to speak. They show us how to relate to our surroundings. They give us the help and the support we need to achieve personal security and mental well-being. Alone, we are relatively frail, defenseless primates; in groups we are astonishingly adaptive and powerful. Yet despite these advantages, well-organized human societies are difficult to achieve. Some species manage to produce social organization genetically. But people are not like bees or ants. We lack the genetically coded directions for behavior that make these insects successful social animals. Although we seem to inherit a general need for social approval, we also harbor individual interests and ambitions that can block or destroy close social ties. To overcome these divisive tendencies, human groups organize around several principles designed to foster cooperation and group loyalty. Kinship is among the strongest of these.

We may define *kinship* as the complex system of culturally defined social relationships based on marriage, the principle of *affinity;* and

113

birth, the principle of *consanguinity*. (Meigs' article in this section expands this definition. She argues that kin can be "made" by the exchange of food and bodily substances, not simply "born" as in our own society.) The study of kinship involves consideration of such principles as descent, kinship statuses and roles, family and other kinship groups, marriage, and residence. In fact, kinship has been such an important organizing factor in many of the societies studied by anthropologists that it is one of the most elaborate areas of the discipline. What are some of the important concepts?

First is descent. *Descent* is based on the notion of common heritage. It is a cultural rule tying together people on the basis of reputed common ancestry. Descent functions to guide inheritance, group loyalty, and, above all, the formation of families and extended kinship groups.

There are three main rules of descent. One is *patrilineal descent*, which links relatives through males only. In patrilineal systems, females are part of their father's line, but their children descend from the husbands. *Matrilineal descent* links relatives through females only. Males belong to their mother's line; the children of males descend from the wives. *Bilateral descent* links a person to kin through both males and females simultaneously. We Americans are said to have bilateral descent, whereas most of the people in India, Japan, and China, are patrilineal. Such groups as the Apache and Trobriand Islanders are matrilineal.

Descent often defines groups called, not surprisingly, *descent groups*. One of these is the *lineage*, a localized group that is based on unilineal (patrilineal or matrilineal) descent and which usually has some corporate powers. In the Marshall Islands, for example, the matriline holds rights to land, which, in turn, it allots to its members. Lineages in India sometimes hold rights to land but are a more important arena for other kinds of decisions such as marriage. Lineage mates must be consulted about the advisability, timing, and arrangements for weddings.

Clans are composed of lineages. Clan members believe they are all descended from a common ancestor, but because clans are larger, members cannot trace their genealogical relationships to everyone in the group. As we saw in Kurin's article in Part II of this volume, clan identity can be of crucial importance to people. In some societies, clans may be linked together in even larger groups called *phratries*. Because phratries are usually large, the feeling of common descent they offer is weaker.

Rammages, or cognatic kin groups, are based on bilateral descent. They often resemble lineages in size and function but provide more recruiting flexibility. An individual can choose membership from among several rammages where he or she has relatives.

Another important kinship group is the family. This unit is more difficult to define than you may think, because people have found so many different ways to organize "family like" groups. Here we will follow anthropologist George P. Murdock's approach and define the *family* as a kin group consisting of at least one married couple sharing the same residence with their children and performing sexual, reproductive, economic, and educational functions. A *nuclear family* consists of a single married couple and their children. An *extended family* consists of two or more married couples and their children. Extended families have a quality all their own and are often found in societies where family performance and honor are paramount to the reputation of individual family members. Extended families are most commonly based on patrilineal descent. Women marry into such families and must establish themselves among the line members and other women who live there. Margery Wolf explores this process in the selection on the Chinese extended family included below.

Marriage, the socially approved union of a man and woman, is a second major principle of kinship. The regulation of marriage takes elaborate forms from one society to the next. Marriage may be *exogamous*, meaning marriage outside any particular named group, or *endogamous* indicating the opposite. Bhil tribals of India, for example, are clan and village exogamous (they should marry outside these groups), but tribal endogamous (they should marry other Bhils).

Marriage may also be *monogamous*, where it is preferred that only one woman should be married to one man at a time, or *polygamous*, meaning that one person may be married to more than one person simultaneously. There are two kinds of polygamy, *polygyny*, the marriage of one man with more than one woman simultaneously, and *polyandry*, the marriage of one woman with more than one man.

Many anthropologists view marriage as a system of alliances between families and descent lines. Viewed in these terms, rules such as endogamy and exogamy can be explained as devices to link or internally strengthen various kinship groups. The *incest taboo*, a legal rule that prohibits sexual intercourse or marriage between particular classes of kin, is often explained as a way to extend alliances between kin groups, and this is the position taken by Yehudi Cohen in his article about the incest taboo found in this section.

Finally, the regulation of marriage falls to the parents and close relatives of eligible young people in many societies. These elders concern themselves with more than wedding preparations; they must also see to it that young people marry appropriately, which means they consider the reputation of prospective spouses and their families' economic strength and social rank. It is easy to accept that Middle Eastern, Indian, and Chinese families try to regulate the marriage of their children. These are kinship-oriented societies. But it is more difficult to imagine that American parents do the same thing. Yet this is just what John Finley Scott argues in "Sororities and the Husband Game" reprinted in this section.

KEY TERMS

kinship	family
consanguinity	nuclear family
affinity	extended family
descent	marriage
patrilineal descent	exogamy
matrilineal descent	endogamy
bilateral descent	monogamy
descent groups	polygamy
lineage	polygyny
clans	polyandry
phratries	incest taboo
rammage	

9

Blood kin and food kin

ANNA S. MEIGS

*Anthropologists usually treat kinship as a complex system of cultur-
ally defined social relationships based on birth and marriage. This
definition rests on the assumption that all human beings feel that kin
are created by the act of conception. In this view, babies are born into
a network of kin who are biologically, thus unalterably, related to
them. Anna Meigs challenges this view. She notes that while many
people hold a biological view of kinship, others, especially those who
live in Highland New Guinea, have a different concept of kinship.
For them, children are built, originally from menstrual blood and
semen, later from substances such as mother's milk, food, and blood.
As the child acquires and incorporates these substances, it gains kinship with those who provided them.*

It is difficult to resist the temptation to think that we understand the
world as it really is, in other words, that we see the world neutrally
and objectively. In fact, though, people perceive their environment
through the set of lenses provided them by their culture. No one sees it
"straight" and "as it truly is." One of the primary goals anthropologists have set themselves is to see through "native" eyes. This is never
easy.

To Americans, kinship is about relationships created through
birth. You are related to:

those people you were born from (mother and father);
any people born from the same people you were born from
(siblings);

This article was written especially for this book. Copyright © 1986 by Anna S. Meigs.

those people born from the same people your parents were born
    from (aunts and uncles);
those people born from you (your children).

And so forth.

This view of kinship manifests itself most clearly in our cultural
fascination with family trees or genealogy. Professional genealogists
are available to lawyers (for tracing out the "real" kin and, thus, the
appropriate inheritors) and to the general public. There are over fifty
do-it-yourself genealogy books in print in the United States with such
titles as *How to Trace Your Family Tree* or *Genealogy Beginner's Manual.*
Family reunions in which large numbers of people who have no connection other than that of common birth (perhaps many generations
back) are a cultural institution. In recent years adopted chidren have
begun to hunt for their "real" parents — a testimony to the power of
our notion that kinship is determined by birth.

This view of kinship, common not only in the United States but
through the West, has worked its way into anthropological studies of
kinship. According to Lewis Henry Morgan, the late-nineteenth-cen-
tury founder of American studies of kinship, kinship is about what a
society does with the phenomena that develop from the biological facts
of sexual intercourse, pregnancy, and parturition. Morgan assumed
that it was this particular set of biological facts (those having to do with
birth) that were universally crucial for understanding kinship. Morgan's contribution lay in his discovery that different cultures order
these facts differently. For example, in one culture it is the fact that you
were born the child of a particular man that is the relevant one for your
kinship (this kind of kinship is called patrilineal), in a second it would
be the fact that you were born the child of a particular woman (matrilineal), and in a third society (one like the United States) both facts
would be relevant to your kinship (cognatic).

This perspective on kinship worked particularly well in societies
in which the local conception of kinship paralleled our own. Some of
the most famous ethnographies, for example Evans-Pritchard's *The
Nuer,* are of African tribal societies organized around the principle of
descent (or birth) from a common ancestor. Many members of these
African descent groups, like their American counterparts, know their
family trees and cherish genealogical information. Similarly, like
Americans they make distinctions between the kinspeople that are
"real" and those that are not.

The Tallensi of West Africa can serve as an example. The Tallensi
believe that real kinship is determined by the male to whom you are

born. You are also related to your mother and her kin but that connection is not as significant in kinship terms as your relationship to your father, and to his father, and so on. These chains of linked connections through males are called lineages or patrilineages (given that this is a patrilineal system). Tallensi villages are agglomerations of lineages. According to Meyer Fortes, the ethnographer of the Tallensi, only those lineages made up of people born through males from an original male ancestor are considered authentic. Where a female ancestor, instead of leaving the village at marriage, stayed and gave birth to sons who themselves gave birth to more sons (and so forth), the lineage that this female established would always be recognized as "attached" rather than as "authentic." (A Tallensi lineage is authentic only if it is made up of people born through males from a common *male* ancestor.) Where a stranger established a lineage in a Tallensi village, its status as an "assimilated" (and nonauthentic) lineage would similarly be preserved ideally for all eternity. Like Americans with their distinction between real and adoptive parents (and children), no amount of common residence, shared experience, and exchange of affection and material goods can erase the basic differences in identity originating in the fact of an unshared ancestor (a noncommon birth).

The idea that kinship is created by birth means that kinship is unchangeable (because it is not possible to change who your parents are). This immutability of kinship identity often has particular significance for a woman, who in patrilineal societies like the Tallensi usually leaves her own kin group to take up residence with her husband's. A Tallensi woman never gains full status as a member of her husband's lineage (you have to be born into it to achieve that). Similarly, she never loses her status as a member of her father's. At death, in testimony to the lack of alteration in kinship identity occasioned by decades of marriage, the Tallensi woman's body is returned to her father's house. This immutability of kinship identity did not seem puzzling to British and American ethnographers. After all, we do not expect marriage or change of residence to alter kinship either.

It was in the 1950s that anthropologists, after decades of work in Africa, first went to the Highlands of New Guinea. Immediately, the kinship there puzzled them. Although the groups appeared to be, for the most part, patrilineal in that at least a core of males were descended by birth from the same male ancestor, most communities contained a good proportion of males not so related. These "immigrants" were called kinsmen and had equal power and status to other males in the group. Unlike the Tallensi and their American ethnographers, these New Guinea Highland groups were not interested in distinguishing between real and not real kin. Similarly they were not interested in family trees and genealogical knowledge.

Anthropologists were puzzled by their casual inattention to the important factor of kinship (i.e., who is born from whom) and were particularly frustrated by their easy inclusion of people not properly born within the groups of people they called kin. To cope with these anomalous inclusions both in New Guinea and elsewhere, anthropologists developed the concept of *fictive kin*. These are people who you know are not linked to you through a common birth but who you *pretend* are. You call them kin and treat them as kin even though the truth is otherwise. A perfect American example is the custom of calling good friends of one's parents *aunt* and *uncle*.

I argue that the device by which immigrants are included in the New Guinea Highland society in which I lived (as well as some others about which I have read) was not a fiction or some kind of pretense but rather a different understanding of kinship.

In the American conception, kinship is created prenatally and established by the act of birth. People "are related" through chains of reproductive acts. In other words, I am related to my first cousin (for example, my mother's brother's son) by the fact that I and my first cousin are both born to people (a brother and a sister) who were themselves born from the same people (my grandparents). In this conception it is the biological phenomena surrounding pregnancy and birth that relate you to other people.

In the new conception of kinship that I, following my Hua informants, am proposing here, people may be related not only through birth but through food, not only through sex but through eating, not only through prenatal but also through postnatal acts. In short, the Hua and others have a different view of what makes people kin to each other.

James Watson, the ethnographer of the Tairora (New Guinea Highlands), describes Tairora social organization in terms that would have been foreign to the anthropologists who studied African tribal groups and who were able to present neat genealogical trees as the ground plan of the society. Watson describes the Tairora as a population constantly in motion, continually cycling itself through the various local groups. Each group he conceives as a kind of funnel taking in outsiders (individuals who, he says, often have little or no claim of kinship by birth) and putting out insiders (people who are uniformly recognized as kin).

The Tairora, according to Watson, are quick to give outsiders full status as kin. They do so, he says, not by some fiction of kinship by common birth, which he calls "nature kinship," but rather through their belief in what he calls "nurture kinship." Nurture kinship is that physiological oneness or communion that is created by postnatal exchanges, in particular of a woman's milk, of food, and of water. In other words, two people not related by birth can create kinship by feeding each other. (The kinship, incidentally, can also be created if the feeding is unilateral.) Immigrants to Tairora communities *become kin* by eating food produced on community lands by its members and by drinking community water.

Nurture kinship among the Hua, a horticultural population of 3,100 with whom I lived, may be illustrated by the progress of a woman's changing relationship to her husband's community. At marriage she enters his community as an outsider, an alien, and one whose body substances are dangerous to many local residents, in particular to her husband and his agemates. She is referred to as *naru'* (wife) by these latter two categories of males. Her body and, as a consequence, all food that she produces or prepares is thought to contain an alien and possibly hostile *nu*. (*Nu* is vital essence, that which is essential to growth, vitality, and sexual potency. It is associated in particular with all body fluids.) No food that this woman produces or prepares may be eaten by any uninitiated person and, in particular, not by her husband or his agemates. She is non-kin *par excellence*, the outsider within the gates.

After about fifteen years of marriage, however, all the proscriptions on eating food that she has produced or prepared are terminated in a public ceremony in which the wife gives her husband some leafy green vegetables (culturally significant repositories of her *nu*), and the husband's classificatory elder brother tells him to eat them freely, as if they came from the hand of his own mother. The wife has been changed from an in-law into a relative.

By what logic does this change occur? Remember the Tallensi wife whose corpse is shipped home to her father's place to be buried with its kin. The Hua woman's situation is very different precisely because the Hua believe in nurture kinship. People are related in their thinking not only by the sexual acts of their forebearers but also by their own eating acts.

In Hua thinking, food contains the *nu* "vital essence" of both its producer and preparer. Any person who grows a food, who labors over it in the garden, invests his or her *nu* in that food. Similarly, the people who prepare the food endow it with some of their self, some of their *nu*. Thus, when you eat a food you are, in Hua thinking, eating some of the *nu* "vital essence" of another person. Eating, by this logic, relates people, makes them kin because it mixes their *nu*.

The Arabs have a similar idea about the effect of eating, according to Robertson Smith, a renowned British scholar of the late-nineteenth century. Their law of hospitality legislates that if you eat the smallest morsel of food with another person, then you and that person are bound not only to do each other no harm but to help and defend each other as if you were brothers. You have a relationship of kinship established by common eating.

Among the Hua, postnatal or nurture kinship can be created through acts other than eating. That which creates kinship in eating is the transfer of *nu*. *Nu* occurs in many forms. In addition to being in the foods people produce or prepare, it is in their blood, sweat, body oils, urine, and saliva and in their feces, hair, breath, and body odor. Any act by which any of these substances is transferred between people serves to relate them at least minimally. Thus a woman married into a Hua community exchanges *nu* with her in-laws in many different ways. Her breath, body odors, sweat, oils, urine, and feces are all, in Hua thinking, continually being released from her body and in small but significant quotients being absorbed by the members of the surrounding community. Conversely she is the recipient of that community's *nu*. She eats blood let from their veins, their hair sprinkled on her food, the flesh of their deceased; in the course of everyday living she absorbs some of their body odor, their sweat, their breath, and so on. In the process her *nu* becomes commingled with the *nu* of her husband's community: they become kin.

Implicit here is a different idea of body than the one to which we are accustomed. Americans think of their bodies as the seat of complicated organs, processes, and substances that are fixed and innate. Given the appropriate fuel (i.e., food), these elaborate and complex inbuilt mechanisms will operate autonomously. Reproduction is one such process. Humans in our conception reproduce themselves through the complex series of physiological events that occur within the testicles, penis, ovaries, fallopian tubes, and uterus. These events are ones that the properly fueled body performs automatically. Once birth has occurred, the act of reproduction is over.

In the Hua conception, reproduction does not end with birth but continues as *nu* is received into the body in postnatal transactions. The difference between the Hua and American conceptions has a lot to do with the power and autonomy attributed to internal states and processes. In American thinking, these are very important, and it is through them that reproduction occurs. In Hua thinking, internal states and processes are accorded very little importance. The body is essentially an empty vessel. (Granted the Hua are aware of the internal organs and do, in fact, have names for them, but they are not aware of the functions of these organs. Perhaps it is more correct to say that to the Hua the body is a functionally empty vessel.) All body states (whether of illness or health) and all body processes (growth, aging, reproduction) are understood as the specific consequence of substances put into and taken out of the body.

Thus in Hua thinking the fetus develops simply out of the coagulation of semen with menstrual blood. It is important that a man have frequent sex with a newly pregnant woman so as to provide sufficient semen for the development of the fetus. (A woman who has sex with more than one male has what the Hua call "a child of the outside," one of ambiguous kinship identity not because it is not known who its "real" father is but because the child is thought to be made of the semen of many men.) The Hua have, to my knowledge, no awareness of sperm, the role of the testes, ovaries, eggs, fertilization, and so forth. In their thinking, reproduction occurs (or begins to occur) when menstrual blood mixes with semen. If this mixture occurs in a male body, for example if a small bit of menstrual blood is swallowed, then in Hua thinking a male can become pregnant. The presence of ovaries, a uterus, and female hormones are not what counts: it is the *nu* substances that are all important.

For the Hua, however, reproduction is not completed by birth but rather is an open process that continues until the child becomes mature. The child is reproduced prenatally by semen and menstrual blood and postnatally by breast milk, blood (let from parents' veins and fed to the child), sweat and body oil (rubbed on the child's skin), flesh (of real and classificatory deceased parents), and of course food. The child in Hua thinking is reproduced not by the autonomous reproductive systems of the parents' bodies but by the real and classificatory parents' prenatal and postnatal donations of *nu* (in form of semen and menstrual blood prenatally and breast milk, blood, sweat, body oil, flesh, and food postnatally).

Where, as with the Hua, reproduction is understood to be a process that continues from conception to maturity (in late adolescence), if not beyond (remember the Hua wife is reproduced as mother), it is consistent that "being related" is similarly open. This is a somewhat difficult concept for Americans to appreciate. We are so accustomed to the idea that reproduction is complete at birth. The child is born "finished," and as such his or her kinship or physiological relatedness to others has been established conclusively by these prenatal events. No postnatal events can alter the child's finished nature or his or her network of kin. It is difficult for us to imagine a concept of reproduction that allows individuals to be continually reproduced by the *nu* that flows into them and, further, that allows their kinship to flow and change as the pattern of their *nu* transactions alters. This is the problem mentioned at the beginning of this paper of seeing with a "native" eye.

Seeing with a Hua eye means understanding kinship as a dynamic and open process determined by transfers of *nu*. These transfers start prior to birth (when the semen and menstrual blood of the parents mix in the womb) but continue until a person dies. Each act of eating, for example, alters the *nu* content of the body and, thus, of kinship. Kinship in this conception is never final or complete. There is, in addition, no such thing as "real" kin. Rather kinship is always in a process of transformation, and "real" kin are those people with whom one is currently exchanging *nu.*

REVIEW QUESTIONS

1. What relationship does Meigs see between the Western view of kinship and the definition customarily used by anthropologists?

2. What is the difference between the biological view of kinship and the nurture view?

3. How do the Hua believe that babies are conceived and "made"? How does this view affect the way they view who their kin are?

4. What does the Hua word *nu* mean? How is it central to the argument Meigs makes in her article?

5. Based on the argument presented here, how might the usual anthropological definition of kinship be changed to fit the data?

10

Marriage, alliance, and the incest taboo

YEHUDI COHEN

The incest taboo, a legal proscription against mating and marriage among certain designated kin, is often considered a human universal. In this article, Yehudi Cohen argues that the taboo as a feature of law may disappear in some societies, because its original functions are being met in other ways. The incest taboo, he claims, originated out of a need for families in technologically and socially simple groups to forge trade alliances. As that need was filled by other institutions, the taboo came to apply to fewer and fewer individuals until, in industrial society, it was limited to primary relatives. For the industrial family, the taboo still prevents isolation and promotes social maturity. Cohen concludes, however, that this function may soon be met in other ways, leading to the demise of the taboo.

Several years ago a minor Swedish bureaucrat, apparently with nothing better to do, was leafing through birth and marriage records, matching people with their natural parents. To his amazement he found a full brother and sister who were married and had several children. The couple were arrested and brought to trial. It emerged that they had been brought up by separate sets of foster parents and never knew of each other's existence. By a coincidence reminiscent of a Greek tragedy, they met as adults, fell in love, and married, learning of their biological tie only after their arrest. The local court declared their marriage illegal and void.

The couple appealed the decision to Sweden's Supreme Court. After lengthy testimony on both sides of the issue, the court overturned the decision on the grounds that the pair had not been reared together. The marriage was declared legal and valid. In the wake of the decision, a committee appointed by Sweden's Minister of Justice to examine the question has proposed that criminal sanctions against incest be repealed. The committee's members were apparently swayed by Carl-Henry Alstrom, a professor of psychiatry. Alstrom argued that psychological deterrents to incest are stronger than legal prohibitions. The question will soon go to Sweden's Parliament, which seems prepared to follow the committee's recommendation.

Aside from illustrating the idea that the most momentous changes in human societies often occur as a result of unforeseen events, this landmark case raises questions that go far beyond Sweden's (or any other society's) borders. Some people may be tempted to dismiss the Swedish decision as an anomaly, as nothing more than a part of Sweden's unusual experiments in public welfare and sexual freedom.

But the probable Swedish decision to repeal criminal laws against incest cannot be regarded so lightly; this simple step reflects a trend in human society that has been developing for several thousand years. When we arrange human societies along a continuum from the least to the most complex, from those with the smallest number of interacting social groups to those with the highest number of groups, from those with the simplest technology to those with the most advanced technology, we observe that the incest taboo applies to fewer and fewer relatives beyond the immediate family.

Though there are exceptions, the widest extension of incest taboos beyond the nuclear family is found in the least complex societies. In a few societies, such as the Cheyenne of North America and the Kwoma of New Guinea, incest taboos extend to many remote relatives, including in-laws and the in-laws of in-laws. In modern industrial societies, incest taboos are usually confined to members of the immediate household. This contraction in the range of incest taboos is reaching the point at which they may disappear entirely.

The source of these changes in incest taboos lies in changing patterns of external trade. Trade is a society's jugular. Because every group lives in a milieu lacking some necessities that are available in other habitats, the flow of goods and resources is a society's lifeblood. But it is never sufficient merely to encourage people to form trade alliances with others in different areas. Incest taboos force people to marry outside their own group, to form alliances and to maintain trade networks. As other institutions — governments, business organizations — begin to organize trade, incest taboos become less necessary for assuring the flow of the society's lifeblood; they start to contract.

Other explanations of the incest taboo do not, under close examination, hold up. The most common assumption is that close inbreeding is biologically deleterious and will lead to the extinction of those who practice it. But there is strong evidence that inbreeding does not materially increase the rate of maladies such as albinism, total color blindness, or various forms of idiocy, which generally result when each parent carries the same recessive gene. In most cases these diseases result from chance combinations of recessive genes or from mutation.

According to Theodosius Dobzhansky, a geneticist, "The increase of the incidence of hereditary diseases in the offspring of marriages between relatives (cousins, uncle and niece or aunt and nephew, second cousins, etc.) over that in marriages between persons not known to be related is slight — so slight that geneticists hesitate to declare such marriages disgenic." Inbreeding does carry a slight risk. The progeny of relatives include more stillbirths and infant and early childhood deaths than the progeny of unrelated people. But most of these deaths are due to environmental rather than genetic factors. Genetic disadvantages are not frequent enough to justify a prohibition. Moreover, it is difficult to justify the biological explanation for incest taboos when many societies prescribe marriage to one cousin and prohibit marriage to another. Among the Lesu of Melanesia a man must avoid sexual contact with his parallel cousins, his mother's sisters' daughters and his father's brothers' daughters, but is supposed to marry his cross cousins, his mother's brothers' daughters and his father's sisters' daughters. Even though both types of cousins have the same genetic relationship to the man, only one kind is included in the incest taboo. The taboo is apparently a cultural phenomenon based on the cultural classification of people and can not be explained biologically.

Genetic inbreeding may even have some advantages in terms of natural selection. Each time a person dies of a hereditary disadvantage, his detrimental genes are lost to the population. By such a process of genetic cleansing, inbreeding may lead to the elimination, or at least to reduced frequencies, of recessive genes. The infant mortality rate may increase slightly at first, but after the sheltered recessive genes are eliminated, the population may stabilize. Inbreeding may also increase the frequency of beneficial recessive genes, contributing to the population's genetic fitness. In the end, inbreeding seems to have only a slight effect on the offspring and a mixed effect, some good and some bad, on the gene pool itself. This mild consequence hardly justifies the universal taboo on incest.

Another explanation of the incest taboo is the theory of natural aversion, first propounded by Edward Westermarck in his 1891 book, *The History of Human Marriage*. According to Westermarck, children reared in the same household are naturally averse to having sexual relations with one another in adulthood. But this theory has major difficulties. First, it has a basic logical flaw: If there were a natural aversion to incest, the taboo would be unnecessary. As James Frazer pointed out in 1910, "It is not easy to see why any deep human instinct should need to be reinforced by law. There is no law commanding men to eat and drink or forbidding them to put their hands in the fire. . . . The law only forbids men to do what their instincts incline them to do; what nature itself prohibits and punishes, it would be superfluous for the law to prohibit and punish. . . . Instead of assuming, therefore, from the legal prohibition of incest that there is a natural aversion to incest, we ought rather to assume that there is a natural instinct in favour of it."

Second, the facts play havoc with the notion of natural aversion. In many societies, such as the Arapesh of New Guinea studied by Margaret Mead, and the Eskimo, young children are betrothed and raised together, usually by the boy's parents, before the marriage is consummated. Arthur Wolf, an anthropologist who studied a village in northern Taiwan, describes just such a custom: "Dressed in the traditional red wedding costume, the bride enters her future husband's home as a child. She is seldom more than three years of age and often less than a year. . . . [The] last phase in the marriage process does not take place until she is old enough to fulfill the role of wife. In the meantime, she and her parents are affinally related to the groom's parents, but she is not in fact married to the groom."

One of the examples commonly drawn up to support Westermarck's theory of aversion is the Israeli *kibbutz*, where children who have been raised together tend to avoid marrying. But this avoidance has been greatly exaggerated. There is some tendency among those who have been brought up in the same age group in a communal "children's house" to avoid marrying one another, but this arises from two regulations that separate young adults from their *kibbutz* at about the age when they might marry. The first is a regulation of the Israel Defense Forces that no married woman may serve in the armed forces. Conscription for men and women is at 18, usually coinciding with their completion of secondary school, and military service is a deeply felt responsibility for most *kibbutz*-reared Israelis. Were women to marry prior to 18, they would be denied one of their principal goals. By the time they complete their military service, many choose urban spouses whom they have met in the army. Thus the probability of marrying a person one has grown up with is greatly reduced.

The second regulation that limits intermarriage on a *kibbutz* is a policy of the federations to which almost all *kibbutzim* belong. Each of the four major federations reserves the right to transfer any member to any other settlement, especially when a new one is being established. These "seeds," as the transferred members are called, are recruited individually from different settlements and most transfers are made during a soldier's third or fourth year of military service. When these soldiers leave the army to live on a *kibbutz*, they may be separated from those they were reared with. The frequency of marriage among people from working-class backgrounds who began and completed school together in an American city or town is probably higher than for an Israeli *kibbutz*; the proclivity among American college graduates to marry outside their neighborhoods or towns is no more an example of exogamy or incest avoidance than is the tendency in Israeli *kibbutzim* to marry out.

Just as marriage within a neighborhood is accepted in the United States, so is marriage within a *kibbutz* accepted in Israel. During research I conducted in Israel between 1967 and 1969, I attended the wedding of two people in a *kibbutz* who supposedly were covered by this taboo or rule of avoidance. As my tape recordings and photographs show, it would be difficult to imagine a more joyous occasion. When I questioned members of the *kibbutz* about this, they told me with condescending smiles that they had "heard of these things the professors say."

A third, "demographic," explanation of the incest taboo was originally set forth in 1950 by Wilson Wallis and elaborated in 1959 by Mariam Slater. According to this theory, mating within the household, especially between parents and children, was unlikely in early human societies because the life span in these early groups was so short that by the time offspring were old enough to mate, their parents would probably have died. Mating between siblings would also have been unlikely because of the average of eight years between children that resulted from breastfeeding and high rates of infant mortality. But even assuming this to have been true for the first human societies, there is nothing to prevent mating among the members of a nuclear family when the life span is lengthened.

A fourth theory that is widely subscribed to focuses on the length of the human child's parental dependency, which is the longest in the animal kingdom. Given the long period required for socializing children, there must be regulation of sexual activity so that children may learn their proper roles. If the nuclear family's members are permitted to have unrestricted sexual access to one another, the members of the unit would be confused about their roles. Parental authority would be undermined, and it would be impossible to socialize children. This interpretation has much to recommend it as far as relationships between parents and children are concerned, but it does not help explain brother-sister incest taboos or the extension of incest taboos to include remote relatives.

The explanation closest to my interpretation of the changes in the taboo is the theory of alliance advocated by the French anthropologist Claude Levi-Strauss, which suggests that people are compelled to marry outside their groups in order to form unions with other groups and promote harmony among them. A key element in the theory is that men exchange their sisters and daughters in marriage with men of other groups. As originally propounded, the theory of alliance was based on the assumption that men stay put while the women change groups by marrying out, moved about by men like pieces on a chessboard. But there are many instances in which the women stay put while the men change groups by marrying out. In either case, the result is the same. Marriage forges alliances.

These alliances freed early human societies from exclusive reliance on their own limited materials and products. No society is self-sustaining or self-perpetuating; no culture is a world unto itself. Each society is compelled to trade with others and this was as true for tribal societies as it is for modern industrial nations. North America, for instance, was crisscrossed with elaborate trade networks before the Europeans arrived. Similar trade networks covered aboriginal New Guinea and Australia. In these trade networks, coastal or riverine groups gave shells and fish to hinterland people in exchange for cultivated foods, wood, and manufactured items.

American Indian standards of living were quite high before the Europeans destroyed the native trade networks, and the same seems to have been true in almost all other parts of the world. It will come as no surprise to economists that the material quality of people's lives improves to the extent that they engage in external trade.

But barter and exchange do not automatically take place when people meet. Exchange involves trust, and devices are needed to establish trust, to distinguish friend from foe, and to assure a smooth, predictable flow of trade goods. Marriage in the tribal world established permanent obligations and reciprocal rights and privileges among families living in different habitats.

For instance, when a young Cheyenne Indian man decided on a

girl to marry, he told his family of his choice. If they agreed that his selection was good, they gathered a store of prized possessions — clothing, blankets, guns, bows and arrows — and carefully loaded them on a fine horse. A friend of the family, usually a respected old woman, led the horse to the tepee of the girl's elder brother. There the go-between spread the gifts for everyone to see while she pressed the suitor's case. The next step was for the girl's brother to assemble all his cousins for a conference to weigh the proposal. If they agreed to it, the cousins distributed the gifts among themselves, the brother taking the horse. Then the men returned to their tepees to find suitable gifts to give in return. Within a day or two, each returned with something roughly equal in value to what he had recieved. While this was happening, the bride was made beautiful. When all arrangements were completed, she mounted one horse while the return gifts were loaded on another. The old woman led both horses to the groom's camp. After the bride was received, her accompanying gifts were distributed among the groom's relatives in accordance with what each had given. The exchanges between the two families did not end with the marriage ceremony, however; they continued as a permanent part of the marriage ties. This continual exchange, which took place periodically, is why the young man's bridal choice was so important for his entire family.

Marriage was not the only integral part of external trade relationships. Another was ritualized friendship, "blood brotherhood," for example. Such bonds were generally established between members of different groups and were invariably trade partnerships. Significantly, these ritualized friendships often included taboos against marriage with the friend's sisters; sometimes the taboo applied to all their close relatives. This extension of a taboo provides an important key for understanding all incest taboos. Sexual prohibitions do not necessarily grow out of biological ties. Both marriage and ritualized friendships in primitive societies promote economic alliances and both are associated with incest taboos.

Incest taboos force people into alliances with others in as many groups as possible. They promote the greatest flow of manufactured goods and raw materials from the widest variety of groups and ecological niches and force people to spread their social nets. Looked at another way, incest taboos prevent localism and economic provincialism; they block social and economic inbreeding.

Incest taboos have their widest extensions outside the nuclear family in those societies in which technology is least well developed and in which people have to carry their own trade goods for barter or exchange with members of other groups. Often in these small societies, everyone in a community is sexually taboo to the rest of the group. When the technology surrounding trade improves and shipments of goods and materials can be concentrated (as when people learn to build and navigate ocean-going canoes or harness pack animals), fewer and fewer people have to be involved in trade. As this happens, incest taboos begin to contract, affecting fewer and fewer people outside the nuclear family.

This process has been going on for centuries. Today, in most industrial societies, the only incest taboos are those that pertain to members of the nuclear family. This contraction of the range of the taboo is inseparable from the fact that we no longer engage in personal alliances and trade agreements to get the food we eat, the clothes we wear, the tools and materials we use, the fuels on which we depend. Goods are brought to distribution points near our homes by a relatively tiny handful of truckers, shippers, merchants, entrepreneurs, and others. Most of us are only vaguely aware of the alliances, negotiations, and relationships that make this massive movement of goods possible. When we compare tribal and contemporary industrialized societies, the correspondence between the range of incest taboos and the material conditions of life cannot be dismissed as mere coincidence.

Industrialization does not operate alone in affecting the degree to which incest taboos extend beyond the nuclear family. In the history of societies, political institutions developed as technology advanced. Improvements in packaging and transportation have led not only to reductions in the number of people involved in external trade, but also to greater and greater concentrations of decision making in the hands of fewer and fewer people. Trade is no longer the responsibility of all members of a society, and the maintenance of relationships between societies has become the responsibility of a few people — a king and his bureaucracy, impersonal governmental agencies, national and multinational corporations.

To the extent that trade is conducted and negotiated by a handful of people, it becomes unnecessary to use incest taboos to force the majority of people into alliances with other groups. Treaties, political alliances, and negotiations by the managers of a few impersonal agencies have replaced marital and other personal alliances. The history of human societies suggests that incest taboos may have outlived their original purpose.

But incest taboos still serve other purposes. For social and emotional reasons rather than economic ones, people in modern industrial societies still need to prevent localism. Psychological well-being in a diversified society depends largely on the ability to tap different ideas, points of view, life styles, and social relationships. The jugulars that must now be kept open by the majority of people may no longer be for goods and resources, but for variety and stimulation. This need for variety is what, in part, seems to underlie the preference of Israelis to marry outside the communities in which they were born and brought up. The taboo against sex within the nuclear family leads young people to explore, to seek new experiences. In a survey of a thousand cases of incest, Christopher Bagley found that incestuous families are cut off from their society's social and cultural mainstream. Whether rural or urban, he writes, "the family seems to withdraw from the general community, and initiates its own 'deviant' norms of sexual behavior, which are contained within the family circle." "Such a family," he continues, "is an isolated cultural unit, relatively untouched by external social norms." This social and cultural inbreeding is the cause of the profound malaise represented by incest.

To illustrate the correspondence between incest and social isolation, let me describe an incestuous family reported by Peter Wilson, an anthropologist. Wilson sketched a sequence of events in which a South American family became almost totally isolated from the community in which it lived, and began to practice almost every variety of incest. The decline into incest began many years before Wilson appeared on the scene to do anthropological research, when the father of five daughters and four sons made the girls (who ranged in age from 18 to 33) sexually available to some sailors for a small sum of money. As a result, the entire household was ostracized by the rest of the village. "But most important," Wilson writes, "the Brown family was immediately cut off from sexual partners. No woman would have anything to do with a Brown man; no man would touch a Brown woman."

The Brown's isolation and incest continued for several years, until the women in the family rebelled — apparently because a new road connecting their hamlet to others provided the opportunity for social contact with people outside the hamlet. At the same time the Brown men began working in new light industry in the area and spending their money in local stores. The family slowly regained some social acceptance in Green Fields, the larger village to which their hamlet belonged. Little by little they were reintegrated into the hamlet and there seems to have been no recurrence of incest among them.

A second example is an upper-middle class, Jewish, urban American family that was described to me by a colleague. The Erva family (a pseudonym) consists of six people — the parents, two daughters aged 19 and 22, and two sons, aged 14 and 20. Mr. Erva is a computer analyst and his wife a dentist. Twenty-five years ago, the Ervas seemed relatively normal, but shortly after their first child was born, Mr. and Mrs. Erva took to wandering naked about their apartment, even when others were present. They also began dropping in on friends for as long as a week; their notion of reciprocity was to refuse to accept food, to eat very little of what was offered them, or to order one member of their family not to accept any food at all during a meal. Their rationale seemed to be that accepting food was receiving a favor, but occupying a bed was not. This pattern was accompanied by intense family bickering and inadvertent insults to their hosts. Not surprisingly, most of their friends wearied of their visits and the family was left almost friendless.

Reflecting Bagley's general description of incestuous families, the Ervas had withdrawn from the norms of the general community after the birth of their first child and had instituted their own "deviant" patterns of behavior. They thereby set the stage for incest.

Mr. Erva began to have intercourse with his daughters when they were 14 and 16 years old. Neither of them was self-conscious about the relationship and it was common for the father to take both girls into bed with him at the same time when they were visiting overnight. Mrs. Erva apparently did not have intercourse with her sons. The incest became a matter of gossip and added to the family's isolation.

The Erva family then moved to the Southwest to start over again. They built a home on a parcel of land that had no access to water. Claiming they could not afford a well of their own, the family began to use the bathrooms and washing facilities of their neighbors. In the end these neighbors, too, wanted nothing to do with them.

Mr. and Mrs. Erva eventually separated, he taking the daughters and she the sons. Later the younger daughter left her father to live alone, but the older daughter still shares a one bedroom apartment with her father.

Social isolation and incest appear to be related, and social maturity and a taboo on incest are also related. Within the modern nuclear family, social and emotional relationships are intense, and sexuality is the source of some of the strongest emotions in human life. When combined with the intensity of family life, sexually stimulated emotions can be overwhelming for children. Incest taboos are a way of limiting family relationships. They are assurances of a degree of emotional insularity, of detachment on which emotional maturity depends.

On balance, then, we can say that legal penalties for incest were first instituted because of the adverse economic effects of incestuous unions on society, but that today the negative consequences of incest affect only individuals. Some will say that criminal penalties should be retained if only to protect children. But legal restraints alone are un-likely to serve as deterrents. Father-daughter incest is regarded by many social workers, judges, and psychiatrists as a form of child abuse, but criminal penalties have not deterred other forms of child abuse. Moreover, incest between brothers and sisters cannot be con-sidered child abuse. Some have even suggested that the concept of abuse may be inappropriate when applied to incest. "Many psycho-therapists," claims psychologist James McCary in *Human Sexuality*, "be-lieve that a child is less affected by actual incest than by seductive behavior on the part of a parent that never culminates in any manifest sexual activity."

Human history suggests that the incest taboo may indeed be ob-solete. As in connection with changing attitudes toward homosexual-ity, it may be maintained that incestuous relations between consenting mature adults are their concern alone and no one else's. At the same time, however, children must be protected. But questions still remain about how they should be protected and until what age.

If a debate over the repeal of criminal laws against incest is to begin in earnest, as it surely will if the Swedish Parliament acts on the proposed reversal, one other important fact about the social history of sexual behavior must be remembered. Until about a century ago, many societies punished adultery and violations of celibacy with death. When it came time to repeal those laws, not a few people favored their retention on the grounds that extramarital sexual relationships would adversely affect the entire society. Someday people may regard incest in the same way they now regard adultery and violations of celibacy. Where the threat of punishment once seemed necessary, social and emotional dissuasion may now suffice.

REVIEW QUESTIONS

1. What is the incest taboo, and why does Cohen believe it might disappear?

2. What explanations of the incest taboo have been suggested by an-thropologists? What are the criticisms of each?

3. What is Cohen's explanation for the taboo, and what supporting evidence does he cite?

4. What is the function of the incest taboo in industrial societies? What is the evidence for this?

5. What social forces (not legal ones) work to prevent incest from occurring in industrial society families?

11

Sororities and the husband game

JOHN FINLEY SCOTT

The concept of function refers to what something does. Social function indicates the effect something has on social organization, particularly its part in the maintenance of society. In this article, John Finley Scott looks at one of the social functions of sororities as these groups existed until the middle 1960s. Arguing that college was a place where young men and women were likely to meet and marry, Scott claims that sororities limited a woman's contact to men of proper social class. This explains why sororities flourished in land-grant universities, which accept men from all social classes, not just the "right" ones, and why sororities, unlike fraternities which have less to do with marriage, are controlled more by older alumnae. He concludes that the marriage game may succumb to the growing competition among males for career training because there is so little time for the lawn parties and leisurely dating required of the system. If he were to write this article in the 1980s, he would have to make that argument for women as well.

Marriages, like births, deaths, or initiations at puberty, are rearrangements of structure that are constantly recurring in any society; they are moments of the continuing social process regulated by custom; there are institutionalized ways of dealing with such events. — A. R. Radcliffe-Brown, *African Systems of Kinship and Marriage*

In many simple societies, the institutionalized ways of controlling marriage run to diverse schemes and devices. Often they include special living quarters designed to make it easy for marriageable women to attract a husband: the Bontok people of the Philippines keep young

Published slightly edited by permission of Transaction, Inc. from *Transaction*, Vol. 2, No. 6, copyright © 1965 by Transaction, Inc.

women in a special house, called the *olag*, where lovers call, sex play is free, and marriage is supposed to result. The Ekoi of Nigeria, who like their women fat, send them away to be specially fattened for marriage. Other peoples, such as the Yao of central Africa and the aborigines of the Canary Islands, send their daughters away to "convents" where old women teach them the special skills and mysteries that a young wife needs to know.

Accounts of such practices have long been a standard topic of anthropology lectures in universities, for their exotic appeal keeps the students, large numbers of whom are sorority members, interested and alert. The control of marriage in simple societies strikes these women as quite different from the freedom that they believe prevails in America. This is ironic, for the American college sorority is a pretty good counterpart in complex societies of the fatting houses and convents of the primitives.

Whatever system they use, parents in all societies have more in mind than just getting their daughters married; they want them married to the *right* man. The criteria for defining the right man vary tremendously, but virtually all parents view some potential mates with approval, some with disapproval, and some with downright horror. Many ethnic groups, including many in America, are *endogamous*, that is, they desire marriage of their young only to those within the group. In *shtetl* society, the Jewish villages of Eastern Europe, marriages were arranged by a *shatchen*, a matchmaker, who paired off the girls and boys with due regard to the status, family connections, wealth, and personal attractions of the participants. But this society was strictly endogamous — only marriage within the group was allowed. Another rule of endogamy relates to social rank or class, for most parents are anxious that their children marry at least at the same level as themselves. Often they hope the children, and especially the daughters, will marry at a higher level. Parents of the *shtetl*, for example, valued *hypergamy* — the marriage of daughters to a man of higher status — and a father who could afford it would offer substantial sums to acquire a scholarly husband (the most highly prized kind) for his daughter.

The marriage problem, from the point of view of parents and of various ethnic groups and social classes, is always one of making sure that women are available for marriage with the right man while at the same time guarding against marriage with the wrong man.

THE UNIVERSITY CONVENT

The American middle class has a particular place where it sends its daughters so they will be easily accessible to the boys — the college campus. Even for the families who worry about the bad habits a nice girl can pick up at college, it has become so much a symbol of middle-class status that the risk must be taken, the girl must be sent. American middle-class society has created an institution on the campus that, like the fatting house, makes the girls more attractive; like the Canary Island convent, teaches skills that middle-class wives need to know; like the *shtetl*, provides matchmakers; and without going so far as to buy husbands of high rank, manages to dissuade the girl from making alliances with lower-class boys. That institution is the college sorority.

A sorority is a private association which provides separate dormitory facilities with a distinctive Greek letter name for selected female college students. Membership is by invitation only, and requires recommendation by former members. Sororities are not simply the feminine counterpart of the college fraternity. They differ from fraternities because marriage is a more important determinant of social position for women than for men in American society, and because standards of conduct associated with marriage correspondingly bear stronger sanctions for women than for men. Sororities have much more "alumnae" involvement than fraternities, and fraternities adapt to local conditions and different living arrangements better than sororities. The college-age sorority "actives" decide only the minor details involved in recruitment, membership, and activities; parent-age alumnae control the important choices. The prototypical sorority is not the servant of youthful interests; on the contrary, it is an organized agency for controlling those interests. Through the sorority, the elders of family, class, ethnic, and religious communities can continue to exert remote control over the marital arrangements of their young girls.

The need for remote control arises from the nature of the educational system in an industrial society. In simple societies, where children are taught the culture at home, the family controls the socialization of children almost completely. In more complex societies, education becomes the province of special agents and competes with the family. The conflict between the family and outside agencies increases as children move through the educational system and is sharpest when the children reach college age. College curricula are even more challenging to family value systems than high school courses, and children frequently go away to college, out of reach of direct family influence. Sometimes a family can find a college that does not challenge family values in any way: devout Catholic parents can send their daughters to Catholic colleges; parents who want to be sure that daughter meets only "Ivy League" men can send her to one of the

"Seven Sisters" — the women's equivalent of the Ivy League, made up of Radcliffe, Barnard, Smith, Vassar, Wellesley, Mt. Holyoke, and Bryn Mawr — if she can get in.

The solution of controlled admissions is applicable only to a small proportion of college-age women, however. There are nowhere near the number of separate, sectarian colleges in the country that would be needed to segregate all the college-age women safely, each with her own kind. Private colleges catering mostly to a specific class can still preserve a woman from meeting her social or economic inferiors, but the fees at such places are steep. It costs more to maintain a daughter in the Vassar dormitories than to pay her sorority bills at a land-grant school. And even if her family is willing to pay the fees, the academic pace at the elite schools is much too fast for many women. Most college girls attend large, tax-supported universities where the tuition is relatively low and where admissions policies let in students from many strata and diverse ethnic backgrounds. It is on the campuses of the free, open, and competitive state universities of the country that the sorority system flourishes.

When a family lets its daughter loose on a large campus with a heterogenous population, there are opportunities to be met and dangers to guard against. The great opportunity is to meet a good man to marry, at the age when daughters are most attractive and the men most amenable. For the daughters, the pressure of time is urgent; though they are often told otherwise, their attractions are in fact primarily physical, and they fade with time. One need only compare the relative handicaps in the marital sweepstakes of a thirty-eight-year-old single male lawyer and a single, female teacher of the same age to realize the urgency of the quest.

The great danger of the public campus is that young girls, however properly reared, are likely to fall in love, and — in our middle-class society at least — love leads to marriage. Love is a potentially random factor, with no regard for class boundaries. There seems to be no good way of preventing young girls from falling in love. The only practical way to control love is to control the type of boys the girl is likely to encounter; she cannot fall dangerously in love with a boy she has never met. Since kinship groups are unable to keep "undesirable" boys off the public campus entirely, they have to settle for control of counter-institutions within the university. An effective counter-institution will protect a girl from the corroding influences of the university environment.

There are roughly three basic functions which a sorority can perform in the interest of kinship groups:

It can ward off the wrong kind of men.

It can facilitate moving-up for middle-status women.

It can solve the "Brahmin problem" — the difficulty of proper marriage that afflicts high-status women.

Kinship groups define the "wrong kind of man" in a variety of ways. Those who use an ethnic definition support sororities that draw an ethnic membership line; the best examples are the Jewish sororities, because among all the ethnic groups with endogamous standards (in America at any rate), only the Jews so far have sent large numbers of daughters away to college. But endogamy along class lines is even more pervasive. It is the most basic mission of the sorority to prevent a woman from marrying out of her group (exogamy) or beneath her class (hypogamy). As one of the founders of a national sorority artlessly put it in an essay titled "The Mission of the Sorority":

> There is a danger, and a very grave danger, that four years' residence in a dormitory will tend to destroy right ideals of home life and substitute in their stead a belief in the freedom that comes from community living . . . culture, broad, liberalizing, humanizing culture, we cannot get too much of, unless while acquiring it we are weaned from home and friends, from ties of blood and kindred.

A sorority discourages this dangerous weaning process by introducing the sisters only to selected boys; each sorority, for example, has dating relations with one or more fraternities, matched rather nicely to the sorority on the basis of ethnicity and/or class. (A particular sorority, for example, will have dating arrangements not with all the fraternities on campus, but only with those whose brothers are a class-match for their sisters.) The sorority's frantically busy schedule of parties, teas, meetings, skits, and exchanges keeps the sisters so occupied that they have neither time nor opportunity to meet men outside the channels the sorority provides.

Marrying up

The second sorority function, that of facilitating hypergamy, is probably even more of an attraction to parents than the simpler preservation of endogamy. American society is not so much oriented to the preservation of the *status quo* as to the pursuit of upward mobility.

In industrial societies, children are taught that if they study hard they can get the kind of job that entitles them to a place in the higher ranks. This incentive actually is appropriate only for boys, but the emphasis on using the most efficient available means to enter the higher levels will not be lost on the girls. And the most efficient means for a girl — marriage — is particularly attractive because it requires so much less effort than the mobility through hard work that is open to boys. To the extent that we do socialize the sexes in different ways, we are more likely to train daughters in the ways of attracting men than to motivate them to do hard, competitive work. The difference in motivation holds even if the girls have the intelligence and talent required for status climbing on their own. For lower-class girls on the make, membership in a sorority can greatly improve the chances of meeting (and subsequently marrying) higher-status boys.

Now we come to the third function of the sorority — solving the Brahmin problem. The fact that hypergamy is encouraged in our society creates difficulties for girls whose parents are already in the upper strata. In a hypergamous system, high status *men* have a strong advantage; they can offer their status to a prospective bride as part of the marriage bargain, and the advantages of high status are often sufficient to offset many personal drawbacks. But a *woman's* high status has very little exchange value because she does not confer it on her husband.

This difficulty of high status women in a hypergamous society we may call the Brahmin problem. Girls of Brahmin caste in India and Southern white women of good family have the problem in common. In order to avoid the horrors of hypogamy, high status women must compete for high status men against women from all classes. Furthermore, high status women are handicapped in their battle by a certain type of vanity engendered by their class. They expect their wooers to court them in the style to which their fathers have accustomed them; this usually involves more formal dating, gift-giving, escorting, taxiing, etc., than many college swains can afford. If upper-stratum men are allowed to find out that the favors of lower-class women are available for a much smaller investment of time, money, and emotion, they may well refuse to court upper-status women.

In theory, there are all kinds of ways for upper-stratum families to deal with surplus daughters. They can strangle them at birth (female infanticide); they can marry several to each available male (polygyny); they can offer money to any suitable male willing to take one off their hands (dowries, groom-service fees). All these solutions have in fact been used in one society or another, but for various reasons none is acceptable in our society. Spinsterhood still works, but marriage is so popular and so well rewarded that everybody hopes to avoid staying single.

The industrial solution to the Brahmin problem is to corner the market, or more specifically to shunt the eligible bachelors into a special marriage market where the upper stratum women are in complete control of the bride-supply. The best place to set up this protected marriage-market is where many suitable men can be found at the age when they are most willing to marry — in short, the college campus. The kind of male collegians who can be shunted more readily into the specialized marriage-market that sororities run, are those who are somewhat uncertain of their own status and who aspire to move into higher strata. These boys are anxious to bolster a shaky self-image by dating obviously high-class sorority girls. The fraternities are full of them.

How does a sorority go about fulfilling its three functions? The first item of business is making sure that the girls join. This is not as simple as it seems, because the values that sororities maintain are more important to the older generation than to the college-age women. Although the sorority image is one of membership denied to the "wrong kind" of girls, it is also true that sororities have quite a problem recruiting the "right kind." Some are pressured into pledging by their parents. Many are recruited straight out of high school, before they know much about what really goes on at college. High school recruiters present sorority life to potential rushees as one of unending gaiety; life outside the sorority is painted as bleak and dateless.

A membership composed of the "right kind" of women is produced by the requirement that each pledge must have the recommendation of, in most cases, two or more alumnae of the sorority. Membership is often passed on from mother to daughter — this is the "legacy," whom sorority actives have to invite whether they like her or not. The sort of headstrong, innovative, or "sassy" female who is likely to organize a campaign inside the sorority against prevailing standards is unlikely to receive alumnae recommendations. This is why sorority women are so complacent about alumnae dominance, and why professors find them so bland and uninteresting as students. Alumnae dominance extends beyond recruitment, into the daily life of the house. Rules, regulations, and policy explanations come to the house from the national association. National headquarters is given to explaining unpopular policy by an available strategem; a favorite device (not limited to the sorority) is to interpret all nonconformity as sexual, so that the woman who rebels against wearing girdle, high heels, and stockings to dinner two or three times a week stands implicitly accused of promiscuity. This sort of argument, based on the shrewdness of many generations, shames into conformity many a woman who otherwise might rebel against the code imposed by her elders. The actives in positions of control (house manager, pledge trainer, or captain) are themselves closely supervised by alumnae. Once the right women are initiated, the organization has mechanisms that make it very difficult for a member to withdraw. Withdrawal can mean difficulty in finding alternative living quarters, loss of prepaid room and board fees, and stigmatization.

Sororities keep their members, and particularly their flighty pledges, in line primarily by filling up all their time with house activities. Pledges are required to study at the house, and they build the big papier-mâché floats (in collaboration with selected fraternity boys) that are a traditional display of "Greek Row" for the homecoming game. Time is encompassed completely; activities are planned long in advance, and there is almost no energy or time available for meeting inappropriate men.

The pledges are taught—if they do not already know—the behavior appropriate to the upper strata. They learn how to dress with expensive restraint, how to make appropriate conversation, how to drink like a lady. There is some variety here among sororities of different rank; members of sororities at the bottom of the social ladder prove their gentility by rigid conformity in dress and manner to the stereotype of the sorority girl, while members of top houses feel socially secure even when casually dressed. If you are born rich you can afford to wear Levi's and sweatshirts.

PRELIMINARY EVENTS

The sorority facilitates dating mainly by exchanging parties, picnics, and other frolics with the fraternities in its set. But to augment this the "fixer-uppers" (the American counterpart of the *shatchen*) arrange dates with selected boys; their efforts raise the sorority dating rate above the independent level by removing most of the inconvenience and anxiety from the contracting of dates.

Dating, in itself, is not sufficient to accomplish the sorority's purposes. Dating must lead to pinning, pinning to engagement, engagement to marriage. In sorority culture, all dating is viewed as a movement toward marriage. Casual, spontaneous dating is frowned upon; formal courtship is still encouraged. Sorority ritual reinforces the progression from dating to marriage. At the vital point in the process, where dating must be turned into engagement, the sorority shores up the structure by the pinning ritual, performed after dinner in the presence of all the sorority sisters (who are required to stay for the ceremony) and attended, in its classic form, by a choir of fraternity boys singing outside. The commitment is so public that it is difficult for either partner to withdraw. Since engagement is already heavily reinforced outside the sorority, pinning ceremonies are more elaborate than engagements.

The social columns of college newspapers faithfully record the successes of the sorority system as it stands today. Sorority members get engaged faster than "independents," and they appear to be marrying more highly ranked men. But what predictions can we make about the system's future?

All social institutions change from time to time, in response to changing conditions. In the mountain villages of the Philippines, the steady attacks of school and mission on the immorality of the *olag* have almost demolished it. Sororities, too, are affected by changes in the surrounding environment. Originally they were places where the few female college students took refuge from the jeers and catcalls of men who thought that nice girls didn't belong on campus. They assumed their present, endogamy-conserving form with the flourishing of the great land-grant universities in the first half of this century.

On the brink

The question about the future of the sorority system is whether it can adapt to the most recent changes in the forms of higher education. At present, neither fraternities nor sororities are in the pink of health. On some campuses there are chapter houses which have been reduced to taking in nonaffiliated boarders to pay the costs of running the property. New sorority chapters are formed, for the most part, on new or low-prestige campuses (where status-anxiety is rife); at schools of high prestige fewer women rush each year and the weaker houses are disbanding.

University administrations are no longer as hospitable to the Greeks as they once were. Most are building extensive dormitories that compete effectively with the housing offered by sororities; many have adopted regulations intended to minimize the influence of the Greeks on campus activities. The campus environment is changing rapidly: academic standards are rising, admission is increasingly competitive and both male and female students are more interested in academic achievement; the proportion of graduate students seriously training for a profession is increasing; campus culture is often so obviously pluralist that the Greek claim to monopolize social activity is unconvincing.

The sorority as it currently stands is ill-adapted to cope with the new surroundings. Sorority houses were built to provide a setting for lawn parties, dances, and dress-up occasions, and not to facilitate study; crowding and noise are severe, and most forms of privacy do not exist. The sorority songs that have to be gone through at rushing and chapter meetings today all seem to have been written in 1915 and are mortifying to sing today. The arcane rituals, so fascinating to high school girls, grow tedious and sophomoric to college seniors.

But the worst blow of all to the sorority system comes from the effect of increased academic pressure on the dating habits of college men. A student competing for grades in a professional school, or even in a difficult undergraduate major, simply has not the time (as he might have had in, say, 1925) to get involved in the sorority forms of courtship. Since these days almost all the "right kind" of men *are* involved in demanding training, the traditions of the sorority are becoming actually inimical to hypergamous marriage. Increasingly, then, sororities do not solve the Brahmin problem but make it worse.

One can imagine a sorority designed to facilitate marriage to men who have no time for elaborate courtship. In such a sorority, the girls — to start with small matters — would improve their telephone arrangements, for the fraternity boy in quest of a date today must call several times to get through the busy signals, interminable paging, and lost messages to the girl he wants. They might arrange a private line with prompt answering and faithfully recorded messages, with an unlisted number given only to busy male students with a promising future. They would even accept dates for the same night as the invitation, rather than, as at present, necessarily five to ten days in advance, for the only thing a first-year law student can schedule that far ahead nowadays is his studies. Emphasis on fraternity boys would have to go, for living in a fraternity and pursuing a promising (and therefore competitive) major field of study are rapidly becoming mutually exclusive. The big formal dances would go (the fraternity boys dislike them now); the football floats would go; the pushcart races would go. The women would reach the hearts of their men not through helping them wash their sports cars but through typing their term papers.

But it is inconceivable that the proud traditions of the sororities that compose the National Panhellenic Council could ever be bent to fit the new design. Their structure is too fixed to fit the changing college and their function is rapidly being lost. The sorority cannot sustain itself on students alone. When parents learn that membership does not benefit their daughters, the sorority as we know it will pass into history.

REVIEW QUESTIONS

1. According to Scott, in what ways did sororities function to regulate marriage?

2. What three special class-related marriage problems did sororities function to solve? How did they do this?

3. Scott claims that fraternities and sororities were not organized in the same way. What were the differences, and have these differences continued to the present?

4. From your own experience, are there other institutions that function to regulate marriage, especially as marriage affects social class, in American society?

5. Is marriage as likely to result from college liaisons today as it was when Scott wrote this article? If not, what are the current functions of sororities?

12

Uterine families and the women's community

MARGERY WOLF

Is the meaning of the family the same for men and women? Margery Wolf answers "no" in this article based on fieldwork in a rural Taiwanese village. For men living in the community, the patrilineal family extends in an unbroken line of ancestors and descendants. Membership is permanent; loyalty assured. For women, the patrilineal family is temporary. Born into one family and married into another, women discover that their happiness and interests depend on their membership in an informal uterine family that grows up inside the household. Family relationships can only be understood if we take the women's as well as the men's views into account.

Few women in China experience the continuity that is typical of the lives of the menfolk. A woman can and, if she is ever to have any economic security, must provide the links in the male chain of descent, but she will never appear in anyone's genealogy as that all-important name connecting the past to the future. If she dies before she is married, her tablet will not appear on her father's altar; although she was a temporary member of his household, she was not a member of his family. A man is born into his family and remains a member of it throughout his life and even after his death. He is identified with the family from birth, and every action concerning him, up to and including his death, is in the context of that group. Whatever other uncertainties may trouble his life, his place in the line of ancestors provides a permanent setting. There is no such secure setting for a woman. She will abruptly leave the household into which she is born, either as an infant or as an adult bride, and enter another whose members treat her with suspicion or even hostility.

A man defines his family as a large group that includes the dead, and not-yet-born, and the living members of his household. But how does a woman define her family? This is not a question that China specialists often consider, but from their treatment of the family in general, it would seem that a woman's family is identical with that of the senior male in the household in which she lives. Although I have never asked, I imagine a Taiwanese man would define a woman's family in very much those same terms. Women, I think, would give quite a different answer. They do not have an unchanging place, assigned at birth, in any group, and their view of the family reflects this.

When she is a child, a woman's family is defined for her by her mother and to some extent by her grandmother. No matter how fond of his daughter the father may be, she is only a temporary member of his household and useless to his family — he cannot even marry her to one of his sons as he could an adopted daughter. Her irrelevance to her father's family in turn affects the daughter's attitude toward it. It is of no particular interest to her, and the need to maintain its continuity has little meaning for her beyond the fact that this continuity matters a great deal to some of the people she loves. As a child she probably accepts to some degree her grandmother's orientation toward the family: the household, i.e., those people who live together and eat together, including perhaps one or more of her father's married brothers and their children. But the group that has the most meaning for her and with which she will have the most lasting ties is the smaller, more cohesive unit centering on her mother, i.e., the uterine family — her mother and her mother's children. Father is important to the group, just as grandmother is important to some of the children, but he is not quite a member of it, and for some uterine families he may even be "the enemy." As the girl grows up and her grandmother dies and a brother or two marries, she discovers that her mother's definition of the family is becoming less exclusive and may even include such outsiders as her brother's new wife. Without knowing precisely when it happened, she finds that her brother's interests and goals have shifted in a direction she cannot follow. Her mother does not push her aside, but when the mother speaks of the future, she speaks in terms of her son's future. Although the mother sees her uterine family as adding new members and another generation, her daughter sees it as dissolving, leaving her with strong particular relationships, but with no group to which she has permanent loyalties and obligations.

When a young woman marries, her formal ties with the household of her father are severed. In one of the rituals of the wedding ceremony the bride's father or brothers symbolically inform her by means of spilt water that she, like the water, may never return, and when her wedding sedan chair passes over the threshold of her father's house, the doors are slammed shut behind her. If she is ill-treated by her husband's family, her father's family may intervene, but unless her parents are willing to bring her home and support her for the rest of her life (and most parents are not), there is little they can do beyond shaming the other family. This is usually enough.

As long as her mother is alive, the daughter will continue her contacts with her father's household by as many visits as her new situation allows. If she lives nearby she may visit every few days, and no matter where she lives she must at least be allowed to return at New Year. After her mother dies her visits may become perfunctory, but her relations with at least one member of her uterine family, the group that centered on her mother, remain strong. Her brother plays an important ritual role throughout her life. She may gradually lose contact with her sisters as she and they become more involved with their own children, but her relations with her brother continue. When her sons marry, he is the guest of honor at the wedding feasts, and when her daughters marry he must give a small banquet in their honor. If her sons wish to divide their father's estate, it is their mother's brother who is called on to supervise. And when she dies, the coffin cannot be closed until her brother determines to his own satisfaction that she died a natural death and that her husband's family did everything possible to prevent it.

With the ritual slam of her father's door on her wedding day, a young woman finds herself quite literally without a family. She enters the household of her husband — a man who in an earlier time, say fifty years ago, she would never have met and who even today, in modern rural Taiwan, she is unlikely to know very well. She is an outsider, and for Chinese an outsider is always an object of deep suspicion. Her husband and her father-in-law do not see her as a member of their family. But they do see her as essential to it; they have gone to great expense to bring her into their household for the purpose of bearing a new generation for their family. Her mother-in-law, who was mainly responsible for negotiating the terms of her entry, may harbor some resentment over the hard bargaining, but she is nonetheless eager to see another generation added to *her* uterine family. A mother-in-law often has the same kind of ambivalence toward her daughter-in-law as she has toward her husband — the younger woman seems a member of her family at times and merely a member of the household at others. The new bride may find that her husband's sister is hostile or at best condescending, both attitudes reflecting the daughter's distress at an outsider who seems to be making her way right into the heart of the family.

Chinese children are taught by proverb, by example, and by experience that the family is the source of their security, and relatives the only people who can be depended on. Ostracism from the family is one of the harshest sanctions that can be imposed on erring youth. One of the reasons mainlanders as individuals are considered so untrustworthy on Taiwan is the fact that they are not subject to the controls of (and therefore have no fear of ostracism from) their families. If a timid new bride is considered an object of suspicion and potentially dangerous because she is a stranger, think how uneasy her own first few months must be surrounded by strangers. Her irrelevance to her father's family may result in her having little reverence for descent lines, but she has warm memories of the security of the family her mother created. If she is ever to return to this certainty and sense of belonging, a woman must create her own uterine family by bearing children, a goal that happily corresponds to the goals of the family into which she has married. She may gradually create a tolerable niche for herself in the household of her mother-in-law, but her family will not be formed until she herself forms it of her own children and grandchildren. In most cases, by the time she adds grandchildren, the uterine family and the household will almost completely overlap, and there will be another daughter-in-law struggling with loneliness and beginning a new uterine family.

The ambiguity of a man's position in relation to the uterine families accounts for much of the hostility between mother-in-law and daughter-in-law. There is no question in the mind of the older woman but that her son *is* her family. The daughter-in-law might be content with this situation once her sons are old enough to represent her interests in the household and in areas strictly under men's control, but until then, she is dependent on her husband. If she were to be completely absorbed into her mother-in-law's family — a rare occurrence unless she is a *simpua* — there would be little or no conflict; but under most circumstances she must rely on her husband, her mother-in-law's son, as her spokesman, and here is where the trouble begins. Since it is usually events within the household that she wishes to affect, and the household more or less overlaps with her mother-in-law's uterine family, even a minor foray by the younger woman suggests to the older one an all-out attack on everything she has worked so hard to build in the years of her own loneliness and insecurity. The birth of grandchildren further complicates their relations, for the one sees them as new members for her family and the other as desperately needed recruits to her own small circle of security.

In summary, my thesis contends . . . that because we have heretofore focused on men when examining the Chinese family — a reasonable approach to a patrilineal system — we have missed not only some of the system's subtleties but also its near-fatal weaknesses. With a male focus we see the Chinese family as a line of descent, bulging to encompass all the members of a man's household and spreading out through his descendants. With a female focus, however, we see the Chinese family not as a continuous line stretching between the vague horizons of past and future, but as a contemporary group that comes into existence out of one woman's need and is held together insofar as she has the strength to do so, or, for that matter, the need to do so. After her death the uterine family survives only in the mind of her son and is symbolized by the special attention he gives her earthly remains and her ancestral tablet. The rites themselves are demanded by the ideology of the patriliny, but the meaning they hold for most sons is formed in the uterine family. The uterine family has no ideology, no formal structure, and no public existence. It is built out of sentiments and loyalties that die with its members, but it is no less real for all that. The descent lines of men are born and nourished in the uterine families of women, and it is here that a male ideology that excludes women makes its accommodations with reality.

Women in rural Taiwan do not live their lives in the walled courtyards of their husbands' households. If they did, they might be as powerless as their stereotype. It is in their relations in the outside world (and for women in rural Taiwan that world consists almost entirely of the village) that women develop sufficient backing to maintain some independence under their powerful mothers-in-law and even occasionally to bring the men's world to terms. A successful venture into the men's world is no small feat when one recalls that the men of a village were born there and are often related to one another, whereas the women are unlikely to have either the ties of childhood or the ties of kinship to unite them. All the same, the needs, shared interests, and common problems of women are reflected in every village in a loosely knit society that can when needed be called on to exercise considerable influence.

Women carry on as many of their activities as possible outside the house. They wash clothes on the riverbank, clean and pare vegetables at a communal pump, mend under a tree that is a known meetingplace, and stop to rest on a bench or group of stones with other women. There is a continual moving back and forth between kitchens, and conversations are carried on from open doorways through the long, hot afternoons of summer. The shy young girl who enters the village as a bride is examined as frankly and suspiciously by the women as an animal that is up for sale. If she is deferential to her elders, does not criticize or compare her new world unfavorably with the one she has left, the older residents will gradually accept her presence on the edge of their conversations and stop changing the topic to general subjects when she brings the family laundry to scrub on the rocks near them. As the young bride meets other girls in her position, she makes allies for the future, but she must also develop relationships with the older women. She learns to use considerable discretion in making and receiving confidences, for a girl who gossips freely about the affairs of her husband's household may find herself labeled a troublemaker. On the other hand, a girl who is too reticent may find herself always on the outside of the group, or worse yet, accused of snobbery. I described in *The House of Lim* the plight of Lim Chui-ieng, who had little village backing in her troubles with her husband and his family as the result of her arrogance toward the women's community. In Peihotien the young wife of the storekeeper's son suffered a similar lack of support. Warned by her husband's parents not to be too "easy" with the other villagers lest they try to buy things on credit, she obeyed to the point of being considered unfriendly by the women of the village. When she began to have serious troubles with her husband and eventually his family, there was no one in the village she could turn to for solace, advice, and most important, peacemaking.

Once a young bride has established herself as a member of the women's community, she has also established for herself a certain amount of protection. If the members of her husband's family step beyond the limits of propriety in their treatment of her — such as refusing to allow her to return to her natal home for her brother's wedding or beating her without serious justification — she can complain to a woman friend, preferably older, while they are washing vegetables at the communal pump. The story will quickly spread to the other women, and one of them will take it on herself to check the facts with another member of the girl's household. For a few days the matter will be thoroughly discussed whenever a few women gather. In a young wife's first few years in the community, she can expect to have her mother-in-law's side of any disagreement given fuller weight than her own — her mother-in-law has, after all, been a part of the community a lot longer. However, the discussion itself will serve to curb many offenses. Even if the older woman knows that public opinion is falling to her side, she will still be somewhat more judicious about refusing her daughter-in-law's next request. Still, the daughter-in-law who hopes to make use of the village forum to depose her mother-in-law or at least gain herself special privilege will discover just how important the prerogatives of age and length of residence are. Although the women can serve as a powerful protective force for their defenseless younger members, they are also a very conservative force in the village.

Taiwanese women can and do make use of their collective power to lose face for their menfolk in order to influence decisions that are ostensibly not theirs to make. Although young women may have little or no influence over their husbands and would not dare express an unsolicited opinion (and perhaps not even a solicited one) to their fathers-in-law, older women who have raised their sons properly retain considerable influence over their sons' actions, even in activities exclusive to men. Further, older women who have displayed years of good judgment are regularly consulted by their husbands about major as well as minor economic and social projects. But even men who think themselves free to ignore the opinions of their women are never free of their own concept, face. It is much easier to lose face than to have face. We once asked a male friend in Peihotien just what "having face" amounted to. He replied, "When no one is talking about a family, you can say it has face." This is precisely where women wield their power. When a man behaves in a way that they consider wrong, they talk about him — not only among themselves, but to their sons and husbands. No one "tells him how to mind his own business," but it becomes abundantly clear that he is losing face and by continuing in this manner may bring shame to the family of his ancestors and descendants. Few men will risk that.

The rules that a Taiwanese man must learn and obey to be a successful member of his society are well developed, clear, and relatively easy to stay within. A Taiwanese woman must also learn the rules, but if she is to be a successful woman, she must learn not to stay within them, but to *appear* to stay within them; to manipulate them, but not to appear to be manipulating them; to teach them to her children, but not to depend on her children for her protection. A truly successful Taiwanese woman is a rugged individualist who has learned to depend largely on herself while appearing to lean on her father, her husband, and her son. The contrast between the terrified young bride and the loud, confident, often lewd old woman who has outlived her mother-in-law and her husband reflects the tests met and passed by not strictly following the rules and by making purposeful use of those who must. The Chinese male's conception of women as "narrow-hearted" and socially inept may well be his vague recognition of this facet of women's power and technique.

The women's subculture in rural Taiwan is, I believe, below the level of consciousness. Mothers do not tell their about-to-be-married daughters how to establish themselves in village society so that they may have some protection from an oppressive family situation, nor do they warn them to gather their children into an exclusive circle under their own control. But girls grow up in village society and see their mothers and sisters-in-law settling their differences to keep them from a public airing or presenting them for the women's community to judge. Their mothers have created around them the meaningful unit in their fathers' households, and when they are desperately lonely and unhappy in the households of their husbands, what they long for is what they have lost. . . . [Some] areas in the subculture of women . . . mesh perfectly into the main culture of the society. The two cultures are not symbiotic because they are not sufficiently independent of one another, but neither do they share identical goals or necessarily use the same means to reach the goals they do share. Outside the village the women's subculture seems not to exist. The uterine family also has no public existence, and appears almost as a response to the traditional family organized in terms of a male ideology.

REVIEW QUESTIONS

1. According to Wolf, what is a uterine family and what relatives are likely to be members?

2. Why is the uterine family important to Chinese women who live in their husband's patrilineal extended families?

3. What is the relationship between a woman's uterine family and her power within her husband's family?

4. Why might the existence of the uterine family contribute to the division of extended families into smaller constituent parts?

5. How do you think a Chinese woman's desire to have a uterine family affects attempts to limit the Chinese population?

V

Sex roles

For most people, social interaction is unconscious and automatic. We associate with other people from the time we are born. Of course we experience moments when we feel socially awkward and out of place, but generally we learn to act toward others with confidence. Yet our unconscious ease masks an enormously complex process. When we enter a social situation, how do we know what to do? What should we say? How are we supposed to act? Are we dressed appropriately? Are we talking to the right person? Without knowing it, we have learned a complex set of cultural categories for social interaction that enable us to estimate the social situation, identify the people in it, act appropriately, and recognize larger groups of people.

Status and role are basic to social intercourse. *Status* refers to the categories of different kinds of people who interact. The old saying, "You can't tell the players without a program," goes for our daily associations as well. Instead of a program, however, we identify the actors by a range of signs from the way they dress to the claims they make about themselves. Most statuses are named, so we may be heard to say things like, "That's President Gavin," or "She's a lawyer," when

155

we explain social situations to others. This identification of actors is a prerequisite for appropriate social interaction.

Social roles are the rules for action associated with particular statuses. We use them to interpret and generate social behavior. For example, a professor plays a role in the classroom. Although often not conscious of this role, the professor will stand, use the blackboard, look at notes, and speak with a slightly more formal air than usual. The professor does not wear blue jeans and a T-shirt, chew gum, sit cross-legged on the podium, or sing. These actions might be appropriate for this person when assuming the identity of "friend" at a party, but they are out of place in the classroom.

People also always relate to each other in *social situations*, the settings in which social interaction takes place. Social situations consist of a combination of times, places, objects, and events. For example, if we see a stranger carrying a television set across campus at four o'clock in the afternoon, we will probably ignore the activity. Most likely someone is simply moving. But if we see the same person carrying the set at four in the morning, we may suspect a theft. Only the time has changed, but it is a significant marker of the social situation. Similarly, we expect classrooms to be associated with lectures, and stethoscopes to be part of medical exams. Such places and objects mark the social situations of which they are part.

Anthropologists regularly describe statuses, roles, and social situations in the course of their fieldwork. Kinship roles, as we saw in the last section, are especially important in the organization of many societies. So are roles associated with economic, political, legal, and religious systems, as we shall see later. In this section we focus on one important aspect of roles, the degree to which sex determines their assignment and content. How are female and male roles different? What accounts for relative variations in equality and inequality between the sexes from one society to the next? Under what circumstances is male dominance most likely to occur? How does this relate to the incidence of rape?

KEY TERMS

status
role
social situation

13

Society and sex roles

ERNESTINE FRIEDL

*Many anthropologists claim that males hold formal authority over fe-
males in every society. Although the degree of masculine authority
may vary from one group to the next, males always have more
power. For some researchers, this unequal male-female relationship is
the result of biological inheritance. As with other primates, they
argue, male humans are naturally more aggressive, females more doc-
ile. Ernestine Friedl challenges this explanation in this selection.
Comparing a variety of hunting and gathering groups, she concludes
that relations between men and women are shaped by a culturally
defined division of labor based on sex, not by inherited predisposition.
Given access to resources that circulate publicly, women can attain
equal or dominant status in any society, including our own.*

"Women must respond quickly to the demands of their husbands,"
says anthropologist Napoleon Chagnon describing the horticultural
Yanomamö Indians of Venezuela. When a man returns from a hunting
trip, "the woman, no matter what she is doing, hurries home and
quietly but rapidly prepares a meal for her husband. Should the wife
be slow in doing this, the husband is within his rights to beat her.
Most reprimands . . . take the form of blows with the hand or with a
piece of firewood. . . . Some of them chop their wives with the sharp
edge of a machete or axe, or shoot them with a barbed arrow in some
nonvital area, such as the buttocks or leg."

Among the Semai agriculturalists of central Malaya, when one
person refuses the request of another, the offended party suffers *pu-*

From *Human Nature,* April 1978. Copyright © 1978 by Human Nature, Inc. Reprinted by
permission of the publisher.

nan, a mixture of emotional pain and frustration. "Enduring *punan* is commonest when a girl has refused the victim her sexual favors," reports Robert Dentan. "The jilted man's 'heart becomes sad.' He loses his energy and his appetite. Much of the time he sleeps, dreaming of his lost love. In this state he is in fact very likely to injure himself 'accidentally.' " The Semai are afraid of violence; a man would never strike a woman.

The social relationship between men and women has emerged as one of the principal disputes occupying the attention of scholars and the public in recent years. Although the discord is sharpest in the United States, the controversy has spread throughout the world. Numerous national and international conferences, including one in Mexico sponsored by the United Nations, have drawn together delegates from all walks of life to discuss such questions as the social and political rights of each sex and even the basic nature of males and females.

Whatever their position, partisans often invoke examples from other cultures to support their ideas about the proper role of each sex. Because women are clearly subservient to men in many societies, like the Yanomamö, some experts conclude that the natural pattern is for men to dominate. But among the Semai no one has the right to command others, and in West Africa women are often chiefs. The place of women in these societies supports the argument of those who believe that sex roles are not fixed, that if there is a natural order, it allows for many different arrangements.

The argument will never be settled as long as the opposing sides toss examples from the world's cultures at each other like intellectual stones. But the effect of biological differences on male and female behavior can be clarified by looking at known examples of the earliest forms of human society and examining the relationship between technology, social organization, environment, and sex roles. The problem is to determine the conditions in which different degrees of male dominance are found, to try to discover the social and cultural arrangements that give rise to equality or inequality between the sexes, and to attempt to apply this knowledge to our understanding of the changes taking place in modern industrial society.

As Western history and the anthropological record have told us, equality between the sexes is rare; in most known societies females are subordinate. Male dominance is so widespread that it is virtually a human universal; societies in which women are consistently dominant do not exist and have never existed.

Evidence of a society in which women control all strategic resources like food and water, and in which women's activities are the most prestigious has never been found. The Iroquois of North America and the Lovedu of Africa came closest. Among the Iroquois, women raised food, controlled its distribution, and helped to choose male political leaders. Lovedu women ruled as queens, exchanged valuable cattle, led ceremonies, and controlled their own sex lives. But among both the Iroquois and Lovedu, men owned the land and held other positions of power and prestige. Women were equal to men; they did not have ultimate authority over them. Neither culture was a true matriarchy.

Patriarchies are prevalent, and they appear to be strongest in societies in which men control significant goods that are exchanged with people outside the family. Regardless of who produces food, the person who gives it to others creates the obligations and alliances that are at the center of all political relations. The greater the male monopoly on the distribution of scarce items, the stronger their control of women seems to be. This is most obvious in relatively simple hunter-gatherer societies.

Hunter-gatherers, or foragers, subsist on wild plants, small land animals, and small river or sea creatures gathered by hand; large land animals and sea mammals hunted with spears, bows and arrows, and blow guns; and fish caught with hooks and nets. The 300,000 hunter-gatherers alive in the world today include the Eskimos, the Australian aborigines, and the Pygmies of Central Africa.

Foraging has endured for two million years and was replaced by farming and animal husbandry only 10,000 years ago; it covers more than 99 percent of human history. Our foraging ancestry is not far behind us and provides a clue to our understanding of the human condition.

Hunter-gatherers are people whose ways of life are technologically simple and socially and politically egalitarian. They live in small groups of 50 to 200 and have neither kings, nor priests, nor social classes. These conditions permit anthropologists to observe the essential bases for inequalities between the sexes without the distortions induced by the complexities of contemporary industrial society.

The source of male power among hunter-gatherers lies in their control of a scarce, hard to acquire, but necessary nutrient — animal protein. When men in a hunter-gatherer society return to camp with game, they divide the meat in some customary way. Among the !Kung San of Africa, certain parts of the animal are given to the owner of the arrow that killed the beast, to the first hunter to sight the game, to the one who threw the first spear, and to all men in the hunting party. After the meat has been divided, each hunter distributes his share to his blood relatives and his in-laws, who in turn share it with others. If an animal is large enough, every member of the band will receive some meat.

Vegetable foods, in contrast, are not distributed beyond the immediate household. Women give food to their children, to their husbands, to other members of the household, and rarely, to the occasional visitor. No one outside the family regularly eats any of the wild fruits and vegetables that are gathered by the women.

The meat distributed by the men is a public gift. Its source is widely known, and the donor expects a reciprocal gift when other men return from a successful hunt. He gains honor as a supplier of a scarce item and simultaneously obligates others to him.

These obligations constitute a form of power or control over others, both men and women. The opinions of hunters play an important part in decisions to move the village; good hunters attract the most desirable women; people in other groups join camps with good hunters; and hunters, because they already participate in an internal system of exchange, control exchange with other groups for flint, salt, and steel axes. The male monopoly on hunting unites men in a system of exchange and gives them power; gathering vegetable food does not give women equal power even among foragers who live in the tropics, where the food collected by women provides more than half the hunter-gatherer diet.

If dominance arises from a monopoly on big-game hunting, why has the male monopoly remained unchallenged? Some women are strong enough to participate in the hunt and their endurance is certainly equal to that of men. Dobe San women of the Kalahari Desert in Africa walk an average of 10 miles a day carrying from 15 to 33 pounds of food plus a baby.

Women do not hunt, I believe, because of four interrelated factors: variability in the supply of game; the different skills required for hunting and gathering; the incompatibility between carrying burdens and hunting; and the small size of seminomadic foraging populations.

Because the meat supply is unstable, foragers must make frequent expeditions to provide the band with gathered food. Environmental factors such as seasonal and annual variation in rainfall often affect the size of the wildlife population. Hunters cannot always find game, and when they do encounter animals, they are not always successful in killing their prey. In northern latitudes, where meat is the primary food, periods of starvation are known in every generation. The irregularity of the game supply leads hunter-gatherers in areas where plant foods are available to depend on these predictable foods a good part of the time. Someone must gather the fruits, nuts, and roots and carry them back to camp to feed unsuccessful hunters, children, the elderly, and anyone who might not have gone foraging that day.

Foraging falls to the women because hunting and gathering cannot be combined on the same expedition. Although gatherers sometimes notice signs of game as they work, the skills required to track game are not the same as those required to find edible roots or plants. Hunters scan the horizon and the land for traces of large game; gatherers keep their eyes to the ground, studying the distribution of plants and the texture of the soil for hidden roots and animal holes. Even if a woman who was collecting plants came across the track of an antelope, she could not follow it; it is impossible to carry a load and hunt at the same time. Running with a heavy load is difficult, and should the animal be sighted, the hunter would be off balance and could neither shoot an arrow nor throw a spear accurately.

Pregnancy and child care would also present difficulties for a hunter. An unborn child affects a woman's body balance, as does a child in her arms, on her back, or slung at her side. Until they are two years old, many hunter-gatherer children are carried at all times, and until they are four, they are carried some of the time.

An observer might wonder why young women do not hunt until they become pregnant, or why mature women and men do not hunt and gather on alternate days, with some women staying in camp to act as wet nurses for the young. Apart from the effects hunting might have on a mother's milk production, there are two reasons. First, young girls begin to bear children as soon as they are physically mature and strong enough to hunt, and second, hunter-gatherer bands are so small that there are unlikely to be enough lactating women to serve as wet nurses. No hunter-gatherer group could afford to maintain a specialized female hunting force.

Because game is not always available, because hunting and gathering are specialized skills, because women carrying heavy loads cannot hunt, and because women in hunter-gatherer societies are usually either pregnant or caring for young children, for most of the last two million years of human history men have hunted and women have gathered.

If male dominance depends on controlling the supply of meat, then the degree of male dominance in a society should vary with the amount of meat available and the amount supplied by the men. Some regions, like the East African grasslands and the North American woodlands, abounded with species of large mammals; other zones, like tropical forests and semideserts, are thinly populated with prey. Many elements affect the supply of game, but theoretically, the less meat provided exclusively by the men, the more egalitarian the society.

All known hunter-gatherer societies fit into four basic types: those in which men and women work together in communal hunts and as teams gathering edible plants, as did the Washo Indians of North America; those in which men and women each collect their own plant foods although the men supply some meat to the group, as do the Hadza of Tanzania; those in which male hunters and female gatherers work apart but return to camp each evening to share their acquisitions, as do the Tiwi of North Australia; and those in which the men provide all the food by hunting large game, as do the Eskimo. In each case the extent of male dominance increases directly with the proportion of meat supplied by individual men and small hunting parties.

Among the most egalitarian of hunter-gatherer societies are the Washo Indians, who inhabited the valleys of the Sierra Nevada in what is now southern California and Nevada. In the spring they moved north to Lake Tahoe for the large fish runs of sucker and native trout. Everyone — men, women, and children — participated in the fishing. Women spent the summer gathering edible berries and seeds while the men continued to fish. In the fall some men hunted deer but the most important source of animal protein was the jackrabbit, which was captured in communal hunts. Men and women together drove the rabbits into nets tied end to end. To provide food for the winter, husbands and wives worked as teams in the late fall to collect pine nuts.

Since everyone participated in most food-gathering activities, there were no individual distributors of food and relatively little difference in male and female rights. Men and women were not segregated from each other in daily activities; both were free to take lovers after marriage; both had the right to separate whenever they chose; menstruating women were not isolated from the rest of the group; and one of the two major Washo rituals celebrated hunting while the other celebrated gathering. Men were accorded more prestige if they had killed a deer, and men directed decisions about the seasonal movement of the group. But if no male leader stepped forward, women were permitted to lead. The distinctive feature of groups such as the Washo is the relative equality of the sexes.

The sexes are also relatively equal among the Hadza of Tanzania but this near-equality arises because men and women tend to work alone to feed themselves. They exchange little food. The Hadza lead a leisurely life in the seemingly barren environment of the East African Rift Gorge that is, in fact, rich in edible berries, roots, and small game.

As a result of this abundance, from the time they are 10 years old, Hadza men and women gather much of their own food. Women take their young children with them into the bush, eating as they forage, and collect only enough food for a light family meal in the evening. The men eat berries and roots as they hunt for small game, and should they bring down a rabbit or a hyrax, they eat the meat on the spot. Meat is carried back to the camp and shared with the rest of the group only on those rare occasions when a poisoned arrow brings down a large animal—an impala, a zebra, an eland, or a giraffe.

Because Hadza men distribute little meat, their status is only slightly higher than that of the women. People flock to the camp of a good hunter and the camp might take on his name because of his popularity, but he is in no sense a leader of the group. A Hadza man and a woman have an equal right to divorce and each can repudiate a marriage simply by living apart for a few weeks. Couples tend to live in the same camp as the wife's mother but they sometimes make long visits to the camp of the husband's mother. Although a man may take more than one wife, most Hadza males cannot afford to indulge in this luxury. In order to maintain a marriage, a man must supply both his wife and his mother-in-law with some meat and trade goods, such as beads and cloth, and the Hadza economy gives few men the wealth to provide for more than one wife and mother-in-law. Washo equality is based on cooperation; Hadza equality is based on independence.

In contrast to both these groups, among the Tiwi of Melville and Bathurst Islands off the northern coast of Australia, male hunters dominate female gatherers. The Tiwi are representative of the most common form of foraging society, in which the men supply large quantities of meat, although less than half the food consumed by the group. Each morning Tiwi women, most with babies on their backs, scatter in different directions in search of vegetables, grubs, worms, and small game such as bandicoots, lizards, and opossums. To track the game, they use hunting dogs. On most days women return to camp with some meat and with baskets full of *korka*, the nut of a native palm, which is soaked and mashed to make a porridge-like dish. The Tiwi men do not hunt small game and do not hunt every day, but when they do they often return with kangaroo, large lizards, fish, and game birds.

The porridge is cooked separately by each household and rarely shared outside the family, but the meat is prepared by a volunteer cook, who can be male or female. After the cook takes one of the parts of the animal traditionally reserved for him or her, the animal's "boss," the one who caught it, distributes the rest to all near kin and then to all others residing with the band. Although the small game supplied by the women is distributed in the same way as the big game supplied by the men, Tiwi men are dominant because the game they kill provides most of the meat.

The power of Tiwi men is clearest in their betrothal practices. Among the Tiwi, a woman must always be married. To ensure this, female infants are betrothed at birth and widows are remarried at the gravesides of their late husbands. Men form alliances by exchanging daughters, sisters, and mothers in marriage and some collect as many as 25 wives. Tiwi men value the quantity and quality of the food many wives can collect and the many children they can produce.

The dominance of the men is offset somewhat by the influence of adult women in selecting their next husbands. Many women are active strategists in the political careers of their male relatives, but to the exasperation of some sons attempting to promote their own futures, widowed mothers sometimes insist on selecting their own partners. Women also influence the marriages of their daughters and granddaughters, especially when the selected husband dies before the bestowed child moves to his camp.

Among the Eskimo, representative of the rarest type of forager society, inequality between the sexes is matched by inequality in supplying the group with food. Inland Eskimo men hunt caribou throughout the year to provision the entire society, and maritime Eskimo men depend on whaling, fishing, and some hunting to feed their extended families. The women process the carcasses, cut and sew skins to make clothing, cook, and care for the young; but they collect no food of their own and depend on the men to supply all the raw materials for their work. Since men provide all the meat, they also control the trade in hides, whale oil, seal oil, and other items that move between the maritime and inland Eskimos.

Eskimo women are treated almost exclusively as objects to be used, abused, and traded by men. After puberty all Eskimo girls are fair game for any interested male. A man shows his intentions by grabbing the belt of a woman and if she protests, he cuts off her trousers and forces himself upon her. These encounters are considered unimportant by the rest of the group. Men offer their wives' sexual services to establish alliances with trading partners and members of hunting and whaling parties.

Despite the consistent pattern of some degree of male dominance among foragers, most of these societies are egalitarian compared with agricultural and industrial societies. No forager has any significant opportunity for political leadership. Foragers, as a rule, do not like to give or take orders, and assume leadership only with reluctance. Shamans (those who are thought to be possessed by spirits) may be either male or female. Public rituals conducted by women in order to celebrate the first menstruation of girls are common, and the symbolism in these rituals is similar to that in the ceremonies that follow a boy's first kill.

In any society, status goes to those who control the distribution of valued goods and services outside the family. Equality arises when both sexes work side by side in food production, as do the Washo, and the products are simply distributed among the workers. In such circumstances, no person or sex has greater access to valued items than do others. But when women make no contribution to the food supply, as in the case of the Eskimo, they are completely subordinate.

When we attempt to apply these generalizations to contemporary industrial society, we can predict that as long as women spend their discretionary income from jobs on domestic needs, they will gain little social recognition and power. To be an effective source of power, money must be exchanged in ways that require returns and create obligations. In other words, it must be invested.

Jobs that do not give women control over valued resources will do little to advance their general status. Only as managers, executives, and professionals are women in a position to trade goods and services, to do others favors, and therefore to obligate others to them. Only as controllers of valued resources can women achieve prestige, power, and equality.

Within the household, women who bring in income from jobs are able to function on a more nearly equal basis with their husbands. Women who contribute services to their husbands and children without pay, as do some middle-class Western housewives, are especially vulnerable to dominance. Like Eskimo women, as long as their services are limited to domestic distribution they have little power relative to their husbands and none with respect to the outside world.

As for the limits imposed on women by their procreative functions in hunter-gatherer societies, childbearing and child care are organized around work as much as work is organized around reproduction. Some foraging groups space their children three to four years apart and have an average of only four to six children, far fewer than many women in other cultures. Hunter-gatherers nurse their infants for extended periods, sometimes for as long as four years. This custom suppresses ovulation and limits the size of their families. Sometimes, although rarely, they practice infanticide. By limiting reproduction, a woman who is gathering food has only one child to carry.

Different societies can and do adjust the frequency of birth and the care of children to accommodate whatever productive activities women customarily engage in. In horticultural societies, where women work long hours in gardens that may be far from home, infants get food to supplement their mothers' milk, older children take care of younger children, and pregnancies are widely spaced. Throughout the world, if a society requires a woman's labor, it finds ways to care for her children.

In the United States, as in some other industrial societies, the accelerated entry of women with preschool children into the labor force has resulted in the development of a variety of child-care arrangements. Individual women have called on friends, relatives, and neighbors. Public and private child-care centers are growing. We should realize that the declining birth rate, the increasing acceptance of childless or single-child families, and de-emphasis on motherhood are adaptations to a sexual division of labor reminiscent of the system of production found in hunter-gatherer societies.

In many countries where women no longer devote most of their productive years to childbearing, they are beginning to demand a change in the social relationship of the sexes. As women gain access to positions that control the exchange of resources, male dominance may become archaic, and industrial societies may one day become as egalitarian as the Washo.

REVIEW QUESTIONS

1. According to Friedl, what factor accounts for the different degrees of dominance and power between males and females found in hunter-gatherer societies?

2. What are the four types of hunter-gatherer societies considered by Friedl in this article, and what is it about the structure of each that relates to the distribution of power and dominance between males and females?

3. Some anthropologists believe that male dominance is inherited. Comment on this assertion in light of Friedl's article.

4. Why does Friedl believe that women will gain equality with men in industrial society?

14

Male and female:
The doctor-nurse game

LEONARD I. STEIN

The characteristics of sex and occupational role are related in this article to inequality. Leonard Stein describes the game played between doctor and nurse in American hospitals, the object of which is for the nurse to transmit recommendations for the treatment of patients to the doctor without appearing to challenge his authority as a male and a physician. Using rules of behavior defined for this purpose in American culture, the nurse must be indirect and deferential as she advises on treatment, while the doctor must be positive and accepting. If either breaks the rules, interaction becomes strained, and effective working relations in the hospital break down.

The relationship between the doctor and the nurse is a very special one. There are few professions where the degree of mutual respect and cooperation between co-workers is as intense as that between the doctor and nurse. Superficially, the stereotype of this relationship has been dramatized in many novels and television serials. When, however, it is observed carefully in an interactional framework, the relationship takes on a new dimension and has a special quality which fits a game model. The underlying attitudes which demand that this game be played are unfortunate. These attitudes create serious obstacles in the path of meaningful communications between physicians and non-medical professional groups.

The physician traditionally and appropriately has total responsi-

From "The Doctor-Nurse Game," *Archives of General Psychiatry* 16 (June 1967): 699-703. Copyright 1967, American Medical Association. Reprinted by permission of the author and the publisher.

bility for making the decisions regarding the management of his patients' treatment. To guide his decisions he considers data gleaned from several sources. He acquires a complete medical history, performs a thorough physical examination, interprets laboratory findings, and at times, obtains recommendations from physician-consultants. Another important factor in his decision making is the recommendations he receives from the nurse. The interaction between doctor and nurse through which these recommendations are communicated and received is unique and interesting.

THE GAME

One rarely hears a nurse say, "Doctor, I would recommend that you order a retention enema for Mrs. Brown." A physician, upon hearing a recommendation of that nature, would gape in amazement at the effrontery of the nurse. The nurse, upon hearing the statement, would look over her shoulder to see who said it, hardly believing the words actually came from her own mouth. Nevertheless, if one observes closely, nurses make recommendations of more import every hour and physicians willingly and respectfully consider them. If the nurse is to make a suggestion without appearing insolent and the doctor is to seriously consider that suggestion, their interaction must not violate the rules of the game.

Object of the game. The object of the game is as follows: the nurse is to be bold, have initiative, and be responsible for making significant recommendations, while at the same time she must appear passive. This must be done in such a manner so as to make her recommendations appear to be initiated by the physician.

Both participants must be acutely sensitive to each other's nonverbal and cryptic verbal communications. A slight lowering of the head, a minor shifting of position in the chair, or a seemingly nonrelevant comment concerning an event which occurred eight months ago must be interpreted as a powerful message. The game requires the nimbleness of a high wire acrobat, and if either participant slips the game can be shattered; the penalties for frequent failure are apt to be severe.

Rules of the game. The cardinal rule of the game is that open disagreement between the players must be avoided at all costs. Thus, the nurse must communicate her recommendations without appearing to be making a recommendation statement. The physician, in requesting a recommendation from a nurse, must do so without appearing to be asking for it. Utilization of this technique keeps anyone from committing themselves to a position before a sub rosa agreement on that position has already been established. In that way open disagreement is avoided. The greater the significance of the recommendation, the more subtly the game must be played.

To convey a subtle example of the game with all its nuances would require the talents of a literary artist. Lacking these talents, let me give you the following example which is unsubtle, but happens frequently. The medical resident on hospital call is awakened by telephone at 1:00 A.M. because a patient on a ward, not his own, has not been able to fall asleep. Dr. Jones answers the telephone and the dialogue goes like this:

> This is Dr. Jones.
>
> (An open and direct communication.)
>
> Dr. Jones, this is Miss Smith on 2W—Mrs. Brown, who learned today of her father's death, is unable to fall asleep.
>
> (This message has two levels. Openly, it describes a set of circumstances, a woman who is unable to sleep and who that morning received word of her father's death. Less openly, but just as directly, it is a diagnostic and recommendation statement; i.e., Mrs. Brown is unable to sleep because of her grief, and she should be given a sedative. Dr. Jones, accepting the diagnostic statement and replying to the recommendation statement, answers.)
>
> What sleeping medication has been helpful to Mrs. Brown in the past?
>
> (Dr. Jones, not knowing the patient, is asking for a recommendation from the nurse, who does know the patient, about what sleeping medication should be prescribed. Note, however, his question does not appear to be asking her for a recommendation. Miss Smith replies.)
>
> Pentobarbital mg 100 was quite effective night before last.
>
> (A disguised recommendation statement. Dr. Jones replies with a note of authority in his voice.)
>
> Pentobarbital mg 100 before bedtime as needed for sleep; got it?
>
> (Miss Smith ends the conversation with the tone of a grateful supplicant.)
>
> Yes, I have, and thank you very much, doctor.

The above is an example of a successfully played doctor-nurse game. The nurse made appropriate recommendations which were accepted by the physician and were helpful to the patient. The game was successful because the cardinal rule was not violated. The nurse was able to make her recommendation without appearing to, and the physician was able to ask for recommendations without conspicuously asking for them.

The scoring system. Inherent in any game are penalties and rewards for the players. In game theory, the doctor-nurse game fits the nonzero sum game model. It is not like chess, where the players compete with each other and whatever one player loses the other wins. Rather, it is the kind of game in which the rewards and punishments are shared by both players. If they play the game successfully they both win rewards, and if they are unskilled and the game is played badly, they both suffer the penalty.

The most obvious reward from the well-played game is a doctor-nurse team that operates efficiently. The physician is able to utilize the nurse as a valuable consultant, and the nurse gains self-esteem and professional satisfaction from her job. The less obvious rewards are no less important. A successful game creates a doctor-nurse alliance; through this alliance the physician gains the respect and admiration of the nursing service. He can be confident that his nursing staff will smooth the path for getting his work done. His charts will be organized and waiting for him when he arrives, the ruffled feathers of patients and relatives will have been smoothed down, and his pet routines will be happily followed, and he will be helped in a thousand and one other ways.

The doctor-nurse alliance sheds its light on the nurse as well. She gains a reputation for being a "damn good nurse." She is respected by everyone and appropriately enjoys her position. When physicians discuss the nursing staff it would not be unusual for her name to be mentioned with respect and admiration. Their esteem for a good nurse is no less than their esteem for a good doctor.

The penalties for a game failure, on the other hand, can be severe. The physician who is an unskilled gamesman and fails to recognize the nurses' subtle recommendation messages is tolerated as a "clod." If, however, he interprets these messages as insolence and strongly indicates he does not wish to tolerate suggestions from nurses, he creates a rocky path for his travels. The old truism "If the nurse is your ally you've got it made, and if she has it in for you, be prepared for misery" takes on life-sized proportions. He receives three times as many phone calls after midnight as his colleagues. Nurses will not accept his telephone orders because "telephone orders are against the rules." Somehow, this rule gets suspended for the skilled players. Soon he becomes like Joe Bfstplk in the "Li'l Abner" comic strip. No matter where he goes, a black cloud constantly hovers over his head.

The unskilled gamesman nurse also pays heavily. The nurse who does not view her role as that of consultant, and therefore does not attempt to communicate recommendations, is perceived as a dullard and is mercifully allowed to fade into the woodwork.

The nurse who does see herself as a consultant but refuses to follow the rules of the game in making her recommendations has hell to pay. The outspoken nurse is labeled a "bitch" by the surgeon. The psychiatrist describes her as unconsciously suffering from penis envy and her behavior is the acting out of her hostility towards men. Loosely translated, the psychiatrist is saying she is a bitch. The employment of the unbright outspoken nurse is soon terminated. The outspoken bright nurse whose recommendations are worthwhile remains employed. She is, however, constantly reminded in a hundred ways that she is not loved.

Genesis of the game

To understand how the game evolved, we must comprehend the nature of the doctors' and nurses' training which shaped the attitudes necessary for the game.

Medical student training. The medical student in his freshman year studies as if possessed. In the anatomy class he learns every groove and prominence on the bones of the skeleton as if life depended on it. As a matter of fact, he literally believes just that. He not infrequently says, "I've got to learn it exactly; a life may depend on me knowing that." A consequence of this attitude, which is carefully nurtured throughout medical school, is the development of a phobia: the over-determined fear of making a mistake. The development of this fear is quite understandable. The burden the physician must carry is at times almost unbearable. He feels responsible in a very personal way for the lives of his patients. When a man dies leaving young children and a widow, the doctor carries some of her grief and despair inside himself; and when a child dies, some of him dies too. He sees himself as a warrior against death and disease. When he loses a battle, through no fault of his own, he nevertheless feels pangs of guilt, and he relentlessly searches himself to see if there might have been a way to alter the outcome. For the physician a mistake leading to a serious consequence is intolerable, and any mistake reminds him of his vulnerability. There is little wonder that he becomes phobic. The classical way in which phobias are managed is to avoid the source of the fear. Since it is impossible to avoid making some mistakes in an active practice of medicine, a substitute defensive maneuver is employed. The physician develops the belief that he is omnipotent and omniscient, and therefore incapable of making mistakes. This belief allows the phobic physician to actively engage in his practice rather than avoid it. The fear of committing an error in a critical field like medicine is unavoidable and appropriately realistic.

The physician, however, must learn to live with the fear rather than handle it defensively through a posture of omnipotence. This defense markedly interferes with his interpersonal professional relationships.

Physicians, of course, deny feelings of omnipotence. The evidence, however, renders their denials to whispers in the wind. The slightest mistake inflicts a large narcissistic wound. Depending on his underlying personality structure the physician may be obsessed for days about it, quickly rationalize it away, or deny it. The guilt produced is unusually exaggerated and the incident is handled defensively. The ways in which physicians enhance and support each other's defenses when an error is made could be the topic of another paper. The feeling of omnipotence becomes generalized to other areas of his life. A report of the Federal Aviation Agency (FAA), as quoted in *Time Magazine* (August 5, 1966), states that in 1964 and 1965 physicians had a fatal-accident rate four times as high as the average for all other private pilots. Major causes of the high death rate were risk-taking attitudes and judgments. Almost all of the accidents occurred on pleasure trips, and were therefore not necessary risks to get to a patient needing emergency care. The trouble, suggested an FAA official, is that too many doctors fly with "the feeling that they are omnipotent." Thus, the extremes to which the physician may go in preserving his self-concept of omnipotence may threaten his own life. This overdetermined preservation of omnipotence is indicative of its brittleness and its underlying foundation of fear of failure.

The physician finds himself trapped in a paradox. He fervently wants to give his patient the best possible medical care, and being open to the nurses' recommendations helps him accomplish this. On the other hand, accepting advice from nonphysicians is highly threatening to his omnipotence. The solution for the paradox is to receive sub rosa recommendations and make them appear to be initiated by himself. In short, he must learn to play the doctor-nurse game.

Some physicians never learn to play the game. Most learn in their internship, and a perceptive few learn during their clerkships in medical school. Medical students frequently complain that the nursing staff treats them as if they had just completed a junior Red Cross first-aid class instead of two years of intensive medical training. Interviewing nurses in a training hospital sheds considerable light on this phenomenon. In their words they said,

> A few students just seem to be with it, they are able to understand what you are trying to tell them, and they are a pleasure to work with; most,

however, pretend to know everything and refuse to listen to anything we
have to say and I guess we do give them a rough time.

In essence, they are saying that those students who quickly learn the
game are rewarded, and those that do not are punished.

Most physicians learn to play the game after they have weathered
a few experiences like the one described below. On the first day of his
internship, the physician and nurse were making rounds. They
stopped at the bed of a fifty-two-year-old woman who, after compli-
menting the young doctor on his appearance, complained to him of her
problem with constipation. After several minutes of listening to her
detailed description of peculiar diets, family home remedies, and special exercises that have helped her constipation in the past, the nurse
politely interrupted the patient. She told her the doctor would take
care of the problem and that he had to move on because there were
other patients waiting to see him. The young doctor gave the nurse a
stern look, turned toward the patient, and kindly told her he would
order an enema for her that very afternoon. As they left the bedside,
the nurse told him the patient has had a normal bowel movement
every day for the past week and that in the twenty-three days the
patient has been in the hospital she has never once passed up an
opportunity to complain of her constipation. She quickly added that *if*
the doctor wanted to order an enema, the patient would certainly
receive one. After hearing this report the intern's mouth fell open and
the wheels began turning in his head. He remembered the nurse's
comment to the patient that "the doctor had to move on," and it
occurred to him that perhaps she was really giving him a message.
This experience and a few more like it, and the young doctor learns to
listen for the subtle recommendations the nurses make.

Nursing student training. Unlike the medical student who usually
learns to play the game after he finishes medical school, the nursing
student begins to learn it early in her training. Throughout her education she is trained to play the doctor-nurse game.

Student nurses are taught how to relate to physicians. They are
told he has infinitely more knowledge than they, and thus he should
be shown the utmost respect. In addition, it was not many years ago
when nurses were instructed to stand whenever a physician entered a
room. When he would come in for a conference the nurse was expected to offer him her chair, and when both entered a room the nurse
would open the door for him and allow him to enter first. Although
these practices are no longer rigidly adhered to, the premise upon

which they were based is still promulgated. One nurse described that premise as, "He's God almighty and your job is to wait on him."

To inculcate subservience and inhibit deviancy, nursing schools, for the most part, are tightly run, disciplined institutions. Certainly there is great variation among nursing schools, and there is little question that the trend is toward giving students more autonomy. However, in too many schools this trend has not gone far enough, and the climate remains restrictive. The student's schedule is firmly controlled and there is very little free time. Classroom hours, study hours, mealtime, and bedtime with lights out are rigidly enforced. In some schools meaningless chores are assigned, such as cleaning bedsprings with cotton applicators. The relationship between student and instructor continues this military flavor. Often their relationship is more like that between recruit and drill sergeant than between student and teacher. Open dialogue is inhibited by attitudes of strict black and white, with few, if any, shades of gray. Straying from the rigidly outlined path is sure to result in disciplinary action.

The inevitable result of these practices is to instill in the student nurse a fear of independent action. This inhibition of independent action is most marked when relating to physicians. One of the students' greatest fears is making a blunder while assisting a physician and being publicly ridiculed by him. This is really more a reflection of the nature of their training than the prevalence of abusive physicians. The fear of being humiliated for a blunder while assisting in a procedure is generalized to the fear of humiliation for making any independent act in relating to a physician, especially the act of making a direct recommendation. Every nurse interviewed felt that making a suggestion to a physician was equivalent to insulting and belittling him. It was tantamount to questioning his medical knowledge and insinuating he did not know his business. In light of her image of the physician as an omniscient and punitive figure, the questioning of his knowledge would be unthinkable.

The student, however, is also given messages quite contrary to the ones described above. She is continually told that she is an invaluable aid to the physician in the treatment of the patient. She is told that she must help him in every way possible, and she is imbued with a strong sense of responsibility for the care of her patient. Thus she, like the physician, is caught in a paradox. The first set of messages implies that the physician is omniscient and that any recommendation she might make would be insulting to him and leave her open to ridicule. The second set of messages implies that she is an important asset to him, has much to contribute, and is duty-bound to make those contributions. Thus, when her good sense tells her a recommendation would be helpful to him she is not allowed to communicate it directly, nor is she allowed not to communicate it. The way out of the bind is to use the doctor-nurse game and communicate the recommendation without appearing to do so.

FORCES PRESERVING THE GAME

Upon observing the indirect interactional system which is the heart of the doctor-nurse game, one must ask the question, "Why does this inefficient mode of communication continue to exist?" The forces mitigating against change are powerful.

Rewards and punishments. The doctor-nurse game has a powerful innate self-perpetuating force — its system of rewards and punishments. One potent method of shaping behavior is to reward one set of behavior patterns and to punish patterns which deviate from it. As described earlier, the rewards given for a well-played game and the punishments meted out to unskilled players are impressive. This system alone would be sufficient to keep the game flourishing. The game, however, has additional forces.

The strength of the set. It is well recognized that sets are hard to break. A powerful attitudinal set is the nurse's perception that making a suggestion to a physician is equivalent to insulting and belittling him. An example of where attempts are regularly made to break this set is seen on psychiatric treatment wards operating on a therapeutic community model. This model requires open and direct communication between members of the team. Psychiatrists working in these settings expend a great deal of energy in urging for and rewarding openness before direct patterns of communication become established. The rigidity of the resistance to break this set is impressive. If the physician himself is a prisoner of a set and therefore does not actively try to destroy it, change is near impossible.

The need for leadership. Lack of leadership and structure in any organization produces anxiety in its members. As the importance of the organization's mission increases, the demand by its members for leadership commensurately increases. In our culture human life is near the top of our hierarchy of values, and organizations which deal with human lives, such as law and medicine, are very rigidly structured. Certainly some of this is necessary for the systematic management of the task. The excessive degree of rigidity, however, is demanded by its members for their own psychic comfort rather than for its utility in efficiently carrying out its mission. The game lends support to this thesis. Indirect communication is an inefficient mode of transmitting information. However, it effectively supports and protects a rigid organizational structure with the physician in clear authority. Maintaining an omnipotent leader provides the other members with a great sense of security.

Sexual roles. Another influence perpetuating the doctor-nurse game is the sexual identity of the players. Doctors are predominately men and nurses are almost exclusively women. There are elements of the game which reinforce the stereotyped roles of male dominance and female passivity. Some nursing instructors explicitly tell their students that their femininity is an important asset to be used when relating to physicians.

THE COMMUNITY

The doctor and nurse have a shared history and thus have been able to work out their game so that it operates more efficiently than one would expect in an indirect system. Major difficulty arises, however, when the physician works closely with other disciplines which are not normally considered part of the medical sphere. With expanding medical horizons encompassing cooperation with sociologists, engineers, anthropologists, computer analysts, etc., continued expectation of a doctor-nurselike interaction by the physician is disastrous. The sociologist, for example, is not willing to play that kind of game. When his direct communications are rebuffed the relationship breaks down.

The major disadvantage of a doctor-nurselike game is its inhibitory effect on open dialogue which is stifling and anti-intellectual. The game is basically a transactional neurosis, and both professions would enhance themselves by taking steps to change the attitudes which breed the game. . . .

REVIEW QUESTIONS

1. According to Stein, what is the object of the doctor-nurse game?

2. What are the special rules of the doctor-nurse game that facilitate effective communication?

3. What mistakes do some nurses make when they communicate with doctors? What mistakes do doctors make?

4. Can you think of other communications games that reflect gender roles in this country?

15

Men's clubs: No girls allowed

THOMAS GREGOR

Men set themselves apart from women in many societies. In Africa, the males of Mbuti Pygmy society reserve most of the sacred molimo ritual, held in honor of the forest, to themselves. Rural Greek men regularly drink together without the presence of women. In this article, Thomas Gregor explores the phenomenon of the men's club. He notes that the prestigious Bohemian Club, an all-men's organization of San Francisco, in many ways resembles the men's house among the tribal Mehinaku of South America. Men's clubs everywhere, he argues, tend to serve as a place for men to relax, joke about women, drop formal rules, guard sacred knowledge and rituals, and display the feminine side of their personalities without fear of outside reproach.

In October of 1980 the California Department of Housing and Fair Employment, an irresistible force in state sex discrimination cases, took aim at an immovable object: the exclusive "men only" Bohemian Club of San Francisco. The club, it was charged, employed 300 men at its Sonoma County Retreat but not one woman. The resulting litigation would have attracted little attention were it not for the prominence of the membership. President Ronald Reagan, Vice-President George Bush, Secretary of Defense Caspar Weinberger, and Attorney General William French Smith are only a few of the better known members.

In the course of the California discrimination proceedings, members of the club explained that having women about spoiled the fun.

Reprinted by permission from the December issue of *Science 82* Magazine. © 1982 by The American Association for the Advancement of Science.

"When women are around," pointed out former California Governor Edmund G. Brown, "any man is more genteel and careful of his words." He would be embarrassed to tell sexual jokes, he said, or to participate in the off-color theatrical revues staged by the members. Not that any of the members dislike women. Far from it. As columnist William Buckley quipped at the same hearing, "I have nothing against E flat, but if I were writing a symphony in D, I would try to do without it."

The Bohemians are an unusually swank and powerful bunch, but they are not the first to try to do without women. Exclusive men's clubs are found in many societies throughout the world among people of all cultural levels. While by no means universal, these clubs are often associated with strongly patriarchal societies.

My own anthropological introduction to a men's club occurred in 1967 among the Mehinaku Indians of central Brazil, a setting far less posh than the one provided by the San Francisco Bohemians. Shortly after I arrived in the Mehinaku village, one of the men took me by the arm and led me to a small house in the center of the community. Inside, the men worked on crafts and oiled and painted each others' bodies with a waxy, red pigment. The mood was loud and boisterous. A shouted remark set off a chorus of laughter, and then a whoop of appreciation from everyone present. Suddenly, one of the men stood up in front of the others and began to address me in a way that claimed everyone's attention. Not understanding a word or knowing how to respond, I glanced at the other men beside me. For the most part they were serious and attentive. After several minutes, the lecture was over. I turned to one of the men who had some knowledge of Portuguese. He explained: "You are in the house of the spirit Kowka. This house is only for men. Women may not see anything in here. If a woman comes in, then all the men take her into the woods and she is raped. It has always been that way."

I had been introduced to a key institution in Mehinaku life. A man's place, when he is not out fishing or working in his garden, is with his comrades in the men's house. A man who spends too much time in his house with his wife and family is called a trash-yard person, a star (because he only comes out to join his comrades at night), or a woman.

Within the men's house, there is an atmosphere of easy informality. "There is no shame in the men's house," say the villagers, meaning that the respect and deference owed in-laws and older kin is suspended in favor of masculine comradeliness. Above all, the men's house is a setting for jokes and laughter. As is true of our own fraternity and locker room comics, the Mehinaku pranksters specialize in sexual and scatological jokes.

Yuma has just entered the men's house. "Yuma," calls one of the men, "how is your 'forest' growing?" (Yuma, unlike most of the Mehinaku, has relatively abundant body hair.) "Any monkeys swinging about in the trees?" shouts another humorist from the opposite end of the house. Soon all the men are in on the joke, speculating on the nature of the dangerous game lurking in poor Yuma's "forest."

But the men's house is not all fun and games. It also serves as an information and labor exchange. A man who has found a good location for fishing generously informs his comrades in the men's house. Here, too, the men organize collective fishing expeditions, house-raisings, and harvests. Less formally, anyone in the men's retreat is fair game for a villager in search of an extra hand. Only an incorrigibly lazy or "tired" man would try to slip away on some pretended errand.

The men's house is a sacred place as well as a social club. It is "the place of spirits." From the rafters hang masks, bullroarers, musical instruments, and costumes crucial to the propitiation of the spirits that live within. The "Chief of the Spirits" is Kowka, the spirit of the sacred flutes. Kowka can take away a person's soul and thus make him seriously ill. To propitiate Kowka and restrain his anger, the men play the flutes several times a week. The main musician, "the master of the songs," carries the melody, while two others, "those who play on the side," accompany him. The songs have names: "Demon Woman," "Sadness," "Evening Song." The flutes have a deep, bassoonlike tone, and the melodies are hauntingly beautiful.

In the family houses, the women may listen to "Kowka's speech," but they never see his flutes or the men who impersonate him. One of the village elders explains: "Look, the men's house now has two sets of Kowka's flutes. The women will not come inside. They are afraid of Kowka. If a woman does come in, someone will say, 'Ah, that one saw Kowka!' Then at night she will be taken, and Kowka will have sex with her. . . . That is the way it has always been, since our grandfathers' day." In fact, no one has been raped since a woman accidentally saw the flutes as they were played on the plaza more than 35 years ago. But the women remember what occurred and know the men are prepared to do it again.

Gang rape is the most dramatic of a much larger set of sanctions and rules that separate men and women among the Mehinaku. These include a nearly ironclad division of labor preventing men and women from doing the same work. Fishing and hunting are men's specializations, while harvesting and processing manioc (the tapioca plant) is women's work. Crafts also fall on either side of the sexual divide, so that men make baskets and arrows and carve wooden benches, while women weave hammocks.

Although separation in work does not imply inequality, Mehinaku culture is uncompromisingly patriarchal. Fish is said to be the best food above all others, while the woman's manioc is "tasteless." Ritual is largely men's ritual, and politics is a man's game. The women, the men claim, are empty-headed and prone to gossip. They cannot recall the myths that make up the villagers' oral tradition, for the words "will not stay in their stomachs." A gossip (male or female) is called a woman mouth.

The men's opinion of femininity is partly shared by women themselves, who are in awe of the men. "I am frightened by the men," explains Kaiyalu, a young woman. "They are fearful. I would not speak on the plaza. I could not go fishing. The line would cut my hands. I am afraid of big animals. We women have no strength, we have no anger. The men are worthy of respect."

The Mehinaku pattern is very similar to other tribal societies scattered throughout South America, Oceania, and Africa. Like the Mehinaku, they have clubhouses that are forbidden to the women. Within are stored sacred instruments: flutes, trumpets, and bells that the women see at pain of gang rape or death. Typically, the atmosphere within the men's club is rowdy and informal, but once outside, the mood changes, and the women are ruled with a firm hand.

The list of similarities extends beyond the general structure of men's organizations to include some of their ritual details. These include the use of the bullroarer and a recurrent myth that ascribes the origin of the men's club to women. Among the Mehinaku the bullroarer is also sacred and a woman's hair will fall out, according to myth, if she should see one. The Mehinaku believe that long ago the women held power and controlled the sacred flutes. A male mutiny chased the women into hiding, and since that time men have ruled life and flutes.

So compelling are the parallels in many tribal men's organizations that they may well have common historical roots whose antiquity goes back to an epoch prior to settlement of the New World. A study of a small tribal group like the Mehinaku thereby reflects on the broader nature of masculine sexual politics and casts a new light on our own society with its fraternities and men's clubs.

Like the Mehinaku, America is a patriarchy. For many, this is an unpalatable conclusion, but a look at the economy and politics of our society shows that it is true. Women make 59 cents for every dollar earned by their male coworkers. A woman with a college degree brings home the salary of a man with a high school education. To a large extent, this economic inequality is explained by occupational segregation. One-fourth of all female workers are found in five relatively underpaid occupations: elementary school teacher, secretary, bookkeeper, waitress, and household worker. In contrast, men permeate and control all sectors of the economy.

In politics, the pattern is just as clear. The higher the political office, the less likely a woman is to fill it. Women are the mayors of only four percent of American cities, and despite affirmative action programs, women make up only two percent of the administrators identified as policy makers within the federal government. In the House of Representatives, they have historically held three percent of the seats and none of the chairmanships of important committees. There have never been more than two female senators in any recent Congress, nor have any of the major parties ever nominated a woman for the office of president or vice-president.

One of the barriers to women's participation in politics and economics is the "old boy network." Men socialize with one another, exchange information, conduct business deals, and recommend their protégés (seldom women) for advancement. American men's houses facilitate this process even though few of them are overtly concerned with money and power. "Weaving spiders, come not here" is the motto of the Bohemian Club. This line from Shakespeare's *A Midsummer Night's Dream* enjoins the members from serious discussions of politics and commerce. But a look at the roster of Bohemians turns up more than a few prodigious weavers. The membership list is a web of America's highly placed and well-connected power elite, according to sociologist G. William Domhoff. The chairmen of America's largest corporations, federal judges, and the founder of Common Cause have all rubbed shoulders in clubby good fellowship at the Bohemian. But do they do business? A congressman told columnist Jack Anderson, "If I were to run for the Senate, I can think of no place where I could spend time more productively."

In the less powerful men's clubs, be they volunteer fire departments or fraternities, observers find the same hidden agenda of exchange of information and influence. In the midst of the high jinks, as the curtains are drawn on the last stag movie, while the trenchermen tuck away the last morsels at the Annual Bull's Balls Lunch — the members are cementing business relationships and angling for position.

The parallels between tribal men's societies and our own clubs include a show of sexual aggression. The hostility toward women found in some tribal men's houses is less overt in American clubs, but it is visible in informal banter. According to a study by William Fry, all-male settings foster highly patterned jokes about women that characterize them as sexually insatiable "dumb blondes," greedy and unfeeling. Beyond this hostility, it is clear that although women are absent from both tribal and American men's clubs they are not forgotten. In many tribal societies, the men's house is strategically located in the center of the community so that the women form an audience (admittedly in distant seats) to the men's aggressive horseplay. In our society the clubs are farther from home, but women remain uppermost in the men's minds. Among the Bohemians, notes Domhoff, "the topic is out-ranked as a subject for light conversation only by remarks about drinking enormous quantities of alcohol and urinating on redwoods."

There is much that is suspect about the exaggeratedly masculine conduct in men's institutions: the hostile perceptions of women, the sexual bravado, and the need to have a secure retreat. The data from tribal societies are especially telling in this regard, since the men are openly fearful of women. Like the Mehinaku, they believe that sexual relations and other contact with women cause disease, stunt growth, weaken wrestlers, and profane sacred rituals. Moreover, despite the hostility and anxiety, some of the men's behavior hints that deep down the masculine personality is alloyed with a feminine identity. Intermixed with the boisterousness of the Mehinaku men's house are rituals in which the men address each other as "husband" and "wife" and scarify their bodies to shed what is regarded as menstrual blood. Rituals of this kind are not rare in societies with men's organizations and have been reported in South America, Melanesia, and elsewhere.

When considered alongside the pattern of aggression and anxiety, these rituals imply that the men are insecure in their masculine roles and frightened by the feminine component of their own personalities. In the arena of ritual, and with the support of their fellows, they can safely express the female side of their male selves. In everyday life, however, this femininity is shouted down by rowdy jokes and masculine camaraderie.

Can the same conclusion be drawn about American men's clubs? Testifying in favor of the Bohemian Club at the California sex discrimination hearings, former Governor Edmund Brown argued that the presence of women would irretrievably alter the character of this organization. Not only would the men feel inhibited from telling off-color jokes, but they would no longer be willing to cross-dress for the comic transvestite revues staged by the members.

Although it stretches the imagination to picture the well-heeled

Bohemians in high heels, comic and often hostile stage characterizations of women are typical of many American men's clubs. It is difficult to generalize about the inner motives of individual participants. Some are in the chorus line simply because it is politic to please a boss who may be directing the show. For others, however, the appeal is the same as it is for many of the Mehinaku. What the tribal men's clubs state in ritual, we Americans often express in comedy: the feminine component of a somewhat insecure masculine identity.

The similarity of men's organizations in several geographically and culturally distant patriarchal societies is evidence of a commonality to the male experience. Even though our college fraternities and volunteer fire departments may not be the lineal descendants of tribal institutions, we recreate within them the same masculine ethos. There is one language for the expression of masculinity, and it is voiced as clearly in American men's houses as it is in those of tribal peoples.

As for the future of our men's clubs, the political and psychological needs they fill make them compellingly attractive and resistant to change. Occasionally, however, even Bohemians must squirm a bit. In 1981 the California Department of Housing and Fair Employment chose to rule against the club despite a judge's recommendation that female staff would "alter the behavior of the members." The case was appealed, however, and the State Superior Court plans to review it. . . . Even if the Bohemians lose, the state will have chipped away only at the edges of female exclusion. The club may hire more women, but the membership will remain all male. The courts cannot yet touch the black-ball that is the heart of the institution: No Girls Allowed.

Review questions

1. According to Thomas Gregor, in what kinds of societies would men's clubs most likely be found?

2. What behaviors occur in the Mehinaku men's club? How does this behavior affect Mehinaku women?

3. In what ways is the Mehinaku men's club like the Bohemian Club of San Francisco? Are there any differences?

4. How do men's clubs meet male needs in patriarchal societies?

16

Rape-free or rape-prone

BERYL LIEFF BENDERLY

*Some Americans view the high incidence of rape as an inevitable fea-
ture of relations between the sexes. Others see it as proof of a weakening national moral fiber. In this study, Beryl Lieff Benderly reports
on a cross-cultural study of rape conducted by anthropologist Peggy
Sanday, which argues that rape is culturally conditioned. Sanday
discovered that rape is present in only about half of the 156 societies
she reviewed, and that in such societies, rape was culturally conditioned. Rape-prone societies, on the one hand, regularly teach aggressive behavior, competitiveness, and the notion that men must overcome women. Such societies seem to be less stable, to face uncertainties that thrust men into the forefront. Rape-free societies, on the
other hand, value feminine qualities and enjoy a stability that nulli-
fies the necessity for male physical prowess.*

The typical American rapist is not, as many people assume, sexually
deprived. Rather he is a hostile, aggressive man who likes to do violence to women. Not until the women's movement, when victims became more willing to report rapes, did social scientists discover that
rape is not so much a sexual act as a violent crime with profoundly
damaging effects. Furthermore, scientists say it is far more pervasive
than they had thought.

One highly significant observation, however, went along unno-
ticed: Rape is not an unavoidable fact of human nature. There are
cultures in the world where it is virtually unknown. American women
are several hundred times as likely to be raped as are women in certain

From *Science 82*, Vol. 3, No. 8, pp. 40-43. Copyright © 1982 by Beryl Lieff Benderly.
Reprinted by permission of the Virginia Barber Literary Agency.

other cultures. But there also are extremely violent societies where women are three times more likely to be attacked than they are in the United States.

New research suggests that the incidence of rape depends in particular on cultural factors: the status of women, the values that govern the relations between the sexes, and the attitudes taught to boys. Although the findings are tentative, they contradict the widely publicized feminist hypothesis that rape is inherent to the relations between men and women, an idea that received considerable attention in Susan Brownmiller's book, *Against Our Will*, published in 1975.

Now comes Peggy Reeves Sanday, a University of Pennsylvania anthropologist who has compared data from scores of cultures to find that rape is anything but universal. It does not stem from a biological drive, she believes, but is rather a conditioned response to the way certain kinds of societies are organized. Sexual violence is no more inherent to masculinity than football. Many American men may express their masculinity by making bone-jarring tackles or watching others do so, but that is because this culture encourages them to perform these strange rituals, not because their inherent nature demands linebacker blitzes or quarterback sneaks. Likewise, Sanday believes, "Human sexual behavior, though based on a biological need, is expressed in cultural terms." Human violence takes many forms, and rape is but one of them.

But what predisposes a culture toward or against rape? To find out, Sanday consulted a cross-cultural sample of 156 societies published in 1969 by George Peter Murdock and Douglas R. White. This sample, while accepted by many anthropologists as a standard basis for cross-cultural comparison, has its drawbacks as a research tool. The societies she referred to were studied at different times by different anthropologists interested in different aspects of each culture. Sensitive information, such as that on rape, might not have been disclosed to a visiting stranger who was not deliberately trying to find out about it. Nevertheless, Sanday found information on rape that she believes to be reliable for 95 of these societies.

Almost half of the reports (47 percent) Sanday studied were rape-free societies with sexual assault "absent or . . . rare." Less than a quarter (17 percent) proved to be "unambiguously rape-prone," displaying "the social use of rape to threaten or punish women or the presence of a high incidence of rape of their own or other women." Reports of rape exist for the remaining 36 percent, but the incidence is not known. Although some of these societies may actually have little rape, Sanday added them to the rape-prone to form the category "rape-present." Thus the split between sample societies that have rape and those that do not is close to even.

A model rape-free society, according to Sanday, is the Ashanti of West Africa. Their principal ethnographer, R. S. Rattray, mentions only a single incidence of rape, although he does not ignore other sexual offenses such as incest and adultery. Ashanti women are respected and influential members of the community. The Ashanti religion emphasizes women's contribution to the general well-being. The main female deity, the Earth Goddess, is believed to be the creator of past and future generations as well as the source of food and water. Women participate fully in religious life, taking as important a ritual role as men.

The Mbuti Pygmies, extensively described by anthropologist Colin Turnbull, present another aspect of rape-free social life. They hunt with nets in the jungle of central Africa and live harmoniously with the forest, which provides all their needs — food, clothing, shelter. The Mbuti believe that the forest takes offense at anger and discord. The people live in cooperative small bands, men and women sharing both work and decisions. No Mbuti attempts to dominate another, nor does the group as a whole seek to dominate nature. Indeed, they refer to the forest in terms of endearment, as they would a parent or lover. Here again women play important symbolic and political roles. The feminine qualities of nurturance and fertility rank among the culture's most valued traits.

Very different traits stand out in rape-prone societies such as the Gusii of Kenya. Anthropologist Robert LeVine reports that judicial authorities counted 47.2 rapes per 100,000 population in a year when the U.S. rate, one of the highest in the industrial world, was 13.85 per 100,000. "Normal heterosexual intercourse between Gusii males and females is conceived as an act in which a man overcomes the resistance of a woman and causes her pain," writes Sanday. It's customary for respectable old ladies to taunt the young bridegroom about his inadequate sexual equipment on the way to his wedding. He retaliates and asserts his manhood by bragging to his friends that he reduced his bride to tears on their wedding night, that she remained in pain the next morning. No wife respects a husband who fails to take her by force.

The degree of tension pervading the Gusii battle of the sexes may be unusual, but the use of rape to conquer unwilling brides or to keep women under tight control is not. Men of certain Plains Indian tribes once invited groups of friends to gang-rape unfaithful wives. Mundurucu men of the Amazon threaten to rape any woman approaching the sacred trumpets, which embody supernatural tribal power and are safeguarded in a special men's house.

As Sanday suspected, she found patterns of behavior common to rape-prone societies, and they differed markedly from traits of rape-free peoples. Societies with a high incidence of rape, she discovered, tolerate violence and encourage men and boys to be tough, aggressive, and competitive. Men in such cultures generally have special, politically important gathering spots off limits to women, whether they be in the Mundurucu men's club or the corner tavern. Women take little or no part in public decision making or religious rituals; men mock or scorn women's practical judgment. They also demean what they consider women's work and remain aloof from childbearing and rearing. These groups usually trace their beginnings to a male supreme being.

Men in such societies, Sanday says, often "perceive themselves as civilized animals." Indeed, the word *macho,* now slang for that attitude, is the Spanish for "male of an animal species," a significant qualification in a language that distinguishes, more carefully than English, the properties of beasts from those of humans.

In short, Sanday concludes, "Rape is not inherent in men's nature but results from their image of that nature." It is a product of a certain set of beliefs, which in turn derive from particular social circumstances. Male dominance, Sanday believes, serves its purpose. Rape-prone societies often have histories of unstable food supplies, warfare, or migration. Such rigors force men to the forefront to repel attackers and compete with others for scarce resources and land. A belief system that glorifies masculine violence, that teaches men to regard strength and physical force as the finest expression of their nature, reconciles them to the necessity of fighting and dying in society's interest. Unstable or threatened societies — gin-ridden, trigger-happy American frontiersmen, Southern planters outnumbered by their restive slaves, children of Israel approaching Canaan, the Azande conquerors of neighboring African tribes — depended for their survival on the physical prowess of their men. Danger brings soldiers and fighters to the front line and encourages the development of male-dominated social structures. And these often include concepts of men as bestial creatures and women as property. It is interesting that a number of rape-prone societies provide restitution to the rape victim's husband rather than to the victim herself.

On the other hand, stable cultures that face no danger from predatory enemies and that harmoniously occupy ancestral surroundings neither need nor condone such violence. Their food supplies usually fluctuate little from season to season or year to year, so they face neither the threat of starvation nor the need to compete with neighbors for resources. Women and men share power and authority because both contribute equally to society's welfare, and fighters are not necessary. Rape-free societies glorify the female traits of nurturance and fertility. Many such peoples believe that they are the offspring of a male and female deity or that they descended from a universal womb.

Although data on hundreds of societies have been available to anthropologists for generations, Sanday is one of the first to dig out broad patterns of behavior relating to rape. Just as the general society paid little attention to rape until Brownmiller's book made the front pages, rape has also been a "nonsubject" in anthropology. But not, anthropologists hope, for long.

The way society trains its boys and girls to think about themselves and each other determines to a large extent how rape-prone or rape-free that society will be. Sanday believes we can mitigate the damage our unconscious biases do by raising boys, for example, with more reverence for nurturance and less for violence. We can encourage women to resist assault. "One must be careful," Sanday says, "in blaming men alone or women alone for the high incidence of rape in our society. In a way we all conspire to perpetuate it. We expect men to attack, just as we expect women to submit."

But we can do something about such patterns of thought. Rape is not inevitable.

REVIEW QUESTIONS

1. According to this article, what is the distribution and incidence of rape in world societies?

2. Why is there a high incidence of rape in some societies and a low incidence or absence in others?

3. How does the anthropological view of rape described in this article compare with the feminist view of such writers as Susan Brownmiller?

4. Given the arguments presented in this article, what changes would have to occur in American culture to reduce the incidence of rape here?

VI

Cultural ecology

Ecology is the relationship of an organism to other elements within its environmental sphere. Every species, no matter how simple or complex, fits into a larger complex ecological system; each adapts to its ecological niche unless rapid environmental alterations outstrip the organism's ability and potential to adapt successfully. An important aim of ecological studies is to show how organisms fit within particular environments. Such studies also look at the effect environments have on the shape and behavior of life forms.

Every species has adapted biologically through genetically produced variation and natural selection. For example, the bipedal (two-footed) locomotion characteristic of humans is one possible adaptation to walking on the ground. It also permitted our ancestors to carry food, tools, weapons, and almost anything else they desired, enabling them to range out from a home base and bring things back for others to share. Some anthropologists believe that the social advantages of carrying and sharing may actually account for our bipedalism.

Biological processes have led to another important human characteristic, the development of a large and complex brain. The human

189

brain is capable of holding an enormous inventory of information. With it, we can classify the parts of our environment and retain instructions for complex ways to deal with the things in our world. Because we can communicate our knowledge symbolically through language, we are able to teach one another. Instead of a genetic code that directs behavior automatically, we operate with a learned cultural code. Culture gives us the ability to behave in a much wider variety of ways, and to change rapidly to new situations. With culture, people have been able to live successfully in almost every part of the world.

Cultural ecology is the way people use their culture to adapt to particular environments. All people live in a *physical environment*, the world they can experience through their senses, but they will conceive of it in terms that seem most important to their adaptive needs and cultural perspective. We call this perspective the *cultural environment*.

Anthropologists classify societies according to basic adaptive strategies. For example, *hunter/gatherers* are those who live in small, nomadic groups and depend for food on wild plants and animals. Richard B. Lee's article in this section describes such a group, the !Kung, who hunt and gather in the African Kalahari Desert. A second group is *horticulturalists*. Its members grow plant foods by gardening, often using digging sticks and other hand implements. *Slash-and-burn agriculture* is a kind of horticulture in which land is cleared and burned over before planting, then left to grow wild when new plots are cleared. *Pastoralists* survive by herding animals such as cattle, sheep, or goats. *Agriculturalists* farm intensively, often with plows and draft animals, irrigation, and sometimes terracing. Unlike horticulture, agriculture involves the farming of permanent fields.

Anthropologists often explain particular customs in terms of their adaptive functions. Michael Harner, for example, believes the high frequency of Aztec human sacrifice was linked to a shortage of dietary animal protein. Aztec wars, he claims, were fought to obtain victims for sacrifice. Once dispatched on the altar, the captives were thrown down the temple steps and butchered for food. Marvin Harris's article in this section takes a similar analytical approach. He accounts for the religious prohibition against eating cattle in India by arguing for their value as fuel producers and draft animals.

Finally, population is an important factor in a society's relationship to its environment. The abundance, location, and seasonal availability of wild foods limit the size and required living space of hunter-gatherers. Horticulture and agriculture, however, permit much larger and more concentrated populations, and this development, combined with the influx of new edible plants from other parts of the world, better control of disease, and more efficient food distribution systems, has caused populations in many parts of the world to skyrocket. Many nations have responded to the increase with birth control programs to limit family size, but as the Freeds show in their article in India, a need for sons to continue the family and provide for parents in their old age far outweighs or at least masks the national benefits of fewer children.

KEY TERMS

ecology	slash-and-burn agriculture
cultural ecology	physical environment
cultural environment	hunting and gathering
horticulture	pastoralism
agriculture	

17

The hunters: Scarce resources in the Kalahari

RICHARD BORSHAY LEE

Peoples who hunt and gather wild foods experience an intimate rela-
tionship with their natural environments. A band's size and struc-
ture, the breadth of its territory, and the frequency and pattern of its
movement depend on the abundance of vegetable foods, game, and
water. For many Western anthropologists, the life of hunter-gatherers
seems precarious and fraught with hardship. Yet, according to Rich-
ard B. Lee, this picture is largely inaccurate. In this article he points
out that the !Kung Bushmen who live in the Kalahari Desert of
South Africa survive well in what Westerners would consider a mar-
ginal habitat. Depending, like most hunter-gatherers, on vegetable
foods for their sustenance, the !Kung actually spend little time at
food collecting, yet they live long and fruitful lives in their desert
home.

The current anthropological view of hunter-gatherer subsistence rests on two questionable assumptions. First is the notion that these people are primarily dependent on the hunting of game animals, and second is the assumption that their way of life is generally a precarious and arduous struggle for existence.

Recent data on living hunter-gatherers show a radically different picture. We have learned that in many societies, plant and marine resources are far more important than are game animals in the diet. More important, it is becoming clear that, with a few conspicuous

Reprinted by permission from Richard Lee and Irvin Devore, editors, *Man the Hunter* (Hawthorne, NY: Aldine Publishing Company); copyright © 1968 Wenner-Gren Foundation for Anthropological Research, Inc.

exceptions, the hunter-gatherer subsistence base is at least routine and reliable and at best surprisingly abundant. Anthropologists have consistently tended to underestimate the viability of even those "marginal isolates" of hunting peoples that have been available to ethnographers.

The purpose of this paper is to analyze the food getting activities of one such "marginal" people, the !Kung Bushmen of the Kalahari Desert. Three related questions are posed: How do the Bushmen make a living? How easy or difficult is it for them to do this? What kinds of evidence are necessary to measure and evaluate the precariousness or security of a way of life? And after the relevant data are presented, two further questions are asked: What makes this security of life possible? To what extent are the Bushmen typical of hunter-gatherers in general?

BUSHMAN SUBSISTENCE

The !Kung Bushmen of Botswana are an apt case for analysis. They inhabit the semi-arid northwest region of the Kalahari Desert. With only six to nine inches of rainfall per year, this is, by any account, a marginal environment for human habitation. In fact, it is precisely the unattractiveness of their homeland that has kept the !Kung isolated from extensive contact with their agricultural and pastoral neighbors.

Field work was carried out in the Dobe area, a line of eight permanent waterholes near the South-West Africa border and 125 miles south of the Okavango River. The population of the Dobe area consists of 466 Bushmen, including 379 permanent residents living in independent camps or associated with Bantu cattle posts, as well as 87 seasonal visitors. The Bushmen share the area with some 340 Bantu pastoralists largely of the Herero and Tswana tribes. The ethnographic present refers to the period of field work: October, 1963–January, 1965.

The Bushmen living in independent camps lack firearms, livestock, and agriculture. Apart from occasional visits to the Herero for milk, these !Kung are entirely dependent upon hunting and gathering for their subsistence. Politically they are under the nominal authority of the Tswana headman, although they pay no taxes and receive very few government services. European presence amounts to one overnight government patrol every six to eight weeks. Although Dobe-area !Kung have had some contact with outsiders since the 1880s, the majority of them continue to hunt and gather because there is no viable alternative locally available to them.

Each of the fourteen independent camps is associated with one of the permanent waterholes. During the dry season (May–October) the entire population is clustered around these wells. Table I shows the numbers at each well at the end of the 1964 dry season. Two wells had

TABLE I. Numbers and distribution of resident Bushmen and Bantu by waterhole*

Name of waterhole	No. of camps	Population of camps	Other Bushmen	Total Bushmen	Bantu
Dobe	2	37	—	37	—
!angwa	1	16	23	39	84
Bate	2	30	12	42	21
!ubi	1	19	—	19	65
!gose	3	52	9	61	18
/ai/ai	5	94	13	107	67
!xabe	—	—	8	8	12
Mahopa	—	—	23	23	73
Total	14	248	88	336	340

*Figures do not include 130 Bushmen outside area on the date of census.

no camp resident and one large well supported five camps. The number of camps at each well and the size of each camp changed frequently during the course of the year. The "camp" is an open aggregate of cooperating persons which changes in size and composition from day to day. Therefore, I have avoided the term "band" in describing the !Kung Bushman living groups.

Each waterhole has a hinterland lying within a six-mile radius which is regularly exploited for vegetable and animal foods. These areas are not territories in the zoological sense, since they are not defended against outsiders. Rather they constitute the resources that lie within a convenient walking distance of a waterhole. The camp is a self-sufficient subsistence unit. The members move out each day to hunt and gather, and return in the evening to pool the collected foods in such a way that every person present receives an equitable share. Trade in foodstuffs between camps is minimal; personnel do move freely from camp to camp, however. The net effect is of a population constantly in motion. On the average, an individual spends a third of his time living only with close relatives, a third visiting other camps, and a third entertaining visitors from other camps.

Because of the strong emphasis on sharing, and the frequency of movement, surplus accumulation of storable plant foods and dried meat is kept to a minimum. There is rarely more than two or three days' supply of food on hand in a camp at any time. The result of this lack of surplus is that a constant subsistence effort must be maintained throughout the year. Unlike agriculturalists who work hard during the planting and harvesting seasons and undergo "seasonal unemployment" for several months, the Bushmen hunter-gatherers collect food every third or fourth day throughout the year.

Vegetable foods comprise from 60–80 per cent of the total diet by weight, and collecting involves two or three days of work per woman per week. The men also collect plants and small animals but their major contribution to the diet is the hunting of medium and large game. The men are conscientious but not particularly successful hunters; although men's and women's work input is roughly equivalent in terms of man-day of effort, the women provide two to three times as much food by weight as the men.

Table II summarizes the seasonal activity cycle observed among the Dobe-area !Kung in 1964. For the greater part of the year, food is locally abundant and easily collected. It is only during the end of the dry season in September and October, when desirable foods have been eaten out in the immediate vicinity of the waterholes that the people have to plan longer hikes of 10–15 miles and carry their own water to those areas where the mongongo nut is still available. The important point is that food is a constant, but distance required to reach food is a variable; it is short in the summer, fall, and early winter, and reaches its maximum in the spring.

This analysis attempts to provide quantitative measures of subsistence status including data on the following topics: abundance and variety of resources, diet selectivity, range size and population density, the composition of the work force, the ratio of work to leisure time, and the caloric and protein levels in the diet. The value of quantitative data is that they can be used comparatively and also may be useful in archeological reconstruction. In addition, one can avoid the pitfalls of subjective and qualitative impressions; for example, statements about food "anxiety" have proven to be difficult to generalize across cultures.

Abundance and variety of resources. It is impossible to define "abundance" of resources absolutely. However, one index of *relative* abundance is whether or not a population exhausts all the food available from a given area. By this criterion, the habitat of the Dobe-area Bushmen is abundant in naturally occurring foods. By far the most important food is the mongongo (mangetti) nut (*Ricinodendron rautanenii* Schinz). Although tens of thousands of pounds of these nuts are harvested and eaten each year, thousands more rot on the ground each year for want of picking.

The mongongo nut, because of its abundance and reliability, alone accounts for 50 per cent of the vegetable diet by weight. In this respect it resembles a cultivated staple crop such as maize or rice. Nutritionally it is even more remarkable, for it contains five times the

TABLE II. The Bushman annual round

Season	Jan.	Feb.	Mar.	April	May	June	July	Aug.	Sept.	Oct.	Nov.	Dec.
		Summer Rains		Autumn Dry			Winter Dry			Spring Dry		First Rains
Availability of water	Temporary summer pools everywhere			Large summer pools			Permanent waterholes only					Summer pools developing
Group moves	Widely dispersed at summer pools			At large summer pools				All population restricted to permanent waterholes				Moving out to summer pools
Men's subsistence activities	1. Hunting with bow, arrows, and dogs (year-round) 2. Running down immatures 3. Some gathering (year-round)						Trapping small game in snares				Running down newborn animals	
Women's subsistence activities	1. Gathering of mongongo nuts (year-round) 2. Fruits, berries, melons						Roots, bulbs, resins				Roots, leafy greens	
Ritual activities	Dancing, trance performances, and ritual curing (year-round)					Boys' initiation*						†
Relative subsistence hardship			Water-food distance minimal				Increasing distance from water to food				Water-food distance minimal	

*Held once every five years; none in 1963–64.

†New Year's: Bushmen join the celebrations of their missionized Bantu neighbors.

196

calories and ten times the proteins per cooked unit of the cereal crops. The average daily per-capita consumption of 300 nuts yields about 1,260 calories and 56 grams of protein. This modest portion, weighing only about 7.5 ounces, contains the caloric equivalent of 2.5 pounds of cooked rice and the protein equivalent of 14 ounces of lean beef.

Furthermore the mongongo nut is drought resistant and it will still be abundant in the dry years when cultivated crops may fail. The extremely hard outer shell protects the inner kernel from rot and allows the nuts to be harvested for up to twelve months after they have fallen to the ground. A diet based on mongongo nuts is in fact more reliable than one based on cultivated foods, and it is not surprising, therefore, that when a Bushman was asked why he hadn't taken to agriculture he replied: "Why should we plant, when there are so many mongongo nuts in the world?"

Apart from the mongongo, the Bushmen have available 84 other species of edible food plants, including 29 species of fruits, berries, and melons and 30 species of roots and bulbs. The existence of this variety allows for a wide range of alternatives in subsistence strategy. During the summer months the Bushmen have no problem other than to choose among the tastiest and most easily collected foods. Many species, which are quite edible but less attractive, are bypassed, so that gathering never exhausts *all* the available plant foods of an area. During the dry season the diet becomes much more eclectic and the many species of roots, bulbs, and edible resins make an important contribution. It is this broad base that provides an essential margin of safety during the end of the dry season when the mongongo nut forests are difficult to reach. In addition, it is likely that these rarely utilized species provide important nutritional and mineral trace elements that may be lacking in the more popular foods.

Diet selectivity. If the Bushmen were living close to the "starvation" level, then one would expect them to exploit every available source of nutrition. That their life is well above this level is indicated by the data in Table III. Here all the edible plant species are arranged in classes according to the frequency with which they were observed to be eaten. It should be noted, that although there are some 85 species available, about 90 percent of the vegetable diet by weight is drawn from only 23 species. In other words, 75 percent of the listed species provide only 10 percent of the food value.

In their meat-eating habits, the Bushmen show a similar selectivity. Of the 223 local species of animals known and named by the Bushmen, 54 species are classified as edible, and of these only 17 species were hunted on a regular basis. Only a handful of the dozens of edible species of small mammals, bird, reptiles, and insects that occur locally are regarded as food. Such animals as rodents, snakes, lizards, termites, and grasshoppers, which in the literature are included in the Bushman dietary, are despised by the Bushmen of the Dobe area.

Range size and population density. The necessity to travel long distances, the high frequency of moves, and the maintenance of populations at low densities are also features commonly associated with the hunting and gathering way of life. Density estimates for hunters in western North America and Australia have ranged from 3 persons/ square mile to as low as 1 person/100 square miles. In 1963–65, the resident and visiting Bushmen were observed to utilize an area of about 1,000 square miles during the course of the annual round for an effective population density of 41 persons/100 square miles. Within this area, however, the amount of ground covered by members of an individual camp was surprisingly small. A day's round-trip of twelve miles serves to define a "core" area six miles in radius surrounding each water point. By fanning out in all directions from their well, the members of a camp can gain access to the food resources of well over 100 square miles of territory within a two-hour hike. Except for a few weeks each year, areas lying beyond this six-mile radius are rarely utilized, even though they are no less rich in plants and game than are the core areas.

Although the Bushmen move their camps frequently (five or six times a year) they do not move them very far. A rainy season camp in the nut forests is rarely more than ten or twelve miles from the home waterhole, and often new campsites are occupied only a few hundred yards away from the previous one. By these criteria, the Bushmen do not lead a free-ranging nomadic way of life. For example, they do not undertake long marches of 30 to 100 miles to get food, since this task can be readily fulfilled within a day's walk of home base. When such long marches do occur they are invariably for visiting, trading, and marriage arrangements, and should not be confused with the normal routine of subsistence.

Demographic factors. Another indicator of the harshness of a way of life is the age at which people die. Ever since Hobbes characterized life in the state of nature as "nasty, brutish and short," the assumption has been that hunting and gathering is so rigorous that members of such societies are rapidly worn out and meet an early death. Silberbauer, for example, says of the Gwi Bushmen of the central Kalahari that "life expectancy . . . is difficult to calculate, but I do not believe that many live beyond 45." And Coon has said of hunters in general:

TABLE III. *!Kung Bushman plant foods*

Food class	Fruit and nut	Bean and root	Fruit and stalk	Root, bulb	Fruit, berry, melon	Resin	Leaves	Seed, bean	Total number of species in class	Estimated contribution by weight to vegetable diet	Estimated contribution of each species
					Part eaten					Totals (percentages)	
I. Primary Eaten daily throughout year (mongongo nut)	1	—	—	—	—	—	—	—	1	c. 50	c. 50*
II. Major Eaten daily in season	1	1	1	1	4	—	—	—	8	c. 25	c. 3
III. Minor Eaten several times per week in season	—	—	—	7	3	2	2	—	14	c. 15	c. 1
IV. Supplementary Eaten when classes I–III locally unavailable	—	—	—	9	12	10	1	—	32	c. 7	c. 0.2
V. Rare Eaten several times per year	—	—	—	9	4	—	—	—	13	c. 3	c. 0.1
VI. Problematic Edible but not observed to be eaten	—	—	—	4	6	4	1	2	17	nil	nil
Total Species	2	1	1	30	29	16	4	2	85	100	—

*1 species constitutes 50 per cent of the vegetable diet by weight. †23 species constitute 90 per cent of the vegetable diet by weight.
‡62 species constitute the remaining 10 per cent of the diet.

The practice of abandoning the hopelessly ill and aged has been observed in many parts of the world. It is always done by people living in poor environments where it is necessary to move about frequently to obtain food, where food is scarce, and transportation difficult. . . . Among peoples who are forced to live in this way the oldest generation, the generation of individuals who have passed their physical peak is reduced in numbers and influence. There is no body of elders to hand on tradition and control the affairs of younger men and women, and no formal system of age grading.

The !Kung Bushmen of the Dobe area flatly contradict this view. In a total population of 466, no fewer than 46 individuals (17 men and 29 women) were determined to be over 60 years of age, a proportion that compares favorably to the percentage of elderly in industrialized populations.

The aged hold a respected position in Bushman society and are the effective leaders of the camps. Senilicide is extremely rare. Long after their productive years have passed, the old people are fed and cared for by their children and grandchildren. The blind, the senile, and the crippled are respected for the special ritual and technical skills they possess. For instance, the four elders at !gose waterhole were totally or partially blind, but this handicap did not prevent their active participation in decision making and ritual curing.

Another significant feature of the composition of the work force is the late assumption of adult responsibility by the adolescents. Young people are not expected to provide food regularly until they are married. Girls typically marry between the ages of 15 and 20, and boys about five years later, so that it is not unusual to find healthy, active teenagers visiting from camp to camp while their older relatives provide food for them.

As a result, the people in the age group 20–60 support a surprisingly large percentage of non-productive young and old people. About 40 per cent of the population in camps contribute little to the food supplies. This allocation of work to young and middle-aged adults allows for a relatively carefree childhood and adolescence and a relatively unstrenuous old age.

Leisure and work. Another important index of ease or difficulty of subsistence is the amount of time devoted to the food quest. Hunting has usually been regarded by social scientists as a way of life in which merely keeping alive is so formidable a task that members of such societies lack the leisure time necessary to "build culture." The !Kung Bushmen would appear to conform to the rule, for as Lorna Marshall says:

It is vividly apparent that among the !Kung Bushmen, ethos, or "the spirit which actuates manners and customs," is survival. Their time and energies are almost wholly given to this task, for life in their environment requires that they spend their days mainly in procuring food.

It is certainly true that getting food is the most important single activity in Bushman life. However, this statement would apply equally well to small-scale agricultural and pastoral societies too. How much time is *actually* devoted to the food quest is fortunately an empirical question. And an analysis of the work effort of the Dobe Bushmen shows some unexpected results. From July 6 to August 2, 1964, I recorded all the daily activities of the Bushmen living at the Dobe waterhole. Because of the coming and going of visitors, the camp population fluctuated in size day by day, from a low of 23 to a high of 40, with a mean of 31.8 persons. Each day some of the adult members of the camp went out to hunt and/or gather while others stayed home or went visiting. The daily recording of all personnel on hand made it possible to calculate the number of man-days of work as a percentage of total number of man-days of consumption.

Although the Bushmen do not organize their activities on the basis of a seven-day week, I have divided the data this way to make them more intelligible. The work-week was calculated to show how many days out of seven each adult spent in subsistence activities (Table IV, Column 7). Week II has been eliminated from the totals since the investigator contributed food. In week I, the people spent an average of 2.3 days in subsistence activities, in week III, 1.9 days, and in week IV, 3.2 days. In all, the adults of the Dobe camp worked about two and a half days a week. Since the average working day was about six hours long, the fact emerges that !Kung Bushmen of Dobe, despite their harsh environment, devote from twelve to nineteen hours a week to getting food. Even the hardest working individual in the camp, a man named ≠oma who went out hunting on sixteen of the 28 days, spent a maximum of 32 hours a week in the food quest.

Because the Bushmen do not amass a surplus of foods, there are no seasons of exceptionally intensive activities such as planting and harvesting, and no seasons of unemployment. The level of work observed is an accurate reflection of the effort required to meet the immediate caloric needs of the group. This work diary covers the midwinter dry season, a period when food is neither at its most plentiful nor at its scarcest levels, and the diary documents the transition from better to worse conditions (see Table II). During the fourth week the gatherers were making overnight trips to camps in the mongongo nut forests

Table IV. *Summary of Dobe work diary*

Week	(1) Mean group size	(2) Adult-days	(3) Child-days	(4) Total man-days of consumption	(5) Man-days of work	(6) Meat (lbs.)	(7) Average work-week/adult	(8) Index of sub-sistence effort
I (July 6–12)	25.6 (23–29)	114	65	179	37	104	2.3	.21
II (July 13–19)	28.3 (23–27)	125	73	198	22	80	1.2	.11
III (July 20–26)	34.3 (29–40)	156	84	240	42	177	1.9	.18
IV (July 27–Aug.2)	35.6 (32–40)	167	82	249	77	129	3.2	.31
4-wk. total	30.9	562	304	866	178	490	2.2	.21
Adjusted total*	31.8	437	231	668	156	410	2.5	.23

*See text

Key: Column 1: Mean group size = $\dfrac{\text{total man-days of consumption}}{7}$

Column 7: Work-week = the number of work days per adult per week.

Column 8: Index of subsistence effort = $\dfrac{\text{man-days of work}}{\text{man-days of consumption}}$ (e.g., in Week I, the value of "S" = 21, i.e., 21 days of work/100 days of consumption or 1 work day produces food for 5 consumption days).

seven to ten miles distant from the waterhole. These longer trips account for the rise in the level of work, from twelve or thirteen to nineteen hours per week.

If food getting occupies such a small proportion of a Bushman's waking hours, then how *do* people allocate their time? A woman gathers on one day enough food to feed her family for three days, and spends the rest of her time resting in camp, doing embroidery, visiting other camps, or entertaining visitors from other camps. For each day at home, kitchen routines, such as cooking, nut cracking, collecting firewood, and fetching water, occupy one to three hours of her time. This rhythm of steady work and steady leisure is maintained throughout the year.

The hunters tend to work more frequently than the women, but their schedule is uneven. It is not unusual for a man to hunt avidly for a week and then do nothing at all for two or three weeks. Since hunting is an unpredictable business and subject to magical control, hunters sometimes experience a run of bad luck and stop hunting for a month or longer. During these periods, visiting, entertaining, and especially dancing are the primary activities of men. (Unlike the Hadza, gambling is only a minor leisure activity.)

The trance-dance is the focus of Bushman ritual life; over 50 per cent of the men have trained as trance-performers and regularly enter trance during the course of the all-night dances. At some camps, trance-dances occur as frequently as two or three times a week and those who have entered trances the night before rarely go out hunting the following day. . . . In a camp with five or more hunters, there are usually two or three who are actively hunting and several others who are inactive. The net effect is to phase the hunting and non-hunting so that a fairly steady supply of meat is brought into camp.

Caloric returns. Is the modest work effort of the Bushmen sufficient to provide the calories necessary to maintain the health of the population? Or have the !Kung, in common with some agricultural peoples, adjusted to a permanently substandard nutritional level?

During my field work I did not encounter any cases of kwashiorkor, the most common nutritional disease in the children of African agricultural societies. However, without medical examinations, it is impossible to exclude the possibility that subclinical signs of malnutrition existed.

Another measure of nutritional adequacy is the average consumption of calories and proteins per person per day. The estimate for the Bushmen is based on observations of the weights of foods of known composition that were brought into Dobe camp on each day of the study period. The per-capita figure is obtained by dividing the total weight of foodstuffs by the total number of persons in the camp. These results are set out in detail elsewhere and can only be summarized here. During the study period 410 pounds of meat were brought in by the hunters of the Dobe camp, for a daily share of nine ounces of meat per person. About 700 pounds of vegetables were gathered and consumed during the same period. Table V sets out the calories and proteins available per capita in the !Kung Bushman dietary from meat, mongongo nuts, and other vegetable sources.

This output of 2,140 calories and 93.1 grams of protein per person per day may be compared with the Recommended Daily Allowances (RDA) for persons of the small size and stature but vigorous activity regime of the !Kung Bushmen. The RDA for Bushmen can be estimated at 1,975 calories and 60 grams of protein per person per day. Thus it is apparent that food output exceeds energy requirements by 165 calories and 33 grams of protein. One can tentatively conclude that even a modest subsistence effort of two or three days work per week is enough to provide an adequate diet for the !Kung Bushmen.

THE SECURITY OF BUSHMAN LIFE

I have attempted to evaluate the subsistence base of one contemporary hunter-gatherer society living in a marginal environment. The !Kung Bushmen have available to them some relatively abundant high-quality foods, and they do not have to walk very far or work very hard to get them. Furthermore this modest work effort provides sufficient calories to support not only active adults, but also a large number of middle-aged and elderly people. The Bushmen do not have to press their youngsters into the service of the food quest, nor do they have to dispose of the oldsters after they have ceased to be productive.

The evidence presented assumes an added significance because this security of life was observed during the third year of one of the most severe droughts in South Africa's history. Most of the 576,000 people of Botswana are pastoralists and agriculturalists. After the crops had failed three years in succession and over 100,000 head of cattle had died on the range for lack of water, the World Food Program of the United Nations instituted a famine relief program which has grown to include 180,000 people, over 30 per cent of the population. This program did not touch the Dobe area in the isolated northwest corner of the country and the Herero and Tswana women there were able to feed their families only by joining the Bushman women to forage for wild foods. Thus the natural plant resources of the Dobe area were carrying a higher proportion of population than would be the case in

TABLE v. *Caloric and protein levels in the !Kung Bushman dietary, July–August, 1964*

Class of food	Percentage contribution to diet by weight	Per capita consumption			Percentage caloric contribution of meat and vegetables
		Weight in grams	Protein in grams	Calories per person per day	
Meat	37	230	34.5	690	33
Mongongo nuts	33	210	56.7	1,260	
Other vegetable foods	30	190	1.9	190	67
Total all sources	100	630	93.1	2,140	100

years when the Bantu harvested crops. Yet this added pressure on the land did not seem to adversely affect the Bushmen.

In one sense it was unfortunate that the period of my field work happened to coincide with the drought, since I was unable to witness a "typical" annual subsistence cycle. However, in another sense, the coincidence was a lucky one, for the drought put the Bushmen and their subsistence system to the acid test and, in terms of adaptation to scarce resources, they passed with flying colors. One can postulate that their subsistence base would be even more substantial during years of higher rainfall.

What are the crucial factors that make this way of life possible? I suggest that the primary factor is the Bushmen's strong emphasis on vegetable food sources. Although hunting involves a great deal of effort and prestige, plant foods provide from 60–80 per cent of the annual diet by weight. Meat has come to be regarded as a special treat; when available, it is welcomed as a break from the routine of vegetable foods, but it is never depended upon as a staple. No one ever goes hungry when hunting fails.

The reason for this emphasis is not hard to find. Vegetable foods are abundant, sedentary, and predictable. They grow in the same place year after year, and the gatherer is guaranteed a day's return of food for a day's expenditure of energy. Game animals, by contrast, are scarce, mobile, unpredictable, and difficult to catch. A hunter has no guarantee of success and may in fact go for days or weeks without killing a large mammal. During the study period, there were eleven men in the Dobe camp, of whom four did no hunting at all. The seven active men spent a total of 78 man-days hunting, and this work input yielded eighteen animals killed, or one kill for every four man-days of hunting. The probability of any one hunter making a kill on a given day was 0.23. By contrast, the probability of a woman finding plant food on a given day was 1.00. In other words, hunting and gathering are not equally felicitous subsistence alternatives.

Consider the productivity per man-hour of the two kinds of subsistence activities. One man-hour of hunting produces about 100 edible calories, and of gathering, 240 calories. Gathering is thus seen to be 2.4 times more productive than hunting. In short, hunting is a *high-risk, low-return* subsistence activity, while gathering is a low-risk, high-return subsistence activity.

It is not at all contradictory that the hunting complex holds a central place in the Bushmen ethos and that meat is valued more highly than vegetable foods. Analogously, steak is valued more highly than potatoes in the food preferences of our own society. In both situations the meat is more "costly" than the vegetable food. In the Bushman case, the cost of food can be measured in terms of time and energy expended. By this standard, 1,000 calories of meat "costs" ten man-hours, while the "cost" of 1,000 calories of vegetable foods is only four man-hours. Further, it is to be expected that the less predictable, more expensive food source would have a greater accretion of myth and ritual built up around it than would the routine staples of life, which rarely if ever fail.

CONCLUSIONS

Three points ought to be stressed. First, life in the state of nature is not necessarily nasty, brutish, and short. The Dobe-area Bushmen live well today on wild plants and meat, in spite of the fact that they are confined to the least productive portion of the range in which Bushman peoples were formerly found. It is likely that an even more substantial subsistence would have been characteristic of these hunters and gatherers in the past, when they had the pick of African habitats to choose from.

Second, the basis of Bushman diet is derived from sources other than meat. This emphasis makes good ecological sense to the !Kung Bushmen and appears to be a common feature among hunters and gatherers in general. Since a 30 to 40 per cent input of meat is such a consistent target for modern hunters in a variety of habitats, is it not reasonable to postulate a similar percentage for prehistoric hunters?

Certainly the absence of plant remains on archeological sites is by itself not sufficient evidence for the absence of gathering. Recently-abandoned Bushman campsites show a similar absence of vegetable remains, although this paper has clearly shown that plant foods comprise over 60 per cent of the actual diet.

Finally, one gets the impression that hunting societies have been chosen by ethnologists to illustrate a dominant theme, such as the extreme importance of environment in the molding of certain cultures. Such a theme can best be exemplified by cases in which the technology is simple and/or the environment is harsh. This emphasis on the dramatic may have been pedagogically useful, but unfortunately it has led to the assumption that a precarious hunting subsistence base was characteristic of all cultures in the Pleistocene. This view of both modern and ancient hunters ought to be reconsidered. Specifically I am suggesting a shift in focus away from the dramatic and unusual cases, and toward a consideration of hunting and gathering as a persistent and well-adapted way of life.

REVIEW QUESTIONS

1. How does Lee assess the day-to-day quality of !Kung life? How does his view compare with the stereotype of hunter-gatherers?

2. Give the evidence that supports Lee's viewpoint about the !Kung.

3. According to Lee, !Kung children are not expected to work until after they are married; old people are supported and respected. How does this arrangement differ from behavior in our own society, and what might explain the difference?

4. What is the key to successful subsistence for the !Kung and other hunter-gatherers?

18

India's sacred cow

MARVIN HARRIS

*Other people's religious practices and beliefs may often appear to be
wasteful. They seem to involve a large expenditure of scarce resources
on ritual; they contain taboos that restrict the use of apparently useful materials. Their existence seems irrational in the face of ecological
needs. One example that many cite in support of this viewpoint is
the religious proscription on the slaughter of cattle in India. How can
people permit millions of cattle to roam about eating, but uneaten, in
a land so continuously threatened by food shortages and starvation?
In this article, Marvin Harris challenges the view that religious value
is ecologically irrational. Dealing with the Indian case, he argues that
Indian cattle, far from being useless, are an essential part of India's
productive base. Religious restrictions on killing cattle are ecologically sensible; they have developed and persisted to ensure a continuous supply of these valuable animals.*

News photographs that came out of India during the famine of the late
1960s showed starving people stretching out bony hands to beg for
food while sacred cattle strolled behind them undisturbed. The Hindu,
it seems, would rather starve to death than eat his cow or even deprive
it of food. The cattle appear to browse unhindered through urban
markets eating an orange here, a mango there, competing with people
for meager supplies of food.

By Western standards, spiritual values seem more important to
Indians than life itself. Specialists in food habits around the world like
Fred Simoons at the University of California at Davis consider Hindu-

From *Human Nature*, February 1978. Copyright © 1978 by Human Nature, Inc. Reprinted
by permission of the publisher.

ism an irrational ideology that compels people to overlook abundant, nutritious foods for scarcer, less healthful foods.

What seems to be an absurd devotion to the mother cow pervades Indian life. Indian wall calendars portray beautiful young women with bodies of fat white cows, often with milk jetting from their teats into sacred shrines.

Cow worship even carries over into politics. In 1966 a crowd of 120,000 people, led by holy men, demonstrated in front of the Indian House of Parliament in support of the All-Party Cow Protection Campaign Committee. In Nepal, the only contemporary Hindu kingdom, cow slaughter is severely punished. As one story goes, the car driven by an official of a United States agency struck and killed a cow. In order to avoid the international incident that would have occurred when the official was arrested for murder, the Nepalese magistrate concluded that the cow had committed suicide.

Many Indians agree with Western assessments of the Hindu reverence for their cattle, the zebu, or *Bos indicus*, a large-humped species prevalent in Asia and Africa. M. N. Srinivas, an Indian anthropologist states: "Orthodox Hindu opinion regards the killing of cattle with abhorrence, even though the refusal to kill the vast number of useless cattle which exists in India today is detrimental to the nation." Even the Indian Ministry of Information formerly maintained that "the large animal population is more a liability than an asset in view of our land resources." Accounts from many different sources point to the same conclusion: India, one of the world's great civilizations, is being strangled by its love for the cow.

The easy explanation for India's devotion to the cow, the one most Westerners and Indians would offer, is that cow worship is an integral part of Hinduism. Religion is somehow good for the soul, even if it sometimes fails the body. Religion orders the cosmos and explains our place in the universe. Religious beliefs, many would claim, have existed for thousands of years and have a life of their own. They are not understandable in scientific terms.

But all this ignores history. There is more to be said for cow worship than is immediately apparent. The earliest Vedas, the Hindu sacred texts from the Second Millennium B.C., do not prohibit the slaughter of cattle. Instead, they ordain it as a part of sacrificial rites. The early Hindus did not avoid the flesh of cows and bulls; they ate it at ceremonial feasts presided over by Brahman priests. Cow worship is a relatively recent development in India; it evolved as the Hindu religion developed and changed.

This evolution is recorded in royal edicts and religious texts writ-

ten during the last 3,000 years of Indian history. The Vedas from the
First Millennium B.C. contain contradictory passages, some referring to
ritual slaughter and others to a strict taboo on beef consumption. A.N.
Bose, in *Social and Rural Economy of Northern India, 600 B.C.–200 A.D.*,
concludes that many of the sacred-cow passages were incorporated
into the texts by priests of a later period.

By 200 A.D. the status of Indian cattle had undergone a spiritual
transformation. The Brahman priesthood exhorted the population to
venerate the cow and forbade them to abuse it or to feed on it. Religious feasts involving the ritual slaughter and consumption of livestock
were eliminated and meat eating was restricted to the nobility.

By 1000 A.D., all Hindus were forbidden to eat beef. Ahimsa, the
Hindu belief in the unity of all life, was the spiritual justification for
this restriction. But it is difficult to ascertain exactly when this change
occurred. An important event that helped to shape the modern complex was the Islamic invasion, which took place in the Eighth Century
A.D. Hindus may have found it politically expedient to set themselves
off from the invaders, who were beefeaters, by emphasizing the need
to prevent the slaughter of their sacred animals. Thereafter, the cow
taboo assumed its modern form and began to function much as it does
today.

The place of the cow in modern India is every place — on posters,
in the movies, in brass figures, in stone and wood carvings, on the
streets, in the fields. The cow is a symbol of health and abundance. It
provides the milk that Indians consume in the form of yogurt and ghee
(clarified butter), which contribute subtle flavors to much spicy Indian
food.

This, perhaps, is the practical role of the cow, but cows provide
less than half the milk produced in India. Most cows in India are not
dairy breeds. In most regions, when an Indian farmer wants a steady,
high-quality source of milk he usually invests in a female water buffalo.
In India the water buffalo is the specialized dairy breed because its milk
has a higher butterfat content than zebu milk. Although the farmer
milks his zebu cows, the milk is merely a by-product.

More vital than zebu milk to South Asian farmers are zebu calves.
Male calves are especially valued because from bulls come oxen, which
are the mainstay of the Indian agricultural system.

Small, fast oxen drag wooden plows through late-spring fields
when monsoons have dampened the dry, cracked earth. After harvest,
the oxen break the grain from the stalk by stomping through mounds
of cut wheat and rice. For rice cultivation in irrigated fields, the male
water buffalo is preferred (it pulls better in deep mud), but for most

other crops, including rainfall rice, wheat, sorghum, and millet, and for transporting goods and people to and from town, a team of oxen is preferred. The ox is the Indian peasant's tractor, thresher, and family car combined; the cow is the factory that produces the ox.

If draft animals instead of cows are counted, India appears to have too few domesticated ruminants, not too many. Since each of the 70 million farms in India requires a draft team, it follows that Indian peasants should use 140 million animals in the fields. But there are only 83 million oxen and male water buffalo on the subcontinent, a shortage of 30 million draft teams.

In other regions of the world, joint ownership of draft animals might overcome a shortage, but Indian agriculture is closely tied to the monsoon rains of late spring and summer. Field preparation and planting must coincide with the rain, and a farmer must have his animals ready to plow when the weather is right. When the farmer without a draft team needs bullocks most, his neighbors are all using theirs. Any delay in turning the soil drastically lowers production.

Because of this dependence on draft animals, loss of the family oxen is devastating. If a beast dies, the farmer must borrow money to buy or rent an ox at interest rates so high that he ultimately loses his land. Every year foreclosures force thousands of poverty-stricken peasants to abandon the countryside for the overcrowded cities.

If a family is fortunate enough to own a fertile cow, it will be able to rear replacements for a lost team and thus survive until life returns to normal. If, as sometimes happens, famine leads a family to sell its cow and ox team, all ties to agriculture are cut. Even if the family survives, it has no way to farm the land, no oxen to work the land, and no cows to produce oxen.

The prohibition against eating meat applies to the flesh of cows, bulls, and oxen, but the cow is the most sacred because it can produce the other two. The peasant whose cow dies is not only crying over a spiritual loss but over the loss of his farm as well.

Religious laws that forbid the slaughter of cattle promote the recovery of the agricultural system from the dry Indian winter and from periods of drought. The monsoon, on which all agriculture depends, is erratic. Sometimes it arrives early, sometimes late, sometimes not at all. Drought has struck large portions of India time and again in this century, and Indian farmers and the zebus are accustomed to these natural disasters. Zebus can pass weeks on end with little or no food and water. Like camels, they store both in their humps and recuperate quickly with only a little nourishment.

During droughts the cows often stop lactating and become barren. In some cases the condition is permanent but often it is only temporary. If barren animals were summarily eliminated, as Western experts in animal husbandry have suggested, cows capable of recovery would be lost along with those entirely debilitated. By keeping alive the cows that can later produce oxen, religious laws against cow slaughter assure the recovery of the agricultural system from the greatest challenge it faces — the failure of the monsoon.

The local Indian governments aid the process of recovery by maintaining homes for barren cows. Farmers reclaim any animal that calves or begins to lactate. One police station in Madras collects strays and pastures them in a field adjacent to the station. After a small fine is paid, a cow is returned to its rightful owner when the owner thinks the cow shows signs of being able to reproduce.

During the hot, dry spring months most of India is like a desert. Indian farmers often complain they cannot feed their livestock during this period. They maintain the cattle by letting them scavenge on the sparse grass along the roads. In the cities cattle are encouraged to scavenge near food stalls to supplement their scant diet. These are the wandering cattle tourists report seeing throughout India.

Westerners expect shopkeepers to respond to these intrusions with the deference due a sacred animal; instead, their response is a string of curses and the crack of a long bamboo pole across the beast's back or a poke at its genitals. Mahatma Gandhi was well aware of the treatment sacred cows (and bulls and oxen) received in India. "How we bleed her to take the last drop of milk from her. How we starve her to emaciation, how we ill-treat the calves, how we deprive them of their portion of milk, how cruelly we treat the oxen, how we castrate them, how we beat them, how we overload them."

Oxen generally receive better treatment than cows. When food is in short supply, thrifty Indian peasants feed their working bullocks and ignore their cows, but rarely do they abandon the cows to die. When cows are sick, farmers worry over them as they would over members of the family and nurse them as if they were children. When the rains return and when the fields are harvested, the farmers again feed their cows regularly and reclaim their abandoned animals. The prohibition against beef consumption is a form of disaster insurance for all India.

Western agronomists and economists are quick to protest that all the functions of the zebu cattle can be improved with organized breeding programs, cultivated pastures, and silage. Because stronger oxen would pull the plow faster, they could work multiple plots of land, allowing farmers to share their animals. Fewer healthy, well-fed cows could provide Indians with more milk. But pastures and silage require arable land, land needed to produce wheat and rice.

A look at Western cattle farming makes plain the cost of adopting advanced technology in Indian agriculture. In a study of livestock production in the United States, David Pimentel of the College of Agriculture and Life Sciences at Cornell University found that 91 percent of the cereal, legume, and vegetable protein suitable for human consumption is consumed by livestock. Approximately three quarters of the arable land in the United States is devoted to growing food for livestock. In the production of meat and milk, American ranchers use enough fossil fuel to equal more than 82 million barrels of oil annually. (See Figure I.)

Indian cattle do not drain the system in the same way. In a 1971 study of livestock in West Bengal, Stewart Odend'hal of the University of Missouri found that Bengalese cattle ate only the inedible remains of subsistence crops — rice straw, rice hulls, the tops of sugar cane, and mustard-oil cake. Cattle graze in the fields after harvest and eat the remains of crops left on the ground; they forage for grass and weeds on the roadsides. The food for zebu cattle costs the human population virtually nothing. "Basically," Odend'hal says, "the cattle convert items of little direct human value into products of immediate utility." (See Figure II.)

In addition to plowing the fields and producing milk, the zebus produce dung, which fires the hearths and fertilizes the fields of India. Much of the estimated 800 million tons of manure produced annually is collected by the farmers' children as they follow the family cows and bullocks from place to place. And when the children see the droppings of another farmer's cattle along the road, they pick those up also. Odend'hal reports that the system operates with such high efficiency that the children of West Bengal recover nearly 100 percent of the dung produced by their livestock.

From 40 to 70 percent of all manure produced by Indian cattle is used as fuel for cooking; the rest is returned to the fields as fertilizer. Dried dung burns slowly, cleanly, and with low heat — characteristics that satisfy the household needs of Indian women. Staples like curry and rice can simmer for hours. While the meal slowly cooks over an unattended fire, the women of the household can do other chores. Cow chips, unlike firewood, do not scorch as they burn.

It is estimated that the dung used for cooking fuel provides the energy-equivalent of 43 million tons of coal. At current prices, it would cost India an extra 1.5 billion dollars in foreign exchange to replace the dung with coal. And if the 350 million tons of manure that are being

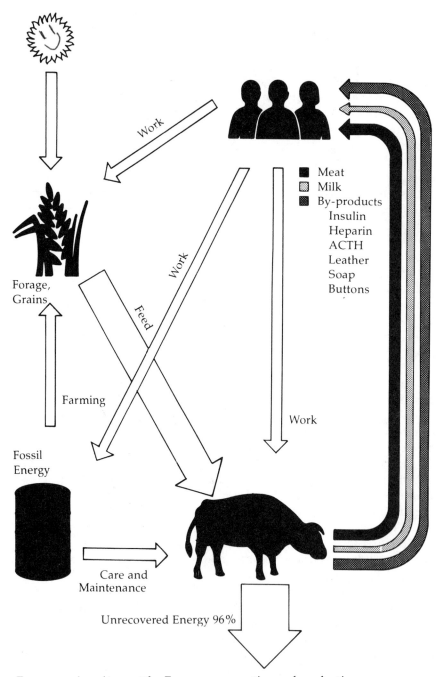

FIGURE I. *American cattle: Energy consumption and production*

214

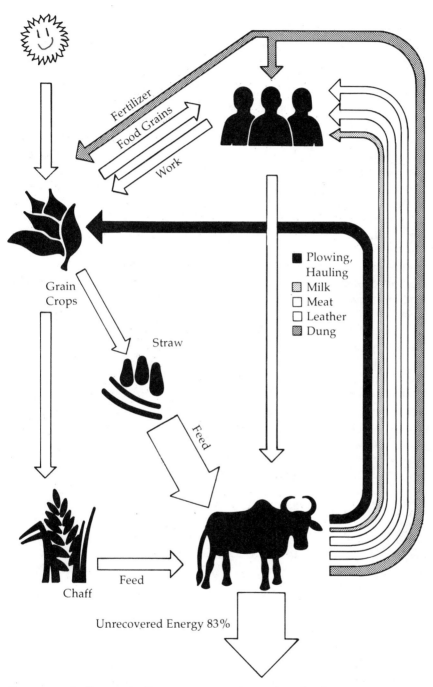

Fertilizer

Food Grains

Work

Grain
Crops

Straw

Feed

■ Plowing,
  Hauling
▨ Milk
☐ Meat
☐ Leather
▨ Dung

Chaff

Feed

Unrecovered Energy 83%

FIGURE II. *Indian cattle: Energy consumption and production*

used as fertilizer were replaced with commercial fertilizers, the expense would be even greater. Roger Revelle of the University of California at San Diego has calculated that 89 percent of the energy used in Indian agriculture (the equivalent of about 140 million tons of coal) is provided by local sources. Even if foreign loans were to provide the money, the capital outlay necessary to replace the Indian cow with tractors and fertilizers for the fields, coal for the fires, and transportation for the family would probably warp international financial institutions for years.

Instead of asking the Indians to learn from the American model of industrial agriculture, American farmers might learn energy conservation from the Indians. Every step in an energy cycle results in a loss of energy to the system. Like a pendulum that slows a bit with each swing, each transfer of energy from sun to plants, plants to animals, and animals to human beings involves energy losses. Some systems are more efficient than others; they provide a higher percentage of the energy inputs in a final, useful form. Seventeen percent of all energy zebus consume is returned in the form of milk, traction and dung. American cattle raised on Western range land return only 4 percent of the energy they consume.

But the American system is improving. Based on techniques pioneered by Indian scientists, at least one commercial firm in the United States is reported to be building plants that will turn manure from cattle feedlots into combustible gas. When organic matter is broken down by anaerobic bacteria, methane gas and carbon dioxide are produced. After the methane is cleansed of the carbon dioxide, it is available for the same purposes as natural gas — cooking, heating, electricity generation. The company constructing the biogasification plant plans to sell its product to a gas-supply company, to be piped through the existing distribution system. Schemes similar to this one could make cattle ranches almost independent of utility and gasoline companies, for methane can be used to run trucks, tractors, and cars as well as to supply heat and electricity. The relative energy self-sufficiency that the Indian peasant has achieved is a goal American farmers and industry are now striving for.

Studies like Odend'hal's understate the efficiency of the Indian cow, because dead cows are used for purposes that Hindus prefer not to acknowledge. When a cow dies, an Untouchable, a member of one of the lowest ranking castes in India, is summoned to haul away the carcass. Higher castes consider the body of the dead cow polluting; if they do handle it, they must go through a rite of purification.

Untouchables first skin the dead animal and either tan the skin themselves or sell it to a leather factory. In the privacy of their homes, contrary to the teachings of Hinduism, untouchable castes cook the meat and eat it. Indians of all castes rarely acknowledge the existence of these practices to non-Hindus, but more are aware that beefeating takes place. The prohibition against beefeating restricts consumption by the higher castes and helps distribute animal protein to the poorest sectors of the population that otherwise would have no source of these vital nutrients.

Untouchables are not the only Indians who consume beef. Indian Muslims and Christians are under no restriction that forbids them beef, and its consumption is legal in many places. The Indian ban on cow slaughter is state, not national, law and not all states restrict it. In many cities, such as New Delhi, Calcutta, and Bombay, legal slaughter-houses sell beef to retail customers and to the restaurants that serve steak.

If the caloric value of beef and the energy costs involved in the manufacture of synthetic leather were included in the estimates of energy, the calculated efficiency of Indian livestock would rise considerably.

As well as the system works, experts often claim that its efficiency can be further improved. Alan Heston, an economist at the University of Pennsylvania, believes that Indians suffer from an overabundance of cows simply because they refuse to slaughter the excess cattle. India could produce at least the same number of oxen and the same quantities of milk and manure with 30 million fewer cows. Heston calculates that only 40 cows are necessary to maintain a population of 100 bulls and oxen. Since India averages 70 cows for every 100 bullocks, the difference, 30 million cows, is expendable.

What Heston fails to note is that sex ratios among cattle in different regions of India vary tremendously, indicating that adjustments in the cow population do take place. Along the Ganges River, one of the holiest shrines of Hinduism, the ratio drops to 47 cows for every 100 male animals. This ratio reflects the preference for dairy buffalo in the irrigated sectors of the Gangetic Plains. In nearby Pakistan, in contrast, where cow slaughter is permitted, the sex ratio is 60 cows to 100 oxen.

Since the sex ratios among cattle differ greatly from region to region and do not even approximate the balance that would be expected if no females were killed, we can assume that some culling of herds does take place; Indians do adjust their religious restrictions to accommodate ecological realities.

They cannot kill a cow but they can tether an old or unhealthy animal until it has starved to death. They cannot slaughter a calf but they can yoke it with a large wooden triangle so that when it nurses it irritates the mother's udder and gets kicked to death. They cannot ship their animals to the slaughterhouse but they can sell them to Muslims, closing their eyes to the fact that the Muslims will take the cattle to the slaughterhouse.

These violations of the prohibition against cattle slaughter strengthen the premise that cow worship is a vital part of Indian culture. The practice arose to prevent the population from consuming the animal on which Indian agriculture depends. During the first Millenium B.C., the Ganges Valley became one of the most densely populated regions of the world.

Where previously there had been only scattered villages, many towns and cities arose and peasants farmed every available acre of land. Kingsley Davis, a population expert at the University of California at Berkeley, estimates that by 300 B.C. between 50 million and 100 million people were living in India. The forested Ganges Valley became a windswept semidesert and signs of ecological collapse appeared; droughts and floods became commonplace, erosion took away the rich topsoil, farms shrank as population increased, and domesticated animals became harder and harder to maintain.

It is probable that the elimination of meat eating came about in a slow, practical manner. The farmers who decided not to eat their cows, who saved them for procreation to produce oxen, were the ones who survived the natural disasters. Those who ate beef lost the tools with which to farm. Over a period of centuries, more and more farmers probably avoided beef until an unwritten taboo came into existence.

Only later was the practice codified by the priesthood. While Indian peasants were probably aware of the role of cattle in their society, strong sanctions were necessary to protect zebus from a population faced with starvation. To remove temptation, the flesh of cattle became taboo and the cow became sacred.

The sacredness of the cow is not just an ignorant belief that stands in the way of progress. Like all concepts of the sacred and the profane, this one affects the physical world; it defines the relationships that are important for the maintenance of Indian society.

Indians have the sacred cow; we have the "sacred" car and the "sacred" dog. It would not occur to us to propose the elimination of automobiles and dogs from our society without carefully considering the consequences, and we should not propose the elimination of zebu cattle without first understanding their place in the social order of India.

Human society is neither random nor capricious. The regularities of thought and behavior called culture are the principal mechanisms by which we human beings adapt to the world around us. Practices and beliefs can be rational or irrational, but a society that fails to adapt to its environment is doomed to extinction. Only those societies that draw the necessities of life from their surroundings, without destroying those surroundings, inherit the earth. The West has much to learn from the great antiquity of Indian civilization, and the sacred cow is an important part of that lesson.

REVIEW QUESTIONS

1. A friend asks, "Why don't Indians eat the millions of cattle that roam loose over their country?" Based on the information in this article, how would you answer?

2. What are the main uses and products of cattle in India? What is most important about cattle for continued human material welfare?

3. How does Harris explain the rise of cattle protection in India?

4. Clearly Indians need bulls and bullocks to plow, but why can't they limit the number of cows to a level just sufficient for breeding?

5. Some anthropologists argue that the sacredness of Indian cattle evolved as part of the religious system, apart from practical considerations. How would Harris respond to this assertion?

19

Population control: One son is no sons

STANLEY A. FREED and
RUTH S. FREED

*As we have seen in the previous selections on hunting and gathering
and the protection of cattle, humans adapt their cultures to meet
basic material needs. In turn, their societies are shaped by material
choices. In this article, Stanley and Ruth Freed explore the effect of
social structure on population growth in India. Unlike many investi-
gators concerned with population control, the Freeds explore the
question largely in terms of culturally defined choices, not statistics.
They argue that social security is provided by the Indian family and
that it is sons who continue the family. Even educated couples who
are part of the modernized Indian economy will rarely stop having
children until they have at least two sons. The result is a high rate of
population growth and a larger percentage of male to female births.*

Devi and her five children were sitting in their village home in north
India watching "Star Trek" on television. Caught up in the adventure,
the children struggled to understand the English words. Their mother,
meanwhile, was explaining why she was not interested in the government's program of birth control. Noting that her first four children had
been girls, Devi said, "I would have gotten sterilized if I had had sons
instead of daughters in the beginning. My six-year-old son is very
weak physically, which is why I want to have one more son. Girls get
married and leave the village to live with their husbands; they are no
longer your own. A son in the family is necessary."

Originally published as "One Son is No Sons." With permission from *Natural History*,
Vol. 94, No. 1; Copyright the American Museum of Natural History, 1984.

Already endowed with five children and intending to have at least one more, Devi and her husband contribute to making India a demographic giant second only to China. In 1981, India had 684 million inhabitants, about 15 percent of the globe's population. This figure includes 136 million persons added since the census of 1971, an increment larger than the total population of Brazil, which ranks sixth in the world. The current annual increase of about 15 million is more than double the population of New York City. India's population, now estimated at 735 million, will approach one billion by 2001 and may surpass China's soon after 2025.

Devi and her husband are not illiterate, poverty-stricken villagers, often thought to be at the heart of India's problem of massive population growth. Devi finished five years of school, and her husband is a high school graduate with a well-paying clerical job in Delhi and a sizable farm in a nearby village. The family is quite prosperous. What impels people like Devi and her husband to continue to have large families in an era of largely free, easily available contraception is that sons are the only dependable insurance against misfortune, poverty, and the disabilities of old age. The vast majority of Indians have no social security, private pension plans, or annuities; they rely instead on their sons. Few couples are satisfied with just one son, for the rate of infant mortality, while steadily declining, is still high enough to make parents with only one son very anxious. "One eye is no eyes, and one son is no sons," runs a popular saying. People try to have two or three sons, hoping that one of them will survive to care for them in their old age.

While a great deal of modernization has taken place in India since independence in 1947, the basic economic arrangements, values, and family roles, which tend to support the desire for a large family, have been generally stable. Even though India's birthrate has dropped and the use of contraception has mounted, India's average annual rate of population growth increased slightly from the 1960s to the 1970s — from 2.20 percent to 2.23 percent — because of lowered mortality. It is this stubbornly high rate of population growth — three times the estimated rate for the United States in 1981 — that the government of India is fighting to control. As the late Prime Minister Indira Gandhi was fond of saying, India adds an Australia a year to her population.

In 1951, the year of the first Indian census after independence, the size of the population was of sufficient concern to lead to a national program of family planning, but it was presented in terms of maternal and child health care rather than fertility control. Serious efforts to reduce fertility did not begin until the mid-1960s. The endeavor to check population growth was most intense during the political Emergency legally proclaimed by Prime Minister Gandhi on June 25, 1975, after a period of political unrest and demands that she resign. During the 21-month period of the Emergency, which lasted until March 21, 1977, couples were strongly urged — by publicity, plus a combination of cash payments and various disincentive measures — to undergo sterilization. The governmental slogan "Two or three children, enough!" was widely disseminated. Because the program was often perceived as coercive, the ruling Congress Party suffered a temporary electoral defeat. Despite the popular reaction against the excesses of the Emergency, however, the government of India did succeed, much faster than might otherwise have happened, in establishing sterilization as a routine and acceptable option for couples wishing to terminate childbearing.

Today sterilization is the principal contraceptive technique used in India. Because it permanently ends childbearing, parents do not use it until they have all the children they want or think they will need. The present government, concerned with fertility control, extols and publicizes the small family of two or three children. Indian parents think in terms of two sons and one daughter as the ideal "small" family; but in trying for at least two sons they end up with an average of about 4.2 children. In general, the minority of Indian parents who choose to be sterilized do so about two children too late from the government's point of view, and the large majority shun sterilization altogether, wanting to be very sure that they will never be left without at least one son. "To be sterilized is to tempt fate" summarizes a common attitude.

The government would like to achieve a family norm of two children by the turn of the century, at which point India's population would begin to stabilize, reaching a plateau of 1.2 billion by the middle of the twenty-first century. Is this goal realistic? The answer must be sought chiefly in India's villages, where 76 percent of the population lives. At various times during the 25-year period from 1958 to 1983, we have had the opportunity to investigate population growth in a north Indian village we call Shanti Nagar (the name is fictitious). The study is of particular interest because it encompasses the demographic watershed between the time that family planning barely existed and the period when fertility control became a serious governmental concern and sterilization was established as the major contraceptive technique. Although one should be cautious about drawing conclusions from a single village, the study of a small community such as Shanti Nagar provides an appreciation of the motives and attitudes that underlie people's everyday decisions about childbearing, family size, and sterilization.

Shanti Nagar is typical of the region that includes the northern states of Punjab, Haryana, western Uttar Pradesh, and the Union Territory of Delhi. From the 1950s to the 1980s, Shanti Nagar has undergone an economic revolution. The village has acquired electricity, brick houses have replaced mud houses, and streets have been paved. In agriculture, bullock power and hand labor have largely given way to machinery. Paved roads and increased bus service make it easier to commute to urban areas, where many men have jobs. Radios are now commonplace, there are some TV sets, and newspapers are delivered daily. The educational level has risen dramatically for both men and women. The village has become more prosperous and better informed about government programs.

Although one would expect that the modernization of education, communications, and the economy would significantly alter family life, the village family has generally maintained its traditional form and functions. A single Indian family may include more people than just a couple and their children: often a family is composed of a couple, their married son (or sons), and his wife and children. Sometimes two or more married brothers live as members of the same family, the eldest brother acting as family head. Families are relatively large by American standards, consisting on average of more than seven members. Men are young when they marry, and women are very young, often beginning their married lives shortly after first menstruation. Men continue to live at their parental home after marriage and bring their brides to live with them. Women are expected to begin childbearing as soon as possible, for both the economic and political strength of a family and a woman's own status depend on the number of sons. "Marriage is not for pleasure," say the villagers. "It is the duty of a wife to have children."

Because attitudes in the 1950s were so strongly in favor of having a goodly number of children, we would have given family planning and, particularly, sterilization little chance of making significant headway. Therefore, when we returned to Shanti Nagar in 1978 after an absence of twenty years, we were startled to hear so many people discussing their own sterilizations or those of their neighbors. We eventually found that there were 68 sterilizations involving both males and females, tantamount to 26 percent of the women of childbearing age (15 to 45 years) at the time. By late 1983, there were 93 sterilized individuals.

Sterilization has run an uneven course in Shanti Nagar. It was accepted slowly at first. From 1968 to 1974, 3.4 individuals on the average were sterilized annually. Then came the twenty-one months of the Emergency, which began in 1975, and the average number of persons who underwent sterilization jumped to about 20 per year. After the Emergency, the figure returned almost to the pre-Emergency norm; from 1977 to late 1983, 4.7 persons were sterilized per year. The big jump in sterilizations during the Emergency was due to the strong campaign mounted by the government. Governmental pressure was especially effective with men holding government jobs. Most of the men sterilized during the Emergency were in government service.

When the Emergency ended, there was a noteworthy change in the proportion of men to women undergoing sterilization. Prior to 1977, 53 percent of the operations were performed on men; for the period from 1977 to late 1983, this figure had fallen to 15 percent. The shift is probably related to the introduction of the surgical technique of laparoscopy, which has made female sterilization easier. The government also suggested a somewhat higher payment to women undergoing sterilization, compared with the incentive to men. Moreover, villagers may not have been entirely convinced that vasectomy was foolproof. If a vasectomy is done improperly, a pregnancy can follow, exposing the unfortunate woman to suspicion of adultery and to village gossip and scorn. Why take that chance when a tubectomy will avoid the problem?

Most of those in Shanti Nagar who discussed reasons for not being sterilized or for postponing the operation cited an insufficient number of sons. On the other hand, the expense of raising children was overwhelmingly the main reason that villagers gave for undergoing sterilization. Couples also frequently cited the governmental sterilization campaign, principally its coercive aspects, as a motive for being sterilized, and a few people mentioned that sterilization was seen as the solution to specific health problems of women.

The emphasis on economic reasons focuses attention on the changing value of child labor. In rural India, where children participate on the family farm from an early age, the value of their labor remains considerable. However, the modernization of agriculture has reduced the need for child labor. At the same time, there has been an increase in employment opportunities that require an educational qualification. Many parents aspire to better jobs for their children and prefer fewer, more educated children to more numerous, uneducated offspring. Few can afford to educate all the children that they can possibly have.

The findings from Shanti Nagar suggest that a significant drop in the growth rate of the population cannot be expected in the near term. The parents in Shanti Nagar who chose sterilization did so generally after having four or five living children, and it must be borne in mind that most couples have not been sterilized. Overall, completed families in the 1970s were larger than those of the 1950s (averaging 5.2 versus 5.0 living children). Even the women who were sterilized (or whose husbands were sterilized) in 1978 had almost as many living childen (an average of 4.9) as had the women with completed families in 1958, almost all of whom used no contraception.

On the other hand, persons who anticipate at least a slight

downturn in the rate of population growth can find some grounds for optimism in the statistics from Shanti Nagar. In 1978, sterilized mothers had fewer living children than nonsterilized mothers who had completed their childbearing (4.9 versus 5.5 on the average). Moreover, the effect of sterilization is becoming more pronounced: from the end of the Emergency in 1977 until late in 1983, couples underwent sterilization at a younger age and had fewer children than before 1977. But they still averaged 4.3 living children, enough to produce a rather high rate of population growth.

Sterilized couples had, on the average, about three sons and two daughters, an imbalance that appears to be increasing. From 1977 to 1983, sterilized couples averaged twice as many sons as daughters. This sexual disparity is no accident: couples aim for between two and three sons before undergoing sterilization, but almost no one desperately wants more than one daughter. It is important to note that sterilization by itself cannot influence the sex of children. However, if either by random chance or active intervention a couple has more sons than daughters, a sterilization operation makes the situation permanent, provided that there are no untimely deaths of sons. As is common in northern India, Shanti Nagar has slightly more males than females, a difference usually explained by the preference for sons and the suspected mistreatment of female children. It is also possible that female infants are undernumerated in censuses. One explanation does not preclude the other, and both may be involved.

From an American and Western European perspective, one might assume that population control could be achieved in India by instituting a system of social security, such as is found in the United States, to reduce the need for so many sons and make the two-child family possible for many couples. In developed countries, much of the economic support and care of the aged comes from outside the family; children may assume minor financial and custodial roles or none at all. This feature of Western society is not of recent origin: it appeared in England, for example, several centuries before the Industrial Revolution, the source of sustenance shifting through the centuries from the manor and the guild to the parish and to the state. But India is a different world, where the care and support of the aged have always been a family affair. Indians do not believe that the government or anyone but their sons will take care of them when they are old. Their experience is that governments and policies change too frequently to be trustworthy in the long term. A family with fewer than two sons makes no sense to most Indians. This attitude would persist even if the resources to institute a system of social security could be found.

Many Western analysts also assume that economic development

to improve the standard of living will solve the problem of population growth in India. However, there is no evidence from Shanti Nagar or elsewhere in India that motivation to limit family size to two or three children develops after a certain economic status has been attained. Even the effect of the education of women — perhaps the most promising of the socioeconomic factors thought to lower fertility — is somewhat ambiguous in India and, in any case, has little impact until women achieve the college level and begin to work outside the home. In all probability, it will be a long time before a significant proportion of rural Indian females are sent to college.

Although sterilization is increasing in India and the birthrate has been declining for some time, these developments do not presage an imminent solution to the problem of India's population growth. For our part, we would be inclined to keep a sharp eye on the average size of completed families, for this statistic will provide greater insight into India's demographic future than the drop of a few points in the birthrate. If parity at completed childbearing shows signs of stabilizing at between four and five children, India will continue to live up to its reputation as a demographic juggernaut. In that case, India's currently voluntary program of family planning might have to be replaced by more Draconian measures, like those instituted in China. The Indian government fell from power when it previously tried to introduce a stringent program of fertility control. The challenge is to try to control population growth in a democracy where families of four or more children are, for very good reasons, considered necessary.

REVIEW QUESTIONS

1. According to the Freeds, how has the annual rate of population growth in India changed from the 1950s to the 1970s?

2. What is the most important form of birth control in India? How has it been used from the 1950s to the present?

3. What motivates Indians to stop having children? What is the average family size?

4. According to the Freeds, why won't a state-run social security system, increased education, and economic development lower the Indian family size in the near future?

5. Using this article as an example, what special kinds of data can anthropologists bring to bear on such large problems as birth control?

VII

Economic systems

People everywhere experience wants that can be satisfied only by the acquisition and use of material goods and the services of others. To meet such wants, humans rely on an aspect of their cultural inventory, the *economic system*, which we will define as the provision of goods and services to meet biological and social wants.

The meaning of the term *want* can be confusing. It can refer to what humans *need* for their survival. We must eat, drink, maintain a constant body temperature, defend ourselves, and deal with injury and illness. The economic system meets these needs by providing food, water, clothing, shelter, weapons, medicines, and the cooperative services of others.

But material goods serve more than just our survival needs: they meet our culturally defined *wants* as well. We need clothes to stay warm, but we want garments of a particular style, cut, and fabric to signal our status, rank, or anything else we wish to socially communicate. We need food to sustain life, but we want particular foods prepared in special ways to fill our aesthetic and social desires. Services and goods may also be exchanged to strengthen ties between people or groups. Birthday

227

presents may not always meet physical needs, but they clearly function to strengthen the ties between the parties to the exchange.

Part of the economic system is concerned with *production*, which means rendering material items useful and available for human consumption. Production systems must designate ways to allocate resources. The *allocation of resources* refers to the cultural rules people use to assign rights to ownership and use of resources. Production systems must also include technologies. Americans usually associate technology with the tools and machines used for manufacturing, rather than with the knowledge for doing it. But many anthropologists link the concept directly to culture. Here we will define *technology* as the cultural knowledge for making and using tools and extracting and refining raw materials.

Production systems also include a *division of labor*, which refers to the rules that govern the assignment of jobs to people. In hunting and gathering societies, labor is most often divided along the lines of gender, and sometimes age. In these societies, almost everyone knows how to produce, use, and collect necessary material goods. In industrial society, however, jobs are highly specialized and labor is divided, at least ideally, on the basis of skill and experience. It is rare that we know how to do someone else's job in our complex society.

The *unit of production*, meaning the persons or groups responsible for producing goods, follows a pattern similar to the way labor is divided in various societies. Among hunter-gatherers, there is little specialization; individuals, families, groups of friends, or sometimes bands form the units of production. But in our own complex society, we are surrounded by groups specially organized to manufacture, transport, and sell goods.

Another part of the economic system is *distribution*. There are three basic modes of distribution: market exchange, reciprocal exchange, and redistribution.

We are most conscious of market exchange because it lies at the heart of our capitalist system. *Market exchange* is the transfer of goods and services based on price, supply, and demand. Every time we enter a store and pay for something, we engage in market exchange. The price of an item may change with the supply. For example, a discount store may lower the price of a television set because it has too many of the appliances on hand. Price may go up, however, if everyone wants the sets when there are few to sell. Money is often used in market systems; it enables people to exchange a large variety of items easily. Barter involves the trading of goods, not money, but it, too, is a form of market exchange because the number of items exchanged can also vary with supply and demand. Market exchange appears in human history when societies become larger and more complex. It is well suited for exchange between strangers who make up these larger groups.

Although we are not so aware of it, we also engage in reciprocal exchange. *Reciprocal exchange* involves the transfer of goods and services between two people or groups based on role obligations. Birthday and holiday gift giving is a fine example of reciprocity. On these occasions we exchange goods not because we necessarily need or want them, but because we are expected to do so as part of our status and role. Parents should give gifts to their children, for example; children should reciprocate. If we fail our reciprocal obligations, we signal an unwillingness to continue the relationship. Small, simply organized societies, such as the !Kung described in the last section, base their exchange systems on reciprocity. Complex ones like ours, although largely organized around the market or redistribution, still manifest reciprocity between kin and close friends.

Finally, there is *redistribution,* the transfer of goods and services between a central collecting source and a group of individuals. Like reciprocity, redistribution is based on role obligation. Taxes typify this sort of exchange in the United States. We must pay our taxes because we are citizens, not because we are buying something. We receive goods and services back — education, transportation, roads, defense — but not necessarily in proportion to the amount we contribute. Redistribution may be the predominant mode of exchange in socialist societies.

The selections included in this section illustrate several of the concepts we have just discussed. Paul Bohannan describes a traditional Tiv economy characterized by three spheres of exchange: one that includes the market exchange of subsistence goods; a second involving the reciprocal exchange of prestige goods; and a third consisting of women exchanged between families at marriage. Elliot Liebow's article deals with the division of labor, specifically with the meaning of jobs to poor black men. The last selection, by Bernard Nietschmann, details the impact of the international market system on a local subsistence economy. Motivated by money, Miskito Indians are now dependent on outsiders for food and find themselves unable to meet their traditional reciprocal obligations.

KEY TERMS

economic system	unit of production
production	distribution
allocation of resources	market exchange
technology	reciprocal exchange
division of labor	redistribution

20

The impact of money on an African subsistence economy

PAUL J. BOHANNAN

In this article Paul Bohannan describes the early colonial economy of the Tiv of Nigeria and shows that it contained three spheres of exchange. These spheres — subsistence, prestige, and women in marriage — were separated by the rule that goods from one could not be used to purchase goods in another without loss of prestige to one party in the exchange. When general-purpose money was introduced from the West, it became possible to equate the values of each sphere, and radical change took place. The author discusses in detail the changes resulting from the introduction of money.

It has often been claimed that money was to be found in much of the African continent before the impact of the European world and the extension of trade made coinage general. When we examine these claims, however, they tend to evaporate or to emerge as tricks of definition. It is an astounding fact that economists have, for decades, been assigning three or four qualities to money when they discuss it with reference to our own society or to those of the medieval and modern world, yet the moment they have gone to ancient history or to the societies and economies studied by anthropologists they have sought the "real" nature of money by allowing only one of these defining characteristics to dominate their definitions.

All economists learned as students that money serves at least

From "The Impact of Money on an African Subsistence Economy," *The Journal of Economic History* 19 (December 1959): 491–503. Reprinted by permission of the publisher and the author. Some footnotes, the bibliographic citations, and the bibliography are omitted.

three purposes. It is a means of exchange, it is a mode of payment, it is a standard of value. Depending on the vintage and persuasion of the author of the book one consults, one may find another money use — storage of wealth. In newer books, money is defined as merely the means of unitizing purchasing power, yet behind that definition still lie the standard, the payment, and the exchange uses of money.

It is interesting that on the fairly rare occasions that economists discuss primitive money at all — or at least when they discuss it with any empirical referent — they have discarded one or more of the money uses in framing their definitions. Paul Einzig,[1] to take one example from many, first makes a plea for "elastic definitions," and goes on to point out that different economists have utilized different criteria in their definitions; he then falls into the trap he has been exposing: he excoriates Menger for utilizing only the "medium of exchange" criterion and then himself omits it, utilizing only the standard and payment criteria, thus taking sides in an argument in which there was no real issue.

The answer to these difficulties should be apparent. If we take no more than the three major money uses — payment, standard, and means of exchange — we will find that in many primitive societies as well as some of the ancient empires, one object may serve one money use while quite another object serves another money use. In order to deal with this situation, and to avoid the trap of choosing one of these uses to define "real" money, Karl Polanyi[2] and his associates have labeled as "general-purpose money" any item which serves all three of these primary money uses, while an item which serves only one or two is "special-purpose money." With this distinction in mind, we can see that special-purpose money was very common in pre-contact Africa, but that general-purpose money was rare.

This paper is a brief analysis of the impact of general-purpose money and increase in trade in an African economy which had known only local trade and had used only special-purpose money.

The Tiv are a people, still largely pagan, who live in the Benue Valley in Central Nigeria, among whom I had the good fortune to live and work for well over two years. They are prosperous subsistence farmers and have a highly developed indigenous market in which they exchanged their produce and handicrafts, and through which they car-

---

[1]Paul Einzig, *Primitive Money in Its Ethnological, Historical and Economic Aspects* (London: Eyre and Spottiswoode, 1949), pp. 319–26.

[2]Karl Polanyi, "The Economy as Instituted Process," in Karl Polanyi, Conrad M. Arensberg, and Harry W. Pearson, eds., *Trade and Market in the Early Empires* (Glencoe, Ill.: The Free Press and The Falcon's Wing Press, 1957), pp. 264–66.

ried on local trade. The most distinctive feature about the economy of the Tiv — and it is a feature they share with many, perhaps most, of the pre-monetary peoples — is what can be called a multi-centric economy. Briefly, a multi-centric economy is an economy in which a society's exchangeable goods fall into two or more mutually exclusive spheres, each marked by different institutionalization and different moral values. In some multi-centric economies these spheres remain distinct, though in most there are more or less institutionalized means of coverting wealth from one into wealth in another.

Indigenously there were three spheres in the multi-centric economy of the Tiv. The first of these spheres is that associated with subsistence, which the Tiv called *yiagh*. The commodities in it include all locally produced foodstuffs: the staple yams and cereals, plus all the condiments, vegetable side-dishes, and seasonings, as well as small livestock — chickens, goats, and sheep. It also includes household utensils (mortars, grindstones, calabashes, baskets, and pots), some tools (particularly those used in agriculture), and raw materials for producing any items in the category.

Within this sphere, goods are distributed either by gift giving or through marketing. Traditionally, there was no money of any sort in this sphere — all goods changed hands by barter. There was a highly developed market organization at which people exchanged their produce for their requirements, and in which today traders buy produce in cheap markets and transport it to sell in dearer markets. The morality of this sphere of the economy is the morality of the free and uncontrolled market.

The second sphere of the Tiv economy is one which is in no way associated with markets. The category of goods within this sphere is slaves, cattle, ritual "offices" purchased from the Jukun, that type of large white cloth known as *tugudu*, medicines and magic, and metal rods. One is still entitled to use the present tense in this case, for ideally the category still exists in spite of the fact that metal rods are today very rare, that slavery has been abolished, that European "offices" have replaced Jukun offices and cannot be bought, and that much European medicine has been accepted. Tiv still quote prices of slaves in cows and brass rods, and of cattle in brass rods and *tugudu* cloth. The price of magical rites, as it has been described in the literature, was in terms of *tugudu* cloth or brass rods (though payment might be made in other items); payment for Jukun titles was in cows and slaves, *tugudu* cloths and metal rods.[3]

---

[3]B. Akiga Sai, *Akiga's Story* (London: International Institute of African Languages and Cultures, 1939), p. 382 and passim.

None of these goods ever entered the market as it was institution-alized in Tivland, even though it might be possible for an economist to find the principle of supply and demand at work in the exchanges which characterized it. The actual shifts of goods took place at ceremonies, at more or less ritualized wealth displays, and on occasions when "doctors" performed rites and prescribed medicines. Tiv refer to the items and the activities within this sphere by the word *shagba*, which can be roughly translated as prestige.

Within the prestige sphere there was one item which took on all of the money uses and hence can be called a general-purpose currency, though it must be remembered that it was of only a *very limited range*. Brass rods were used as means of exchange *within the sphere*; they also served as a standard of value within it (though not the only one), and as a means of payment. However, this sphere of the economy was tightly sealed off from the subsistence goods and its market. After European contact, brass rods occasionally entered the market, but they did so only as means of payment, not as medium of exchange or as standard of valuation. Because of the complex institutionalization and morality, no one ever sold a slave for food; no one, save in the depths of extremity, ever paid brass rods for domestic goods.

The supreme and unique sphere of exchangeable values for the Tiv contains a single item: rights in human beings other than slaves, particularly rights in women. Even twenty-five years after official abolition of exchange marriage, it is the category of exchange in which Tiv are emotionally most entangled. All exchanges within this category are exchanges of rights in human beings, usually dependent women and children. Its value is expressed in terms of kinship and marriage.

Tiv marriage is an extremely complex subject. Again, economists might find supply and demand principles at work, but Tiv adamantly separate marriage and market. Before the coming of the Europeans all "real" marriages were exchange marriages. In its simplest form, an exchange marriage involves two men exchanging sisters. Actually, this simple form seldom or never occurred. In order for every man to have a ward (*ingol*) to exchange for a wife, small localized agnatic lineages formed ward-sharing groups ("those who eat one Ingol" — *mbaye ingol i mom*). There was an initial "exchange" — or at least, distribution — of wards among the men of this group, so that each man became the guardian (*tien*) of one or more wards. The guardian, then, saw to the marriage of his ward, exchanging her with outsiders for another woman (her "partner" or *ikyar*) who becomes the bride of the guardian or one of his close agnatic kinsmen, or — in some situations — becomes a ward in the ward-sharing group and is exchanged for yet another woman who becomes a wife.

Tiv are, however, extremely practical and sensible people, and they know that successful marriages cannot be made if women are not consulted and if they are not happy. Elopements occurred, and sometimes a woman in exchange was not forthcoming. Therefore, a debt existed from the ward-sharing group of the husband to that of the guardian.

These debts sometimes lagged two or even three generations behind actual exchanges. The simplest way of paying them off was for the eldest daughter of the marriage to return to the ward-sharing group of her mother, as ward, thus, cancelling the debt.

Because of its many impracticalities, the system had to be buttressed in several ways in order to work: one way was a provision for "earnest" during the time of the lag, another was to recognize other types of marriage as binding to limited extents. These two elements are somewhat confused with one another, because of the fact that right up until the abolition of exchange marriage in 1927, the inclination was always to treat all non-exchange marriages as if they were "lags" in the completion of exchange marriages.

When lags in exchange occurred, they were usually filled with "earnests" of brass rods, or occasionally, it would seem, of cattle. The brass rods or cattle in such situations were *never* exchange equivalents (*ishe*) for the woman. The only "price" of one woman is another woman.

Although Tiv decline to grant it antiquity, another type of marriage occurred at the time Europeans first met them — it was called "accumulating a woman/wife" (*kem kwase*). It is difficult to tell today just exactly what it consisted in because the terminology of this union has been adapted to describe the bridewealth marriage that was declared by an administrative fiat of 1927 to be the only legal form.

Kem marriage consisted in acquisition of sexual, domestic and economic rights in a woman — but not the rights to filiate her children to the social group of the husband. Put in another way, in exchange marriage, both rights *in genetricem* (rights to filiate a woman's children) and rights *in uxorem* (sexual, domestic and economic rights in a woman) automatically were acquired by husbands and their lineages. In *kem* marriage, only rights *in uxorem* were acquired. In order to affiliate the *kem* wife's children, additional payments had to be made to the woman's guardians. These payments were for the children, not for the rights *in genetricem* in their mother, which could be acquired only by exchange of equivalent rights in another woman. *Kem* payments were paid in brass rods. However, rights in women had no equivalent or "price" in brass rods or in any other item — save, of course, identical rights in another woman. *Kem* marriage was similar to but showed important differences from bridewealth marriage as it is known in South and East Africa. There rights in women and rights in cattle form a single economic sphere, and could be exchanged directly for one another. Among Tiv, however, conveyance of rights in women necessarily involved direct exchange of another woman. The Tiv custom that approached bridewealth was not an exchange of equivalents, but payment in a medium that was specifically not equivalent.

Thus, within the sphere of exchange marriage there was no item that fulfilled any of the uses of money; when second-best types of marriage were made, payment was in an item which was specifically not used as a standard of value.

That Tiv do conceptualize exchange articles as belonging to different categories, and that they rank the categories on a moral basis, and that most but not all exchanges are limited to one sphere, gives rise to the fact that two different kinds of exchanges may be recognized: exchange of items contained within a single category, and exchanges of items belonging to different categories. For Tiv, these two different types of exchange are marked by separate and distinct moral attitudes.

To maintain this distinction between the two types of exchanges which Tiv mark by different behavior and different values, I shall use separate words. I shall call those exchanges of items within a single category "conveyances" and those exchanges of items from one category to another "conversions." Roughly, conveyances are morally neutral; conversions have a strong moral quality in their rationalization.

Exchanges within a category—particularly that of subsistence, the only one intact today—excite no moral judgments. Exchanges between categories, however, do excite a moral reaction: the man who exchanges lower category goods for higher category goods does not brag about his market luck but about his "strong heart" and his success in life. The man who exchanges high category goods for lower rationalizes his action in terms of high-valued motivation (most often the needs of his kinsmen).

The two institutions most intimately connected with conveyance are markets and marriage. Conveyance in the prestige sphere seems (to the latter-day investigator, at least) to have been less highly institutionalized. It centered on slave dealing, on curing, and on the acquisition of status.

Conversion is a much more complex matter. Conversion depends on the fact that some items of every sphere could, on certain occasions, be used in exchanges in which the return was *not* considered equivalent (*ishe*). Obviously, given the moral ranking of the spheres, such a situation leaves one party to the exchange in a good position, and the other in a bad one. Tiv says that it is "good" to trade food for brass rods, but that it is "bad" to trade brass rods for food, that it is good to trade your cows or brass rods for a wife, but very bad to trade your marriage ward for cows or brass rods.

Seen from the individual's point of view, it is profitable and possible to invest one's wealth if one converts it into a morally superior category: to convert subsistence wealth into prestige wealth and both into women is the aim of the economic endeavor of individual Tiv. To put it into economists' terms: conversion is the ultimate type of maximization.

We have already examined the marriage system by which a man can convert his brass rods to a wife: he could get a *kem* wife and *kem* her children as they were born. Her daughters, then, could be used as wards in his exchange marriages. It is the desire of every Tiv to "acquire a woman" (*ngoho kwase*) either as wife or ward in some way other than sharing in the ward-sharing group. A wife whom one acquires in any other way is not the concern of one's marriage-ward sharing group because the woman or other property exchanged for her did not belong to the marriage-ward group. The daughters of such a wife are not divided among the members of a man's marriage-ward group, but only among his sons. Such a wife is not only indicative of a man's ability and success financially and personally, but rights in her are the only form of property which is not ethically subject to the demands of his kinsmen.

Conversion from the prestige sphere to the kinship sphere was, thus, fairly common; it consisted in all the forms of marriage save exchange marriage, usually in terms of brass rods.

Conversion from the subsistence sphere to the prestige sphere was also usually in terms of metal rods. They, on occasion, entered the market place as payment. If the owner of the brass rods required an unusually large amount of staples to give a feast, making too heavy a drain on his wives' food supplies, he might buy it with brass rods.

However, brass rods could not possibly have been a general currency. They were not divisible. One could not receive "change" from a brass rod. Moreover, a single rod was worth much more than the usual market purchases for any given day of most Tiv subsistence traders. Although it might be possible to buy chickens with brass rods, one would have to have bought a very large quantity of yams to equal one rod, and to buy an item like pepper with rods would be laughable.

Brass rods, thus, overlapped from the prestige to the subsistence sphere on some occasions, but only on special occasions and for large purchases.

Not only is conversion possible, but it is encouraged — it is, in fact, the behavior which proves a man's worth. Tiv are scornful of a man who is merely rich in subsistence goods (or, today, in money). If, having adequate subsistence, he does not seek prestige in accordance with the old counters, or if he does not strive for more wives, and hence more children, the fault must be personal inadequacy. They also note that they all try to keep a man from making conversions; jealous kinsmen of a rich man will bewitch him and his people by fetishes, in order to make him expend his wealth on sacrifices to repair the fetishes, thus maintaining economic equality. However, once a conversion has been made, demands of kinsmen are not effective — at least, they take a new form.

Therefore, the man who successfully converts his wealth into higher categories is successful — he has a "strong heart." He is both feared and respected.

In this entire process, metal rods hold a pivotal position, and it is not surprising that early administrators considered them money. Originally imported from Europe, they were used as "currency" in some parts of southern Nigeria in the slave trade. They are dowels about a quarter of an inch in diameter and some three feet long; they can be made into jewelry, and were used as a source of metal for castings.

Whatever their use elsewhere, brass rods in Tivland had some but not all of the attributes of money. Within the prestige sphere, they were used as a standard of equivalence, and they were a medium of exchange; they were also a mode for storage of wealth, and were used as payment. In short, brass rods were a general-purpose currency *within the prestige sphere.* However, outside of the prestige sphere — markets and marriage were the most active institutions of exchange outside it — brass rods fulfilled only one of these functions of money: payment. We have examined in detail the reasons why equivalency could not exist between brass rods and rights in women, between brass rods and food.

We have, thus, in Tivland, a multi-centric economy of three spheres, and we have a sort of money which was general-purpose money within the limited range of the prestige sphere, and a special-purpose money in the special transactions in which the other spheres overlapped it.

The next question is: what happened to this multi-centric economy and to the morality accompanying it when it felt the impact of the expanding European economy in the nineteenth and early twentieth centuries, and when an all-purpose money of very much greater range was introduced?

The Western impact is not, of course, limited to economic institutions. Administrative organizations, missions and others have been as effective instruments of change as any other.

One of the most startling innovations of the British administration was a general peace. Before the arrival of the British, one did not venture far beyond the area of one's kinsmen or special friends. To do so was to court death or enslavement.

With government police systems and safety, road-building was also begun. Moving about the country has been made both safe and comparatively easy. Peace and the new road network led to both increased trade and a greater number of markets.

Not only has the internal marketing system been perturbed by the introduction of alien institutions, but the economic institutions of the Tiv have in fact been put into touch with world economy. Northern Nigeria, like much of the rest of the colonial world, was originally taken over by trading companies with governing powers. The close linkage of government and trade was evident when taxation was introduced into Tivland. Tax was originally paid in produce, which was transported and sold through Hausa traders, who were government contractors. A few years later, coinage was introduced; taxes were demanded in that medium. It became necessary for Tiv to go into trade or to make their own contract with foreign traders in order to get cash. The trading companies, which had had "canteens" on the Benue for some decades, were quick to cooperate with the government in introducing a "cash crop" which could be bought by the traders in return for cash to pay taxes, and incidentally to buy imported goods. The crop which proved best adapted for this purpose in Tivland was beniseed (*sesamum indicum*,) a crop Tiv already grew in small quantities. Acreage need only be increased and facilities for sale established.

There is still another way in which Tiv economy is linked, through the trading companies, to the economy of the outside world. Not only do the companies buy their cash crops, they also "stake" African traders with imported goods. There is, on the part both of the companies and the government, a desire to build up "native entrepreneurial classes." Imported cloth, enamelware, and ironmongery are generally sold through a network of dependent African traders. Thus, African traders are linked to the companies, and hence into international trade.

Probably no single factor has been so important, however, as the introduction of all-purpose money. Neither introduction of cash crops and taxes nor extended trading has affected the basic congruence between Tiv ideas and their institutionalization to the same extent as has money. With the introduction of money the indigenous ideas of maximization — that is, conversion of all forms of wealth into women and children — no longer leads to the result it once did.

General-purpose money provides a common denominator among all the spheres, thus making the commodities within each expressible in terms of a single standard and hence immediately exchangeable. This new money is misunderstood by Tiv. They use it as a standard of value in the subsistence category, even when — as is often the case — the exchange is direct barter. They use it as a means of payment of bridewealth under the new system, but still refuse to admit that a woman has a "price" or can be valued in the same terms as food. At the same time, it has become something formerly lacking in all save the prestige sphere of Tiv economy — a means of exchange. Tiv have tried to categorize money with the other new imported goods and place them all in a fourth economic sphere, to be ranked morally below subsistence. They have, of course, not been successful in so doing.

What in fact happened was that general-purpose money was introduced to Tivland, where formerly only special-purpose money had been known.

It is in the nature of a general-purpose money that it standardizes the exchangeability value of every item to a common scale. It is precisely this function which brass rods, a "limited-purpose money" in the old system, did not perform. As we have seen, brass rods were used as a standard in some situations of conveyance in the intermediate or "prestige" category. They were also used as a means of payment (but specifically not as a standard) in some instances of conversion.

In this situation, the early Administrative officers interpreted brass rods as "money," by which they meant a general-purpose money. It became a fairly easy process, in their view, to establish by fiat an exchange rate between brass rods and a new coinage, "withdraw" the rods, and hence "replace" one currency with another. The actual effect, as we have seen, was to introduce a general-purpose currency in place of a limited-purpose money. Today all conversions and most conveyances are made in terms of coinage. Yet Tiv constantly express their distrust of money. This fact, and another — that a single means of exchange has entered all the economic spheres — has broken down the major distinctions among the spheres. Money has created in Tivland a uni-centric economy. Not only is the money a general-purpose money, but it applies to the full range of exchangeable goods.

Thus, when semi-professional traders, using money, began trading in the foodstuffs marketed by women and formerly solely the province of women, the range of the market was very greatly increased and hence the price in Tiv markets is determined by supply and demand far distant from the local producer and consumer. Tiv react to this situation by saying that foreign traders "spoil" their markets. The overlap of marketing and men's long-distance trade in staples also results in truckload after truckload of foodstuffs exported from major Tiv markets every day they meet. Tiv say that food is less plentiful today than it was in the past, though more land is being farmed. Tiv elders deplore this situation and know what is happening, but they do not know just where to fix the blame. In attempts to do something about it, they sometimes announce that no women are to sell any food at all. But when their wives disobey them men do not really feel that they were wrong to have done so. Tiv sometimes discriminate against non-Tiv traders in attempts to stop export of food. In their condemnation of the situation which is depriving them of their food faster than they are able to increase production, Tiv elders always curse money itself. It is money which, as the instrument for selling one's life subsistence, is responsible for the worsened situation — money and the Europeans who brought it.

Of even greater concern to Tiv is the influence money has had on marriage institutions. Today every women's guardian, in accepting money as bridewealth, feels that he is converting down. Although attempts are made to spend money which is received in bridewealth to acquire brides for one's self and one's sons, it is in the nature of money, Tiv insist, that it is most difficult to accomplish. The good man still spends his bridewealth receipts for brides — but good men are not so numerous as would be desirable. Tiv deplore the fact that they are required to "sell" (te) their daughters and "buy" (yam) wives. There is no dignity in it since the possibility of making a bridewealth marriage into an exchange marriage has been removed.

With money, thus, the institutionalization of Tiv economy has become uni-centric, even though Tiv still see it with multi-centric values. The single sphere takes many of its characteristics from the market, so that the new situation can be considered a spread of the market. But throughout these changes in institutionalization, the basic Tiv value of maximization — converting one's wealth into the highest category, women and children — has remained. And in this discrepancy between values and institutions, Tiv have come upon what is to them a paradox, for all that Westerners understand it and are familiar with it. Today it is easy to sell subsistence goods for money to buy prestige articles and women, thereby aggrandizing oneself at a rapid rate. The food so sold is exported, decreasing the amount of subsistence goods available for consumption. On the other hand, the number of women is limited. The result is that bridewealth gets higher: rights in women have entered the market, and since the supply is fixed, the price of women has become inflated.

The frame of reference given me by the organizer of this symposium asked for comments on the effects of increased monetization on trade, on the distribution of wealth and indebtedness. To sum up the situation in these terms, trade has vastly increased with the introduction of general-purpose money but also with the other factors brought by a colonial form of government. At the same time, the market has expanded its range of applicability in the society. The Tiv are, indigenously, a people who valued egalitarian distribution of wealth to the extent that they believe they bewitched one another to whittle down the wealth of one man to the size of that of another. With money, the degree and extent of differentiation by wealth has greatly increased and will probably continue to increase. Finally, money has brought a new form of indebtedness — one which we know, only too well. In the indigenous system, debt took either the form of owing marriage wards and was hence congruent with the kinship system, or else took the form of decreased prestige. There was no debt in the sphere of subsistence because there was no credit there save among kinsmen and neighbors whose activities were aspects of family status, not acts of money-lenders. The introduction of general-purpose money and the concomitant spread of the market has divorced debt from kinship and status and has created the notion of debt in the subsistence sphere divorced from the activities of kinsmen and neighbors.

In short, because of the spread of the market and the introduction of general-purpose money, Tiv economy has become a part of the world economy. It has brought about profound changes in the institutionalization of Tiv society. Money is one of the shatteringly simplifying ideas of all time, and like any other new and compelling idea, it creates its own revolution. The monetary revolution, at least in this part of Africa, is the turn away from the multi-centric economy. Its course may be painful, but there is very little doubt about its outcome.

REVIEW QUESTIONS

1. What is Bohannan's definition of money? What is the difference between general- and special-purpose money?

2. What does Bohannan mean by *economic spheres*? How were these spheres traditionally related in the Tiv economy?

3. What does Bohannan mean by *conveyance* and *conversion?* How could Tiv men use conversion to increase their power and prestige?

4. In what ways are Tiv marriage customs part of the economic system? Do you think American marriage customs also fall within the economic system in some way? How?

5. Explain the effects of European money on the Tiv economic system.

21

Men and jobs

ELLIOT LIEBOW

*In our complex Western economy, the jobs people have and the value
society places on them determine productive capability and self-
esteem. In this classic work, Elliot Liebow examines the cultural
meaning of jobs to men in the black ghetto. Like millions of today's
poor, most black "corner men" have little motivation to work. Realistic assessment tells them that pay will be too low. Higher-paying jobs
usually require physical stamina, health, training, experience, and
personal transportation—all things corner men may lack. And just
as important, corner men place the same low value on the menial jobs
they can get as do the more affluent members of our society; they are
not motivated by current or future prospects for work.*

A pickup truck drives slowly down the street. The truck stops as it
comes abreast of a man sitting on a cast-iron porch and the white
driver calls out, asking if the man wants a day's work. The man shakes
his head and the truck moves on up the block, stopping again whenever idling men come within calling distance of the driver. At the
Carry-out corner, five men debate the question briefly and shake their
heads no to the truck. The truck turns the corner and repeats the same
performance up the next street. In the distance, one can see one man,
then another, climb into the back of the truck and sit down. It starts
and stops, the truck finally disappears.

What is it we have witnessed here? A labor scavenger rebuffed by
his would-be prey? Lazy, irresponsible men turning down an honest
day's pay for an honest day's work? Or a more complex phenomenon

From *Tally's Corner: A Study of Negro Streetcorner Men* by Elliot Liebow. Copyright © 1967
by Little, Brown and Company, Inc. By permission of Little, Brown and Company.

marking the intersection of economic forces, social values, and individual states of mind and body?

Let us look again at the driver of the truck. He has been able to recruit only two or three men from each twenty or fifty he contacts. To him, it is clear that the others simply do not choose to work. Singly or in groups, belly-empty or belly-full, sullen or gregarious, drunk or sober, they confirm what he has read, heard and knows from his own experience: these men wouldn't take a job if it were handed to them on a platter.[1]

Quite apart from the question of whether or not this is true of some of the men he sees on the street, it is clearly not true of all of them. If it were, he would not have come here in the first place; or having come, he would have left with an empty truck. It is not even true of most of them, for most of the men he sees on the street this weekday morning do, in fact, have jobs. But since, at the moment, they are neither working nor sleeping, and since they hate the depressing room or apartment they live in, or because there is nothing to do there,[2] or because they want to get away from their wives or anyone else living there, they are out on the street, indistinguishable from those who do not have jobs or do not want them. Some, like Boley, a member of a trash-collection crew in a suburban housing development, work Saturdays and are off on this weekday. Some, like Sweets, work nights cleaning up middle-class trash, dirt, dishes, and garbage, and mopping the floors of the office buildings, hotels, restaurants, toilets, and other public places dirtied during the day. Some men work for retail businesses such as liquor stores which do not begin the day until ten o'clock. Some laborers, like Tally, have already come back from the job because the ground was too wet for pick and shovel or because the weather was too cold for pouring concrete. Other employed men stayed off the job today for personal reasons: Clarence to go to a funeral at eleven this morning and Sea Cat to answer a subpoena as a witness in a criminal proceeding.

Also on the street, unwitting contributors to the impression taken away by the truck driver, are the halt and the lame. The man on the

[1]By different methods, perhaps, some social scientists have also located the problem in the men themselves, in their unwillingness or lack of desire to work: "To improve the underprivileged worker's performance one must help him to learn *to want* . . . higher social goals for himself and his children. . . . The problem of changing the work habits and motivation of [lower class] people . . . is a problem of changing the goals, the ambitions, and the level of cultural and occupational aspiration of the underprivleged worker." (Emphasis in original.) Allison Davis, "The Motivation of the Underprivileged Worker," p. 90.

[2]The comparison of sitting at home alone with being in jail is commonplace.

cast-iron steps strokes one gnarled arthritic hand with the other and says he doesn't know whether or not he'll live long enough to be eligible for Social Security. He pauses, then adds matter-of-factly, "Most times, I don't care whether I do or don't." Stoopy's left leg was polio-withered in childhood. Raymond, who looks as if he could tear out a fire hydrant, coughs up blood if he bends or moves suddenly. The quiet man who hangs out in front of the Saratoga apartments has a steel hook strapped onto his left elbow. And had the man in the truck been able to look into the wine-clouded eyes of the man in the green cap, he would have realized that the man did not even understand he was being offered a day's work.

Others, having had jobs and been laid off, are drawing unemployment compensation (up to $44 per week) and have nothing to gain by accepting work which pays little more than this and frequently less.

Still others, like Bumdoodle the numbers man, are working hard at illegal ways of making money, hustlers who are on the street to turn a dollar any way they can: buying and selling sex, liquor, narcotics, stolen goods, or anything else that turns up.

Only a handful remains unaccounted for. There is Tonk, who cannot bring himself to take a job away from the corner, because, according to the other men, he suspects his wife will be unfaithful if given the opportunity. There is Stanton, who has not reported to work for four days now, not since Bernice disappeared. He bought a brand new knife against her return. She had done this twice before, he said, but not for so long and not without warning, and he had forgiven her. But this time, "I ain't got it in me to forgive her again." His rage and shame are there for all to see as he paces the Carry-out and the corner, day and night, hoping to catch a glimpse of her.

And finally, there are those like Arthur, able-bodied men who have no visible means of support, legal or illegal, who neither have jobs nor want them. The truck driver, among others, believes the Arthurs to be representative of all the men he sees idling on the street during his own working hours. They are not, but they cannot be dismissed simply because they are a small minority. It is not enough to explain them away as being lazy or irresponsible or both because an able-bodied man with responsibilities who refuses work is, by the truck driver's definition, lazy and irresponsible. Such an answer begs the question. It is descriptive of the facts; it does not explain them.

Moreover, despite their small numbers, the don't-work-and-don't-want-to-work minority is especially significant because they represent the strongest and clearest expression of those values and attitudes associated with making a living which, to varying degrees, are found throughout the streetcorner world. These men differ from the others in degree rather than in kind, the principal difference being that they are carrying out the implications of their values and experiences to their logical, inevitable conclusions. In this sense, the others have yet to come to terms with themselves and the world they live in.

Putting aside, for the moment, what the men say and feel, and looking at what they actually do and the choices they make, getting a job, keeping a job, and doing well at it is clearly of low priority. Arthur will not take a job at all. Leroy is supposed to be on his job at 4:00 P.M. but it is already 4:10 and he still cannot bring himself to leave the free games he has accumulated on the pinball machine in the Carry-out. Tonk started a construction job on Wednesday, worked Thursday and Friday, then didn't go back again. On the same kind of job, Sea Cat quit in the second week. Sweets had been working three months as a busboy in a restaurant, then quit without notice, not sure himself why he did so. A real estate agent, saying he was more interested in getting the job done than in the cost, asked Richard to give him an estimate on repairing and painting the inside of a house, but Richard, after looking over the job, somehow never got around to submitting an estimate. During one period, Tonk would not leave the corner to take a job because his wife might prove unfaithful; Stanton would not take a job because his woman had been unfaithful.

Thus, the man-job relationship is a tenuous one. At any given moment, a job may occupy a relatively low position on the streetcorner scale of real values. Getting a job may be subordinated to relations with women or to other non-job considerations; the commitment to a job one already has is frequently shallow and tentative.

The reasons are many. Some are objective and reside principally in the job; some are subjective and reside principally in the man. The line between them, however, is not a clear one. Behind the man's refusal to take a job or his decision to quit one is not a simple impulse or value choice but a complex combination of assessments of objective reality on the one hand, and values, attitudes and beliefs drawn from different levels of his experience on the other.

Objective economic considerations are frequently a controlling factor in a man's refusal to take a job. How much the job pays is a crucial question but seldom asked. He knows how much it pays. Working as a stock clerk, a delivery boy, or even behind the counter of liquor stores, drug stores, and other retail businesses pays one dollar an hour. So, too, do most busboy, car-wash, janitorial, and other jobs available to him. Some jobs, such as dishwasher, may dip as low as eighty cents an hour and others, such as elevator operator or work in a junk yard, may offer $1.15 or $1.25. Take-home pay for jobs such as these ranges from $35 to $50 a week, but a take-home pay of over $45 for a five-day week is the exception rather than the rule.

One of the principal advantages of these kinds of jobs is that they offer fairly regular work. Most of them involve essential services and are therefore somewhat less responsive to business conditions than are some higher paying, less menial jobs. Most of them are also inside jobs not dependent on the weather, as are construction jobs and other higher-paying outside work.

Another seemingly important advantage of working in hotels, restaurants, office and apartment buildings, and retail establishments is that they frequently offer an opportunity for stealing on the job. But stealing can be a two-edged sword. Apart from increasing the cost of the goods or services to the general public, a less obvious result is that the practice usually acts as a depressant on the employee's own wage level. Owners of small retail establishments and other employers frequently anticipate employee stealing and adjust the wage rate accordingly. Tonk's employer explained why he was paying Tonk $35 for a 55–60 hour workweek. These men will all steal, he said. Although he keeps close watch on Tonk, he estimates that Tonk steals from $35 to $40 a week.[3] What he steals, when added to his regular earnings, brings his take-home pay to $70 or $75 per week. The employer said he did not mind this because Tonk is worth that much to the business. But if he were to pay Tonk outright the full value of his labor, Tonk would still be stealing $35–$40 per week and this, he said, the business simply would not support.

This wage arrangement, with stealing built-in, was satisfactory to both parties, with each one independently expressing his satisfaction. Such a wage-theft system, however, is not as balanced and equitable as it appears. Since the wage level rests on the premise that the employee will steal the unpaid value of his labor, the man who does not steal on the job is penalized. And furthermore, even it he does not steal, no one would believe him; the employer and others believe he steals because the system presumes it.

Nor is the man who steals, as he is expected to, as well off as he believes himself to be. The employer may occasionally close his eyes to the worker's stealing but not often and not for long. He is, after all, a

[3]Exactly the same estimate as the one made by Tonk himself. On the basis of personal knowledge of the stealing routine employed by Tonk, however, I suspect the actual amount is considerably smaller.

businessman and cannot always find it within himself to let a man steal from him, even if the man is stealing his own wages. Moreover, it is only by keeping close watch on the worker that the employer can control how much is stolen and thereby protect himself against the employee's stealing more than he is worth. From this viewpoint, then, the employer is not in wage-theft collusion with the employee. In the case of Tonk, for instance, the employer was not actively abetting the theft. His estimate of how much Tonk was stealing was based on what he thought Tonk was able to steal despite his own best efforts to prevent him from stealing anything at all. Were he to have caught Tonk in the act of stealing, he would, of course, have fired him from the job and perhaps called the police as well. Thus, in an actual if not in a legal sense, all the elements of entrapment are present. The employer knowingly provides the conditions which entice (force) the employee to steal the unpaid value of his labor, but at the same time he punishes him for theft if he catches him doing so.

Other consequences of the wage-theft system are even more damaging to the employee. Let us, for argument's sake, say that Tonk is in no danger of entrapment; that his employer is willing to wink at the stealing and that Tonk, for his part, is perfectly willing to earn a little, steal a little. Let us say, too, that he is paid $35 a week and allowed to steal $35. His money income—as measured by the goods and services he can purchase with it—is, of course, $70. But not all of his income is available to him for all purposes. He cannot draw on what he steals to build his self-respect or to measure his self-worth. For this, he can draw only on his earnings—the amount given him publicly and voluntarily in exchange for his labor. His "respect" and "self-worth" income remains at $35—only half that of the man who also receives $70 but all of it in the form of wages. His earnings publicly measure the worth of his labor to his employer, and they are important to others and to himself in taking the measure of his worth as a man.[4]

With or without stealing, and quite apart from any interior processes going on in the man who refuses such a job or quits it casually and without apparent reason, the objective fact is that menial jobs in retailing or in the service trades simply do not pay enough to support a man and his family. This is not to say that the worker is underpaid; this may or may not be true. Whether he is or not, the plain fact is that, in such a job, he cannot make a living. Nor can he take much comfort in the fact that these jobs tend to offer more regular, steadier work. If

---

[4]Some public credit may accrue to the clever thief but not respect.

he cannot live on the $45 or $50 he makes in one week, the longer he works, the longer he cannot live on what he makes.[5]

Construction work, even for unskilled laborers, usually pays better, with the hourly rate ranging from $1.50 to $2.60 an hour.[6] Importantly, too, good references, a good driving record, a tenth grade (or any high school) education, previous experience, the ability to "bring police clearance with you" are not normally required of laborers as they frequently are for some of the jobs in retailing or in the service trades.

Construction work, however, has its own objective disadvantages. It is, first of all, seasonal work for the great bulk of the laborers, beginning early in the spring and tapering off as winter weather sets in.[7] And even during the season the work is frequently irregular. Early or late in the season, snow or temperatures too low for concrete fre-

[5]It might be profitable to compare, as Howard S. Becker suggests, gross aspects of income and housing costs in this particular area with those reported by Herbert Gans for the low-income working class in Boston's West End. In 1958, Gans reports, median income for the West Enders was just under $70 a week, a level considerably higher than that enjoyed by the people in the Carry-out neighborhood five years later. Gans himself rented a six-room apartment in the West End for $46 a month, about $10 more than the going rate for long-time residents. In the Carry-out neighborhood, rooms that could accommodate more than a cot and a miniature dresser — that is, rooms that qualified for family living — rented for $12 to $22 a week. Ignoring differences that really can't be ignored — the privacy and self-contained efficiency of the multi-room apartment as against the fragmented, public living of the rooming-house "apartment," with a public toilet on a floor always different from the one your room is on (no matter, it probably doesn't work, anyway) — and assuming comparable states of disrepair, the West Enders were paying $6 or $7 a month for a room that cost the Carry-outers at least $50 a month, and frequently more. Looking at housing costs as a percentage of income — and again ignoring what cannot be ignored: that what goes by the name of "housing" in the two areas is not at all the same thing — the median income West Ender could get a six-room apartment for about 12 percent of his income, while his 1963 Carry-out counterpart, with a weekly income of $60 (to choose a figure from the upper end of the income range), often paid 20–33 percent of his income for one room. See Herbert J. Gans, *The Urban Villagers*, pp. 10–13.

[6]The higher amount is 1962 union scale for building laborers. According to the Wage Agreement Contract for Heavy Construction Laborers (Washington, D.C., and vicinity) covering the period from May 1, 1963 to April 30, 1966, minimum hourly wage for heavy construction laborers was to go from $2.75 (May 1963) by annual increments to $2.92, effective November 1, 1965.

[7]"Open-sky" work, such as building overpasses, highways, etc., in which the workers and materials are directly exposed to the elements, traditionally begins in March and ends around Thanksgiving. The same is true for much of the street repair work and the laying of sewer, electric, gas, and telephone lines by the city and public utilities, all important employers of laborers. Between Thanksgiving and March, they retain only skeleton crews selected from their best, most reliable men.

quently sends the laborers back home, and during late spring or summer, a heavy rain on Tuesday or Wednesday, leaving a lot of water
and mud behind it, can mean a two or three day workweek for the
pick-and-shovel men and other unskilled laborers.[8]

The elements are not the only hazard. As the project moves from
one construction stage to another, laborers — usually without warning — are laid off, sometimes permanently or sometimes for weeks at a
time. The more fortunate or the better workers are told periodically to
"take a walk for two, three days."

Both getting the construction job and getting to it are also relatively more difficult than is the case for the menial jobs in retailing and
the service trades. Job competition is always fierce. In the city, the
large construction projects are unionized. One has to have ready cash
to get into the union to become eligible to work on these projects and,
being eligible, one has to find an opening. Unless one "knows somebody," say a foreman or a laborer who knows the day before that they
are going to take on new men in the morning, this can be a difficult
and disheartening search.

Many of the nonunion jobs are in suburban Maryland or Virginia.
The newspaper ads say, "Report ready to work to the trailer at the
intersection of Rte. 11 and Old Bridge Rd., Bunston, Virginia (or Maryland)," but this location may be ten, fifteen, or even twenty-five miles
from the Carry-out. Public transportation would require two or more
hours to get there, if it services the area at all. Without access to a car
or to a car-pool arrangement, it is not worthwhile reading the ad. So
the men do not. Jobs such as these are usually filled by word of mouth
information, beginning with someone who knows someone or who is
himself working there and looking for a paying rider. Furthermore,
nonunion jobs in outlying areas tend to be smaller projects of relatively
short duration and to pay somewhat less than scale.

Still another objective factor is the work itself. For some men,

---

[8]In a recent year, the crime rate in Washington for the month of August jumped
18 percent over the preceding month. A veteran police officer explained the increase to
David L. Bazelon, Chief Judge, U.S. Court of Appeals for the District of Columbia. "It's
quite simple. . . . You see, August was a very wet month. . . . These people wait on the
street corner each morning around 6:00 or 6:30 for a truck to pick them up and take them
to a construction site. If it's raining, that truck doesn't come, and the men are going to be
idle that day. If the bad weather keeps up for three days . . . we know we are going to
have trouble on our hands — and sure enough, there invariably follows a rash of purse-
snatchings, house-breakings and the like. . . . These people have to eat like the rest of
us, you know." David L. Bazelon, Address to the Federal Bar Association, p.3.

whether the job be digging, mixing mortar, pushing a wheelbarrow, unloading materials, carrying and placing steel rods for reinforcing concrete, or building or laying concrete forms, the work is simply too hard. Men such as Tally and Wee Tom can make such work look like child's play; some of the older work-hardened men, such as Budder and Stanton, can do it too, although not without showing unmistakable signs of strain and weariness at the end of the workday. But those who lack the robustness of a Tally or the time-inured immunity of a Budder must either forego jobs such as these or pay a heavy toll to keep them. For Leroy, in his early twenties, almost six feet tall but weighing under 140 pounds, it would be as difficult to push a loaded wheelbarrow, or to unload and stack 96-pound bags of cement all day long, as it would be for Stoopy and his withered leg.

Heavy, backbreaking labor of the kind that used to be regularly associated with bull gangs or concrete gangs is no longer characteristic of laboring jobs, especially those with the larger, well-equipped construction companies. Brute strength is still required from time to time, as on smaller jobs where it is not economical to bring in heavy equipment or where the small, undercapitalized contractor has none to bring in. In many cases, however, the conveyor belt has replaced the wheelbarrow or the Georgia buggy, mechanized forklifts have eliminated heavy, manual lifting, and a variety of digging machines have replaced the pick and shovel. The result is fewer jobs for unskilled laborers and, in many cases, a work speed-up for those who do have jobs. Machines now set the pace formerly set by men. Formerly, a laborer pushed a wheelbarrow of wet cement to a particular spot, dumped it, and returned for another load. Another laborer, in hip boots, pushed the wet concrete around with a shovel or a hoe, getting it roughly level in preparation for the skilled finishers. He had relatively small loads to contend with and had only to keep up with the men pushing the wheelbarrows. Now, the job for the man pushing the wheelbarrow is gone and the wet concrete comes rushing down a chute at the man in the hip boots who must "spread it quick or drown."

Men who have been running an elevator, washing dishes, or "pulling trash" cannot easily move into laboring jobs. They lack the basic skills for "unskilled" construction labor, familiarity with tools and materials, and tricks of the trade without which hard jobs are made harder. Previously unused or untrained muscles rebel in pain against the new and insistent demands made upon them, seriously compromising the man's performance and testing his willingness to see the job through.

A healthy, sturdy, active man of good intelligence requires from two to four weeks to break in on a construction job.[9] Even if he is willing somehow to bull his way through the first few weeks, it frequently happens that his foreman or the craftsman he services with materials and general assistance is not willing to wait that long for him to get into condition or to learn at a glance the difference in size between a rough 2" x 8" and a finished 2" x 10". The foreman and the craftsman are themselves "under the gun" and cannot "carry" the man when other men, who are already used to the work and who know the tools and materials, are lined up to take the job.

Sea Cat was "healthy, sturdy, active and of good intelligence." When a judge gave him six weeks in which to pay his wife $200 in back child-support payments, he left his grocery-store job in order to take a higher-paying job as a laborer, arranged for him by a foreman friend. During the first week the weather was bad and he worked only Wednesday and Friday, cursing the elements all the while for cheating him out of the money he could have made. The second week, the weather was fair but he quit at the end of the fourth day, saying frankly that the work was too hard for him. He went back to his job at the grocery store and took a second job working nights as a dishwasher in a restaurant,[10] earning little if any more at the two jobs than he would have earned as a laborer, and keeping at both of them until he had paid off his debts.

Tonk did not last as long as Sea Cat. No one made any predictions when he got a job in a parking lot, but when the men on the corner learned he was to start on a road construction job, estimates of how long he would last ranged from one to three weeks. Wednesday was his first day. He spent that evening and night at home. He did the same on Thursday. He worked Friday and spent Friday evening and part of Saturday draped over the mailbox on the corner. Sunday afternoon, Tonk decided he was not going to report on the job the next morning. He explained that after working three days, he knew enough about the job to know that it was too hard for him. He knew he wouldn't be able to keep up and he'd just as soon quit now as get fired later.

Logan was a tall, two-hundred-pound man in his late twenties. His back used to hurt him only on the job, he said, but now he can't

[9]Estimate of Mr. Francis Greenfield, President of the International Hod Carriers, Building and Common Laborers' District Council of Washington, D.C., and Vicinity. I am indebted to Mr. Greenfield for several points in these paragraphs dealing with construction laborers.

[10]Not a sinecure, even by streetcorner standards.

straighten up for increasingly longer periods of time. He said he had traced this to the awkward walk he was forced to adopt by the loaded wheelbarows which pull him down into a half-stoop. He's going to quit, he said, as soon as he can find another job. If he can't find one real soon, he guesses he'll quit anyway. It's not worth it, having to walk bent over and leaning to one side.

Sometimes, the strain and effort is greater than the man is willing to admit, even to himself. In the early summer of 1963, Richard was rooming at Nancy's place. His wife and children were "in the country" (his grandmother's home in Carolina), waiting for him to save up enough money so that he could bring them back to Washington and start over again after a disastrous attempt to "make it" in Philadelphia. Richard had gotten a job with a fence company in Virginia. It paid $1.60 an hour. The first few evenings, when he came home from work, he looked ill from exhaustion and the heat. Stanton said Richard would have to quit, "he's too small [thin] for that kind of work." Richard said he was doing O.K. and would stick with the job.

At Nancy's one night, when Richard had been working about two weeks, Nancy and three or four others were sitting around talking, drinking, and listening to music. Someone asked Nancy when was Richard going to bring his wife and children up from the country. Nancy said she didn't know, but it probably depended on how long it would take him to save up enough money. She said she didn't think he could stay with the fence job much longer. This morning, she said, the man Richard rode to work with knocked on the door and Richard didn't answer. She looked in his room. Richard was still asleep. Nancy tried to shake him awake. "No more digging!" Richard cried out. "No more digging! I can't do no more God-damn digging!" When Nancy finally managed to wake him, he dressed quickly and went to work.

Richard stayed on the job two more weeks, then suddenly quit, ostensibly because his pay check was three dollars less than what he thought it should have been.

In summary of objective job considerations, then, the most important fact is that a man who is able and willing to work cannot earn enough money to support himself, his wife, and one or more children. A man's chances for working regularly are good only if he is willing to work for less than he can live on, and sometimes not even then. On some jobs, the wage rate is deceptively higher than on others, but the higher the wage rate, the more difficult it is to get the job, and the less the job security. Higher-paying construction work tends to be seasonal and, during the season, the amount of work available is highly sensitive to business and weather conditions and to the changing require-

ments of individual projects.[11] Moreover, high-paying construction jobs
are frequently beyond the physical capacity of some of the men, and
some of the low-paying jobs are scaled down even lower in accordance
with the self-fulfilling assumption that the man will steal part of his
wages on the job.[12]

Bernard assesses the objective job situation dispassionately over a
cup of coffee, sometimes poking at the coffee with his spoon, sometimes staring at it as if, like a crystal ball, it holds tomorrow's secrets.
He is twenty-seven years old. He and the woman with whom he lives
have a baby son, and she has another child by another man. Bernard
does odd jobs—mostly painting—but here it is the end of January,
and his last job was with the Post Office during the Christmas mail
rush. He would like postal work as a steady job, he says. It pays well
(about $2.00 an hour) but he has twice failed the Post Office examina-
tion (he graduated from a Washington high school) and has given up
the idea as an impractical one. He is supposed to see a man tonight
about a job as a parking attendant for a large apartment house. The
man told him to bring his birth certificate and driver's license, but his
license was suspended because of a backlog of unpaid traffic fines. A
friend promised to lend him some money this evening. If he gets it, he
will pay the fines tomorrow morning and have his license reinstated.
He hopes the man with the job will wait till tomorrow night.

A "security job" is what he really wants, he said. He would like
to save up money for a taxicab. (But having twice failed the postal
examination and having a bad driving record as well, it is highly
doubtful that he could meet the qualifications or pass the written test.)
That would be "a good life." He can always get a job in a restaurant or
as a clerk in a drugstore but they don't pay enough, he said. He needs
to take home at least $50 to $55 a week. He thinks he can get that much

[11]The overall result is that, in the long run, a Negro laborer's earnings are not
substantially greater—and may be less—than those of the busboy, janitor, or stock
clerk. Herman P. Miller, for example, reports that in 1960, 40 percent of all jobs held by
Negro men were as laborers or in the service trades. The average annual wage for
nonwhite nonfarm laborers was $2,400. The average earning of nonwhite service workers
was $2,500 (*Rich Man, Poor Man*, p. 90). Francis Greenfield estimates that in the Washing-
ton vicinity, the 1965 earnings of the union laborer who works whenever work is available will be about $3,200. Even this figure is high for the man on the streetcorner. Union
men in heavy construction are the aristocrats of the laborers. Casual day labor and jobs
with small firms in the building and construction trades, or with firms in other indus-
tries, pay considerably less.

[12]For an excellent discussion of the self-fulfilling assumption (or prophecy) as a
social force, see "The Self-Fulfilling Prophecy," Ch. XI, in Robert K. Merton's *Social
Theory and Social Structure*.

driving a truck somewhere . . . Sometimes he wishes he had stayed in the army . . . A security job, that's what he wants most of all, a real security job . . .

When we look at what the men bring to the job rather than at what the job offers the men, it is essential to keep in mind that we are not looking at men who come to the job fresh, just out of school perhaps, and newly prepared to undertake the task of making a living, or from another job where they earned a living and are prepared to do the same on this job. Each man comes to the job with a long job history characterized by his not being able to support himself and his family. Each man carries this knowledge, born of his experience, with him. He comes to the job flat and stale, wearied by the sameness of it all, convinced of his own incompetence, terrified of responsibility — of being tested still again and found wanting. Possible exceptions are the younger men not yet, or just, married. They suspect all this but have yet to have it confirmed by repeated personal experience over time. But those who are or have been married know it well. It is the experience of the individual and the group; of their fathers and probably their sons. Convinced of their inadequacies, not only do they not seek out those better-paying jobs which test their resources, but they actively avoid them, gravitating in a mass to the menial, routine jobs which offer no challenge — and therefore pose no threat — to the already diminished images they have of themselves.

Thus Richard does not follow through on the real estate agent's offer. He is afraid to do on his own — minor plastering, replacing broken windows, other minor repairs, and painting — exactly what he had been doing for months on a piecework basis under someone else (and which provided him with a solid base from which to derive a cost estimate).

Richard once offered an important clue to what may have gone on in his mind when the job offer was made. We were in the Carry-out, at a time when he was looking for work. He was talking about the kind of jobs available to him.

> I graduated from high school [Baltimore] but I don't know anything. I'm dumb. Most of the time I don't even say I graduated, 'cause then somebody asks me a question and I can't answer it, and they think I was lying about graduating. . . . They graduated me but I didn't know anything. I had lousy grades but I guess they wanted to get rid of me.
>
> I was at Margaret's house the other night and her little sister asked me to help her with her homework. She showed me some fractions and I knew right away I couldn't do them. I was ashamed so I told her I had to go to the bathroom.

And so it must have been, surely, with the real estate agent's offer. Convinced that "I'm dumb . . . I don't know anything," he "knew right away" he couldn't do it, despite the fact that he had been doing just this sort of work all along.

Thus, the man's low self-esteem generates a fear of being tested and prevents him from accepting a job with responsibilities or, once on a job, from staying with it if responsibilities are thrust on him, even if the wages are commensurately higher. Richard refuses such a job, Leroy leaves one, and another man, given more responsibility and more pay, knows he will fail and proceeds to do so, proving he was right about himself all along. The self-fulfilling prophecy is everywhere at work. In a hallway, Stanton, Tonk and Boley are passing a bottle around. Stanton recalls the time he was in the service. Everything was fine until he attained the rank of corporal. He worried about everything he did then. Was he doing the right thing? Was he doing it well? When would they discover their mistake and take his stripes (and extra pay) away? When he finally lost his stripes, everything was all right again.

Lethargy, disinterest, and general apathy on the job, so often reported by employers, has its streetcorner counterpart. The men do not ordinarily talk about their jobs or ask one another about them.[13] Although most of the men know who is or is not working at any given time, they may or may not know what particular job an individual man has. There is no overt interest in job specifics as they relate to this or that person, in large part perhaps because the specifics are not especially relevant. To know that a man is working is to know approximately how much he makes and to know as much as one needs or wants to know about how he makes it. After all, how much difference does it make to know whether a man is pushing a mop or pulling trash in an apartment house, a restaurant, or an office building, or delivering groceries, drugs, or liquor, or, if he's a laborer, whether he's pushing a wheelbarrow, mixing mortar, or digging a hole. So much does one job look like every other that there is little to choose between them. In large part, the job market consists of a narrow range of nondescript chores calling for nondistinctive, undifferentiated, unskilled labor. "A job is a job."

A crucial factor in the streetcorner man's lack of job commitment

[13]This stands in dramatic contrast to the leisure-time conversation of stable, working-class men. For the coal miners (of Ashton, England), for example, "the topic [of conversation] which surpasses all others in frequency is work—the difficulties which have been encountered in the day's shift, the way in which a particular task was accomplished, and so on." Josephine Klein, *Samples from English Cultures*, Vol. I, p.88.

is the overall value he places on the job. *For his part, the streetcorner man puts no lower value on the job than does the larger society around him.* He knows the social value of the job by the amount of money the employer is willing to pay him for doing it. In a real sense, every pay day, he counts in dollars and cents the value placed on the job by society at large. He is no more (and frequently less) ready to quit and look for another job than his employer is ready to fire him and look for another man. Neither the streetcorner man who performs these jobs nor the society which requires him to perform them assess the job as one "worth doing and worth doing well." Both employee and employer are contemptuous of the job. The employee shows his contempt by his reluctance to accept it or keep it, the employer by paying less than is required to support a family.[14] Nor does the low-wage job offer prestige, respect, interesting work, opportunity for learning or advancement, or any other compensation. With few exceptions, jobs filled by the streetcorner men are at the bottom of the employment ladder in every respect, from wage level to prestige. Typically, they are hard, dirty, uninteresting, and underpaid. The rest of society (whatever its ideal values regarding the dignity of labor) holds the job of the dishwasher or janitor or unskilled laborer in low esteem if not outright contempt.[15] So does the streetcorner man. He cannot do otherwise. He cannot draw from a job those social values which other people do not put into it.[16]

Only occasionally does spontaneous conversation touch on these matters directly. Talk about jobs is usually limited to isolated statements of intention, such as "I think I'll get me another gig [job]," "I'm going to look for a construction job when the weather breaks," or "I'm going to quit. I can't take no more of his shit." Job assessments typi-

---

[14]It is important to remember that the employer is not entirely a free agent. Subject to the constraints of the larger society, he acts for the larger society as well as for himself. Child labor laws, safety and sanitation regulations, minimum wage scales in some employment areas, and other constraints, are already on the books; other control mechanisms, such as a guaranteed annual wage, are to be had for the voting.

[15]See, for example, the U.S. Bureau of the Census, *Methodology and Scores of Socioeconomic Status*. This assignment of the lowest SES ratings to men who hold such jobs is not peculiar to our own society. A low SES rating for "the shoeshine boy or garbage man . . . seems to be true for all [industrial] countries." Alex Inkeles, "Industrial Man," p. 8.

[16]That the streetcorner man downgrades manual labor should occasion no surprise. Merton points out that "the American stigmatization of manual labor . . . *has been found to hold rather uniformly in all social classes*" (emphasis in original; *Social Theory and Social Structure*, p. 145). That he finds no satisfaction in such work should also occasion no surprise: "[There is] a clear positive correlation between the over-all status of occupations and the experience of satisfaction in them." Inkeles, "Industrial Man," p. 12.

cally consist of nothing more than a noncommittal shrug and "It's O.K." or "It's a job."

One reason for the relative absence of talk about one's job is, as suggested earlier, that the sameness of job experience does not bear reiteration. Another and more important reason is the emptiness of the job experience itself. The man sees middle-class occupations as a primary source of prestige, pride, and self-respect; his own job affords him none of these. To think about his job is to see himself as others see him, to remind him of just where he stands in this society.[17] And because society's criteria for placement are generally the same as his own, to talk about his job can trigger a flush of shame and a deep, almost physical ache to change places with someone, almost anyone, else.[18] The desire to be a person in his own right, to be noticed by the world he lives in, is shared by each of the men on the streetcorner. Whether they articulate this desire (as Tally does below) or not, one can see them position themselves to catch the attention of their fellows in much the same way as plants bend or stretch to catch the sunlight.[19]

Tally and I were in the Carry-out. It was summer, Tally's peak earning season as a cement finisher, a semiskilled job a cut or so above that of the unskilled laborer. His take-home pay during these weeks was well over a hundred dollars—"a lot of bread." But for Tally, who no longer had a family to support, bread was not enough.

> "You know that boy came in last night? That Black Moozlem? That's what I ought to be doing. I ought to be in his place."
> "What do you mean?"
> "Dressed nice, going to [night] school, got a good job."
> "He's no better off than you, Tally. You make much more than he does."

[17]"[In our society] a man's work is one of the things by which he is judged, and certainly one of the more significant things by which he judges himself. . . . A man's work is one of the more important parts of his social identity, of his self; indeed, of his fate in the one life he has to live." Everett C. Hughes, *Men and Their Work*, pp. 42–43.

[18]Noting that lower-class persons "are constantly exposed to evidence of their own irrelevance," Lee Rainwater spells out still another way in which the poor are poor: "The identity problems of lower class persons make the soul-searching of middle class adolescents and adults seem rather like a kind of conspicuous consumption of psychic riches" ("Work and Identity in the Lower Class," p. 3).

[19]Sea Cat cuts his pants legs off at the calf and puts a fringe on the raggedy edges. Tonk breaks his "shades" and continues to wear the horn-rimmed frames minus the lenses. Richard cultivates a distinctive manner of speech. Lonny gives himself a birthday party. And so on.

"It's not the money. [Pause] It's position, I guess. He's got position. When he finish school he gonna be a supervisor. People respect him. . . . Thinking about people with position and education gives me a feeling right here [pressing his fingers into the pit of his stomach]."

"You're educated, too. You have a skill, a trade. You're a cement finisher. You can make a building, pour a sidewalk."

"That's different. Look, can anybody do what you're doing? Can anybody just come up and do your job? Well, in one week I can teach you cement finishing. You won't be as good as me 'cause you won't have the experience but you'll be a cement finisher. That's what I mean. Anybody can do what I'm doing and that's what gives me this feeling. [Long pause] Suppose I like this girl. I go over to her house and I meet her father. He starts talking about what he done today. He talks about operating on somebody and sewing them up and about surgery. I know he's a doctor 'cause of the way he talks. Then she starts talking about what she did. Maybe she's a boss or a supervisor. Maybe she's a lawyer and her father says to me, 'And what do you do, Mr. Jackson?' [Pause] You remember at the courthouse, Lonny's trial? You and the lawyer was talking in the hall? You remember? I just stood there listening. I didn't say a word. You know why? 'Cause I didn't even know what you was talking about. That's happened to me a lot."

"Hell, you're nothing special. That happens to everybody. Nobody knows everything. One man is a doctor, so he talks about surgery. Another man is a teacher, so he talks about books. But doctors and teachers don't know anything about concrete. You're a cement finisher and that's your specialty."

"Maybe so, but when was the last time you saw anybody standing around talking about concrete?"

The streetcorner man wants to be a person in his own right, to be noticed, to be taken account of, but in this respect, as well as in meeting his money needs, his job fails him. The job and the man are even. The job fails the man and the man fails the job.

Furthermore, the man does not have any reasonable expectation that, however bad it is, his job will lead to better things. Menial jobs are not, by and large, the starting point of a track system which leads to even better jobs for those who are able and willing to do them. The busboy or dishwasher in a restaurant is not on a job track which, if negotiated skillfully, leads to chef or manager of the restaurant. The busboy or dishwasher who works hard becomes, simply, a hard-working busboy or dishwasher. Neither hard work nor perseverance can conceivably carry the janitor to a sitdown job in the office building he cleans up. And it is the apprentice who becomes the journeyman electrician, plumber, steam fitter or bricklayer, not the common unskilled Negro laborer.

Thus, the job is not a stepping-stone to something better. It is a dead end. It promises to deliver no more tomorrow, next month or next year than it does today.

Delivering little, and promising no more, the job is "no big thing." The man appears to treat the job in a cavalier fashion, working and not working as the spirit moves him, as if all that matters is the immediate satisfaction of his present appetites, the surrender to present moods, and the indulgence of whims with no thought for the cost, the consequences, the future. To the middle-class observer, this behavior reflects a "present-time orientation" — an "inability to defer gratification." It is this "present-time" orientation — as against the "future orientation" of the middle-class person — that "explains" to the outsider why Leroy chooses to spend the day at the Carry-out rather than report to work; why Richard, who was paid Friday, was drunk Saturday and Sunday and penniless Monday; why Sweets quit his job today because the boss looked at him "funny" yesterday.

But from the inside looking out, what appears as a "present-time" orientation to the outside observer is, to the man experiencing it, as much a future orientation as that of his middle-class counterpart.[20] The difference between the two men lies not so much in their different orientations to time as in their different orientations to future time or, more specifically, to their different futures.[21]

The future orientation of the middle-class person presumes, among other things, a surplus of resources to be invested in the future and a belief that the future will be sufficiently stable both to justify his investment (money in a bank, time and effort in a job, investment of himself in marriage and family, etc.) and to permit the consumption of his investment at a time, place and manner of his own choosing and to his greater satisfaction. But the streetcorner man lives in a sea of want. He does not, as a rule, have a surplus of resources, either economic or psychological. Gratification of hunger and the desire for simple creature comforts cannot be long deferred. Neither can support for one's flagging self-esteem. Living on the edge of both economic and psycho-

[20]Taking a somewhat different point of view, S. M. Miller and Frank Riessman suggest that "the entire concept of deferred gratification may be inappropriate to understanding the essence of workers' lives" ("The Working Class Subculture: A New View," p. 87).

[21]This sentence is a paraphrase of a statement made by Marvin Cline at a 1965 colloquium at the Mental Health Study Center, National Institute of Mental Health.

logical subsistence, the streetcorner man is obliged to expend all his resources on maintaining himself from moment to moment.[22]

As for the future, the young streetcorner man has a fairly good picture of it. In Richard or Sea Cat or Arthur he can see himself in his middle twenties; he can look at Tally to see himself at thirty, at Wee Tom to see himself in his middle thirties, and at Budder and Stanton to see himself in his forties. It is a future in which everything is uncertain except the ultimate destruction of his hopes and the eventual realization of his fears. The most he can reasonably look forward to is that these things do not come too soon. Thus, when Richard squanders a week's pay in two days it is not because, like an animal or a child, he is "present-time oriented," unaware of or unconcerned with his future. He does so precisely because he is aware of the future and the hopelessness of it all.

Sometimes this kind of response appears as a conscious, explicit choice. Richard had had a violent argument with his wife. He said he was going to leave her and the children, that he had had enough of everything and could not take any more, and he chased her out of the house. His chest still heaving, he leaned back against the wall in the hallway of his basement apartment.

> "I've been scuffling for five years," he said. "I've been scuffling for five years from morning till night. And my kids still don't have anything, my wife don't have anything, and I don't have anything.
>
> "There," he said, gesturing down the hall to a bed, a sofa, a couple of chairs and a television set, all shabby, some broken. "There's everything I have and I'm having trouble holding onto that."
>
> Leroy came in, presumably to petition Richard on behalf of Richard's wife, who was sitting outside on the steps, afraid to come in. Leroy started to say something but Richard cut him short.

[22]And if, for the moment, he does sometimes have more money than he chooses to spend or more food than he wants to eat, he is pressed to spend the money and eat the food anyway since his friends, neighbors, kinsmen, or acquaintances will beg or borrow whatever surplus he has or, failing this, they may steal it. In one extreme case, one of the men admitted taking the last of a woman's surplus food allotment after she had explained that, with four children, she could not spare any food. The prospect that consumer soft goods not consumed by oneself will be consumed by someone else may be related to the way in which portable consumer durable goods, such as watches, radios, television sets, or phonographs, are sometimes looked at as a form of savings. When Shirley was on welfare, she regularly took her television set out of pawn when she got her monthly check. Not so much to watch it, she explained, as to have something to fall back on when her money runs out toward the end of the month. For her and others, the television set or the phonograph is her savings, the pawnshop is where she banks her savings, and the pawn ticket is her bankbook.

"Look, Leroy, don't give me any of that action. You and me are entirely different people. Maybe I look like a boy and maybe I act like a boy sometimes but I got a man's mind. You and me don't want the same things out of life. Maybe some of the same, but you don't care how long you have to wait for yours and *I — want — mine — right — now.*"[23]

Thus, apparent present-time concerns with consumption and indulgences — material and emotional — reflect a future-time orientation. "I want mine right now" is ultimately a cry of despair, a direct response to the future as he sees it.[24]

In many instances, it is precisely the streetcorner man's orientation to the future — but to a future loaded with "trouble" — which not only leads to a greater emphasis on present concerns ("I want mine right now") but also contributes importantly to the instability of employment, family and friend relationships, and to the general transient quality of daily life.

Let me give some concrete examples. One day, after Tally had gotten paid, he gave me four twenty-dollar bills and asked me to keep

[23]This was no simple rationalization for irresponsibility. Richard had indeed "been scuffling for five years" trying to keep his family going. Until shortly after this episode, Richard was known and respected as one of the hardest-working men on the street. Richard had said, only a couple of months earlier, "I figure you got to get out there and try. You got to try before you can get anything." His wife Shirley confirmed that he had always tried. "If things get tough, with me I'll get all worried. But Richard get worried, he don't want me to see him worried. . . . He *will* get out there. He's shoveled snow, picked beans, and he's done some of everything. . . . He's not ashamed to get out there and get us something to eat." At the time of the episode reported above, Leroy was just starting marriage and raising a family. He and Richard were not, as Richard thought, "entirely different people." Leroy had just not learned, by personal experience over time, what Richard had learned. But within two years Leroy's marriage had broken up and he was talking and acting like Richard. "He just let go completely," said one of the men on the street.

[24]There is no mystically intrinsic connection between "present-time" orientation and lower-class persons. Whenever people of whatever class have been uncertain, skeptical or downright pessimistic about the future, "I want mine right now" has been one of the characteristic responses, although it is usually couched in more delicate terms: e.g., Omar Khayyam's "Take the cash and let the credit go," or Horace's "*Carpe diem.*" In wartime, especially, all classes tend to slough off conventional restraints on sexual and other behavior (i.e., become less able or less willing to defer gratification). And when inflation threatens, darkening the fiscal future, persons who formerly husbanded their resources with commendable restraint almost stampede one another rushing to spend their money. Similarly, it seems that future-time orientation tends to collapse toward the present when persons are in pain or under stress. The point here is that, the label notwithstanding (what passes for) present-time orientation appears to be a situation-specific phenomenon rather than a part of the standard psychic equipment of Cognitive Lower Class Man.

them for him. Three days later he asked me for the money. I returned it and asked why he did not put his money in a bank. He said that the banks close at two o'clock. I argued that there were four or more banks within a two-block radius of where he was working at the time and that he could easily get to any one of them on his lunch hour. "No, man," he said, "you don't understand. They close at two o'clock and they closed Saturday and Sunday. Suppose I get into trouble and I got to make it [leave]. Me get out of town, and everything I got in the world layin' up in that bank? No good! No good!"

In another instance, Leroy and his girl friend were discussing "trouble." Leroy was trying to decide how best to go about getting his hands on some "long green" (a lot of money), and his girl friend cautioned him about "trouble." Leroy sneered at this, saying he had had "trouble" all his life and wasn't afraid of a little more. "Anyway," he said, "I'm famous for leaving town."[25]

Thus, the constant awareness of a future loaded with "trouble" results in a constant readiness to leave, to "make it," to "get out of town," and discourages the man from sinking roots into the world he lives in.[26] Just as it discourages him from putting money in the bank, so it discourages him from committing himself to a job, especially one whose payoff lies in the promise of future rewards rather than in the present. In the same way, it discourages him from deep and lasting commitments to family and friends or to any persons, places or things, since such commitments could hold him hostage, limiting his freedom of movement and thereby compromising his security which lies in that freedom.

What lies behind the response to the driver of the pickup truck, then, is a complex combination of attitudes and assessments. The street-corner man is under continuous assault by his job experiences and job fears. His experiences and fears feed on one another. The kind of job he can get—and frequently only after fighting for it, if then— steadily confirms his fears, depresses his self-confidence and self-esteem until finally, terrified of an opportunity even if one presents itself, he stands defeated by his experiences, his belief in his own self-worth destroyed and his fears a confirmed reality.

[25]And proceeded to do just that the following year when "trouble"—in this case, a grand jury indictment, a pile of debts, and a violent separation from his wife and children—appeared again.

[26]For a discussion of "trouble" as a focal concern of lower-class culture, see Walter Miller, "Lower Class Culture as a Generating Milieu of Gang Delinquency," pp. 7, 8.

REVIEW QUESTIONS

1. According to Liebow, how do middle-class Americans view the personal industry of corner men?

2. What are the reasons corner men turn down offers to work by day-labor recruiters?

3. How do corner men assess the work they can get? How does this assessment affect their motivation to work?

4. What values and experiences do corner men bring to their view of work? How do these values and experiences affect their motivation?

5. Recently, some government officials and social scientists have begun to speak of a permanent American underclass. Using the information provided in this article, evaluate this assertion.

22

Subsistence and market: When the turtle collapses

BERNARD NIETSCHMANN

Subsistence economies were once common in the world. People hunted and gathered or farmed largely for their own needs. But the world market economy has penetrated even the most remote areas and has brought with it a change from subsistence economies to production for money. In this article, Bernard Nietschmann traces the disturbing effect of the international market for green sea turtles on the Miskito Indians, who once harpooned the large sea reptiles only for food. Trapped in a vicious circle, Indians began to catch the turtles to sell rather than to eat. With no turtle meat to eat came a need for money to buy food. Money came only from catching and selling more turtles. The need for cash also reduced the Indians' ability to perform reciprocal economic obligations. In the end, the new economy began to disappear because of a diminished catch of overexploited turtles, leaving the Miskito without even their original means of subsistence.

In the half-light of dawn, a sailing canoe approaches a shoal where nets have been set the day before. A Miskito turtleman stands in the bow and points to a distant splash that breaks the gray sheen of the Caribbean waters. Even from a hundred yards, he can tell that a green turtle has been caught in one of the nets. His two companions quickly bring the craft alongside the turtle, and as they pull it from the sea, its glistening shell reflects the first rays of the rising sun. As two men work to remove the heavy reptile from the net, the third keeps the canoe headed into the swells and beside the anchored net. After its fins have been pierced and lashed with bark fiber cord, the 250-pound turtle is placed on its back in the bottom of the canoe. The turtlemen are happy. Perhaps their luck will be good today and their other nets will also yield many turtles.

These green turtles, caught by Miskito Indian turtlemen off the eastern coast of Nicaragua, are destined for distant markets. Their butchered bodies will pass through many hands, local and foreign, eventually ending up in tins, bottles, and freezers far away. Their meat, leather, shell, oil, and calipee, a gelatinous substance that is the base for turtle soup, will be used to produce goods consumed in more affluent parts of the world.

The coastal Miskito Indians are very dependent on green turtles. Their culture has long been adapted to utilizing the once vast populations that inhabited the largest sea turtle feeding grounds in the Western Hemisphere. As the most important link between livelihood, social interaction, and environment, green turtles were the pivotal resource around which traditional Miskito Indian society revolved. These large reptiles also provided the major source of protein for Miskito subsistence. Now this priceless and limited resource has become a prized commodity that is being exploited almost entirely for economic reasons.

In the past, turtles fulfilled the nutritional needs as well as the social responsibilities of Miskito society. Today, however, the Miskito depend mainly on the sale of turtles to provide them with the money they need to purchase household goods and other necessities. But turtles are a declining resource; overdependence on them is leading the Miskito into an ecological blind alley. The cultural control mechanisms that once adapted the Miskito to their environment and faunal resources are now circumvented or inoperative, and they are caught up in a system of continued intensification of turtle fishing, which threatens to provide neither cash nor subsistence.

I have been studying this situation for several years, unraveling its historical context and piecing together its past and future effect on Miskito society, economy, and diet, and on the turtle population.

The coastal Miskito Indians are among the world's most adept small-craft seamen and turtlemen. Their traditional subsistence system provided dependable yields from the judicious scheduling of resource procurement activities. Agriculture, hunting, fishing, and gathering were organized in accordance with seasonal fluctuations in weather and resource availability and provided adequate amounts of food and materials without overexploiting any one species or site. Women cultivated the crops while men hunted and fished. Turtle fishing was the backbone of subsistence, providing meat throughout the year.

Miskito society and economy were interdependent. There was no economic activity without a social context and every social act had a reciprocal economic aspect. To the Miskito, meat, especially turtle meat, was the most esteemed and valuable resource, for it was not only a mainstay of subsistence, it was the item most commonly distributed to relatives and friends. Meat shared in this way satisfied mutual obligations and responsibilities and smoothed out daily and seasonal differences in the acquisition of animal protein. In this way, those too young, old, sick, or otherwise unable to secure meat received their share, and a certain balance in the village was achieved: minimal food requirements were met, meat surplus was disposed of to others, and social responsibilities were satisfied.

Today, the older Miskito recall that when meat was scarce in the village, a few turtlemen would put out to sea in their dugout canoes for a day's harpooning on the turtle feeding grounds. In the afternoon, the men would return, sailing before the northeast trade wind, bringing meat for all. Gathered on the beach, the villagers helped drag the canoes into thatched storage sheds. After the turtles were butchered and the meat distributed, everyone returned home to the cooking fires.

Historical circumstances and a series of boom-bust economic cycles disrupted the Miskito's society and environment. In the seventeenth and eighteenth centuries, intermittent trade with English and French buccaneers — based on the exchange of forest and marine resources for metal tools and utensils, rum, and firearms — prompted the Miskito to extend hunting, fishing, and gathering beyond subsistence needs to exploitative enterprises.

During the nineteenth and early twentieth centuries, foreign-owned companies operating in eastern Nicaragua exported rubber, lumber, and gold, and initiated commercial banana production. As alien economic and ecological influences were intensified, contract wage labor replaced seasonal, short-term economic relationships; company commissaries replaced limited trade goods; and large-scale exploitation of natural resources replaced sporadic, selective extraction. During economic boom periods the relationship between resources, subsistence, and environment was drastically altered for the Miskito. Resources became a commodity with a price tag, market exploitation a livelihood, and foreign wages and goods a necessity.

For more than 200 years, relations between the coastal Miskito and the English were based on sea turtles. It was from the Miskito that the English learned the art of turtling, which they then organized into intensive commercial exploitation of Caribbean turtle grounds and nesting beaches. Sea turtles were among the first resources involved in trade relations and foreign commerce in the Caribbean. Zoologist

Archie Carr, an authority on sea turtles, has remarked that "more than any other dietary factor, the green turtle supported the opening up of the Caribbean." The once abundant turtle populations provided sustenance to ships' crews and to the new settlers and plantation laborers.

The Cayman Islands, settled by the English, became in the seventeenth and eighteenth centuries the center of commercial turtle fishing in the Caribbean. By the early nineteenth century, pressure on the Cayman turtle grounds and nesting beaches to supply meat to Caribbean and European markets became so great that the turtle population was decimated. The Cayman Islanders were forced to shift to other turtle areas off Cuba, the Gulf of Honduras, and the coast of eastern Nicaragua. They made annual expeditions, lasting four to seven weeks, to the Miskito turtle grounds to net green turtles, occasionally purchasing live ones, dried calipee, and the shells of hawksbill turtles (*Eretmochelys imbricata*) from the Miskito Indians. Reported catches of green turtles by the Cayman turtlers generally ranged between 2,000 and 3,000 a year up to the early 1960s, when the Nicaraguan government failed to renew the islanders' fishing privileges.

Intensive resource extraction by foreign companies led to seriously depleted and altered environments. By the 1940s, many of the economic booms had turned to busts. As the resources ran out and operating costs mounted, companies shut down production and moved to other areas in Central America. Thus, the economic mainstays that had helped provide the Miskito with jobs, currency, markets, and foreign goods were gone. The company supply ships and commissaries disappeared, money became scarce, and store-bought items expensive.

In the backwater of the passing golden boom period, the Miskito were left with an ethic of poverty, but they still had the subsistence skills that had maintained their culture for hundreds of years. Their land and water environment was still capable of providing reliable resources for local consumption. As it had been in the past, turtle fishing became a way of life, a provider of life itself. But traditional subsistence culture could no longer integrate Miskito society and environment in a state of equilibrium. Resources were now viewed as having a value and labor a price tag. All that was needed was a market.

Recently, two foreign turtle companies began operations along the east coast of Nicaragua. One was built in Puerto Cabezas in late 1968, and another was completed in Bluefields in 1969. Both companies were capable of processing and shipping large amounts of green turtle meat and by-products to markets in North America and Europe. Turtles were acquired by purchase from the Miskito. Each week company boats visited coastal Miskito communities and offshore island turtle camps to buy green turtles. The "company" was back, money

was again available, and the Miskito were expert in securing the desired commodity. Another economic boom period was at hand. But the
significant difference between this boom and previous ones was that
the Miskito were now selling a subsistence resource.

As a result, the last large surviving green turtle population in the
Caribbean was opened to intensive, almost year-round exploitation.
Paradoxically, it would be the Miskito Indians, who once caught only
what they needed for food, who would conduct the assault on the
remaining turtle population. . . .

Green turtles, *Chelonia mydas,* are large, air-breathing, herbivo-
rous marine reptiles. They congregate in large populations and graze
on underwater beds of vegetation in relatively clear, shallow, tropical
waters. A mature turtle can weigh 250 pounds or more and when
caught, can live indefinitely in a saltwater enclosure or for a couple of
weeks if kept in shade on land. Green turtles have at least six behavioral characteristics that are important in their exploitation: they occur
in large numbers in localized areas; they are air breathing, so they
have to surface; they are mass social nesters; they have an acute
location-finding ability; when mature, they migrate seasonally on an
overlapping two- or three-year cycle for mating and nesting; and they
exhibit predictable local distributional patterns.

The extensive shallow shelf off eastern Nicaragua is dotted with
numerous small coral islands, thousands of reefs, and vast underwater
pastures of marine vegetation called "turtle banks." During the day, a
large group of turtles may be found feeding at one of the many turtle
banks, while adjacent marine pastures may have only a few turtles.
They graze on the vegetation, rising periodically to the surface for air
and to float for a while before diving again. In the late afternoon,
groups of turtles will leave the feeding areas and swim to shoals, some
up to four or five miles away, to spend the night. By five the next
morning, they gather to depart again for the banks. The turtles' pre-
cise, commuterlike behavior between sleeping and feeding areas is well
known to the Miskito and helps insure good turtling.

Each coastal turtling village exploits an immense sea area, containing many turtle banks and shoals. For example, the Miskito of
Tasbapauni utilize a marine area of approximately 600 square miles,
with twenty major turtle banks and almost forty important shoals.

Having rather predictable patterns of movement and habitat preference, green turtles are commonly caught by the Miskito in three
ways: on the turtle banks with harpoons; along the shoal-to-feeding
area route with harpoons; and on the shoals using nets, which en-
tangle the turtles when they surface for air.

The Miskito's traditional means of taking turtles was by harpoon—an eight- to ten-foot shaft fitted with a detachable short point tied to a strong line. The simple technology pitted two turtlemen in a small, seagoing canoe against the elusive turtles. Successful turtling with harpoons requires an extensive knowledge of turtle behavior and habits and tremendous skill and experience in handling a small canoe in what can be very rough seas. Turtlemen work in partnerships: a "strikerman" in the bow; the "captain" in the stern. Together, they make a single unit engaged in the delicate and almost silent pursuit of a wary prey, their movements coordinated by experience and rewarded by proficiency. Turtlemen have mental maps of all the banks and shoals in their area, each one named and located through a complex system of celestial navigation, distance reckoning, wind and current direction, and the individual surface-swell motion over each site. Traditionally, not all Miskito were sufficiently expert in seamanship and turtle lore to become respected "strikermen," capable of securing turtles even during hazardous sea conditions. Theirs was a very specialized calling. Harpooning restrained possible overexploitation since turtles were taken one at a time by two men directly involved in the chase, and there were only a limited number of really proficient "strikermen" in each village.

Those who still use harpoons must leave early to take advantage of the land breeze and to have enough time to reach the distant offshore turtle grounds by first light. Turtlemen who are going for the day, or for several days, will meet on the beach by 2:00 A.M. They drag the canoes on bamboo rollers from beachfront sheds to the water's edge. There, in the swash of spent breakers, food, water, paddles, lines, harpoons, and sails are loaded and secured. Using a long pole, the standing bowman propels the canoe through the foaming surf while the captain in the stern keeps the craft running straight with a six-foot mahogany paddle. Once past the inside break, the men count the dark rolling seas building outside until there is a momentary pause in the sets; then with paddles digging deep, they drive the narrow, twenty-foot canoe over the cresting swells, rising precipitously on each wave face and then plunging down the far side as the sea and sky seesaw into view. Once past the breakers, they rig the sail and, running with the land breeze, point the canoe toward a star in the eastern sky.

A course is set by star fix and by backsight on a prominent coconut palm on the mainland horizon. Course alterations are made to correct for the direction and intensity of winds and currents. After two or three hours of sailing the men reach a distant spot located between a turtle sleeping shoal and feeding bank. There they intercept and follow the turtles as they leave for specific banks.

On the banks the turtlemen paddle quietly, listening for the sound of a "blowing" turtle. When a turtle surfaces for air it emits a hissing sound audible for fifty yards or more on a calm day. Since a turtle will stay near the surface for only a minute or two before diving to feed, the men must approach quickly and silently, maneuvering the canoe directly in front of or behind the turtle. These are its blind spots. Once harpooned, a turtle explodes into a frenzy of action, pulling the canoe along at high speeds in its hopeless, underwater dash for escape until it tires and can be pulled alongside the canoe.

But turtle harpooning is a dying art. The dominant method of turtling today is the use of nets. Since their introduction, the widespread use of turtle nets has drastically altered turtling strategy and productivity. Originally brought to the Miskito by the Cayman Islanders, nets are now extensively distributed on credit by the turtle companies. This simple technological change, along with a market demand for turtles, has resulted in intensified pressure on green turtle populations.

Buoyed by wooden floats and anchored to the bottom by a single line, the fifty-foot-long by fourteen-foot-wide nets hang from the surface like underwater flags, shifting direction with the current. Nets are set in place during midday when the turtlemen can see the dark shoal areas. Two Miskito will set five to thirty nets from one canoe, often completely saturating a small shoal. In the late afternoon, green turtles return to their shoals to spend the night. There they will sleep beside or beneath a coral outcrop, periodically surfacing for air where a canopy of nets awaits them.

Catching turtles with nets requires little skill; anyone with a canoe can now be a turtleman. The Miskito set thousands of nets daily, providing continuous coverage in densely populated nocturnal habitats. Younger Miskito can become turtlemen almost overnight simply by following more experienced men to the shoal areas, thus circumventing the need for years of accumulated skill and knowledge that once were the domain of the "strikermen." All one has to do is learn where to set the nets, retire for the night, remove the entangled turtles the next morning, and reset the nets. The outcome is predictable: more turtlemen, using more effective methods, catch more turtles.

With an assured market for turtles, the Miskito devote more time to catching turtles, traveling farther and staying at sea longer. Increased dependence on turtles as a source of income and greater time inputs have meant disruption of subsistence agriculture and hunting and fishing. The Miskito no longer produce foodstuffs for themselves; they buy imported foods with money gained from the sale of turtles. Caught between contradictory priorities — their traditional subsistence system and the market economy — the Miskito are opting for cash.

The Miskito are now enveloped in a positive feedback system where change spawns change. Coastal villages rely on turtles for a livelihood. Decline of subsistence provisioning has led to the need to secure food from local shopkeepers on credit to feed the families in the villages and the men during their turtling expeditions. Initial high catches of turtles encouraged more Miskito to participate, and by 1972 the per person and per day catch began to decline noticeably.

In late 1972, several months after I had returned to Michigan, I received a letter from an old turtleman, who wrote: "Turtle is getting scarce, Mr. Barney. You said it would happen in five or ten years but it is happening now."

Burdened by an overdependence on an endangered species and with accumulating debts for food and nets, the Miskito are finding it increasingly difficult to break even, much less secure a profit. With few other economic alternatives, the inevitable step is to use more nets and stay out at sea longer.

The turtle companies encourage the Miskito to expand turtling activities by providing them with building materials so that they can construct houses on offshore cays, thereby elminating the need to return to the mainland during rough weather. On their weekly runs up and down the coast, company boats bring food, turtle gear, and cash for turtles to fishing camps from the Miskito Cays to the Set Net Cays. Frequent visits keep the Miskito from becoming discouraged and returning to their villages with the turtles. On Saturdays, villagers look to sea, watching for returning canoes. A few men will bring turtle for their families; the majority will bring only money. Many return with neither.

Most Miskito prefer to be home on Sunday to visit with friends and for religious reasons. (There are Moravian, Anglican, and Catholic mission churches in many of the villages.) But more and more, turtlemen are staying out for two to four weeks. The church may promise salvation, but only the turtle companies can provide money.

Returning to their villages, turtlemen are confronted with a complex dilemma: how to satisfy both social and economic demands with a limited resource. Traditional Miskito social rules stipulate that turtle meat should be shared among kin, but the new economic system requires that turtles be sold for personal economic gain. Kin expect gifts of meat, and friends expect to be sold meat. Turtlemen are besieged with requests forcing them to decide between who will or will not receive meat. This is contrary to the traditional Miskito ethic, which is based on generosity and mutual concern for the well-being of others. The older Miskito ask why the turtlemen should have to allocate a food that was once abundant and available to all. Turtlemen sell and give to other turtlemen, thereby ensuring reciprocal treatment for themselves, but there simply are not enough turtles to accommodate other economic and social requirements. In order to have enough turtles to sell, fewer are butchered in the villages. This means that less meat is being consumed than before the turtle companies began operations. The Miskito presently sell 70 to 90 percent of the turtles they catch; in the near future they will sell even more and eat less. . . .

Social tension and friction are growing in the villages. Kinship relationships are being strained by what some villagers interpret as preferential and stingy meat distribution. Rather than endure the trauma caused by having to ration a limited item to fellow villagers, many turtlemen prefer to sell all their turtles to the company and return with money, which does not have to be shared. However, if a Miskito sells out to the company, he will probably be unable to acquire meat for himself in the village, regardless of kinship or purchasing power. I overheard an elderly turtleman muttering to himself as he butchered a turtle: "I no going to sell, neither give dem meat. Let dem eat de money."

The situation is bad and getting worse. Individuals too old or sick to provide for themselves often receive little meat or money from relatives. Families without turtlemen are families without money or access to meat. The trend is toward the individualization of nuclear families, operating for their own economic ends. Miskito villages are becoming neighborhoods rather than communities.

The Miskito diet has suffered in quality and quantity. Less protein and fewer diverse vegetables and fruits are consumed. Present dietary staples — rice, white flour, beans, sugar, and coffee — come from the store. In one Miskito village, 65 percent of all food eaten in a year was purchased.

Besides the nutritional significance of what is becoming a largely carbohydrate diet, dependence on purchased foods has also had major economic reverberations. Generated by national and international scarcities, inflationary fallout has hit the Miskito. Most of their purchased foods are imported, much coming from the United States. In the last five years prices for staples have increased 100 to 150 percent. This has had an overwhelming impact on the Miskito, who spend 50 to 75 percent of their income for food. Consequently, their entry into the market by selling a subsistence resource, diverting labor from agriculture, and intensifying exploitation of a vanishing species has resulted in their living off poorer-quality, higher-priced foods.

The Miskito now depend on outside systems to supply them with money and materials that are subject to world market fluctuations.

They have lost their autonomy and their adaptive relationship with their environment. Life is no longer socially rewarding nor is their diet satisfying. The coastal Miskito have become a specialized and highly vulnerable sector of the global market economy.

Loss of turtle market would be a serious economic blow to the Miskito, who have almost no other means of securing cash for what have now become necessities. Nevertheless, continued exploitation will surely reduce the turtle population to a critical level.

National and international legislation is urgently needed. At the very least, commercial turtle fishing must be curtailed for several years until the *Chelonia* population can rebound and exploitation quotas can be set. While turtle fishing for subsistence should be permitted, exportation of sea turtle products used in the gourmet, cosmetic, or jewelry trade should be banned.

Restrictive environmental legislation, however, is not a popular subject in Nicaragua, a country that has recently been torn by earthquakes, volcanic eruption, and hurricanes. A program for sea turtle conservation submitted to the Nicaraguan government for consideration ended up in a pile of rubble during the earthquake that devastated Managua in December, 1972, adding a sad footnote to the Miskito–sea turtle situation. With other problems to face, the government has not yet reviewed what is happening on the distant east coast, separated from the capital by more than 200 miles of rain forest—and years of neglect.

As it is now, the turtles are going down and along with them, the Miskito—seemingly, a small problem in terms of the scale of ongoing ecological and cultural change in the world. But each localized situation involves species and societies with long histories and, perhaps, short futures. They are weathervanes in the conflicting winds of economic and environmental priorities. As Bob Dylan sang: "You don't need a weatherman to tell which way the wind blows."

Review questions

1. What does Nietschmann mean by *subsistence economy?*

2. How has the Miskito Indians' exploitation of the green sea turtle affected their economy?

3. What does Nietschmann mean when he says that the Miskito Indian economy is "enveloped in a positive feedback system"?

4. How has the world market affected the Miskito economy?

VIII

Law and politics

Ideally, culture provides the blueprint for a smoothly oiled social machine whose parts work together under all circumstances. But human society is not like a rigidly constructed machine. It is made of individuals who have their own special needs and desires. Personal interest, competition for scarce resources, and simple accident can cause nonconformity and disputes, resulting in serious social disorganization.

One way we manage social disruption is through the socialization of children. As we acquire our culture, we learn the appropriate ways to look at experience, to define our existence, and to feel about life. Each system of cultural knowledge contains implicit values of what is desirable, and we come to share these values with other people. Slowly, with the acquisition of culture, most people find they *want* to do what they *must* do; the requirements of an orderly social life become personal goals.

Enculturation, however, is rarely enough. Disputes among individuals regularly occur in all societies, and how such disagreements are handled defines what anthropologists mean by the legal system. Some disputes are *infralegal;* they never reach a point where they are settled

275

by individuals with special authority. Neighbors, for example, would engage in an infralegal dispute if they argued over who should pay for the damage caused by water that runs off one's land into the other's basement. So long as they don't take the matter to court or resort to violence, the dispute will remain infralegal. This dispute may become *extralegal*, however, if it occurs outside the law and escalates into violence. Had the neighbors come to blows over the waterlogged basement, the dispute would have become extralegal. Feuds and wars are the best examples of this kind of dispute.

Legal disputes, on the other hand, involve socially approved mechanisms for their settlement. *Law* is the cultural knowledge that people use to settle disputes by means of agents who have recognized authority to do so. Thus, if the argument between neighbors cited above ended up in court before a judge or referee, it would have become legal.

Although we Americans often think of courts as synonymous with the legal system, societies have evolved a variety of structures for settling disputes. For example, some disputes may be settled by *self-redress*, meaning that wronged individuals are given the right to settle matters themselves. *Contests* requiring physical or mental combat between disputants may also be used to settle disputes. A trusted third party, or *go-between*, may be asked to negotiate with each side until a settlement is achieved. In some societies, supernatural power or beings may be used. In parts of India, for example, disputants are asked to take an oath in the name of a powerful deity or (at least in the past) to submit to a supernaturally controlled, painful, or physically dangerous test, called an *ordeal*. Disputes may also be taken to a *moot*, an informal community meeting where conflict may be aired. At the moot, talk continues until a settlement is reached. Finally, as we saw above, disputes are often taken to *courts*, which are formally organized and include officials with authority to make and enforce decisions. The first selection in this section discusses the legal dispute settlement process in a Mexican Zapotec court.

Political systems are closely related to legal ones and often involve some of the same offices and actors. The *political system* contains the process for making and carrying out public policy according to cultural categories and rules; *policy* refers to guidelines for action. The *public* are the people affected by the policy. Every society must make decisions that affect all or most of its members. The Mbuti Pygmies of the Ituri Forest described by anthropologist Colin Turnbull, for example, occasionally decide to conduct a communal hunt. Hunters set their nets together and wait for the appearance of forest game. Men, women, and children must work together as beaters to drive the animals toward the nets. When the Mbuti decide to hold a hunt, they make a political decision.

The political process requires that people make and abide by a particular policy, often in the face of competing plans. To do so a policy must have *support*, which is anything that contributes to its adoption and enforcement. Anthropologists recognize two main kinds of support, legitimacy and coercion. *Legitimacy* refers to people's positive evaluation of public officials and public policy. A college faculty, for example, may decide to institute the quarter system because a majority feels that quarters rather than semesters represent the "right length" for courses. Theirs is a positive evaluation of the policy. Some faculty members will oppose the change but will abide by the decision because they value the authority of faculty governance. For them the decision, although unfortunate, is legitimate.

Coercion, on the other hand, is support derived from the threat or use of force or the promise of short-term gain. Had the faculty members adopted the quarter system because they had been threatened with termination by the administration, they would have acted under coercion.

There are also other important aspects of the political process. Some members of a society may be given *authority*, the right to make and enforce public policy. In our country, elected officials are given authority to make certain decisions and exercise particular powers. However, formal political offices with authority do not occur in every society. Most hunting and gathering societies lack such positions, as do many horticulturalists. *Leadership*, which is the ability to influence others to act, must be exercised informally in these societies.

As we noted above, legal and political systems cannot be thought of as separate parts of any culture, except for analytical purposes. In practice, both are backed by legitimate power and authority, and in many instances the two systems operate together. As the following selections will demonstrate, the forms legal and political systems take vary from one society to the next.

KEY TERMS

infralegal	political system
extralegal	policy
law	public
self-redress	support

contest	legitimacy
go-between	coercion
ordeal	authority
moot	leadership
court	

23

Law and order

JAMES P. SPRADLEY and
DAVID W. McCURDY

*When we consider American law, we are likely to think of formal
written statutes, police, courts, lawyers, strict rules of evidence, the
determination of guilt, and punishment. In our large society the system seems technical and impersonal. In this selection, Spradley and
McCurdy discuss the structure of law in the context of fieldwork
conducted by anthropologist Laura Nader, who did research in the
Zapotec community of Ralu'a. They discuss several legal cases to illustrate such concepts as substantive and procedural law, legal levels,
and legal principles. They conclude with Nader's argument that
Zapotec law seeks "to make the balance," to attempt a settlement
between disputants that will promote social harmony.*

The land rover disappeared in a cloud of dust on its way back to
Oaxaca City. The anthropologist adjusted the shoulder straps on the
backpack, turned away from the end of the road, and began to follow
the two Zapotec Indian guides. The trail led north, climbing along the
edge of steep valleys, crossing over mountain ridges, and winding
back and forth to make a steady gain in altitude. Accustomed to living
at 5000 feet above sea level, the two guides walked rapidly, oblivious to
the hard breathing of their American companion. In every direction,
scattered over much of the 36,000 square miles of Oaxaca State in
southern Mexico, the anthropologist knew there were small Zapotec
villages. The three of them headed toward the Rincon district, which
means "the corner," calling attention to the fact that the area is par-

"Law and Order" (abridged) by James P. Spradley and David W. McCurdy from *Anthropology: The Cultural Perspective*, 2nd edition. Copyright © 1980 John Wiley and Sons, Inc.
Reprinted by permission of Random House, Inc.

tially encircled by three high mountain peaks. As they walked, the anthropologist could see the distant and formidable Zempoateptl Mountain reaching to more than 10,000 feet; Maceta and El Machin, the two other peaks, would come into view before they reached their destination, the pueblo of Ralu'a. One of the Zapotec men spoke Spanish and had told the anthropologist as they started, "We are called the people of the corner, *Rinconeros*, because we live between the peaks." The sun was high on this day in early May 1957 and the sky clear; it was several weeks before the rainy season would begin. Wild orchids were in bloom everywhere. The mountains had a kind of awesome beauty for the anthropologist, particularly since she had anticipated the sight for many months. As she walked behind the guides, she wondered why no other social scientist had ever come before to this place, to live and study among these people.

The Zapotec guides pushed on, stopping only for water now and then at the edge of fast-flowing mountain streams. During the first hour they had passed scattered fields of coffee plants in bloom and sugarcane, evidence that a pueblo or homestead was nearby, enfolded in some mountain niche. The anthropologist would like to have stopped to inquire about these settlements and to rest, but the two guides never hesitated, pressing on toward their destination. The sun had already disappeared behind the highest peak when, after a 3½-hour walk, they came to Ralu'a, a pueblo of 2000 people. Unexpectedly, as they came over a rise, houses appeared everywhere; children played on the paths, and women could be seen carrying firewood. The anthropologist felt a sense of excitement as she looked down on the town that would be her home for many months to come. Here she would live and work and make friends; from here she would travel to other villages and nearby settlements in her efforts to discover the cultural ways of the Zapotec; and here she would try to understand Zapotec law, to describe the cultural rules these people used when settling disputes.

As they entered the edge of the pueblo, she wondered how these people would receive her. Would they understand why she had come? In Oaxaca City she had met an engineer, a government employee who had friends in Ralu'a. He had made tentative arrangements for her to stay with a family while she conducted her field study. All was excitement at the home of her hosts, for a fiesta was in progress to celebrate the return of religious pilgrims from the Sanctuario in Veracruz. Her hosts seemed polite but not enthusiastic as they invited her to join them in the fiesta meal of special foods. After they had eaten, the head of the household came to her and asked, "Are you a Catholic? If you are not a Catholic, you cannot stay here. We do not want Protestants in our town." Surprised by this question, she explained her role and assured him that she belonged to the original Catholic church (Eastern Orthodox).

It would be many weeks before she would fully appreciate what lay behind this simple question about her religion. She was to discover that it concerned authority, conflict, and the process of law and dispute settlement, the very areas she had come to investigate. Before two weeks had elapsed a message came from the priest: she was to come to his house immediately. She entered and, after a brief exchange in Spanish, he said, "You are a Protestant missionary! Why have you come to our pueblo?" Nothing would convince him that it was not so; even the letter of recommendation that she brought from a priest in Oaxaca was dismissed as a fake, and a wire of confirmation from that priest that she was an anthropologist and a good Christian did not convince him. Although others would eventually accept her, the priest in Ralu'a would remain unconvinced, spreading the word from the pulpit and in the streets that she was really a Protestant missionary. Several years earlier some missionaries had come to Ralu'a and, as a result of winning converts, conflicts erupted that led to burning of Protestant homes. The dispute reached enormous proportions for this small pueblo and was only settled through the process of law when the state government forced the town to pay heavy fines for damage inflicted.

When the anthropologist was called to the home of the priest in the Zapotec pueblo of Ralu'a, she became a party to a dispute. He accused her of being a Protestant missionary; she denied it. Although she appealed to another priest to confirm her identity, he did not have the authority to settle the dispute. Like many troubles that beset human interaction, this dispute was never settled, and the anthropologist had to work around the difficulties it created with other individuals in the village. The dispute remained below the level of the law, but it is conceivable that the priest or the anthropologist could have appealed to some agent whose authority was recognized and who could settle the case. It would then have become a legal matter.

One of the earliest disputes that came to the anthropologist's attention occurred at a Ralu'a well several months after she arrived among the Zapotec. She awoke as usual one morning to the sound of the women in the household getting ready to go to the mill. It was 5:00 A.M., and each morning at this time the women in Ralu'a arose to take their corn to nearby mills. The men were still asleep as the anthropologist dressed and prepared to go with the women. It was not yet light at this hour of the morning, but the daily walk to the mill was exhilarating. Other women greeted them and, at the mill, while they waited to have their corn ground, they visited with each other. Soon each would return home to prepare tortillas, fix breakfast for the family, and make lunches for the men who must walk many miles to their fields for a day of work. But now they caught up on the local news and enjoyed visiting.

This morning two women were earnestly discussing an argument that had occurred on the previous day at Los Remedios, one of the town wells. Carmen had gone to the well to wash the family clothes, and instead of using the flat slab of stone that belonged to her, she selected one near a friend so they could visit as they worked. Like other women she looked forward to this task because it enabled her to visit and gossip with others in the neighborhood, a pleasant change from working alone inside her house. But hardly 20 minutes had passed when the owner of the washing stone appeared, and instead of taking another place she angrily asked Carmen to move. As Carmen began to gather her wet clothes together, she loudly commented on the other woman's generosity. Insults began to fly, and the situation became especially tense when Carmen "accidentally" splashed water on the newcomer's dress as she went off to finish washing on her own slab. Some said Carmen should have moved to her own stone without comment; others declared that the second woman was wrong and should have gone quietly to another place to wash. Someone recalled a similar conflict several years earlier when a woman had taken the matter to the *municipio*, or town hall, where the *presidente* had settled the dispute. Some of the women wondered whether the trouble of yesterday would go that far.

It was the end of the summer before the dispute over washing stones reached the boiling point and became a case of law, but it did not happen in the way the anthropologist had expected, for no one took the dispute to the *municipio*. The incident at the well did not die down; the two women continued to make insulting remarks in public, and others began to take sides. Then a similar conflict arose between several other women who were not using the stones that belonged to them. At night in the *cantina* as the men drank *mescal*, an alcoholic drink made from the fermented juice of agave plants, they talked of the disputes they had learned about from their wives. Some men reported that at the wells where their wives washed clothes no such fights had occurred; everyone agreed that the problem was primarily at Los Remedios.

The bickering and fighting continued until one day people not-

ater at Los Remedios had begun to dry up. Some said
d by the fighting. The men who belonged to the Well
group that worked to maintain the wells, called a special
lecided that they must take action to save the water.
They formed a work party and improved the well to ensure more
water, but they also removed all the slabs of stone used for washing. In
place of these privately owned washing places they constructed 24
shallow tubs from cement and announced that no one could own or
reserve one of these spaces. They belonged to the well and were to be
used on a first-come, first-serve basis. The priest blessed the new well,
and the disputes were settled. Although some women complained that
they liked the old way better, everyone recognized the authority of the
men's Well Association, and the change was accepted. . . .

The ethnographer who investigates the process of law in a non-
Western society must collect data on all kinds of disputes. Since any
conflict can be transformed overnight into a legal dispute involving
some agent with recognized authority, it is important to examine the
range of ways that people handle such troubles. By means of various
ethnographic discovery procedures, one begins to focus more and
more on legal cases, those that are settled by people or groups with
authority.

THE STRUCTURE OF LEGAL CULTURE

By examining dispute cases, observing their outcome, and questioning the parties involved, one can describe a goodly portion of the
law ways of a community. Such legal knowledge can be analyzed into
three different aspects. First, the most explicit aspect of legal knowledge
includes *substantive law* and *procedural law,* which are interrelated. At a
more implicit level, underlying these rules, are the fundamental *legal
principles* that determine the shape of the law in a particular society.
Finally, there is a common core of *cultural values* that influence the legal
principles and link the law of any culture to other domains of that
culture. . . .

Substantive law. The term "law" is most often used in our own
society to refer to substantive law, the legal statutes that define right
and wrong. Phrases such as, "He broke the law" or "It is illegal to
bring liquor across the state line," refer to substantive law. It is easy for
us to assume that substantive rules can be equated with written statutes, but this is not always the case in our own society, and most of the
world's cultures do not have written laws at all. But all people have
agreed-on substantive rules. Let us look at an example of an unwritten
law from our own society.

Until recently every city in the United States had passed legislatu that made it a crime to appear drunk in public. For many years in the city of Seattle this substantive rule was used to make more than 10,000 arrests each year. Although the law against public drunkenness seems clear and simple, ethnographic investigation of individual cases in Seattle shows that many other substantive rules of a complex nature were actually being used. In practice, the police used their own discretion to arrest some drunks but not others. The unwritten rule was, "If you see a poor man on skid row who is drunk, arrest him; those of the middle and upper class who are drunk in other parts of town need not be arrested." A tramp from skid row who had been arrested many times reported the following experience. Standing outside the University Club located several blocks from skid row, he observed men coming out of the club in states of obvious intoxication. A policeman not only saw the same men, but assisted them into cabs for transportation home.

The substantive law of Ralu'a contains many specific rules. Some are part of a written legal code, others must be inferred from what people say and do in dispute cases. Many cases end up in the town hall, the *municipio*, a two-room, adobe building in the center of town. Here certain officials hold a kind of court to settle disputes. Thirteen respected men make up an advisory group for the pueblo, the *principales*. Each year this group nominates three men for the position of village chairman, or *presidente*, one of whom is elected by the village to serve for 1 year. The *presidente*, in turn, appoints these same *principales* for another 1-year term. Working closely with the *presidente* is a man elected to the office of *sindico*, who runs the communal work program of the pueblo and is also head of the town police. There are 12 *policia* who serve under two lieutenants and a chief of police. Each year the outgoing men of this police force nominate other men, generally those who have been the biggest troublemakers during the year, to take over as replacements. They are then elected by the village as a whole, and the roughest man of all becomes the chief of police for the year. The *presidente* and the *sindico*, working together, handle minor disputes such as drunkenness, fighting, flirting, slander, boundary trespass, and theft. There is a third elected official, the *alcalde*, a kind of justice of the peace, who presides over more serious disputes. The *presidente* will often pass more serious cases as well as any cases that he cannot resolve directly to the *alcalde*. More serious cases or those that the *alcalde* cannot resolve are passed on to the district court. While the *presidente* and the *sindico* have various duties, the *alcalde* deals only with legal matters. We can see substantive law in action among the Zapotec if we examine two specific cases.

The case of the flirting husband. The first dispute involves a violation of rules that prohibit flirting. An unmarried woman, Señorita Zoalage, came to the *presidente* early on a Tuesday morning. She complained that a married man, Señor Huachic, had flirted with her. He appeared outside her house and made the equivalent of American wolf-calls shortly after dark on Monday night on his way home from the market. The *presidente* talked over the matter with the *sindico,* and someone was sent to notify Señor Huachic to appear in court that afternoon. It was now 2:00 P.M. and the *presidente* sat behind a long table at the front of the *presidencia,* one of the rooms in the town hall. Both Señor Huachic and Señorita Zoalage sat before him. After presenting the complaint to Señor Huachic, the *presidente* waited for his response. "Yes," he admitted, "I did what she said, but only because this woman here, Señorita Zoalage, flirted with me last week! She even invited me to come with her to collect firewood!" After some discussion about the particulars of the case the *presidente* said, "Señorita Zoalage, I am going to fine you 30 pesos for flirting with Señor Huachic. And Señor Huachic, you are fined 60 pesos for flirting with Señorita Zoalage. You are a married man and should have been at home with your wife." After warning them to refrain from further exhibitions of such behavior he dismissed them, they paid their fines, and returned to their homes. Each had violated a substantive rule that holds flirting to be illegal. In some cases individuals refuse to pay fines and, as a result, may be detained in jail or compelled to work on a community project.

The case of the disobedient son. The second case sheds light on substantive rules involving the relationships between parents and children. It was relatively easy to elicit cultural rules for this relationship. For example, one evening after the anthropologist had been in Ralu'a for 8 months, she was having dinner with a Zapotec family. The father had just told the others about a son who had been sent to jail in the district capital because when his father had beat him he had struck back, hitting his father. The anthropologist asked quizzically, "And for this they sent him to jail?"

"Of course," he said, looking rather surprised that she would ask such a stupid question.

"But," she said, seeking to enlarge on the discussion, "many men beat their wives, and they never go to jail for that!"

"Yes," the father responded, "but wives are one thing, fathers another."

It seemed a good place to introduce a hypothetical question and so she asked, "But what if the father beats his son harshly, and the father is in the wrong? Is it still wrong for the son to strike his father?"

The son in the family spoke up, entering the discussion with a serious tone. "Fathers are never in the wrong for beating their sons. They always do it for their own good."

Still not satisfied, the anthropologist asked one last question, "All right, but sons grow up and become men. Under your law could a father ever be proved guilty for doing wrong to a son, even if he is a grown man?"

The father's answer brought looks of agreement from the others, "A father cannot do wrong with his children." There the discussion ended, but several days later she observed a case in the *presidencia* that underscored this substantive rule of Zapotec law.[1]

Señor Benjamin Mendoza Cruz had complained to the court about his son, Clemente Mendoza, who was 25 years of age. Because the complaint had been made several days earlier, both men were sitting before the *presidente*. Señor Cruz repeated his charge. "I have coffee planted on my land near one of the neighboring *ranchos*. Someone harvested some of my ripe coffee beans, and I thought the thief was from the neighboring pueblo, but a woman who has the land next to mine said she saw my son harvesting the coffee. I demand that he repay me for the coffee he has stolen."

The *presidente* turned to the son, Clemente Mendoza, waiting for him to speak. His eyes were on the floor; he did not look at the *presidente* or his father as he spoke. "Yes," he said, "I admit that I went to his field and cut some coffee. A year ago he allowed me to cut some coffee on his property, and I was confident he would give the coffee to me, but I am at fault, and now he can decide how to punish me. I have committed a crime against him and now I wish he would forgive me." There was a long pause when the son finished speaking. The *presidente* sat silently as the secretary continued writing. Then the father spoke slowly. "I am, as his father, very sad that my son Clemente should have done this wickedness to me. I did not believe that it was he until the woman told me. Now I will leave it to his *Municipio Presidente* to decide what is suitable. As his father I have to help him and look after him, but he should not act this way, disposing of the fruit of my harvest without my consent."

Another period of silence followed; flies buzzed noisily around the room. It was warm and the *presidente* thought about the man and

---

[1]This case is presented in the excellent ethnographic film *To Make the Balance*, Berkeley: University of California Extension Media Center, and also in "Styles of Court Procedure: To Make the Balance," in *Law in Culture and Society*, Laura Nader (editor), Chicago: Aldine, 1969.

his son, how he would settle the case. He recalled that fathers should provide for their sons when they came asking for a bride price, but Señor Cruz had already given more than once to his son for this purpose; Clemente had spent it on other things. Yes, it was the son who was at fault. He turned to him now. "Now you heard what your father said, and I will tell you that your father does not have an obligation to give you, his son, *anything.*" He raised his voice on the last word as if to emphasize the great distance between fathers and sons. He continued, "Nor is a father obliged to give you what is his. If a father loves his son very much, he may give him something, but nobody can force him to do so. Now, you have abused him and, as you have admitted, there is no reason why your father should help you because you committed this wrong." Clemente Mendoza had been afraid of his father all of his life. After his mother died, his father remarried, and he found it even more difficult to get along with the old man. Now he sat in silence, his eyes shifting nervously, focused on the floor most of the time as he listened to the *presidente* ask, "Are you now both ready to come to an agreement?" They would accept his settlement.

"Clemente Mendoza," the *presidente* addressed the guilty son, "you shall repay your father for the coffee that you took without permission. Without delay you have to deliver the 25 pounds of dried coffee to your father, and the deadline is Friday, the 21st of this month, and for the wrong you have committed I impose on you a 200-peso fine, which you have to pay today." The secretary prepared an agreement that finalized the ending of the dispute, and it was soon ready for signing. More than an hour had passed since they first appeared before the *presidente.* The agreement showed the amount Clemente would repay his father as well as the fine payable to the *municipio.* The agreement was shown to both parties, and the *presidente* addressed them one more time.

"Clemente Mendoza, you should realize that both you and your father are bound by this agreement; you should not inflict reprisals on your father or stepmother, and you must realize that your father has the right, as a father, to correct any of your faults. You, as his son, must ask him for full permission to harvest some coffee or give you anything else, to avoid being offensive to your father. You should now go and behave as a good son should behave."

Turning to the father he said, "Señor Cruz, whenever you desire you can dispose of your property and give it to your son, you can help him in mutual agreement, but the father does not have any obligation to give his son anything; on the other hand, the son cannot demand his father to give him any of his property. It is entirely in the hands of the father whether he wants to give or not."

The two men, father and son, signed the agreement and turned to walk out of the *municipio*. It had been a rare occurrence for a father to bring his son to court. Most disputes of this sort are easily settled by the authority of the father. Although all sons feel the constraints of the father's authority, they know they will one day marry and have sons of their own and, like their father, require total obedience.

Procedural law. When a dispute moves into the settlement stage, numerous procedural rules come into play. Procedural law refers to the agreed-on ways to settle a dispute. They guide not only the *presidente*, the *sindico*, the *alcalde*, or other authority agent, but also the parties to a dispute. Take, for example, the unwritten procedural rule about *who* should bring family disputes to the court. Although a large number of family cases are brought to the *presidente's* court, only certain classes of persons would think of settling such disputes in the court. The *principales*, for example, are some of the most respected men in Ralu'a, and they take pride in their respectable families. Undoubtedly their authority in the pueblo enhances their authority within their families, giving them the power to arbitrate and settle any disputes that may arise. If any member complained about family problems in court, it would bring shame and dishonor to the entire family. There is, therefore, considerable social pressure to keep members abiding by the unwritten procedural rule that says that *principales and their families should not use the court to settle family disputes.* If the wife of a *principale* were to appear in court making a complaint against her husband, the *presidente* would be greatly surprised, and news of this event would quickly spread throughout the pueblo. Everyone would know that she had violated an implicit procedural rule of Zapotec law.

Procedural rules in U.S. society. Procedural rules in our own legal system are not always clearly specified. The ethnographer seeks to make these rules explicit, thereby shedding light on substantive rules and the entire process of law. The ethnographic research among the tramps in Seattle, Washington, mentioned earlier, revealed an implicit procedural rule that held enormous significance for this population. It involves a procedural rule for sentencing that can be stated as follows.

> *If a man is poor and has been arrested many times for being drunk in public, he shall be sentenced with greater severity than those with money or with no record of previous arrests for drunkenness.*

On the basis of this rule, two men could be arrested at 10:00 P.M. on Monday on the same block in Seattle and plead guilty in court to public drunkenness. One would be given a 2-day suspended sentence and would walk out of the courtroom a free man. The other would be given 90 days in jail. Why this difference? The first man had not been arrested for this crime during the preceding 6 months, whereas the other had been arrested seven times.

The most significant part of this procedural rule, however, involves differences in wealth. Take two men, for example, who were arrested 10 to 15 times each year for public drunkenness. Each time they were picked up by the Seattle police they had to spend several hours in the jail "drying out." Then both men were allowed to post a $20 bail, *if they had the money.* Only one of the men had this amount, and he alone was immediately released from jail. He might be arrested again within a few days or weeks and repeat the process. Over the course of 15 or 20 years such a man might spend several thousand dollars for bail, each time walking away from jail after a few hours of sleep. Although a man who posted bail was expected to appear in court for his arraignment, no one did, choosing instead to forfeit this money than face a judge and possible jail sentence. The man who could not post bail, on the other hand, waited several days in the drunk tank, appeared in court, pleaded guilty, received his sentence, and then returned to the jail to serve his time. Thus violation of the same *substantive rule* can lead to enormously different consequences, depending on the nature of related *procedural rules. . . .*

LEGAL LEVELS

In every culture the existence of different kinds of authority agents means that disputes can be settled at different levels. In our own society a dispute between a teacher and a student can be settled by the school principal. If the dispute continues, it could go to the town board of education. If still unsettled, it might go to the local court and even be appealed to a series of higher courts.

Among the Zapotec, several levels for settling disputes exist. Disputes can be settled by family elders, witches, local officials, the priest, supernatural beings, or officials in the *municipio.* If all else fails, the dispute can be taken to the district court in Villa Alta. Consider the following case.

Mariano's son Pedro married the only daughter of a family in the pueblo and went to live with her family. Mariano was pleased with the arrangement because he had helped decide the marriage. But soon trouble began to develop between his son and the new wife. It came to his attention directly when his daughter-in-law came to him and complained, "Your son Pedro is always drunk, he does not work now, and he argues with me all the time in the home of my parents." Mariano talked with her for some time and, on the following day, he warned Pedro that he should drink less and live at peace with his new wife. Like any son in Ralu'a, Pedro promised his father that he would change his behavior. However, within a month Mariano's daughter-in-law was back again with the same complaint. This time Mariano was angry. "She is back again so soon," he thought. "This son of mine does not learn from words." Mariano found his son and this time, amidst stern warnings, he whipped Pedro harshly.

The weeks passed and still Pedro did not change. His wife now turned to the *padrinos de pano*, the godparents of the marriage. But their warnings to Pedro were to no avail, and so she went to the priest. He talked to Pedro several times, and it seemed the penitent husband might change with his intervention. Then one night Pedro came home very drunk and began cursing at his wife and threatening her. Then he beat her, and she lay awake most of the night wondering what to do next. The fact that he had beat her was less important than that it was another stage in their deteriorating relationship and evidence that Pedro had not changed. Early in the morning while Pedro was still asleep she went to the *municipio* and made a complaint to the *presidente*. Pedro was cited and appeared in court later that same afternoon. He told the *presidente* that he had been drunk and did not know what he was doing, that he would change his ways, and that he would begin to work regularly in his fields. Pedro paid a fine of 50 pesos and signed an agreement that he would live at peace with his wife.

Disputes such as this can be resolved at various levels and through various remedy agents such as male family heads, church officials, village officials, and even by appeals directly to supernatural beings and individuals who are witches. For example, a man who is having trouble with his wife may go to a witch and say, "Somebody is gossiping about me and every time I come home my wife is after me because she is so upset. Can you do something about this person who is spreading bad tales about me?" The witch will reply, "Pay me 5 pesos and I'll find out who it is and do something about it." But whether a man goes to a witch or to the *presidente*, or whether a woman goes to her father-in-law is not left to happenstance. The procedural rules of a culture's law help define which authorities should be employed for various kinds of disputes.

LEGAL PRINCIPLES AND CULTURAL VALUES

Underlying the settlement of disputes in every society we find legal principles based on the fundamental values of a culture. A legal principle is a broad conception of some desirable state of affairs that gives rise to many substantive and procedural rules. The witness is asked, "Do you promise to tell the truth, the whole truth, and nothing but the truth, so help you God?" We accept the value of telling the objective truth, getting at the facts, and we believe that humans are capable of telling the truth. In some societies, however, people hold different assumptions, asserting that it is not possible to tell objective truth. In other cultures the value placed on the facts is small when compared to the importance of restoring amicable relationships. In order to understand the decisions authorities make to settle disputes, we need to grasp the legal principles of a culture.

When the Zapotec talk about the characteristics of those wise men who have settled disputes in the proper way, they say, "He knows how to *make the balance.*" This principle means that fault-finding in a particular trouble case is not as important as balancing the demands of all parties and restoring conditions of peaceful coexistence. The men's Well Association did not concern itself with seeking culprits who had violated rules about the use of private property. Instead, they sought to restore peace and prevent future conflicts at Los Remedios. Their goal—*hacer el balance*—to make the balance, was achieved.

The principle of balance does not mean people are never at fault, never violate substantive rules. Instead, it means that disputes are not settled merely by establishing the facts of the case, finding the guilty party, and administering punishment. When Clemente Mendoza harvested his father's coffee without permission, he was clearly in the wrong. But the *presidente,* acting as a kind of father to the citizens of Ralu'a, sought to restore the balance, to mend the relationship between father and son, eliciting a signed agreement from them that they would not hold grudges and continue the dispute.

The case of fright. To the Zapotec, making the balance means settling disputes with an eye to the future of the relationships involved, not merely an examination of past events. Disputes create difficulties for people, financial losses, bitter feelings, and disrupted relationships. It would be possible to settle disputes without rectifying any of these conditions, but for the Zapotec this would not be sufficient, although the guilty person were given a life sentence for his or her crime. Take the case of Señora Juan. She complained to the *presidente* that she had been working, cutting coffee in the field of Señora Quiroz, when a young boy, Teodora Garcia, had picked on her 6-year-old boy, hitting him. The experience had been so disconcerting to the smaller boy that he had come down with *susto*, or magical fright, an illness involving the loss of one's soul. "My little boy got frightened," she told the *presidente*, "and now he yells during the night and has diarrhea because of the fright. I am asking the *presidente* to help me make my little son well again." The *presidente* asked Teodoro Garcia about the dispute, and he answered that the son of Señora Juan was always calling him names and taunting him while he worked. Back and forth the discussion went, but the *presidente* did not seek to discover what really happened; *his goal was not to find out the facts.* He allowed people to express their feelings in the matter. It was difficult to tell who was at fault, but he could easily see that this upset had disturbed the equilibrium in social relationships of all those involved. A boy had *susto* as a result, and the *presidente* knew he could do something about that, restoring the balance required. The poor mother said she needed 30 pesos for the curer. After negotiation, Teodoro Garcia offered to settle for 20 pesos. The case was resolved, the boy taken to a curer, and the balance restored.

Cultural values. Underlying the legal principles of a society are the values that form the basis of social life. Making the balance in settling disputes is based on a widely held Zapotec cultural value of maintaining equilibrium. Direct confrontation between individuals in which one loses and another wins is unsettling to Zapotecans. As expressed by Laura Nader:

> This concern for equilibrium is evident through Ralu'a. Upon my making inquiries as to the motives for witchcraft in Ralu'a an informant reported the following as causes: "because one works too much or not enough; because one is too pretty or too ugly or too rich; for being an only child; for being rich and refusing to lend money; for being antisocial—for example, for refusing to greet people." These are all situations that some-how upset the balance as Ralu'ans see it. It is no wonder that the zero-sum game (win or lose) as we know it in some American courts would be a frightening prospect to a plaintiff, even though all "right" might be on his side. The plaintiff need not worry, however, for the *presidente* is equally reluctant to make such a clear-cut zero-sum game decision for a variety of reasons—among them that witchcraft is an all too possible tool of retaliation for such behavior. If a plaintiff wanted to play the zero-sum game he would go to a witch and not to the courts, where behavior is far too public.[2]

[2]"Styles of Court Procedure: To Make the Balance," in *Law in Culture and Society*, Laura Nader (editor), Chicago: Aldine, 1969, pp. 73–74.

No doubt on that first day when the anthropologist entered the pueblo she had somehow upset some unseen sense of equilibrium in this Zapotec pueblo. A strange woman, dressed in strange clothes, with a strange reason for being there, asking strange questions; she must be a Protestant missionary, a person with supernatural power, at least someone to arouse suspicion. However, after weeks of persistently defining her role and participating in the daily round of life, she had overcome most of the suspicion and fear. Then one warm day when the excitement of a fiesta filled the air of Ralu'a, she had purchased a large barrel of *mescal* and donated it to the pueblo celebrations. It was a simple token, but the citizens of Ralu'a responded with enthusiasm. Public officials lauded her generosity and declared that she was now a true member of the pueblo. Others apologized for their suspicions and unfriendliness as they drank and laughed together. Without calculation she had *hacer el balance.* . . .

REVIEW QUESTIONS

1. What are the definitions of law, substantive law, procedural law, legal levels, and legal principles? What Zapotec dispute cases illustrate these concepts? Can you think of examples from our own society?

2. Based on the examples cited in this selection, how does Zapotec law differ from American law? Illustrate your answer with specific examples.

3. Some anthropologists believe that every society has some *informal* substantive and procedural legal rules. Comment on this assertion using the Zapotec and American cases presented in this article.

4. Why do you think Zapotec law emphasizes "making the balance" while American law seems more concerned with determining guilt?

24

Yanomamö: The fierce people

NAPOLEON A. CHAGNON

Every society provides a basis for authority and ways to gain support for such authority. In this article, Napoleon Chagnon describes the Yanomamö, a group which bases its authority structure on a continuum of violence and on claims to fierceness or willingness to do violence.

The Yanomamö Indians are a tribe in Venezuela and Brazil who practice a slash-and-burn way of horticultural life. Traditionally, they have been an inland "foot" tribe, avoiding larger rivers and settling deep in the tropical jungle. Until about 1950 they had no sustained contact with other peoples except, to a minor extent, with another tribe, the Carib-speaking Makiritaris to the northeast.

I recently lived with the Yanomamö for more than a year, doing research sponsored by the U.S. Public Health Service, with the cooperation of the Venezuela Institute for Scientific Research. My purpose was to study Yanomamö social organization, language, sex practices, and forms of violence, ranging from treacherous raids to chest-pounding duels.

Those Yanomamö who have been encouraged to live on the larger rivers (Orinoco, Mavaca, Ocamo, and Padamo) are slowly beginning to realize that they are not the only people in the world; there is also a place called Caraca-tedi (Caracas), from whence come foreigners of an entirely new order. These foreigners speak an incomprehensible language, probably a degenerate form of Yanomamö. They bring malaria

With permission from *Natural History*, Vol. 76, No. 1; Copyright the American Museum of Natural History, 1967.

pills, machetes, axes, cooking pots, and *copetas* ("guns"), have curious ideas about indecency, and speak of a new "spirit."

However, the Yanomamö remain a people relatively unadulterated by outside contacts. They are also fairly numerous. Their population is roughly 10,000, the larger portion of them distributed throughout southern Venezuela. Here, in basins of the upper Orinoco and all its tributaries, they dwell in some 75 scattered villages, each of which contains from 40 to 300 individuals.

The largest, most all-embracing human reality to these people is humanity itself; Yanomamö means true human beings. Their conception of themselves as the only true "domestic" beings (those that dwell in houses) is demonstrated by the contempt with which they treat non-Yanomamö, who, in their language, are "wild." For instance, when referring to themselves, they use an honorific pronoun otherwise reserved for important spirits and headmen; when discussing *nabäs* ("non-Yanomamö"), an ordinary pronoun is enough. Again, in one of the myths about their origin, the first people to be created were the Yanomamö. All others developed by a process of degeneration and are, therefore, not quite on a par with the Yanomamö.

In addition to meaning "people," Yanomamö also refers to the language. Their tribal name does not designate a politically organized entity but is more or less equivalent to our concept of humanity. (This, of course, makes their most outstanding characteristic — chronic warfare, of which I shall speak in detail — seem rather an anomaly.) Sub-Yanomamö groupings are based on language differences, historical separation, and geographical location.

For instance, two distinguishable groups, Waika (from *waikaö* — "to kill off") and Shamatari, speak nearly identical dialects; they are differentiated mostly on the basis of a specific event that led to their separation. The Shamatari, the group I know best, occupy the area south of the Orinoco to, and including portions of, northern Brazil. Their differentiation from the Waika probably occurred in the past 75 years.

According to the Indians, there was a large village on a northern tributary of the upper Orinoco River, close to its headwaters. The village had several factions, one of which was led by a man called Kayabawä (big tree). A notably corpulent man, he also had the name Shamatari, derived from *shama*, the "tapir," a robust ungulate found throughout tropical South America. As the story goes, Shamatari's faction got into a fight with the rest of the village over the possession of a woman, and the community split into two warring halves. Gradually the fighting involved more villages, and Shamatari led his faction south, crossed the Orinoco, and settled there. He was followed by members of other villages that had taken his part in the fight.

Those who moved to the south side of the Orinoco came to be called Shamataris by those living on the north side, and the term is now applied to any village in this area, whether or not it can trace its origin to the first supporters of Shamatari.

For the Yanomamö, the village is the maximum political unit and the maximum sovereign body, and it is linked to other villages by ephemeral alliances, visiting and trade relationships, and intermarriages. In essence, the village is a building — a continuous, open-roofed lean-to built on a circular plan and surrounded by a protective palisade of split palm logs. The roof starts at or near ground level, ascends at an angle of about 45 degrees, and reaches a height of some 20 to 25 feet. Individual segments under the continuous roof are not partitioned; from a hammock hung anywhere beneath it one can see (and hear, thanks to the band shell nature of the structure) all that goes on within the village.

The palisade, about three to six feet behind the base of the roof, is some ten feet high and is usually in various stages of disrepair, depending on the current warfare situation. The limited number of entrances are covered with dry palm leaves in the evening; if these are moved even slightly, the sound precipitates the barking of a horde of ill-tempered, underfed dogs, whose bad manners preadapt the stranger to what lies beyond the entrance.

A typical "house" (a segment under the continuous roof) shelters a man, his wife or wives, their children, perhaps one or both of the man's parents, and, farther down, the man's brothers and their families. The roof is alive with cockroaches, scorpions, and spiders, and the ground is littered with the debris of numerous repasts — bird, fish, and animal bones; bits of fur; skulls of monkeys and other animals, banana and plantain peelings; feathers; and the seeds of palm fruits. Bows and arrows stand against housepoles all over the village, baskets hang from roof rafters, and firewood is stacked under the lower part of the roof where it slopes to the ground. Some men will be whittling arrow points with agouti-tooth knives or tying feathers to arrow shafts. Some women will be spinning cotton, weaving baskets, or making hammocks or cotton waistbands. The children, gathered in the center of the village clearing, frequently tie a string to a lizard and entertain themselves by shooting the animal full of tiny arrows. And, of course, many people will be outside the compound, working in their gardens, fishing, or collecting palm fruits in the jungle.

If it is a typical late afternoon, most of the older men are gathered in one part of the village, blowing one of their hallucinatory drugs (*ebene*) up each other's nostrils by means of a hollow tube and chanting to the forest demons (*hekuras*) as the drug takes effect. Other men may be curing a sick person by sucking, massaging, and exhorting the evil spirit from him. Everybody in the village is swatting vigorously at the voracious biting gnats, and here and there groups of people delouse each other's heads and eat the vermin.

In composition, the village consists of one or more groups of patrilineally related kinsmen (*mashis*), but it also contains other categories, including people who have come from other villages seeking spouses. All villages try to increase their size and consider it desirable for both the young men and young women to remain at home after marriage. Since one must marry out of his *mashi*, villages with only one patrilineage frequently lose their young men to other villages; they must go to another village to *siohamou* (to "son-in-law") if they want wives. The parents of the bride-to-be, of course, want the young man to remain in their village to help support them in their old age, particularly if they have few or no sons. They will frequently promise a young man one or more of the sisters of his wife in order to make his stay more attractive.

He, on the other hand, would rather return to his home village to be with his own kinsmen, and the tendency is for postmarital residence to be patrilocal (with the father of the groom). If a village is rich in axes and machetes, it can and does coerce its poorer trading partners into permitting their young women to live permanently with the richer village. The latter thus obtains more women, while the poorer village gains some security in the trading network. The poor village then coerces other villages even poorer, or they raid them and steal their women.

The patrilineages that maintain the composition of the villages, rich or poor, include a man and his brothers and sisters, his children and his brothers' children, and the children of his sons and brothers' sons. The ideal marriage pattern is for a group of brothers to exchange sisters with another group of brothers. Furthermore, it is both permissible and desirable for a man to marry his mother's brother's daughter (his matrilateral cross-cousin) and/or his father's sister's daughter (his patrilateral cross-cousin) and, as we have seen earlier, to remain in his parents' village. Hence, the "ideal" village would have at least two patrilineages that exchanged marriageable people.

There is a considerable amount of adherence to these rules, and both brother-sister exchange and cross-cousin marriage are common.

However, there are also a substantial number of people in each village who are not related in these ways. For the most part they are women and their children who have been stolen from other villages, segments of lineages that have fled from their own village because of fights, and individuals — mostly young men — who have moved in and attached themselves to the household of one of the lineage (*mashi*) leaders.

Even if the sex ratio is balanced, there is a chronic shortage of women. A pregnant woman or one who is still nursing her children must not have sexual relationships. This means that for as many as three years, even allowing for violations of the taboos, a woman is asexual as far as the men are concerned. Hence, men with pregnant wives, and bachelors too, are potentially disruptive in every village because they constantly seek liaisons with the wives of other men. Eventually such relationships are discovered and violence ensues.

The woman, even if merely suspected of having affairs with other men, is beaten with a club; burned with a glowing brand; shot with a barbed arrow in a non-vital area, such as the buttocks, so that removal of the barb is both difficult and painful; or chopped on the arms or legs with a machete or ax. Most women over thirty carry numerous scars inflicted on them by their enraged husbands. My study of genealogies also indicates that not a few women have been killed outright by their husbands. The woman's punishment for infidelity depends on the number of brothers she has in the village, for if her husband is too brutal, her brothers may club him or take her away and give her to someone else.

The guilty man, on the other hand, is challenged to a fight with clubs. This duel is rarely confined to the two parties involved, for their brothers and supporters join the battle. If nobody is seriously injured, the matter may be forgotten. But if the incidents are frequent, the two patrilineages may decide to split while they are still on relatively "peaceable" terms with each other and form two independent villages. They will still be able to reunite when threatened by raid from a larger village.

This is only one aspect of the chronic warfare of the Yanomamö — warfare that has a basic effect on settlement pattern and demography, intervillage political relationships, leadership, and social organization. The collective aggressive behavior is caused by the desire to accent "sovereignty" — the capacity to initiate fighting and to demonstrate this capacity to others.

Although the Yanomamö are habitually armed with lethal bows and arrows, they have a graded system of violence within which they can express their *waiteri*, or "fierceness." The form of violence is determined by the nature of the affront or wrong to be challenged. The most benign form is a duel between two groups, in which an individual from each group stands (or kneels) with his chest stuck out, head up in the air, and arms held back and receives a hard blow to the chest. His opponent literally winds up and delivers a close-fist blow from the ground, striking the man on the left pectoral muscle just above the heart. The impact frequently drops the man to his knees, and participants may cough up blood for several days after such a contest. After receiving several such blows, the man then has his turn to strike his opponent, while the respective supporters of each antagonist gather around and frenziedly urge their champion on.

All men in the two villages are obliged to participate as village representatives, and on one occasion I saw some individuals take as many as three or four turns of four blows each. Duels of this type usually result from minor wrongs, such as a village being guilty of spreading bad rumors about another village, questioning its generosity or fierceness, or accusing it of gluttony at a feast. A variant of this form of duel is side slapping, in which an open-handed blow is delivered across the flank just above the pelvis.

More serious are the club fights. Although these almost invariably result from cases in which a wife has been caught in an affair with another man, some fights follow the theft of food within the village. The usual procedure calls for a representative from each belligerent group. One man holds a ten-foot club upright, braces himself by leaning on the club and spreading his feet, then holds his head out for his opponent to strike. Following this comes his turn to do likewise to his adversary. These duels, more often than not, end in a free-for-all in which everybody clubs everybody else on whatever spot he can hit. Such brawls occasionally result in fatalities. However, since headmen of the respective groups stand by with bows drawn, no one dares deliver an intentionally killing blow, for if he does, he will be shot. The scalps of the older men are almost incredible to behold, covered as they are by as many as a dozen ugly welts. Yet, most of them proudly shave the top of their heads to display their scars.

Also precipitated by feuds over women are spear fights, which are even more serious than club fights. Members of a village will warn those of the offending village that they are coming to fight with spears. They specify that they are not planning to shoot arrows unless the others shoot first. On the day of the fight, the attackers enter the other village, armed with five or six sharpened clubs or slender shafts some eight feet long and attempt to drive the defenders out. If successful, the invaders steal all the valuable possessions — hammocks, cooking pots, and machetes — and retreat. In the spear fight that occurred while I was studying the tribe, the attackers were successful, but they wounded several individuals so badly that one of them died. The fighting then escalated to a raid, the penultimate form of violence.

Such raids may be precipitated by woman stealing or the killing of a visitor (visitors are sometimes slain because they are suspected of having practiced harmful magic that has led to a death in the host's village). Raids also occur if a man kills his wife in a fit of anger; her natal village is then obliged to avenge the death. Most raids, however, are in revenge for deaths that occurred in previous raids, and once the vendetta gets started, it is not likely to end for a long time. Something else may trigger a raid. Occasionally an ambitious headman wearies of peaceful times — a rarity, certainly — and deliberately creates a situation that will demonstrate his leadership.

A revenge raid is preceded by a feast in which the ground bones of the person to be avenged are mixed in a soup of boiled, ripe plantains (the mainstay of Yanomamö diet) and swallowed. Yanomamö are endocannibals, which means they consume the remains of members of their own group. This ceremony puts the raiders in the appropriate state of frenzy for the business of warfare. A mock raid — rather like a dress rehearsal — is conducted in their own village on the afternoon before the day of the raid, and a life-size effigy of an enemy, constructed of leaves or a log, is slain. That evening all the participants march, one at a time, to the center of the village clearing, while clacking their bows and arrows and screaming their versions of the calls of carnivorous birds, mammals, and even insects.

When all have lined up facing the direction of the enemy village, they sing their war song, "I am a meat-hungry buzzard," and shout several times in unison until they hear the echo return from the jungle. They then disperse to their individual sections of the village to vomit the symbolic rotten flesh of the enemy that they, as symbolic carnivorous vultures and wasps, partook of in the lineup. The same thing, with the exception of the song, is repeated at dawn the following morning. Then the raiders, covered with black paint made of chewed charcoal, march out of the village in single file and collect the hammocks and plantains that their women have previously set outside the village for them. On each night they spend en route to the enemy they fire arrows at a dummy in a mock raid. They approach the enemy village itself under cover of darkness, ambush the first person they catch, and retreat as rapidly as possible. If they catch a man and his family, they will shoot the man and steal the woman and her children.

At a safe distance from her village, each of the raiders rapes the woman, and when they reach their own village, every man in the village may, if he wishes, do likewise before she is given to one of the men as a wife. Ordinarily she attempts to escape, but if caught, she may be killed. So constant is the threat of raids that every woman leaves her village in the knowledge that she may be stolen.

The supreme form of violence is the *nomohoni* — the "trick." During the dry season, the Yanomamö do a great deal of visiting. An entire village will go to another village for a ceremony that involves feasting, dancing, chanting, curing, trading, and just plain gossiping. Shortly after arrival, the visitors are invited to recline in the hammocks of the hosts. By custom they lie motionless to display their fine decorations while the hosts prepare food for them. But now suppose that a village has a grudge to settle with another, such as deaths to avenge. It enlists the support of a third village to act as accomplice. This third village, which must be on friendly terms with the intended victims, will invite them to a feast. While the guests recline defenseless in the hammocks, the hosts descend on them with axes and sharpened poles, treacherously killing as many as they can. Those that manage to escape the slaughter inside the village are shot outside the palisade by the village that instigated the *nomohoni*. The women and children will be shared between the two accomplices.

Throughout all this ferocity there are two organizational aspects of violence. One concerns leadership: A man must be able to demonstrate his fierceness if he is to be a true leader. It is equally important, however, that he have a large natural following — that is, he must have many male kinsmen to support his position and a quantity of daughters and sisters to distribute to other men. Lineage leaders cannot accurately be described as unilateral initiators of activities; rather, they are the vehicles through which the group's will is expressed. For example, when a certain palm fruit is ripe and is particularly abundant in an area some distance from the village, everybody knows that the whole village will pack its belongings and erect a temporary camp at that spot to collect the fruit. The headman does little more than set the date. When his kinsmen see him packing, they know that the time has come to leave for the collecting trip. True, the headman does have some initiative in raiding, but not even this is completely independent of the attitudes of his followers, which dictate that a death must be avenged. However, when the purpose of a raid is to steal women, the headman does have some freedom to act on his own initiative.

As a general rule, the smaller his natural following, the more he is obliged to demonstrate his personal qualities of fierceness and leadership. Padudiwä, the headman of one of the lineages in Bisaasi-tedi, took pains to demonstrate his personal qualities whenever he could; he had only two living brothers and four living sisters in his group. Most of his demonstrations of ferocity were cruel beatings he administered to his four wives, none of whom had brothers in the village to take their part. Several young men who attached themselves to his household admired him for this.

Padudiwä was also responsible for organizing several raids while I lived with the villagers of Bisaasi-tedi. Every one of them was against Patanowä-tedi, a village that was being raided regularly by some seven or eight other villages, so that the danger of being raided in return was correspondingly reduced. On one occasion, when three young men from Patanowä-tedi arrived as emissaries of peace, Padudiwä wanted to kill them, although he had lived with them at one time and they were fairly close relatives. The murder was prevented by the headman of the other — and larger — lineage in the village, who warned that if an attempt were made on the lives of the visitors he himself would kill Padudiwä.

Obviously then, Padudiwä's reputation was built largely on calculated acts of fierceness, which carefully reduced the possibility of personal danger to himself and his followers, and on cunning and cruelty. To some extent he was obliged by the smallness of his gathering to behave in such a way, but he was certainly a man to treat with caution.

Despite their extreme aggressiveness, the Yanomamö have at least two qualities I admired. They are kind and indulgent with children and can quickly forget personal angers. (A few even treated me almost as an equal — in their culture this was a considerable concession.) But to portray them as "noble savages" would be misleading. Many of them are delightful and charming people when confronted alone and on a personal basis, but the greater number of them are much like Padudiwä — or strive to be that way. As they frequently told me, *Yanomamö täbä waiteri!* — "Yanomamö are fierce!"

REVIEW QUESTIONS

1. What is the most important value for men among the Yanomamö, and how is it acted out in the world of conflict and social control?

2. Describe the Yanomamö social and political organization. What accounts for the proliferation of Yanomamö villages over the past seventy-five years?

3. What are the different kinds of Yanomamö combat? Rank them according to their severity.

4. What are the major causes of disputes that set off physical combat among the Yanomamö?

5. How do men attain positions of leadership among the Yanomamö?

25

Poor man, rich man, big-man, chief

MARSHALL D. SAHLINS

Melanesia and Polynesia provide an interesting contrast in political complexity, as Marshall Sahlins describes in the following article. The Melanesian "big-man" is the self-made leader of his small localized kinship group, whereas the Polynesian chief is a "born" leader. The Polynesian system, which depends upon the ascribed right of its chief to lead, attains far larger proportions than the Melanesian structure, which depends on the ability of certain individuals to influence others.

With an eye to their own life goals, the native peoples of Pacific Islands unwittingly present to anthropologists a generous scientific gift: an extended series of experiments in cultural adaptation and evolutionary development. They have compressed their institutions within the confines of infertile coral atolls, expanded them on volcanic islands, created with the means history gave them cultures adapted to the deserts of Australia, the mountains and warm coasts of New Guinea, the rain forests of the Solomon Islands. From the Australian Aborigines, whose hunting and gathering existence duplicates in outline the cultural life of the later Paleolithic, to the great chiefdoms of Hawaii, where society approached the formative levels of the old Fertile Crescent civilizations, almost every general phase in the progress of primitive culture is exemplified.

Marshall D. Sahlins, "Poor Man, Big-Man, Rich Man, Chief: Political Types in Melanesia and Polynesia" in *Comparative Studies in Society and History*, Vol. 5., No. 3, pp. 285–303. Copyright by Cambridge University Press. Reprinted by permission of the Cambridge University Press. Many footnotes, the bibliographic citations, and bibliography are omitted.

Where culture so experiments, anthropology finds its laboratories — makes its comparisons.

In the southern and eastern Pacific two contrasting cultural provinces have long evoked anthropological interest: *Melanesia*, including New Guinea, the Bismarcks, Solomons, and island groups east to Fiji; and *Polynesia*, consisting in its main portion of the triangular constellation of lands between New Zealand, Easter Island, and the Hawaiian Islands. In and around Fiji, Melanesia and Polynesia intergrade culturally, but west and east of their intersection the two provinces pose broad contrasts in several sectors: in religion, art, kinship groupings, economics, political organization. The differences are the more notable for the underlying similarities from which they emerge. Melanesia and Polynesia are both agricultural regions in which many of the same crops — such as yams, taro, breadfruit, bananas, and coconuts — have long been cultivated by many similar techniques. Some recently presented linguistic and archaeological studies indeed suggest that Polynesian cultures originated from an eastern Melanesian hearth during the first millennium B.C. Yet in anthropological annals the Polynesians were to become famous for elaborate forms of rank and chieftianship, whereas most Melanesian societies broke off advance on this front at more rudimentary levels.

It is obviously imprecise, however, to make out the political contrast in broad culture-area terms. Within Polynesia, certain of the islands, such as Hawaii, the Society Islands and Tonga, developed unparalleled political momentum. And not all Melanesian polities, on the other side, were constrained and truncated in their evolution. In New Guinea and nearby areas of western Melanesia, small and loosely ordered political groupings are numerous, but in eastern Melanesia, New Caledonia and Fiji for example, political approximations of the Polynesian condition become common. There is more of an upward west to east slope in political development in the southern Pacific than a step-like, quantum progression. It is quite revealing, however, to compare the extremes of this continuum, the western Melanesian underdevelopment against the greater Polynesian chiefdoms. While such comparison does not exhaust the evolutionary variations, it fairly establishes the scope of overall political achievement in this Pacific phylum of cultures.

Measurable along several dimensions, the contrast between developed Polynesian and underdeveloped Melanesian polities is immediately striking for differences in scale. H. Ian Hogbin and Camilla Wedgwood concluded from a survey of Melanesian (most western

Melanesian) societies that ordered, independent political bodies in the region typically include seventy to three hundred persons; more recent work in the New Guinea Highlands suggests political groupings of up to a thousand, occasionally a few thousand, people.[1] But in Polynesia sovereignties of two thousand or three thousand are run-of-the-mill, and the most advanced chiefdoms, as in Tonga or Hawaii, might claim ten thousand, even tens of thousands. Varying step by step with such differences in size of the polity are differences in territorial extent: from a few square miles in western Melanesia to tens or even hundreds of square miles in Polynesia.

The Polynesian advance in political scale was supported by advance over Melanesia in political structure. Melanesia presents a great array of social-political forms: here political organization is based upon patrilineal descent groups, there on cognatic groups, or men's clubhouses recruiting neighborhood memberships, on a secret ceremonial society, or perhaps on some combination of these structural principles. Yet a general plan can be discerned. The characteristic western Melanesian "tribe," that is, the ethnic-cultural entity, consists of many autonomous kinship-residential groups. Amounting on the ground to a small village or a local cluster of hamlets, each of these is a copy of the others in organization, each tends to be economically self-governing, and each is the equal of the others in political status. The tribal plan is one of politically unintegrated segments — segmental. But the political geometry in Polynesia is pyramidal. Local groups of the order of self-governing Melanesian communities appear in Polynesia as subdivisions of a more inclusive political body. Smaller units are integrated into larger through a system of intergroup ranking, and the network of representative chiefs of the subdivisions amounts to a coordinating political structure. So instead of the Melanesian scheme of small, separate, and equal political blocs, the Polynesian polity is an extensive pyramid of groups capped by the family and following of a paramount chief. (This Polynesian political upshot is often, although not always, facilitated by the development of ranked lineages. Called *conical clan* by Kirchhoff, at one time *ramage* by Firth and *status lineage* by Goldman, the Polynesian ranked lineage is the same in principle as the so-called *obok* system widely distributed in Central Asia, and it is at least analogous to the Scottish clan, the Chinese clan, certain Central African Bantu lineage systems, the housegroups of Northwest Coast Indians, perhaps even the "tribes" of the Israelites.

[1]H. Ian Hogbin and Camilla H. Wedgwood, "Local Groupings in Melanesia," *Oceania* 23 (1952–53): 241–276; 24 (1953–54): 58–76.

Genealogical ranking is its distinctive feature: members of the same descent unit are ranked by genealogical distance from the common ancestor; lines of the same group become senior and cadet branches on this principle; related corporate lineages are relatively ranked, again by genealogical priority.)

Here is another criterion of Polynesian political advance: historical performance. Almost all of the native peoples of the South Pacific were brought up against intense European cultural pressure in the late eighteenth and nineteenth centuries. Yet only the Hawaiians, Tahitians, Tongans, and to a lesser extent the Fijians, successfully defended themselves by evolving countervailing, native-controlled states. Complete with public governments and public law, monarchs and taxes, ministers and minions, these nineteenth-century states are testimony to the native Polynesian political genius, to the level and the potential of indigenous political accomplishments.

Embedded within the grand differences in political scale, structure and performance is a more personal contrast, one in quality of leadership. An historically particular type of leader-figure, the "big-man" as he is often locally styled, appears in the underdeveloped settings of Melanesia. Another type, a chief properly so-called, is associated with the Polynesian advance. Now these are distinct sociological types, that is to say, differences in the powers, privileges, rights, duties, and obligations of Melanesian big-men and Polynesian chiefs are given by the divergent societal contexts in which they operate. Yet the institutional distinctions cannot help but be manifest also in differences in bearing and character, appearance and manner — in a word, personality. It may be a good way to begin the more rigorous sociological comparison of leadership with a more impressionistic sketch of the contrast in the human dimension. Here I find it useful to apply characterizations — or is it caricature? — from our own history to big-men and chiefs, however much injustice this does to the historically incomparable backgrounds of the Melanesians and Polynesians. The Melanesian big-man seems so thoroughly bourgeois, so reminiscent of the free-enterprising rugged individual of our own heritage. He combines with an ostensible interest in the general welfare a more profound measure of self-interested cunning and economic calculation. His gaze, as Veblen might have put it, is fixed unswervingly to the main chance. His every public action is designed to make a competitive and invidious comparison with others, to show a standing above the masses that is product of his own personal manufacture. The historical caricature of the Polynesian chief, however, is feudal rather than capitalist. His ap-

pearance, his bearing is almost regal; very likely he just *is* a big man—
" 'Can't you see he is a chief? See how big he is?' "[2] In his every public
action is a display of the refinements of breeding, in his manner always
that *noblesse oblige* of true pedigree and an incontestable right of rule.
With his standing not so much a personal achievement as a just social
due, he can afford to be, and he is, every inch a chief.

In the several Melanesian tribes in which big-men have come
under anthropological scrutiny, local cultural differences modify the
expression of their personal powers. But the indicative quality of big-
man authority is everywhere the same: it is *personal* power. Big-men do
not come to office; they do not succeed to, nor are they installed in,
existing positions of leadership over political groups. The attainment of
big-man status is rather the outcome of a series of acts which elevate a
person above the common herd and attract about him a coterie of loyal,
lesser men. It is not accurate to speak of "big-man" as a political title,
for it is but an acknowledged standing in interpersonal relations—a
"prince among men" so to speak as opposed to "The Prince of Danes."
In particular Melanesian tribes the phrase might be "man of importance" or "man of renown," "generous rich-man," or "center-man," as
well as "big-man."

A kind of two-sidedness in authority is implied in this series of
phrases, a division of the big-man's field of influence into two distinct
sectors. "Center-man" particularly connotes a cluster of followers
gathered about an influential pivot. It socially implies the division of
the tribe into political in-groups dominated by outstanding personalities. To the in-group, the big-man presents this sort of picture:

> The place of the leader in the district group [in northern Malaita] is well
> summed up by his title, which might be translated as "center-man." . . .
> He was like a banyan, the natives explain, which, though the biggest and
> tallest in the forest, is still a tree like the rest. But, just because it exceeds
> all others, the banyan gives support to more lianas and creepers, pro-
> vides more food for the birds, and gives better protection against sun and
> rain.[3]

But "man of renown" connotes a broader tribal field in which a man is
not so much a leader as he is some sort of hero. This is the side of the
big-man facing outward from his own faction, his status among some

[2]Edward Winslow Gifford, *Tongan Society* (Honolulu: Bernice P. Bishop Museum
Bulletin 61, 1926).

[3]H. Ian Hogbin, "Native Councils and Courts in the Solomon Islands," *Oceania* 14
(1943–44): 258–283.

or all of the other political clusters of the tribe. The political sphere of the big-man divides itself into a small internal sector composed of his personal satellites — rarely over eighty men — and a much larger external sector, the tribal galaxy consisting of many similar constellations.

As it crosses over from the internal into the external sector, a big-man's power undergoes qualitative change. Within his faction a Melanesian leader has true command ability, outside of it only fame and indirect influence. It is not that the center-man rules his faction by physical force, but his followers do feel obliged to obey him, and he can usually get what he wants by haranguing them — public verbal suasion is indeed so often employed by center-men that they have been styled "harangueutans." The orbits of outsiders, however, are set by their own center-men. " 'Do it yourself. I'm not *your* fool,' " would be the characteristic response to an order issued by a center-man to an outsider among the Siuai.[4] This fragmentation of true authority presents special political difficulties, particularly in organizing large masses of people for the prosecution of such collective ends as warfare or ceremony. Big-men do instigate mass action, but only by establishing both extensive renown and special personal relations of compulsion or reciprocity with other center-men.

Politics is in the main personal politicking in these Melanesian societies, and the size of a leader's faction as well as the extent of his renown are normally set by competition with other ambitious men. Little or no authority is given by social ascription: leadership is a creation — a creation of followership. "Followers," as it is written of the Kapauku of New Guinea, "stand in various relations to the leader. Their obedience to the headman's decisions is caused by motivations which reflect their particular relations to the leader."[5] So a man must be prepared to demonstrate that he possesses the kinds of skills that command respect — magical powers, gardening prowess, mastery of oratorical style, perhaps bravery in war and feud. Typically decisive is the deployment of one's skills and efforts in a certain direction: towards amassing goods, most often pigs, shell monies and vegetable foods, and distributing them in ways which build a name for cavalier generosity, if not for compassion. A faction is developed by informal private assistance to people of a locale. Tribal rank and renown are developed by great public giveaways sponsored by the rising big-man,

[4]Douglas Oliver, *A Solomon Islands Society* (Cambridge: Harvard University Press, 1955).

[5]Leopold Pospisil, *Kapauku Papuans and Their Law* (New Haven: Yale University Publications in Anthropology, no. 54, 1958).

often on behalf of his faction as well as himself. In different Melanesian tribes, the renown-making public distribution may appear as one side of a delayed exchange of pigs between corporate kinship groups; a marital consideration given a bride's kinfolk; a set of feasts connected with the erection of a big-man's dwelling, or of a clubhouse for himself and his faction, or with the purchase of higher grades of rank in secret societies; the sponsorship of a religious ceremony; a payment of subsidies and blood compensations to military allies; or perhaps the giveaway is a ceremonial challenge bestowed on another leader in the attempt to outgive and thus outrank him (a potlatch).

The making of the faction, however, is the true making of the Melanesian big-man. It is essential to establish relations of loyalty and obligation on the part of a number of people such that their production can be mobilized for renown-building external distribution. The bigger the faction the greater the renown; once momentum in external distribution has been generated the opposite can also be true. Any ambitious man who can gather a following can launch a societal career. The rising big-man necessarily depends initially on a small core of followers, principally his own household and his closest relatives. Upon these people he can prevail economically: he capitalizes in the first instance on kinship dues and by finessing the relation of reciprocity appropriate among close kinsmen. Often it becomes necessary at an early phase to enlarge one's household. The rising leader goes out of his way to incorporate within his family "strays" of various sorts, people without familial support themselves, such as widows and orphans. Additional wives are especially useful. The more wives a man has the more pigs he has. The relation here is functional, not identical: with more women gardening there will be more food for pigs and more swineherds. A Kiwai Papuan picturesquely put to an anthropologist in pidgin the advantages, economic and political, of polygamy: " 'Another woman go garden, another woman go take firewood, another woman go catch fish, another woman cook him — husband he sing out plenty people come kaikai [i.e., come to eat].' "[6] Each new marriage, incidentally, creates for the big-man an additional set of in-laws from whom he can exact economic favors. Finally, a leader's career sustains its upward climb when he is able to link other men and their families to his faction, harnessing their production to his ambition. This is done by calculated generosities, by placing others in gratitude and obligation through helping them in some big way. A common technique is payment of bridewealth on behalf of young men seeking wives.

[6]Gunnar Landtman, *The Kiwai Papuans of British New Guinea* (London: Macmillan, 1927).

The great Malinowski used a phrase in analyzing primitive political economy that felicitously describes just what the big-man is doing: amassing a "fund of power." A big-man is one who can create and use social relations which give him leverage on others' production and the ability to siphon off an excess product — or sometimes he can cut down their consumption in the interest of the siphon. Now although his attention may be given primarily to short-term personal interests, from an objective standpoint the leader acts to promote long-term societal interests. The fund of power provisions activities that involve other groups of the society at large. In the greater perspective of that society at large, big-men are indispensable means of creating supralocal organization: in tribes normally fragmented into small independent groups, big-men at least temporarily widen the sphere of ceremony, recreation and art, economic collaboration, of war too. Yet always this greater societal organization depends on the lesser factional organization, particularly on the ceilings on economic mobilization set by relations between center-men and followers. The limits and the weaknesses of the political order in general are the limits and weaknesses of the factional in-groups.

And the personal quality of subordination to a center-man is a serious weakness in factional structure. A personal loyalty has to be made and continually reinforced; if there is discontent it may well be severed. Merely to create a faction takes times and effort, and to hold it, still more effort. The potential rupture of personal links in the factional chain is at the heart of two broad evolutionary shortcomings of western Melanesian political orders. First, a comparative instability. Shifting dispositions and magnetisms of ambitious men in a region may induce fluctuations in factions, perhaps some overlapping of them, and fluctuations also in the extent of different renowns. The death of a center-man can become a regional political trauma: the death undermines the personally cemented faction, the group dissolves in whole or in part, and the people re-group finally around rising pivotal big-men. Although particular tribal structures in places cushion the disorganization, the big-man political system is generally unstable over short terms: in its superstructure it is a flux of rising and falling leaders, in its substructure of enlarging and contracting factions. Secondly, the personal political bond contributes to the containment of evolutionary advance. The possibility of their desertion, it is clear, often inhibits a leader's ability to forceably push up his followers' output, thereby placing constraints on higher political organization, but there is more to it than that. If it is to generate great momentum, a big-man's quest for the summits of renown is likely to bring out a contradiction in his relations to followers, so that he finds himself encouraging defection — or worse, an egalitarian rebellion — by encouraging production.

One side of the Melanesian contradiction is the initial economic reciprocity between a center-man and his followers. For his help they give their help, and for goods going out through his hands other goods (often from outside factions) flow back to his followers by the same path. The other side is that a cumulative build-up of renown forces center-men into economic extortion of the faction. Here it is important that not merely his own status, but the standing and perhaps the military security of his people depend on the big-man's achievements in public distribution. Established at the head of a sizeable faction, a center-man comes under increasing pressure to extract goods from his followers, to delay reciprocities owing them, and to deflect incoming goods back into external circulation. Success in competition with other big-men particularly undermines internal-factional reciprocities: such success is precisely measurable by the ability to give outsiders more than they can possibly reciprocate. In well-delineated big-man polities, we find leaders negating the reciprocal obligations upon which their following had been predicated. Substituting extraction for reciprocity, they must compel their people to "eat the leader's renown," as one Solomon Island group puts it, in return for productive efforts. Some center-men appear more able than others to dam the inevitable tide of discontent that mounts within their factions, perhaps because of charismatic personalities, perhaps because of the particular social organizations in which they operate. But paradoxically the ultimate defense of the center-man's position is some slackening of his drive to enlarge the funds of power. The alternative is much worse. In the anthropological record there are not merely instances of big-man chicanery and of material deprivation of the faction in the interests of renown, but some also of overloading of social relations with followers: the generation of antagonisms, defections, and in extreme cases the violent liquidation of the center-man. Developing internal constraints, the Melanesian big-man political order brakes evolutionary advance at a certain level. It sets ceilings on the intensification of political authority, on the intensification of household production by political means, and on the diversion of household outputs in support of wider political organization. But in Polynesia these constraints were breached, and although Polynesian chiefdoms also found their developmental plateau, it was not before political evolution had been carried above the Melanesian ceilings. The fundamental defects of the Melanesian plan were overcome in Polynesia. The division between small internal and larger external political sectors, upon which all big-man politics hinged, was suppressed in Polynesia by the growth of an enclaving chiefdom-at-large. A chain of command subordinating lesser chiefs and groups to greater, on the basis of inherent societal rank, made local blocs or personal followings (such as were independent in Melanesia) merely dependent parts of the larger Polynesian chiefdom. So the nexus of the Polynesian chiefdom became an extensive set of offices, a pyramid of higher and lower chiefs holding sway over larger and smaller sections of the polity. Indeed the system of ranked and subdivided lineages (conical clan system), upon which the pyramid was characteristically established, might build up through several orders of inclusion and encompass the whole of an island or group of islands. While the island or the archipelago would normally be divided into several independent chiefdoms, high-order lineage connections between them, as well as kinship ties between their paramount chiefs, provided structural avenues for at least temporary expansion of political scale, for consolidation of great into even greater chiefdoms.

The pivotal paramount chief as well as the chieftains controlling parts of a chiefdom were true office holders and title holders. They were not, like Melanesian big-men, fishers of men: they held positions of authority over permanent groups. The honorifics of Polynesian chiefs likewise did not refer to a standing in interpersonal relations, but to their leadership of political divisions — here "The Prince of Danes" *not* "The prince among men." In western Melanesia the personal superiorities and inferiorities arising in the intercourse of particular men largely defined the political bodies. In Polynesia there emerged suprapersonal structures of leadership and followership, organizations that continued independently of the particular men who occupied positions in them for brief mortal spans.

And these Polynesian chiefs did not make their positions in society — they were installed in societal positions. In several of the islands, men did struggle to office against the will and stratagems of rival aspirants. But then they came *to* power. Power resided in the office; it was not made by the demonstration of personal superiority. In other islands, Tahiti was famous for it, succession to chieftainship was tightly controlled by inherent rank. The chiefly lineage ruled by virtue of its genealogical connections with divinity, and chiefs were succeeded by first sons, who carried "in the blood" the attributes of leadership. The important comparative point is this: the qualities of command that had to reside in men in Melanesia, that had to be personally demonstrated in order to attract loyal followers, were in Polynesia socially assigned to office and rank. In Polynesia, people of high rank and office *ipso facto* were leaders, and by the same token the qualities of leadership were automatically lacking—theirs was not to question why—among the underlying population. Magical powers such as a Melanesian big-man might acquire to sustain his position, a Polynesian high chief inherited by divine descent as the *mana* which sanctified his rule and protected his person against the hands of the commonalty. The productive ability the big-man laboriously had to demonstrate was effortlessly given Polynesian chiefs as religious control over agricultural fertility, and upon the ceremonial implementation of it the rest of the people were conceived dependent. Where a Melanesian leader had to master the compelling oratorical style, Polynesian paramounts often had trained "talking chiefs" whose voice was the chiefly command.

In the Polynesian view, a chiefly personage was in the nature of things powerful. But this merely implies the objective observation that his power was of the group rather than of himself. His authority came from the organization, from an organized acquiescence in his privileges and organized means of sustaining them. A kind of paradox resides in evolutionary developments which detach the exercise of authority from the necessity to demonstrate personal superiority: organizational power actually extends the role of personal decision and conscious planning, gives it greater scope, impact, and effectiveness. The growth of a political system such as the Polynesian constitutes advance over Melanesian orders of interpersonal dominance in the human control of human affairs. Especially significant for society at large were privileges accorded Polynesian chiefs which made them greater architects of funds of power than ever was any Melanesian big-man.

Masters of their people and "owners" in a titular sense of group resources, Polynesian chiefs had rights of call upon the labor and agricultural produce of households within their domains. Economic mobilization did not depend on, as it necessarily had for Melanesian big-men, the *de novo* creation by the leader of personal loyalties and economic obligations. A chief need not stoop to obligate this man or that man, need not by a series of individual acts of generosity induce others to support him, for economic leverage over a group was the inherent chiefly due. Consider the implications for the fund of power of the widespread chiefly privilege, related to titular "ownership" of land, of placing an interdiction, a tabu, on the harvest of some crop by way of reserving its use for a collective project. By means of the tabu the chief directs the course of production in a general way: households of his domain must turn to some other means of subsistence. He delivers a stimulus to household production: in the absence of the tabu further labors would not have been necessary. Most significantly, he has generated a politically utilizable agricultural surplus. A subsequent call on this surplus floats chieftainship as a going concern, capitalizes the fund of power. In certain islands, Polynesian chiefs controlled great storehouses which held the goods congealed by chiefly pressures on the commonalty. David Malo, one of the great native custodians of old Hawaiian lore, felicitously catches the political significance of the chiefly magazine in his well-known *Hawaiian Antiquities:*

> It was the practice for kings [i.e., paramount chiefs of individual islands] to build store-houses in which to collect food, fish, tapas [bark cloth], malos [men's loin cloths] pa-us [woman's loin skirts], and all sorts of goods. These store-houses were designed by the Kalaimoku [the chief's principal executive] as a means of keeping the people contented, so they would not desert the king. They were like the baskets that were used to entrap the *hinalea* fish. The *hinalea* thought there was something good within the basket, and he hung round the outside of it. In the same way the people thought there was food in the store-houses, and they kept their eyes on the king. As the rat will not desert the pantry . . . where he thinks food is, so the people will not desert the king while they think there is food in his store-house.[7]

Redistribution of the fund of power was the supreme art of Polynesian politics. By well-planned *noblesse oblige* the large domain of a paramount chief was held together, organized at times for massive projects, protected against other chiefdoms, even further enriched. Uses of the chiefly fund included lavish hospitality and entertainments for outside chiefs and for the chief's own people, and succor of individuals or the underlying population at large in times of scarcities — bread and circuses. Chiefs subsidized craft production, promoting in Polynesia a division of technical labor unparalleled in extent and expertise in most of the Pacific. They supported also great technical construction, as of irrigation complexes, the further returns to which swelled the chiefly fund. They initiated large-scale religious construction too, subsidized the great ceremonies, and organized logistic support for extensive military campaigns. Larger and more easily replenished than their western Melanesian counterparts, Polynesian funds of power permitted greater political regulation of a greater range of social activities on greater scale.

In the most advanced Polynesian chiefdoms, as in Hawaii and Tahiti, a significant part of the chiefly fund was deflected away from general redistribution towards the upkeep of the institution of chief-

---

[7]David Malo, *Hawaiian Antiquities* (Honolulu: Hawaiian Gazette Co., 1903).

tainship. The fund was siphoned for the support of a permanent administrative establishment. In some measure, goods and services contributed by the people precipitated out as the grand houses, assembly places, and temple platforms of chiefly precincts. In another measure, they were appropriated for the livelihood of circles of retainers, many of them close kinsmen of the chief, who clustered about the powerful paramounts. These were not all useless hangers-on. They were political cadres: supervisors of the stores, talking chiefs, ceremonial attendants, high priests who were intimately involved in political rule, envoys to transmit directives through the chiefdom. There were men in these chiefly retinues — in Tahiti and perhaps Hawaii, specialized warrior corps — whose force could be directed internally as a buttress against fragmenting or rebellious elements of the chiefdom. A Tahitian or Hawaiian high chief had more compelling sanctions than the harangue. He controlled a ready physical force, an armed body of executioners, which gave him mastery particularly over the lesser people of the community. While it looks a lot like the big-man's faction again, the differences in functioning of the great Polynesian chief's retinue are more significant than the superficial similarities in appearance. The chief's coterie, for one thing, is economically dependent upon him rather than he upon them. And in deploying the cadres politically in various sections of the chiefdom, or against the lower orders, the great Polynesian chiefs sustained command where the Melanesian big-man, in his external sector, had at best renown.

This is not to say that the advanced Polynesian chiefdoms were free of internal defect, of potential or actual malfunctioning. The large political-military apparatus indicates something of the opposite. So does the recent work of Irving Goldman[8] on the intensity of "status rivalry" in Polynesia, especially when it is considered that much of the status rivalry in developed chiefdoms, as the Hawaiian, amounted to popular rebellion against chiefly despotism rather than mere contest for position within the ruling-stratum. This suggests that Polynesian chiefdoms, just as Melanesian big-man orders, generate along with evolutionary development countervailing anti-authority pressures, and that the weight of the latter may ultimately impede further development.

The Polynesian contradiction seems clear enough. On one side, chieftainship is never detached from kinship moorings and kinship economic ethics. Even the greatest Polynesian chiefs were conceived

[8]Irving Goldman, "Status Rivalry and Cultural Evolution in Polynesia," *American Anthropologist* 57 (1957): 680–697; "Variations in Polynesian Social Organization," *Journal of the Polynesian Society* 66 (1957): 374–390.

superior kinsmen to the masses, fathers of their people, and generosity was morally incumbent upon them. On the other side, the major Polynesian paramounts seemed inclined to "eat the power of the government too much," as the Tahitians put it, to divert an undue proportion of the general wealth toward the chiefly establishment. The diversion could be accomplished by lowering the customary level of general redistribution, lessening the material returns of chieftianship to the community at large — tradition attributes the great rebellion of Mangarevan commoners to such cause. Or the diversion might — and I suspect more commonly did — consist in greater and more forceful exactions from lesser chiefs and people, increasing returns to the chiefly apparatus without necessarily affecting the level of general redistribution. In either case, the well-developed chiefdom creates for itself the dampening paradox of stoking rebellion by funding its authority.

In Hawaii and other islands cycles of political centralization and decentralization may be abstracted from traditional histories. That is, larger chiefdoms periodically fragmented into smaller and then were later reconstituted. Here would be more evidence of a tendency to overtax the political structure. But how to explain the emergence of a developmental stymie, of an inability to sustain political advance beyond a certain level? To point to a chiefly propensity to consume or a Polynesian propensity to rebel is not enough: such propensities are promoted by the very advance of chiefdoms. There is reason to hazard instead that Parkinson's notable law is behind it all: that progressive expansion in political scale entailed more-than-proportionate accretion in the ruling apparatus, unbalancing the flow of wealth in favor of the apparatus. The ensuing unrest then curbs the chiefly impositions, sometimes by reducing chiefdom scale to the nadir of the periodic cycle. Comparison of the requirements of administration in small and large Polynesian chiefdoms helps make the point.

A lesser chiefdom, confined say as in the Marquesas Islands to a narrow valley, could be almost personally ruled by a headman in frequent contact with the relatively small population. Melville's partly romanticized — also for its ethnographic details, partly cribbed — account in *Typee* makes this clear enough. But the great Polynesian chiefs had to rule much larger, spatially dispersed, internally organized populations. Hawaii, an island over four thousand square miles with an aboriginal population approaching one hundred thousand, was at times a single chiefdom, at other times divided into two to six independent chiefdoms, and at all times each chiefdom was composed of large subdivisions under powerful subchiefs. Sometimes a chiefdom in the Hawaiian group extended beyond the confines of one of the islands, incorporating part of another through conquest. Now, such extensive chiefdoms would have to be coordinated; they would have to be centrally tapped for a fund of power, buttressed against internal disruption, sometimes massed for distant, perhaps overseas, military engagements. All of this to be implemented by means of communication still at the level of word-of-mouth, and means of transportation consisting of human bodies and canoes. (The extent of certain larger chieftianships, coupled with the limitations of communication and transportation, incidentally suggests another possible source of political unrest: that the burden of provisioning the governing apparatus would tend to fall disproportionately on groups within easiest access of the paramount.) A tendency for the developed chiefdom to proliferate in executive cadres, to grow top-heavy, seems in these circumstances altogether functional, even though the ensuing drain on wealth proves the chiefdom's undoing. Functional also, and likewise a material drain on the chiefdom at large, would be widening distinctions between chiefs and people in style of life. Palatial housing, ornamentation and luxury, finery and ceremony, in brief, conspicuous consumption, however much it seems mere self-interest always has a more decisive social significance. It creates those invidious distinctions between rulers and ruled so conducive to a passive — hence quite economical! — acceptance of authority. Throughout history, inherently more powerful political organizations than the Polynesian, with more assured logistics of rule, have turned to it — including in our time some ostensibly revolutionary and proletarian governments, despite every pre-revolutionary protestation of solidarity with the masses and equality for the classes.

In Polynesia then, as in Melanesia, political evolution is eventually shortcircuited by an overload on the relations between leaders and their people. The Polynesian tragedy, however, was somewhat the opposite of the Melanesian. In Polynesia, the evolutionary ceiling was set by extraction from the population at large in favor of the chiefly faction, in Melanesia by extraction from the big-man's faction in favor of distribution to the population at large. Most importantly, the Polynesian ceiling was higher. Melanesian big-men and Polynesian chiefs not only reflect different varieties and levels of political evolution, they display in different degrees the capacity to generate and to sustain political progress.

Especially emerging from their juxtaposition is the more decisive impact of Polynesian chiefs on the economy, the chiefs' greater leverage on the output of the several households of society. The success of any primitive political organization is decided here, in the control that can be developed over household economies. For the household is not merely the principal productive unit in primitive societies, it is often quite capable of autonomous direction of its own production, and it is oriented towards production for its own, not societal consumption. The greater potential of Polynesian chieftainship is precisely the greater pressure it could exert on household output, its capacity both to generate a surplus and to deploy it out of the household towards a broader division of labor, cooperative construction, and massive ceremonial and military action. Polynesian chiefs were the more effective means of societal collaboration on economic, political, indeed all cultural fronts. Perhaps we have been too long accustomed to perceive rank and rule from the standpoint of the individuals involved, rather than from the perspective of the total society, as if the secret of the subordination of man to man lay in the personal satisfactions of power. And then the breakdowns too, or the evolutionary limits, have been searched out in men, in "weak" kings or megalomaniacal dictators—always, "who is the matter?" An excursion into the field of primitive politics suggests the more fruitful conception that the gains of political developments accrue more decisively to society than to individuals, and the failings as well are of structure not men.

REVIEW QUESTIONS

1. What is the difference between a Melanesian big-man and a Polynesian chief? How does each acquire and maintain power?

2. What are the bases of political integration for the big-man and chiefly political systems?

3. What is the role of kinship in the Melanesian and Polynesian political systems?

4. How does Sahlins support his argument that the chiefly system of Polynesia permits larger political aggregates?

26

Big-men on Capitol Hill

JACK McIVER WEATHERFORD

As we saw in the last article, Melanesian big-men gather followers and power by personal, usually face-to-face, effort. In this article, Jack Weatherford shows how the road to power is the same for U.S. senators as it is for New Guinea big-men. Both start with few supporters and resources. Both must acquire more followers and valuable items to rise in power. Each must give "pork" to followers to increase power. For congressmen, the rise to power requires the acquisition of substantive jurisdictions, staff, and other beholden senators.

Ongka, a tribal elder of the Kawelka in Highland New Guinea, knew that he had finally arrived as a big-man when he was able to give the biggest *moka* the region had ever witnessed. At this huge feast, Ongka made speeches to all of his assembled relatives, friends, and allies. Dressed in his finest feathers and decorations, he distributed the roasted pigs and yam puddings made by his wives, and to cement his position as a leader and patron, he presented a great many gifts to the assembled tribesmen. To some went live pigs or a bird; a few got cows and cassowaries. In addition to these traditional gifts, Ongka gave away a motorbike and a Toyota Landcruiser, making his *moka* without doubt the finest and most modern ever known in New Guinea: as such, it was the culmination of a lifetime of hard work to become a big-man.

In parts of tribal New Guinea and Melanesia where there are no hereditary chiefs, politics are dominated by these successful old warri-

This article was written especially for this book. Copyright © 1986 by Jack McIver Weatherford.

ors known as big-men. The arduous path to become a big-man is one of hard work and careful strategy. It is a path open only to males, but any young man who applies himself to the task can attain this preeminent status. The young politician begins life, as do most of his peers, with a meager patrimony of a small garden plot and a wife to work it. The yam crop from this garden feeds not only the fledgling family but their pigs as well. If the young couple works hard, they can produce an excess of yams, which can be used to raise more pigs. As they become prosperous, the young warrior acquires another wife, who can help to grow even more yams and more pigs. The repetitive acquisition of wives, pigs, and yams lies at the heart of his political power. Through the distribution of pork to other less successful men, he acquires followers, and through his marriages to new wives and the carefully orchestrated marriages of his own children, he acquires allies.

By the time he becomes a senior warrior, he can thereby head a large group of fellow tribesmen bound to him by these pig alliances. He has become a big-man. The great *mokas* crown the process like a combination election and inaugural celebration. Even though the raiding parties that traditionally centered on these big-men have now been outlawed, the practices have never been completely banished from the hinterlands, where big-men are still known by the title "Slayers of Pigs and Men."

The political path to becoming a big-man in the United States Congress resembles the route followed by Ongka and other big-men in New Guinea. As in New Guinea, the role of big-man has been usually reserved for males, but in the United States a few women have broken into these ranks. The baked-chicken dinners and paper hats of American politics may lack some of the color of roasting pigs and cassowary feather headdresses, and American oratory may pale before the eloquent rhetoric of a New Guinea big-man, but underneath the process remains the same. The distribution of pork represents the heart of the organization in both cases, even if the Americans have substituted a metaphorical distribution of grants in aid and water projects for the living, squealing variety. The more pork he distributes, the more followers he attracts, and the more followers he attracts, the more pork he acquires to distribute.

In New Guinea and on Capitol Hill alike, the system rests on a delicately synchronized spiral of growth, in which followers and goods increase each other. Any boost to one part creates a chain reaction that increases all the other parts. By the same set of interrelations, however, a breakdown at any single point in the process can reverse the whole spiral, rapidly depleting power, production, and followers. A sudden plague that wipes out the pigs, a yam blight, massive budget cuts, or the abolition of a favorite program can destroy a lifetime of careful work and orchestration. Similarly, a rupture in domestic relations and the departure of several wives amid much rumor and gossip or an ethics scandal with public ridicule can deprive a big-man of his reputation, labor force, and thereby his political clout as well.

Few men in New Guinea survive the ravages of jungle disease and war to become senior members of their tribes, much less big-men. In the United States Congress, a few politicians survive the vicissitudes of voter opinion long enough to become senior congressmen. Of those who do survive, fewer still have the combination of ability and luck to become congressional big-men. The key to their success lies in their ability to organize and run a personal political organization within the congress. Most congressmen get some training for this by putting together an electoral organization in the home district, but in contemporary politics an inept politician who is rich can just buy an election campaign staff, public relations firm, and lots of advertising. Once he gets in the Congress, however, he must learn to pit his own organizational skills against other congressmen for control of the resources available. His ability to do this determines whether or not he will ever become a big-man.

Every New Guinea big-man's career originates from his ability to organize his domestic household to produce as many yams and pigs as possible. From this rather undramatic skill develops his opportunity to be a real leader of men in politics, war, and in the big hunt. In parallel fashion, every congressional Big Man's career originates from his capacity to organize his personal staff to maximize his political output. This basic skill provides him with the means to be a real political leader within the Congress. The congressman does not begin his legislative career as a leader of other politicians; he begins as the leader of a small staff. Only if he plays the game correctly can he turn his group into one that includes other politicians as well as staff.

The size of each congressman's personal staff is fairly standardized, while those of senators vary according to the population of the state, with only modest room for manipulation. For the freshmen and sophomores, particularly in the House, there is little opportunity for political expansion. Most of their efforts focus on the home district rather than on congressional politics. For senators and representatives who survive the first few terms, playing the insider game of congressional politics begins when they vie for subcommittee jurisdiction and for the accompanying staff. If a member is to expand his following, he must do so in either the committee or the party organization. It is there that both jurisdiction and staff are available.

Until the reforms of the Watergate era, a new senator joining a committee could do nothing but wait until the years passed to chair that committee. Today, however, senators expect and get a small piece of the action from the beginning. How they handle this responsibility will determine how quickly they rise in the power structure. Initial authority comes in the form of a subcommittee chairmanship. The three essentials for a subcommittee are (1) a staff to run it, (2) space in which to operate, and (3) a piece of jurisdiction to manage. These are acquired through a form of "United Fund Drive." The senior senators on the committee, who all chair their own subcommittees, are expected to donate something in one of these three categories to the freshman member. One senator may have a small room he uses for storage in the annex building; he donates that for an office. Another senator has oversight over the census, but since there will not be another census for several years, he hands over that jurisdiction. A third senator is responsible for consumer fraud; since consumer issues generate so much crank mail with very little press attention, he is willing to donate that piece of jurisdiction and the sole accompanying clerical position. The chairman of the committee has been having trouble with the subchairmen and thinks it might be beneficial to win over the freshman as an ally, so in a generous spirit the chairman throws in another clerical position and responsibility for a sewage program that has lost its funding.

If each of the senior senators donates something to this United Fund Drive, bit by bit a subcommittee can be assembled. It may have only one staffer and one secretary, a storage room for an office, and jurisdiction over an area for which there are no bills or pending legislation, but nevertheless it is a start. This miniature chimera is decorated with a title — preferably one that reflects a trendy topic or a relevant campaign issue. The title does not necessarily have to reflect the function of the subcommittee because the subcommittee does not necessarily have to have any function.

By means of a United Fund Drive for each of the two or three committees on which a new member serves, a freshman senator within a few months of election can be chairman of two or three very impressive-sounding subcommittees. Senator Max Baucus of Montana entered the Senate in 1979. From a United Fund Drive in the Senate Finance Committee, he was made chairman of the Subcommittee on Oversight of the Internal Revenue Service. This was a perfect subcommittee. The title sounded important, since every voter knows how important taxes and the Internal Revenue Service are. It was also highly relevant to the big issue of tax cutting. At the same time it was very specific; unlike vague issues such as consumerism, this subcommittee was concerned with one particular government agency — the IRS. The subcommittee was tailored to impress voters. Only a government insider would know that the mention of "oversight" in the title is a code word for powerlessness. In the Congress only "authorizations," which create programs, and "appropriations," which fund them, are a part of the power structure. "Oversight" implies the right to look but not to touch.

Senator Baucus also served on the Judiciary Committee. From the United Fund Drive there, he became chairman of the Limitations of Contracted and Delegated Authority Subcommittee. The name alone is formidable enough to prevent anyone, inside or outside the government, from bothering to ask what it means. If Baucus was to be chairman, however, he needed someone over whom to preside. The Judiciary Committee then assigned the other freshman, Senator Howell Heflin. In the spirit of reciprocity, Baucus joined Heflin's newly created subcommittee on Jurisprudence and Governmental Relations.

Members of the minority party are entitled to their proportion of all committee and subcommittee seats, so Senator Baucus's subcommittee needed a member of the "opposition." Freshman Republican Thad Cochran was assigned to the subcommittee and as the only Republican was made ranking minority member. Baucus and Heflin could then have an opposition faction to represent the minority view of the limitations of contracted and delegated authority, just in case the issue ever came up for discussion. And if they did not do anything, they had a member of the other party on the committee, and they could always blame him for interference.

This modern procedure assures that no one is left out of the power facade. Gone are the days when it took two decades of sitting on one's hands and waiting for the elders to die before a chairmanship became available. In the 96th Congress, the 60 Democrats divided among themselves 105 chairmanships; there were a corresponding 105 ranking minority-member positions for the 40 Republicans. Every man a chairman. With the Republican majority in 1981, the proportions changed, so that Republicans became the chairmen and the Democrats took the ranking minority positions. Nevertheless each senator can be the *head* of two separate subcommittees, or, as was the case with Senator James Abdnor, the freshman may get three subcommittees from the United Fund Campaign.

Be it ever so humble, the first subcommitte chairmanship initiates a senator's political career. Like a young New Guinea man beginning his political career with an older widow as a wife, a poor parcel of a yam field, and a crippled hog, it may not be much, but it is a start. Hard work might turn even that into a family of several young wives, acres of lush fields, and a herd of prize porkers, just as a hardworking senator may eventually build a powerful congressional clan from his meager subcommittee.

Every two years, in January following the November elections, Congress goes through a reorganization. The jurisdictions of departing members are divided up, after which the crumbs are gathered in the United Fund Drive and presented to an entering freshman as a subcommittee. Even though the freshman has to take what is given the first time, in subsequent reorganizations he will be able to increase his meager share of what the departing big-men left behind. He will also use that opportunity to fob off insignificant parts of his jurisdiction on the new cohort of freshmen.

When Donald Riegle of Michigan moved from the House of Representatives to the Senate in the 95th Congress, he joined Senator Proxmire's Committee on Banking, Housing, and Urban Affairs. His United Fund Subcommittee was given the then hot title of Consumer Affairs. When consumer issues gave way in the press to more severe economic problems, Riegle used the reorganization of the 96th Congress to expand his title to Economic Stabilization Subcommittee. The same pressing economic concerns moved Senator Paul Sarbanes from chairman of the Western Hemisphere Affairs Subcommittee of the Foreign Relations Committee to that committee's International Economic Policy Subcommittee. The Foreign Affairs panel tries to keep a stable subcommittee nomenclature (in the interest of better international relations), so Sarbane's old subcommittee title was passed unchanged to committee newcomer Edward Zorinsky of Nebraska.

For the first few organizations in a senator's career, the "gains in jurisdiction" are more apparent than substantial. Reorganization is a public relations exercise of senior members trying to make the juniors look and feel more important. Gradually, however, the senator is able to acquire a bailiwick of real jurisdiction. The process by which he does this is more one of slow accretion and aggrandizement than of dramatic political coups. For the first few terms the gains come as superficial name trades, exchanging words like "application" for "oversight" and "consumer issues" for "economic affairs." Eventually, the senator acquires small bits of the real authorization and appropriations process. Once this begins, the senator loses interest in the subcommittee name. If he has a piece of real power, people will know it, and he does not need to impress them with a fancy name. At this point in his career any old name will suffice, as he abandons word games for power politics.

When a senator captures another staff position, he immediately fires the employee who occupies the job and fills the position with one of his own clients. Every congressional reorganization involves a major shuffle of staff. When control of the Congress changes parties, as the Senate did after the 1980 elections, these staff changes reach monumental proportions. Within hours after the election returns were announced, Senator Strom Thurmond, as the incoming chairman of the Judiciary Committee, the largest employer in the Senate, put all of Senator Ted Kennedy's staff on notice to vacate their jobs. Thurmond was moving in his own people in a quantum jump in power. Over the next three months corresponding chain reactions reverberated through all the committees and subcommittees of the Senate, as Republicans took over each of the chairmanships.

Committee and staff shuffling continues throughout the politician's congressional career. If he is not vigilant in protecting or expanding his staff, he will forfeit it to more aggressive senators. This happened in 1981 when Strom Thurmond successfully abolished the antitrust subcommittee, which Senator Charles Mathias was taking over as chairman. In abolishing it, Thurmond assumed responsibility for the issues and the staff in his capacity as full Judiciary Committee chairman. The same scenario was played out on the Banking and Urban Affairs Committee when Chairman Jake Garn managed to appoint his own staffer to be director over Senator Richard Lugar's subcommittee. Refusing to be chairman in name only, Lugar resigned from the subcommittee. On the House side, Commerce Committee Chairman John Dingell managed to abolish the consumer affairs subcommittee, thereby taking away the staff of the second-ranking committee member, James H. Scheuer of New York.

Occasionally, this game of musical chairs forces the politician to transfer jurisdiction from one of his committees, where it is in danger, to another better fortified one. This is what Senator William Fulbright did when he surrendered the chairmanship of the Banking Committee for Foreign Relations. On the Banking Committee he had spent years acquiring control over the World Bank and the International Monetary Fund. Rather than abandoning them when he gave up the chairmanship of that committee, he simply moved jurisdiction for them to his Foreign Relations Committee. Subsequent banking chairmen, like William Proxmire, have been fighting unsuccessfully ever since to get these programs back in their original committee.

That kind of juggling, however, is less necessary in the wake of recent committee reforms. Subcommittee chairmen can be much more independent today. Were Fulbright around now, he could take over Foreign Relations and still keep his banking interests within a subcommittee. When Fulbright made his move, however, relinquishing the Banking Committee chairmanship meant relinquishing all of the power in it. Today as a subcommittee chairman, he could retain that power within both spheres. The big struggles now are within committees rather than among them. Subcommittee chairmen struggle against each other and against the chairman of the full committee, while committees fight less against each other. In this Congress of rapidly changing jurisdictions, in which some changes are substantive and some are pretense, how is it possible to tell where power actually is? Is the power in the committee or the subcommittee? Is it in the hands of the chairman, or divided among the subchairmen?

The nominal jurisdictions and the titles belong to the facade of Congress. As part of that facade they are rearranged every other year, when new shingles are made and hung out to represent the shifts of public concern and media attention. Behind this variable facade, however, is a simple arrangement that clarifies the location of power. Power is where the staff is.

No matter how grandiose the name and the official jurisdiction, if a subcommittee has only one young counsel and a single secretary, it is obviously not equipped to exercise much power. By the same token, no matter how innocuous the name and how vague the title, if it has a dozen lawyers, three Ph.D.'s, a battery of secretaries, and four interns, it is certain that some real power is being exercised. It may not be immediately apparent what they command, but staff is a sure sign of dominion over something.

A junior senator may fuss over his subcommittee name and supposed territory, but the middle-level senators — the rising comers — go straight to the heart of the matter; they fuss over staff. As Stephen Isaacs of *The Washington Post* described it, senators are "scrambling after staff bodies like hunters in pursuit of prey, hungering for the impact that extra staff person, or two, or three, or even dozens can give to them and their political careers."

Rochelle Jones and Peter Woll call staff "the surrogates of power." As they explain it, "Committees . . . are mere symbols of power, not power itself, unless they are accompanied by adequate staff. A good staff is necessary if a senator wants to wield power through his committees. If he wants to exert influence beyond his committees, a capable staff is essential. Staff and power go together. . . ." Not only is a senator's staff size directly correlated to the amount of public attention he receives in the news media, it is also related to the amount of work he can get done. Having broad jurisdiction and no staff is like a New Guinea tribesman's having a claim to two large yam fields but no wives to tend them. The fields then belong to the jungle, and they will be expropriated by someone who does have wives and children to cultivate them.

Conceptually, the scheme is simple. Like the tribal politicians of New Guinea and the complex of wives, land, and pigs, congressional politicians have to unite the variables of staff, jurisdiction, and pork. The synthesis depends on skill, luck, and hard work. Most important of all, it depends on the strategy devised and pursued by the individual politician. All the politicians know the basic ingredients of power, but each one must conjure up a plan appropriate to his or her own needs, goals, and abilities.

REVIEW QUESTIONS

1. What are the specific steps senators take to acquire power?

2. How are the steps to power taken by U.S. senators like those taken by New Guinea big-men? What are the differences?

3. What part does "pork" play in the acquisition of power by U.S. senators and Melanesian big-men?

4. How is power acquired by people in other kinds of organizations? Use your own experience to answer.

IX

Religion, magic, and world view

People seem most content when they are confident about themselves and the order of things around them. Uncertainty breeds debilitating anxiety; insecurity saps people's sense of purpose and their willingness to participate in social activity. Most of the time cultural institutions serve as a lens through which to view and interpret the world and respond realistically to its demands. But from time to time the unexpected or contradictory intervenes to shake people's assurance. A farmer may wonder about his skill when a properly planted and tended crop fails to grow. A wife may feel bewildered when the man she has treated with tenderness and justice for many years runs off with another woman. Death, natural disaster, and countless other forms of adversity strike without warning, eating away at the foundations of confidence. At these crucial points in life, many people use religion to help account for the vagaries of their experience.

Religion is the cultural knowledge of the supernatural that people use to cope with the ultimate problems of human existence.[1] In this

[1]This definition draws on the work of Milton Yinger, *Religion, Society, and the Individual: An Introduction to the Sociology of Religion,* (New York: Macmillan, 1957).

definition, the term *supernatural* refers to a realm beyond normal experience. Belief in gods, spirits, ghosts, and magical power often defines the supernatural, but the matter is complicated by cultural variation and the lack of a clear distinction in many societies between a natural and supernatural world. *Ultimate problems*, on the other hand, emerge from universal features of human life and include life's meaning, death, evil, and transcendent values. People everywhere wonder why they are alive, why they must die, and why evil strikes some individuals and not others. In every society, people's personal desires and goals may conflict with the values of the larger group. Religion often provides a set of *transcendent values* that override differences and unify the group.

An aspect of religion that is more difficult to comprehend is its link to emotion. Ultimate problems "are more appropriately seen as deep-seated emotional needs," not as conscious, rational constructs, according to sociologist Milton Yinger.[2] Anthropologists may describe and analyze religious ritual and belief but find it harder to get at religion's deeper meanings and personal feelings.

Anthropologists have identified two kinds of supernatural power, personified and impersonal. *Personified supernatural force* resides in supernatural beings, in the deities, ghosts, ancestors, and other beings found in the divine world. For the Bhils of India, a *bhut*, or ghost, has the power to cause skin lesions and wasting diseases. *Bhagwan*, the equivalent of the Christian Deity, controls the universe. Both possess and use personified supernatural force.

Impersonal supernatural force is a more difficult concept to grasp. Often called *mana*, the term used in Polynesian and Melanesian belief, it represents a kind of free-floating force lodged in many things and places. The concept is akin to the Western term *luck* and works like an electrical charge that can be introduced into things or discharged from them. Melanesians, for example, might attribute the spectacular growth of yams to some rocks lying in the fields. The rocks possess mana, which is increasing fertility. If yams fail to grow in subsequent years, they may feel that the stones have lost their power.

Supernatural force, both personified and impersonal, may be used by people in many societies. *Magic* refers to the strategies people use to control supernatural power. Magicians have clear ends in mind when they perform magic, and use a set of well-defined procedures to control and manipulate supernatural forces. For example, a Trobriand Island religious specialist will ensure a sunny day for a political event by repeating powerful sayings thought to affect the weather.

[2]Ibid., 9.

Sorcery uses magic to cause harm. For example, some Bhil *bhopas*, who regularly use magic for positive purposes, may also be hired to work revenge. They will recite powerful *mantras* (ritual sayings) over effigies to cause harm to their victims.

Witchcraft is closely related to sorcery because both use supernatural force to cause evil. But many anthropologists use the term to designate envious individuals who are born with or acquire evil power and who knowingly or unknowingly project it to hurt others. The Azande of Africa believe that most unfortunate events are due to witchcraft, and most Azande witches claim they were unaware of their power and apologize for its use.

Most religions possess ways to influence supernatural power or, if spirits are nearby, to communicate with it directly. For example, people may say *prayers* to petition supernatural beings. They may also give gifts in the form of *sacrifices* and offerings. Direct communication takes different forms. *Spirit possession* occurs when a supernatural being enters and controls the behavior of a human being. With the spirit in possession, others may talk directly with someone from the divine world. *Divination* is a second way to communicate with the supernatural. It usually requires material objects or animals to provide answers to human-directed questions. The Bhils of India, for example, predict the abundance of summer rainfall by watching where a small bird specially caught for the purpose lands when it is released. If it settles on something green, rainfall will be plentiful; if it rests on something brown, the year will be dry.

Almost all religions involve people with special knowledge who either control supernatural power outright or facilitate others in their attempt to influence it. *Shamans* are religious specialists who directly control supernatural power. They may have personal relationships with spiritual beings or know powerful secret medicines and sayings. They are usually associated with curing. *Priests* are religious specialists who mediate between people and supernatural beings. They don't control divine power; instead, they lead congregations in ceremonies and help others to petition the gods.

World view refers to a system of concepts and often unstated assumptions about life. It usually contains a *cosmology* about the way things are and a *mythology* about how things have come to be. World view presents answers to the ultimate questions: life, death, evil, and conflicting values.

The first two articles in this section deal with the use of magic to reduce uncertainty. In Philip Newman's article, it is the anxiety surrounding illness that receives attention; in George Gmelch's article, it is the irregularities of American baseball. The third article, by Lloyd Warner, is an analysis of the sacred national symbols associated with the American Memorial Day ritual. These function to generate national solidarity in the face of numerous conflicting values and group goals. In the final article, William Merrill describes how a Mexican Indian group has transformed a foreign religion, Catholicism, to fit its original cultural beliefs and world view, creating a whole new way to celebrate Easter.

KEY TERMS

religion	prayer
supernatural	sacrifice
ultimate problems	spirit possession
transcendent values	divination
personified supernatural force	shaman
mana	priest
magic	world view
sorcery	cosmology
witchcraft	mythology

27

When technology fails: Magic and religion in New Guinea

PHILIP L. NEWMAN

All people experience anxiety when confronted with situations they cannot control, and in many societies natural methods of influencing and predicting events work only part of the time. In such instances, supernatural forces are invoked to account for such events and our relation to them. In this article, Philip Newman describes the use of magic and witchcraft by a highland New Guinea people and shows that they employ such practices throughout their lives whenever faced with uncertainty. He suggests that magical procedures can be ranked according to their ability to release tension, and that the choice of particular magical practices correlates with the degree of anxiety to be reduced.

Man has created many forms in his quest for means of dealing with the world around him. Whether these forms be material tools, social groups, or intangible ideas, they are all, in a sense, "instruments": each is a means to some end; each has a purpose that it fulfills. When we think of such things as magical rites, a belief in ghosts, or accusations of sorcery, however, the matter of purpose becomes less obvious. In the descriptions and in the case history that follow, we will try both to show something of the magical and religious beliefs of a New Guinea people and to demonstrate the purposes that these beliefs have for the men who hold them.

In the mountainous interior of Australian New Guinea, the Asaro River has its headwaters some thirty miles to the north of Goroka, a

Originally published as "Sorcery, Religion, and the Man." With permission from *Natural History*, Vol. 71, No. 2; Copyright the American Museum of Natural History, 1962.

European settlement that serves as the administrative center for the Central Highlands District. Near Goroka, the Asaro flows through a wide valley where the ground cover is mostly grasses and reeds. In its upper reaches, this valley narrows into a gorge where steep, heavily forested ridges reach out toward the river from mountain masses on either side. Some 12,000 people live on this part of the river, occupying an area of approximately 200 square miles. While these people are culturally and linguistically similar, they do not form a single political unit. Indeed, before contact with Europeans, the area was characterized by incessant intertribal warfare. Even now, when active warfare is no longer part of their lives, the pattern of alliances and animosities among the tribes is a factor in social intercourse.

Except for the cessation of warfare, life in the valley today is little changed from what it was before the Australian government began active pacification of the area after the end of World War II. Almost daily, the people climb up from the valley floor to enter the dense forest on the mountain slopes. It is here that building wood is gathered; birds and small marsupials are shot for meat, plumage, or fur; plants that provide for many needs are collected.

Below an altitude of some 7,000 feet, the forest has been cut back to make room for gardens that cling to the sides of steep ridges and crowd together in the narrow valley floors. These gardens provide the people's staple foods — sweet potatoes, yams, sugar cane, and a variety of green vegetables. A woman spends most of her time at garden work, preparing new planting areas, weeding the crop, and harvesting the mature plants. In fallow areas nearby she can turn loose the pigs her husband has entrusted to her care. If they wander too far afield by evening, her call will bring them back on the run. They know that a meal awaits them, as well as a snooze by the fire in their "mother's" house.

While each family may have one or more houses near the forest or in their garden, the center of social life is the village. The villages are located on the tops of ridges in spots usually selected with an eye to their defensibility against enemies. The fifteen to twenty houses that compose each village usually march in single file along the narrow ridge. But, if space permits, they are formed into a square. All the houses are much alike — round, about fifteen feet in diameter, made of double rows of five-foot stakes. The space between the stakes is filled with grass and the outside covered with strips of bark. The roof is thatched and topped with a long, tasseled pole.

Two or three houses always stand out. They are larger, they are not in line with the rest, and they may have as many as eight poles protruding through their roofs. These are the men's houses. As a rule, men and women do not live together, for the men fear that too much contact with women is weakening. For this reason, a man builds a house for his wife — or each of them, if he has more than one — and then helps in the construction of the larger house where he and the other men of the village will sleep apart. Ideally, all the men who live together in a single house can trace their descent back to a known, common ancestor. They thus constitute a lineage. Such a lineage is connected to the other village men's houses by descent links, but in many cases the links are so amorphous that no one can actually tell what they are. Similarly, several villages will be linked together into a clan, but genealogical ties may be more imputed than real.

Just as the forest and the garden represent the physical framework within which each individual lives, so too these various orders of grouping — the lineage, the village, the clan, and the tribe — represent the social framework of existence. The members of these groups are the people with whom each individual is in daily contact. They nurture him, teach him, and assist him in times of crisis. It is from these groups that he derives such things as his name, his rights to the land for gardening and hunting, and the financial help that he needs when it is time to purchase a wife. They hail his birth and mourn his death.

In turn, each individual has obligations to the other members of these groups. He acts as a representative of his group when dealing with outsiders. In this way, he enters into a whole series of relationships with individuals and groups outside his own immediate circle. He may visit a neighboring clan to help one of his own clansmen win the admiration of a prospective bride by sitting up all night near the hot fire singing love songs to her. Or a trip may take him to a nearby tribe, where he dances mightily with other men to show that his group is appreciative of the gift of food and valuables they are about to receive. He may walk several days over difficult ground to reach a completely alien group, where he can barter for shells, plumes, or foodstuffs not available in his own group. As in all societies, the groups comprising the society provide for the individual, while the individual, in turn, contributes some of his efforts to the life of the group.

Man not only has his tools and his society to help cope with the world: he also has his ideas. There are some problems presented by the environment for which the people of the upper Asaro have not yet devised a mechanical or technical solution. There are other problems for which a technical solution seems not enough. Finally, there are problems for which an idea seems to be an inherently better solution than a physical or social tool. It is here that we enter the realm of magic and religion.

A great many of the activities among the upper Asaro people have a magical or religious component. When a child is born, it is cleaned, fed, and covered with grease to help protect it from the cool mountain air. It is also protected, nonphysically, by burying its umbilical cord in some secluded spot—so that sorcerers cannot later use this piece of the newformed being to cause illness or death by magical means. During the first few days of life, the infant is also made to accept, via magic, his first social responsibility—not to cry at night and disturb its mother. A small bundle of sweet-smelling grass is placed on the mother's head and her desire for uninterrupted slumber is blown into the grass by an attendant. The grass is then crushed over the head of the child and its pungent odor released so that the infant will breathe in the command along with the scent of the plant.

Throughout an individual's life there will be magical rites to protect him from various dangers, to overcome difficulties, and to assist his growth. When a young boy kills his first animal, his hand will be magically "locked" in the position that first sent an arrow on a true course. When he reaches puberty and moves out of his mother's house to begin his life in the men's house, he will be ritually cleansed of the contamination he has been subjected to during his years of association with women. If he were not so cleansed, he would never become strong enough to engage in men's activities. During the years when a young man is trying to win the favor of a girl, he not only relies on his prowess in singing love songs and his decorations, but on his knowledge of love magic as well. If all the usual spells and potions fail, he may utilize one especially powerful form that is thought to make him appear to his beloved with an entirely new face—the face of someone he knows she likes.

In his mature years, when a man's attention turns to the growth of pigs and gardens, he will have magical as well as technical skills to help him. Gardens are not difficult to grow in this fertile land, but it is still wise to put a certain series of leaves across one's fences, so that any thief will find his arms and legs paralyzed should he decide to raid the garden. It also behooves one whose gardens are near the main trails and settlements to give them magical assistance, for a slow-growing garden in such a conspicuous place could be an embarrassment.

The raising of pigs is a more difficult matter, and it is here that magical and religious rites become greatly elaborated. Some of these rites are performed by an individual for his own pigs. It may be a simple performance, as when smoke is blown into the ear of a wild pig to tame it. The theory is that the smoke cools and dries the pig's "hot" disposition. On the other hand, these individual rites may attain considerable complexity, as in the propitiation of forest spirits called *nokondisi*. These spirits are capricious in nature — sometimes playing malicious tricks on men and sometimes performing acts of kindness. Each man, therefore, maintains a small, fenced enclosure in which he builds a miniature earth oven and a tiny house. By placing food in the earth oven he may be able to entice a *nokondisi* to come live near his pigs and watch after them. In return for the food, the spirit will help bring in lost pigs, protect the herd from thieves, and carry the animals safely across flooded streams during the rainy season.

In addition to the magic performed by an individual on behalf of his own pigs, some rather elaborate rites are performed by the lineage and clan for all the pigs belonging to these groups. The largest of these is the *gerua* ceremony, performed at intervals of from five to seven years. In this ritual, hundreds of pigs are killed and used to pay off various kinds of economic obligations to other clans. It is a time for feasting and dancing, for courting and reunion. It is also a time for propitiating the ghosts of the dead in the hope that they will help the living grow their pigs. All the pigs are killed in the name of particular ghosts. The songs are pleas for ghostly assistance. The wooden *gerua* boards, with their colorful geometric designs, are visible symbols to the ghosts that they have not been forgotten. It is not tender sentiment that motivates this display, however. Rather, it is the fear that failure to do so will engender the wrath of the ever watchful dead.

The magical and religious beliefs that we have so far examined are all used in conjunction with other practices of a nonmagical nature. There are some areas, however, where no purely technical solutions are available, and where magic and religion are the only "tools" available. One such area is sickness. The people of the upper Asaro are not generally aware of modern medical practices, although efforts are being made in that direction. The nonmagical techniques available to them, such as inhaling the steam from fragrant plants to relieve a stopped-up nose, are few. These remedies do not extend to more serious maladies. When serious illness strikes, the only recourse is to magic.

The magical solutions available are many and varied. There are herbs with magical properties that are administered in much the same way as are medicines in our own society. I made a cursory check, however, which seems to show that few of the plants possess any curative value.

Ghosts and forest spirits are frequently thought to be the causes of illness, for they are deemed capable of entering the body and devouring a person's inner organs. Cures for such illnesses usually involve propitiation of the offending supernatural.

Witches and sorcerers are believed to be another major cause of illness, for they are supposedly capable of injecting foreign bodies into a victim, or performing black magic on objects that have been in association with the victim. To cure illness caused in this way involves calling in a magical specialist who can either extract the foreign bodies or retrieve the objects being operated upon.

While the ideas and rites listed here do not exhaust the entire inventory available to the group under discussion, they give some sense of the variety that exists. The notions are interesting in themselves, but the question of how an individual makes use of these notions is even more fascinating. Let us look at a crisis in the life of one of these people, and see how he picks and chooses among the various "tools" at his disposal.

Ombo was a young man in his early thirties. He has been married for about five years, but was childless. Early one April, it was announced in the traditional style that his wife, Magara, was with child. On such an occasion, a food distribution is held in the village and the announcement, along with gifts of food, was sent out to related villages. Ombo was instructed in the food taboos he would have to undergo during the period of his wife's pregnancy to protect himself from her increased contamination.

All went well for the first few weeks and then Magara became ill. It is doubtful that her illness was associated with her pregnancy, for her symptoms were the classic signs of malaria — a rather rare disease in this part of the highlands. The first attempts to cure her involved a variety of highly regarded pseudomedications.

A potion of sweet-smelling leaves was administered. A command to the effect that the illness should depart was blown into the leaves, and the leaves were eaten. It was thought that the command, thus internalized, would drive out the illness.

At various other times, attempts were made to relieve her headaches and body pains by rubbing the afflicted areas with stinging nettles. It was held that when the welts and the pain caused by the nettles subsided, the pains in her body would also leave. On one occasion her husband blew smoke over her during a period of fever because, as we have seen, smoke is held to have a cooling and drying effect. He also painted various parts of her body with mud in an effort to cause the pain to dry up at the same time the mud dried.

This kind of treatment continued until early May without any noticeable improvement in Magara's condition. After almost a month had passed and it became apparent that the illness was not going away, Ombo began to speculate on a possible cause. During the next few weeks he came up with several solutions. While he had been away from the village, working for Europeans in Goroka, he had acquired some charms to help him win at a card game popular among the sophisticated younger men.

One of these charms was fairly new and he was worried that he might not have gained sufficient control over it. Since he kept it hidden in his wife's house, his conclusion was that the charm was exerting its influence on her and causing the illness. He therefore removed it from her house and sent it away to a friend in another tribe. There was no improvement in his wife's condition.

Ombo's next action was to destroy his spirit house. He had not kept it in good repair and had not been diligent in feeding the *nokondisi* that lived there. His father suggested that the angered spirit was taking revenge on Magara. By destroying the house of the spirit, Ombo caused it to retreat to the forest where it could do no harm. Finally, he burned the costly paraphernalia of a potent sorcery technique he had purchased some years before, fearing it affected his wife.

By now it was late in May. Magara had become so ill that she stopped all but the most minimal work in her garden. Concern about her illness began to increase, and people outside the immediate family began to speculate about its cause. Ombo's older brother mentioned one day that a malevolent ghost might be behind it. It was not long after this that a meeting was held in the men's house and Fumai, a member of the lineage, recounted a dream he had had the night before. In it, he had seen the ghost of Ombo's great-grandmother sitting in the forest near the spot where *gerua* boards are displayed for the ancestors. She had covered herself with ashes and, in a fit of self-pity, was wailing loudly because no one had made a *gerua* board in her honor at the last *gerua* ceremony, and no one had killed a pig in her name. Since ashes are put on at the death of a near relative as a sign of mourning, while clay is put on if the deceased is more distantly related, and since ghosts are thought to be capable of causing death, it was concluded that the dream was prophetic. It implied the imminent death of Magara at the great-grandmother's hands unless something were done.

The next day, Ombo and his wife, along with his parents and siblings, set out for the spot where the ghost had been "seen." A pig was killed there in honor of the ghost. It was cooked in an earth oven filled with valued food items—the largest sweet potatoes, the most succulent yams, and the most highly prized varieties of taro. While water was being poured into the oven, a speech was addressed to the ghost. It was pointed out that the food had been prepared and donated in her honor at considerable trouble to those present. The feeling was expressed that she should be satisfied with the amount and the quality of the offering. She was then told to refrain from causing trouble in the future. As the food steamed in the oven, a *gerua* board was made in the ghost's honor and placed among others in a nearby tree. Some of the food was eaten and the rest was later distributed among members of the lineage.

Things seemed to go well for the next few weeks. Magara improved and was able to return to her work in the garden. Discussion of the topic was dropped. Then, late in June, she suddenly became ill again. Ombo was greatly upset. I suggested to him that she might have malaria and should be taken to the medical aid post. But Ombo did not want to do this, for by now he was convinced that his wife was being attacked by a sorcerer. To deal with this threat, a magical specialist had to be called in. It was several days before he arrived, for he lived some distance away in another tribe. As with any good "doctor," his first acts were aimed at relieving his patient's pain and fever. With much physical strain, he literally pulled the pain from her body and cast it into the ground where it could do no further harm. His next task was to find out what was causing her illness. For over two hours he sat chatting with Ombo and Magara, discussing the history of the illness, the treatments that had been used, and their own life histories. All the while, he puffed on a tobacco pipe made of a bamboo tube. The degree of irritation caused by the smoke in his throat signalized the appearance in the conversation of significant diagnostic events. Finally, he announced his conclusion—illness by black magic.

To eliminate the effects of the imputed black magic, the object being manipulated by the sorcerer had to be recovered. To do this, the magical specialist first had a bundle of long, thin leaves prepared. Into the bundle were put cooked pork and a variety of plants with magical properties. The specialist never directly touched the bundle himself, but directed Ombo in its preparation. When the bundle was completed, it and a specially prepared bamboo tube were both carried into Magara's house. She was given the tube to hold and the bundle was hung in the rafters near the center pole. After a rite to protect her from further sorcery, Ombo and Magara were locked together in the house.

The specialist remained outside. He walked round and round the house, reciting spells and whirling a special plant around his head. He was pulling the unknown object away from the sorcerer and bringing it back home. The ceremony became a real struggle: the object would come tantalizingly close, only to slip away. Then the specialist announced that the object had arrived. Magara was instructed to open the bundle in the rafters. Inside, among the bits of meat, were a small spider and a piece of string of the type used to hang ornaments around the neck.

The spider, Magara and Ombo were told, was an assistant to the specialist. It had taken the string out of the sorcerer's house and into the open where the specialist could reach it with his powers. The sorcerer was thought to be a young man who had once wanted to marry Magara. The existence of a disappointed suitor was one fact that had come out during the specialist's long interview. When Magara had married Ombo, the suitor had become angry and cut a bit of her necklace string to use for sorcery. The specialist placed the recovered string in the bamboo tube that Magara had been holding, and the tube was then hidden away among the thatch.

From that time until late September, when I left the area, Magara did not experience any further attacks of illness, although she was not in the best of health. The community considered her cured. Significantly, her child was born prematurely in September and died two days later, but no one saw any connection between this death and her illness.

What, then, can we say about the purpose of such ideas and behavior patterns? A situation such as Magara's creates a great deal of tension in an individual who experiences it. If magic does nothing more, it allows the bearer of this tension to act. Both the patient and those concerned feel that something is being done. The pioneer anthropologist Bronislaw Malinowski long ago made the point: "Magic expresses the greater value for man of confidence over doubt, of steadfastness over vacillation, of optimism over pessimism."

It is a rare man indeed, however, who can maintain his confidence and optimism in the face of repeated failure. The question then arises, why is it that magic is not more readily given up? Three answers have traditionally been given to this question, all of them valid. In the first place, for people such as these, there is no alternative. Secondly, for the believer in the efficacy of magic, the occasional chance successes are more significant than repeated failure. Finally, explanations for failures are always at hand. Inadvertent errors in spells or formulas that must be performed precisely, or imagined countermagic, are ready explanations that are necessarily built into the very nature of magic.

The case history we have seen suggests still a fourth answer. This answer becomes apparent, however, only if we examine the way in which an individual makes use of the magical notions available to him. In the progression of the various magical techniques and explanations employed by Ombo, we can see that they call for behavior patterns allowing for increasingly aggressive release of the tension built up in him by the failure of previously selected techniques.

The simple pseudomedicinal rites, such as rubbing with nettles and painting with mud, were enough to reduce the tension of the initial crisis. The treatment was symptomatic and there was no attempt to identify the cause of the illness. When it became apparent that these techniques had failed, we find Ombo resorting to the more drastic measure of destroying valuable property. The frustration was not yet great enough to cause him to seek outlets in other people: that which he destroyed and removed from his use belonged only to him. In the next phase, we find that a ghost is predicated as the causative agent. One need not be nice to ghosts. They, like the living, are thought to be a mercenary lot who do not much care what is said about them as long as they get their just due. The speech made to the great-grandmother was studded with commands and expressions of anger at the trouble the ghost had caused. This was an excellent mechanism for the release of tension, just as was the physical act of killing the pig.

Finally, we see the most aggressive act of all—accusing a specific individual of sorcery. The accused individual was a member of an enemy tribe and lived some distance away. It was, therefore, unlikely that accuser and accused would often meet. But if the two had come together, a fight would have been inevitable. In former times, this could have led to open warfare. Thus, Ombo not only used magic as a tool against disease, but also selected the magical tools in such an order that his own increasing anxiety was relieved by increasingly aggressive actions. It is thus not only the forms created by man that enable him to cope with the world he meets, but the very way in which he manipulates those forms that are available to him.

REVIEW QUESTIONS

1. According to Newman, what is the function of magic?

2. Why do the Asaro use magic? What kinds of things do they use it on?

3. Why did the husband depicted in this article use stronger and stronger magic to cure his wife as time went by?

4. How does Newman explain the fact that people continue to use magic even when it fails?

28

Baseball magic

GEORGE GMELCH

Americans pride themselves on their "scientific" approach to life and problem solving. But as George Gmelch demonstrates in this article, American baseball players, much like the New Guinea Highlanders described in the last article by Philip Newman, also depend to a great extent on supernatural forces to ensure success in their athletic endeavors. He demonstrates that the findings of anthropologists in distant cultures shed light on our own cultural practices.

On each pitching day for the first three months of a winning season, Dennis Grossini, a pitcher on a Detroit Tiger farm team, arose from bed at exactly 10 A.M. At 1 P.M. he went to the nearest restaurant for two glasses of iced tea and a tuna fish sandwich. Although the afternoon was free, he changed into the sweat shirt and supporter he wore during his last winning game, and one hour before the game he chewed a wad of Beech-Nut chewing tobacco. During the game he touched his letters (the team name on his uniform) after each pitch and straightened his cap after each ball. Before the start of each inning he replaced the pitcher's rosin bag next to the spot where it was the inning before. And after every inning in which he gave up a run he would wash his hands.

I asked him which part of the ritual was most important. He responded, "You can't really tell what's most important so it all becomes important. I'd be afraid to change anything. As long as I'm winning, I do everything the same. Even when I can't wash my hands

Reprinted by permission of the author. Published by permission from Transaction, Inc., from *Transaction*, Vol. 8, No. 8. Copyright © 1971 by Transaction, Inc.

[this would occur when he had to bat], it scares me going back to the mound. . . . I don't feel quite right."

Trobriand Islanders, according to anthropologist Bronislaw Malinowski, felt the same way about their fishing magic. Among the Trobrianders, fishing took two forms. In the inner lagoon, fish were plentiful and there was little danger; on the open sea, fishing was dangerous and yields varied widely. Malinowski found that magic was not used in lagoon fishing, where men could rely solely on their knowledge and skill. But when fishing on the open sea, Trobrianders used a great deal of magical ritual to ensure safety and increase their catch.

Baseball, the American national sport, is an arena in which the players behave remarkably like Malinowski's Trobriand fishermen. To professional baseball players, baseball is more than a game. It is an occupation. Since their livelihood depends on how well they perform, they use magic to try to control or eliminate the chance and uncertainty built into baseball.

To control uncertainty, ex-San Francisco Giant pitcher Ron Bryant added a new stick of bubble gum to the collection in his bulging back pocket after each game he won. Jim Ohms, my teammate on the Daytona Beach Islanders in 1966, used to put another penny in the pouch of his supporter after each win. Clanging against the hard plastic genital cup, the pennies made an audible sound as the pitcher ran the bases toward the end of a winning season. Fred Caviglia, former Kansas City minor-league pitcher, used to eat the same food before each game he pitched.

Whether they are professional baseball players, Trobriand fishermen, soldiers, or farmers, people resort to magic in situations of chance, when they believe they have limited control over the success of their activities. In technologically advanced societies that pride themselves on a scientific approach to problem solving, as well as in simple societies, rituals of magic are common. Magic is a human attempt to impose order and certainty on a chaotic, uncertain situation. This attempt is irrational in that there is no causal connection between the instruments of magic and the desired consequences of the magical practice. But it is rational in that it creates in the practitioner a sense of confidence, competence, and control, which in turn is important to successfully executing a specific activity and achieving a desired result.

I have long had a close relationship with baseball, first as a participant and then as an observer. I devoted much of my youth to the game and played professionally as a first baseman for five teams in the Detroit Tiger organization over three years. I also spent two years in

the Quebec Provincial League. For additional information about baseball magic, I interviewed 28 professional ballplayers and sportswriters.
There are three essential activities in baseball—pitching, hitting,
and fielding. The first two, pitching and hitting, involve a great deal of
chance and are comparable to the Trobriand fishermen's open sea; in
them, players use magic and ritual to increase their chances for success. The third activity, fielding, involves little uncertainty, and is similar to the Trobriander inner lagoon; fielders find it unnecessary to
resort to magic.

The pitcher is the player least able to control the outcome of his
own efforts. His best pitch may be hit for a home run, and his worst
pitch may be hit directly into the hands of a fielder for an out or be
swung at and missed for a third strike. He may limit the opposing
team to a few hits yet lose the game, or he may give up a dozen hits
and win. Frequently pitchers perform well and lose, and perform
poorly and win. One has only to look at the frequency with which
pitchers end a season with poor won-lost records but good earned run
averages (a small number of runs given up per game), or vice versa.
For example, in 1977 Jerry Koosman of the Mets had an abysmal won-
lost record of 8 and 20, but a competent 3.49 earned run average, while
Larry Christenson of the Phillies had an unimpressive earned run average of 4.07 and an excellent won-lost record of 19 and 6. Regardless of
how well he performs, the pitcher depends upon the proficiency of his
teammates, the inefficiency of the opposition, and caprice.

An incredible example of bad luck in pitching occurred some
years ago involving former Giant outfielder Willie Mays. Mays intentionally "dove for the dirt" to avoid being hit in the head by a fastball.
While he was falling the ball hit his bat and went shooting down the
left-field line. Mays jumped up and ran, turning the play into a double.
Players shook their heads in amazement—most players can't hit when
they try to, but Mays couldn't avoid hitting even when he tried not to.
The pitcher looked on in disgust.

Hitting is also full of risk and uncertainty—Red Sox outfielder
and Hall of Famer Ted Williams called it the most difficult single task in
the world of sports. Consider the forces and time constraints operating
against the batter. A fastball travels from the pitcher's mound to the
batter's box, just 60½ feet, in three to four tenths of a second. For only
three feet of the journey, an absurdly short 2/100ths of a second, the
ball is in a position where it can be hit. And to be hit well, the ball
must be neither too close to the batter's body nor too far from the
"meat" of his bat. Any distraction, any slip of a muscle or change in

stance can throw a swing off. Once the ball is hit, chance plays a large role in determining where it will go — into a waiting glove, whistling past a fielder's diving stab, or into the wide-open spaces. While the pitcher who threw the fastball to Mays was suffering, Mays was collecting the benefits of luck.

Batters also suffer from the fear of being hit by a pitch — specifically, by a fastball that often travels at speeds exceeding 90 miles per hour. Throughout baseball history the great fastball pitchers — men like Sandy Koufax, Walter Johnson, Bob Gibson, and currently Nolan Ryan of the California Angels — have thrived on this fear and on the level of distraction it causes hitters. The well-armed pitcher inevitably captures the advantage in the psychological war of nerves that characterizes the ongoing tension between pitcher and hitter, and that determines who wins and loses the game. If a hitter is crowding the plate in order to reach balls on the outside corner, or if the batter has been hitting unusually well, pitchers try to regain control of their territory. Indeed, many pitchers intentionally throw at or "dust" a batter in order to instill this sense of fear (what hitters euphemistically call "respect") in him. On one occasion Dock Ellis of the Pittsburgh Pirates, having become convinced that the Cincinnati Reds were dominating his team, intentionally hit the first three Reds' batters he faced before his manager removed him from the game.

In fielding, on the other hand, the player has almost complete control over the outcome. Once a ball has been hit in his direction, no one can intervene and ruin his chances of catching it for an out. Infielders have approximately three seconds in which to judge the flight of the ball, field it cleanly, and throw it to first base. Outfielders have almost double that amount of time to track down a fly ball. The average fielding percentage (or success rate) of .975, compared with a .250 success rate for hitters (the average batting percentage), reflects the degree of certainty in fielding. Compared with the pitcher or the hitter, the fielder has little to worry about. He knows that in better than 9.7 times out of 10 he will execute his task flawlessly.

In keeping with Malinowski's hypothesis about the relationship between magic and uncertainty, my research shows that baseball players associate magic with hitting and pitching, but not with fielding. Despite the wide assortment of magic — which includes rituals, taboos, and fetishes — associated with both hitting and pitching, I have never observed any directly connected to fielding. In my experience I have known only one player, a shortstop with fielding problems, who reported any ritual even remotely connected with fielding.

The most common form of magic in professional baseball is personal ritual — a prescribed form of behavior that players scrupulously observe in an effort to ensure that things go their way. These rituals, like those of Malinowski's Trobriand fishermen, are performed in a routine, unemotional manner, much as players do nonmagical things to improve their play: rubbing pine tar on the hands to improve a grip on the bat, or rubbing a new ball to make it more comfortable and responsive to the pitcher's grip. Rituals are infinitely varied since ball-players may formalize any activity that they consider important to performing well.

Rituals usually grow out of exceptionally good performances. When a player does well he seldom attributes his success to skill alone. Although his skill remains constant, he may go hitless in one game and in the next get three or four hits. Many players attribute the inconsistencies in their performances to an object, item of food, or form of behavior outside their play. Through ritual, players seek to gain control over their performance. In the 1920s and '30s sportswriters reported that a player who tripped en route to the field would often retrace his steps and carefully walk over the stumbling block for "insurance."

The word "taboo" comes from a Polynesian term meaning prohibition. Failure to observe a taboo or prohibition leads to undesirable consequences or bad luck. Most players observe a number of taboos. Taboos usually grow out of exceptionally poor performances, which players often attribute to a particular behavior or food. Certain uniforms may become taboo. If a player has a poor spring training season or an unsuccessful year, he may refuse to wear the same number again. During my first season of professional baseball I ate pancakes before a game in which I struck out four times. Several weeks later I had a repeat performance, again after eating pancakes. The result was a pancake taboo — I never ate pancakes during the season from that day on. Another personal taboo, against holding a baseball during the national anthem (the usual practice for first basemen, who must warm up the other infielders), had a similar origin.

In earlier decades some baseball players believed that it was bad luck to go back and fasten a missed buttonhole after dressing for a game. They simply left missed buttons on shirts or pants undone. This taboo is not practiced by modern ballplayers.

Fetishes or charms are material objects believed to embody supernatural powers that aid or protect the owner. Good-luck fetishes are standard equipment for many ballplayers. They include a wide assortment of objects: horsehide covers from old baseballs, coins, bobby pins (Hall of Fame pitcher Rube Waddell collected these), crucifixes, and old

bats. Ordinary objects acquire power by being connected to exceptionally hot batting or pitching streaks, especially ones in which players get
all the breaks. The object is often a new possession or something a
player finds and holds responsible for his good fortune. A player who
is in a slump might find a coin or an odd stone just before he begins a
hitting streak, attribute an improvement in his performance to the influence of the new object, and regard it as a fetish.

While playing for Spokane, a Dodger farm team, Alan Foster
forgot his baseball shoes on a road trip and borrowed a pair from a
teammate. That night he pitched a no-hitter, which he attributed to the
borrowed shoes. After he bought them from his teammate, they became a prized possession.

During World War II, American soldiers used fetishes in much
the same way. Social psychologist Samuel Stouffer and his colleagues
found that in the face of great danger and uncertainty soldiers developed magical practices, particularly the use of protective amulets and
good-luck charms (crosses, Bibles, rabbits' feet, medals), and jealously
guarded articles of clothing they associated with past experiences of
escape from danger. Stouffer also found that prebattle preparations
were carried out in a fixed "ritual" order, much as ballplayers prepare
for a game.

Because most pitchers play only once every four days, they perform rituals less frequently than hitters. The rituals they do perform,
however, are just as important. A pitcher cannot make up for a poor
performance the next day, and having to wait three days to redeem
oneself can be miserable. Moreover, the team's win or loss depends
more on the performance of the pitcher than on any other single
player. Considering the pressures to do well, it is not surprising that
pitchers' rituals are often more complex than those of hitters.

A 17-game winner last year in the Texas Ranger organization,
Mike Griffin, begins his ritual preparation a full day before he pitches,
by washing his hair. The next day, although he does not consider
himself superstitious, he eats bacon for lunch. When Griffin dresses for
the game he puts on his clothes in the same order, making certain he
puts the slightly longer of his two outer, or "stirrup," socks on his
right leg. "I just wouldn't feel right mentally if I did it the other way
around," he explains. He always wears the same shirt under his uniform on the days he pitches. During the game he takes off his cap after
each pitch, and between innings he sits in the same place on the
dugout bench.

Steve Hamilton, formerly a relief pitcher for the Yankees, used to
motion with his pitching hand as he left the mound after an inning. He
would make a fist, holding it at arm's length by his side, and pull it

upward, as if he were pulling a chain—which is what the announcers used to call it. Tug McGraw, relief pitcher for the Phillies, slaps his thigh with his glove with each step he takes leaving the mound at the end of an inning. This began as a means of saying hello to his wife in the stands, but has since become a ritual. McGraw now slaps his thigh whether his wife is there or not.

Many of the rituals pitchers engage in—tugging their caps between pitches, touching the rosin bag after each bad pitch, smoothing the dirt on the mound before each new batter or inning (as the Tigers' Mark Fidrych does)—take place on the field. Most baseball fans observe this behavior regularly, never realizing that it may be as important to the pitcher as actually throwing the ball.

Uniform numbers have special significance for some pitchers. Many have a lucky number, which they request. Since the choice is usually limited, pitchers may try to get a number that at least contains their lucky number, such as 14, 24, 34, or 44 for the pitcher whose lucky number is 4. Oddly enough, there is no consensus about the effect of wearing number 13. Some pitchers will not wear it; others, such as Oakland's John "Blue Moon" Odom and Steve Barber, formerly of the Orioles, prefer it. (During a pitching slump, however, Odom asked for a new number. Later he switched back to 13.)

The way in which number preferences emerge varies. Occasionally a pitcher requests the number of a former professional star, hoping that—in a form of imitative magic—it will bring him the same measure of success. Or he may request a favorite number that he has always associated with good luck. Vida Blue, formerly with Oakland and now playing for San Francisco, changed his uniform number from 35 to 14, the number he wore as a high-school quarterback. When the new number did not produce the better pitching performance he was looking for, he switched back to his old number.

One of the sources of his good fortune, Blue believed, was the baseball hat he had worn since 1974. Several American League umpires refused to let him wear the faded and soiled cap last season. When Blue persisted, he was threatened with a fine and suspension from a game. Finally he conceded, but not before he ceremoniously burned the hat on the field before a game.

On the days they are scheduled to appear, many pitchers avoid activities that they believe sap their strength and therefore detract from their effectiveness, or that they otherwise generally link with poor performance. Many pitchers avoid eating certain foods on their pitching days. Some pitchers refuse to walk anywhere on the day of the game in the belief that every little exertion subtracts from their playing strength. One pitcher would never put on his cap until the game started and would not wear it at all on the days he did not pitch. Another had a movie taboo. He refused to watch movies on the day of the game. And until this season Al Hrabosky, recently traded from the St. Louis Cardinals to the Kansas City Royals, had an even more encompassing taboo: Samsonlike, he refused to cut his hair or beard during the entire season—hence part of the reason for his nickname, the "Mad Hungarian."

Many hitters go through a series of preparatory rituals before stepping into the batter's box. These include tugging on their caps, touching their uniform letters or medallions, crossing themselves, tapping or bouncing the bat on the plate, swinging the weighted warm-up bat a prescribed number of times, and smoothing the dirt in the batter's box. Rocky Colavito, a colorful home-run hitter active in the 1950s and '60s, used to stretch his arms behind his back and cross himself when he came to the plate. A player in the Texas Ranger organization draws a triangle in the dirt outside the batter's box, with the peak pointing toward center field. Other players are careful never to step on the chalk lines of the batter's box when standing at the plate.

Clothing, both the choice of clothes and the order in which they are put on, is often ritualized. During a batting streak many players wear the same clothes and uniforms for each game and put them on in exactly the same order. Once I changed sweat shirts midway through the game for seven consecutive games to keep a hitting streak going. During a 16-game winning streak in 1954 the New York Giants wore the same clothes in each game and refused to let them be cleaned for fear that their good fortune might be washed away with the dirt. Taking this ritual to the extreme, Leo Durocher, managing the Brooklyn Dodgers to a pennant in 1941, spent three and a half weeks in the same black shoes, gray slacks, blue coat, and knitted blue tie.

The opposite may also occur. Several of the Oakland A's players bought new street clothing last year in an attempt to break a 14-game losing streak. Most players, however, single out one or two lucky articles or quirks of dress rather than ritualizing all items of clothing. After hitting two home runs in a game, infielder Jim Davenport of the San Francisco Giants discovered that he had missed a buttonhole while dressing for the game. For the remainder of his career he left the same button undone.

A popular ritual associated with hitting is tagging a base when leaving and returning to the dugout during each inning. Mickey Mantle was in the habit of tagging second base on the way to or from the outfield. During a successful month of the season one player stepped on third base on his way to the dugout after the third, sixth, and ninth innings of each game. Asked if he ever purposely failed to step on the bag he replied, "Never! I wouldn't dare. It would destroy my confidence to hit." A hitter who is playing poorly may try different combinations of tagging and not tagging particular bases in an attempt to find a successful combination.

Another component of a hitter's ritual may be tapping the plate with his bat. A teammate of mine described a variation of this in which he gambled for a certain hit by tapping the plate with his bat a fixed number of times: one tap for a single, two for a double, and so on. He even built in odds that prevented him from asking for a home run each time at bat. The odds of hitting a home run with four taps were one in 12.

When their players are not hitting, some managers will rattle the bat bin, the large wooden box containing the team's bats, as if the bats were asleep or in a stupor and could be aroused by a good shaking. Similarly, some hitters rub their hands or their own bats along the handles of the bats protruding from the bin, presumably in hopes of picking up some power or luck from bats that are getting hits for their owners.

There is a taboo against crossing bats, against permitting one bat to rest on top of another. Although this superstition appears to be dying out among professional ballplayers, it was religiously observed by some of my teammates a decade ago. And in some cases it was elaborated even further. One former Detroit minor leaguer became quite annoyed when a teammate tossed a bat from the batting cage and it landed on top of his bat. Later he explained that the top bat might steal hits from the lower one. In his view, bats contained a finite number of hits, a sort of zero-sum game or baseball "image of limited good." For Pirate shortstop Honus Wagner, a charter member of baseball's Hall of Fame, each bat contained only a certain number of hits, and never more than 100. Regardless of the quality of the bat, he would discard it after its 100th hit.

Hall of Famer Johnny Evers, of the Cub double-play trio Tinker to Evers to Chance, believed in saving his luck. If he was hitting well in practice, he would suddenly stop and retire to the bench to "save" his batting for the game. One player told me that many of his teammates on the Asheville Tourists in the Class A Western Carolinas League would not let pitchers touch or swing their bats, not even to loosen up. The traditionally poor-hitting pitchers were believed to contaminate or weaken the bats.

Food often forms part of a hitter's ritual repertoire. Eating certain foods before a game is supposed to give the ball "eyes," that is, the ability to seek the gaps between fielders after being hit. In hopes of maintaining a batting streak, I once ate chicken every day at 4 P.M. until the streak ended. Hitters — like pitchers — also avoid certain foods that are believed to sap their strength during the game.

There are other examples of hitters' ritualized behavior. I once kept my eyes closed during the national anthem in an effort to prolong a batting streak. And a teammate of mine refused to read anything on the day of a game because he believed that reading weakened his eyesight when batting.

These are personal taboos. There are some taboos, however, that all players hold and that do not develop out of individual experiences or misfortunes. These taboos are learned, some as early as Little League. Mentioning a no-hitter while one is in progress is a widely known example. It is believed that if a pitcher hears the words "no-hitter," the spell will be broken and the no-hitter lost. Until recently this taboo was also observed by sports broadcasters, who used various linguistic subterfuges to inform their listeners that the pitcher had not given up a hit, never mentioning "no-hitter."

Most professional baseball coaches or managers will not step on the chalk foul lines when going onto the field to talk to their pitchers. Cincinnati's manager Sparky Anderson jumps over the line. Others follow a different ritual. They intentionally step on the lines when they are going to take a pitcher out of a game.

How do these rituals and taboos get established in the first place? B. F. Skinner's early research with pigeons provides a clue. Like human beings, pigeons quickly learn to associate their behavior with rewards or punishment. By rewarding the birds at the appropriate time, Skinner taught them such elaborate games as table tennis, miniature bowling, or to play simple tunes on a toy piano.

On one occasion he decided to see what would happen if pigeons were rewarded with food pellets every 15 seconds, regardless of what they did. He found that the birds tended to associate the arrival of food with a particular action — tucking the head under a wing, hopping from side to side, or turning in a clockwise direction. About 10 seconds after the arrival of the last pellet, a bird would begin doing whatever it had associated with getting the food and keep it up until the next pellet arrived.

In the same way, baseball players tend to believe there is a causal connection between two events that are linked only temporally. If a superstitious player touches his crucifix and then gets a hit, he may decide the gesture was responsible for his good fortune and follow the same ritual the next time he comes to the plate. If he should get another hit, the chances are good that he will begin touching the crucifix each time he bats and that he will do so whether or not he hits safely each time.

The average batter hits safely approximately one quarter of the time. And, if the behavior of Skinner's pigeons — or of gamblers at a Las Vegas slot machine — is any guide, that is more often than necessary to keep him believing in a ritual. Skinner found that once a pigeon associated one of its actions with the arrival of food or water, sporadic rewards would keep the connection going. One bird, which apparently believed hopping from side to side brought pellets into its feeding cup, hopped 10,000 times without a pellet before it gave up.

Since the batter associates his hits at least in some degree with his ritual touching of a crucifix, each hit he gets reinforces the strength of the ritual. Even if he falls into a batting slump and the hits temporarily stop, he will persist in touching the crucifix in the hope that this will change his luck.

Skinner's and Malinowski's explanations are not contradictory. Skinner focuses on how the individual comes to develop and maintain a particular ritual, taboo, or fetish. Malinowski focuses on why human beings turn to magic in precarious or uncertain situations. In their attempts to gain greater control over their performance, baseball players respond to chance and uncertainty in the same way as do people in simple societies. It is wrong to assume that magical practices are a waste of time for either group. The magic in baseball obviously does not make a pitch travel faster or more accurately, or a batted ball seek the gaps between fielders. Nor does the Trobriand brand of magic make the surrounding seas calmer and more abundant with fish. But both kinds of magic give their practitioners a sense of control — and an important element in any endeavor is confidence.

REVIEW QUESTIONS

1. What is magic and why do people practice it, according to Gmelch?

2. How does Gmelch account for American baseball players practicing magic?

3. In what parts of the game is magic most likely to be used? Why?

4. How are Malinowski's and Skinner's theories of magic alike and different?

29

An American sacred ceremony

W. LLOYD WARNER

All societies suffer the disruptive effects of interpersonal and sub-group competition. The ambitions of one individual are likely to con-flict with those of others. The tenets of one subgroup, such as a club, political party, or church, may also contradict those of others, leading to division. Yet the larger society exists and must continue in the face of such divisiveness. In this selection, W. Lloyd Warner argues that Memorial Day in America is a sacred ceremony designed to transcend individual and subgroup differences and to provide a sense of collective well-being in the presence of death. By using such symbols as Lincoln and the dead soldiers themselves, the ceremony unifies people around the themes of sacrifice for the common good and equality.

Memorial day and symbolic behavior

Every year in the springtime when the flowers are in bloom and the trees and shrubs are most beautiful, citizens of the Union celebrate Memorial Day. Over most of the United States it is a legal holiday. Being both sacred and secular, it is a holy day as well as a holiday and is accordingly celebrated.

For some it is part of a long holiday of pleasure, extended out-ings, and great athletic events; for others it is a sacred day when the dead are mourned and sacred ceremonies are held to express their sorrow; but for most Americans, especially in the smaller cities, it is both sacred and secular. They feel the sacred importance of the day

From William Lloyd Warner, "An American Sacred Ceremony." Reprinted with slight abridgment from W. Lloyd Warner, *American Life,* pp. 1–26. Copyright 1953 University of Chicago Press. Reprinted by permission of The University of Chicago Press.

when they, or members of their family, participate in the ceremonies; but they also enjoy going for an automobile trip or seeing or reading about some important athletic event staged on Memorial Day. This chapter will be devoted to the analysis and interpretation of Memorial Day to learn its meanings as an American sacred ceremony, a rite that evolved in this country and is native to it.

Memorial Day originated in the North shortly after the end of the Civil War as a sacred day to show respect for the Union soldiers who were killed in the War between the States. Only since the last two wars has it become a day for all who died for their country. In the South only now are they beginning to use it to express southern respect and obligation to the nation's soldier dead.

Memorial Day is an important occasion in the American ceremonial calendar and as such is a unit of this larger ceremonial system of symbols. Close examination discloses that it, too, is a symbol system in its own right existing within the complexities of the larger one.

Symbols include such familiar things as written and spoken words, religious beliefs and practices, including creeds and ceremonies, the several arts, such familiar signs as the cross and the flag, and countless other objects and acts which stand for something more than that which they are. The red, white, and blue cloth and the crossed sticks in themselves and as objects mean very little, but the sacred meanings which they evoke are of such deep significance to some that millions of men have sacrificed their lives for the first as the Stars and Stripes and for the second as the Christian Cross.

The ceremonial calendar of American society, this yearly round of holidays and holy days, partly sacred and partly secular, but more sacred than secular, is a symbol system used by all Americans. Christmas and Thanksgiving, Memorial Day and the Fourth of July, are days in our ceremonial calendar which allow Americans to express common sentiments about themselves and share their feelings with others on set days pre-established by the society for this very purpose. This calendar functions to draw all people together to emphasize their similarities and common heritage; to minimize their differences; and to contribute to their thinking, feeling, and acting alike. All societies, simple or complex, possess some form of ceremonial calendar, if it be no more than the seasonal alternation of secular and ceremonial periods, such as that used by the Australian aborigines in their yearly cycle.

The integration and smooth functioning of the social life of a modern community are very difficult because of its complexity. American communities are filled with churches, each claiming great authority and each with its separate sacred symbol system. Many of them are in conflict, and all of them in opposition to one another. Many associations, such as the Masons, the Odd Fellows, and the like, have sacred symbol systems which partly separate them from the whole community. The traditions of foreign-born groups contribute to the diversity of symbolic life. The evidence is clear for the conflict among these systems.

It is the thesis of this chapter that the Memorial Day ceremonies and subsidiary rites (such as those of Armistice Day) of today, yesterday, and tomorrow are rituals of a sacred symbol system which functions periodically to unify the whole community, with its conflicting symbols and its opposing, autonomous churches and associations. It is contended here that in the Memorial Day ceremonies the anxieties which man has about death are confronted with a system of sacred beliefs about death which gives the individuals involved and the collectivity of individuals a feeling of well-being. Further, the feeling of triumph over death by collective action in the Memorial Day parade is made possible by re-creating the feeling of well-being and the sense of group strength and individual strength in the group power, which is felt so intensely during the wars when the veterans' associations are created and when the feeling so necessary for the Memorial Day's symbol system is originally experienced.

Memorial Day is a cult of the dead which organizes and integrates the various faiths and national and class groups into a sacred unity. It is a cult of the dead organized around the community cemeteries. Its principal themes are those of the sacrifice of the soldier dead for the living and the obligation of the living to sacrifice their individual purposes for the good of the group, so that they, too, can perform their spiritual obligations.

MEMORIAL DAY CEREMONIES

We shall first examine the Memorial Day ceremony of an American town for evidence. The sacred symbolic behavior of Memorial Day, in which scores of the town's organizations are involved, is ordinarily divided into four periods. During the year separate rituals are held by many of the associations for their dead, and many of these activities are connected with later Memorial Day events. In the second phase, preparations are made during the last three or four weeks for the ceremony itself, and some of the associations perform public rituals. The third phase consists of the scores of rituals held in all the cemeteries, churches, and halls of the associations. These rituals consist of speeches and highly ceremonialized behavior. They last for two days and are climaxed by the fourth and last phase, in which all the separate celebrants gather in the center of the business district on the afternoon of Memorial Day. The separate organizations, with their members in uniform or with fitting insignia, march through the town, visit the shrines and monuments of the hero dead, and, finally, enter the cemetery. Here dozens of ceremonies are held, most of them highly symbolic and formalized. Let us examine the actual ritual behavior in these several phases of the ceremony.

The two or three weeks before the Memorial Day ceremonies are usually filled with elaborate preparations by each participating group. Meetings are held, and patriotic pronouncements are sent to the local paper by the various organizations which announce what part each organization is to play in the ceremony. Some of the associations have Memorial Day processions, memorial services are conducted, the schools have patriotic programs, and the cemeteries are cleaned and repaired. Graves are decorated by families and associations and new gravestones purchased and erected. The merchants put up flags before their establishments, and residents place flags above their houses.

All these events are recorded in the local paper, and most of them are discussed by the town. The preparation of public opinion for an awareness of the importance of Memorial Day and the rehearsal of what is expected from each section of the community are done fully and in great detail. The latent sentiments of each individual, each family, each church, school, and association for its own dead are thereby stimulated and related to the sentiments for the dead of the nation.

One of the important events observed in the preparatory phase in the community studied occurred several days before Memorial Day, when the man who had been the war mayor wrote an open letter to the commander of the American Legion. It was published in the local paper. He had a city-wide reputation for patriotism. He was an honorary member of the American Legion. The letter read: "Dear Commander: The approaching Poppy Day (when Legion supporters sold poppies in the town) brings to my mind a visit to the war zone in France on Memorial Day, 1925, reaching Belleau Wood at about 11 o'clock. On this sacred spot we left floral tributes in memory of our town's boys—Jonathan Dexter and John Smith, who here had made the supreme sacrifice, that the principle that 'might makes right' should not prevail."

Three days later the paper in a front-page editorial told its readers: "Next Saturday is the annual Poppy Day of the American Legion. Everybody should wear a poppy on Poppy Day. Think back to those terrible days when the red poppy on Flanders Field symbolized the blood of our boys slaughtered for democracy." The editor here explicitly states the symbolism involved.

Through the early preparatory period of the ceremony, through all its phases and in every rite, the emphasis in all communities is always on sacrifice — the sacrifice of the lives of the soldiers of the city, willingly given for democracy and for their country. The theme is always that the gift of their lives was voluntary; that it was freely given and therefore above selfishness or thoughts of self-preservation; and, finally, that the "sacrifice on the altars of their country" was done for everyone. The red poppy became a separate symbol from McCrae's poem "In Flanders Fields." The poem expressed and symbolized the sentiments experienced by the soldiers and people of the country who went through the first war. The editor makes the poppy refer directly to the "blood of the boys slaughtered." In ritual language he then recites the names of some of the city's "sacrificed dead," and "the altars" (battles) where they were killed. "Remember Dexter and Smith killed at Belleau Wood," he says." "Remember O'Flaherty killed near Château-Thierry, Stulavitz killed in the Bois D'Ormont, Kelley killed at Côte de Châtillon, Jones near the Bois de Montrebeaux, Kilnikap in the St.-Mihiel offensive, and the other brave boys who died in camp or on stricken fields. Remember the living boys of the Legion on Saturday."

The names selected by the editor covered most of the ethnic and religious groups of the community. They included Polish, Russian, Irish, French-Canadian, and Yankee names. The use of such names in this context emphasized the fact that the voluntary sacrifice of a citizen's life was equalitarian. They covered the top, middle, and bottom of the several classes. The newspapers throughout the country each year print similar lists, and their editorials stress the equality of sacrifice by all classes and creeds.

The topic for the morning services of the churches on the Sunday before Memorial Day ordinarily is the meaning of Memorial Day to the town and to the people as Christians. All the churches participate. Because of space limitations, we shall quote from only a few sermons from one Memorial Day to show the main themes; but observations of Memorial Day behavior since the Second World War show no difference in the principal themes expressed before and after the war started. Indeed, some of the words are almost interchangeable. The Rev. Hugh McKellar chose as his text, "Be thou faithful until death." He said:

"Memorial Day is a day of sentiment and when it loses that, it loses all its value. We are all conscious of the danger of losing that sentiment. What we need today is more sacrifice, for there can be no achievement without sacrifice. There are too many out today preaching selfishness. Sacrifice is necessary to a noble living. In the words of our Lord, 'Whosoever shall save his life shall lose it and whosoever shall lose his life in My name shall save it.' It is only those who sacrifice personal gain and will to power and personal ambition who ever accomplish anything for their nation. Those who expect to save the nation will not get wealth and power for themselves.

"Memorial Day is a religious day. It is a day when we get a vision of the unbreakable brotherhood and unity of spirit which exists and still exists, no matter what race or creed or color, in the country where all men have equal rights."

The minister of the Congregational Church spoke with the voice of the Unknown Soldier to emphasize his message of sacrifice:

"If the spirit of that Unknown Soldier should speak, what would be his message? What would be the message of a youth I knew myself who might be one of the unknown dead? I believe he would speak as follows: 'It is well to remember us today, who gave our lives that democracy might live, we know something of sacrifice.' "

The two ministers in different language expressed the same theme of the sacrifice of the individual for national and democratic principles. One introduces divine sanction for this sacrificial belief and thereby succeeds in emphasizing the theme that the loss of an individual's life rewards him with life eternal. The other uses one of our greatest and most sacred symbols of democracy and the only very powerful one that came out of the First World War — the Unknown Soldier. The American Unknown Soldier is Everyman; he is the perfect symbol of equalitarianism.

There were many more Memorial Day sermons, most of which had this same theme. Many of them added the point that the Christian God had given his life for all. That afternoon during the same ceremony the cemeteries, memorial squares named for the town's dead, the lodge halls, and the churches had a large number of rituals. Among them was the "vacant chair." A row of chairs decorated with flags and wreaths, each with the name of a veteran who had died in the last year, was the center of this ceremony held in a church. Most of the institutions were represented in the ritual. We shall give only a small selection from the principal speech:

"Now we come to pay tribute to these men whose chairs are vacant, not because they were eminent men, as many soldiers were not, but the tribute we pay is to their attachment to the great cause. We are living in the most magnificent country on the face of the globe, a country planted and fertilized by a Great Power, a power not political or economic but religious and educational, especially in the North. In the South they had settlers who were there in pursuit of gold, in search of El Dorado, but the North was settled by people seeking religious principles and education."

In a large city park, before a tablet filled with the names of war dead, one of our field workers shortly after the vacant-chair rite heard a speaker in the memorial ritual eulogize the two great symbols of American unity — Washington and Lincoln. The orator said:

"No character except the Carpenter of Nazareth has ever been honored the way Washington and Lincoln have been in New England. Virtue, freedom from sin, and righteousness were qualities possessed by Washington and Lincoln, and in possessing these characteristics both were true Americans, and we would do well to emulate them. Let us first be true Americans. From these our friends beneath the sod we receive their message, 'Carry on.' Though your speaker will die, the fire and spark will carry on. Thou are not conqueror, death, and thy pale flag is not advancing."

In all the other services the same themes were used in the speeches, most of which were in ritualized, oratorical language, or were expressed in the ceremonials themselves. Washington, the father of his country, first in war and peace, had devoted his life not to himself but to his country. Lincoln had given his own life, sacrificed on the altar of his country. Most of the speeches implied or explicitly stated that divine guidance was involved and that these mundane affairs had supernatural implications. They stated that the revered dead had given the last ounce of devotion in following the ideals of Washington and Lincoln and the Unknown Soldier and declared that these same principles must guide us, the living. The beliefs and values of which they spoke referred to a world beyond the natural. Their references were to the supernatural.

On Memorial Day morning the separate rituals, publicly performed, continued. The parade formed in the early afternoon in the business district. Hundreds of people, dressed in their best, gathered to watch the various uniformed groups march in the parade. Crowds collected along the entire route. The cemeteries, carefully prepared for the event, and the graves of kindred covered with flowers and flags and wreaths looked almost gay.

The parade marched through the town to the cemeteries. The various organizations spread throughout the several parts of the graveyards, and rites were performed. In the Greek quarter ceremonies were held; others were performed in the Polish and Russian sections; the Boy

Scouts held a memorial rite for their departed; the Sons and Daughters of Union Veterans went through a ritual, as did the other men's and women's organizations. All this was part of the parade in which everyone from all parts of the community could and did participate.

Near the end of the day all the men's and women's organizations assembled about the roped-off grave of General Fredericks. The Legion band played. A minister uttered a prayer. The ceremonial speaker said:

"We meet to honor those who fought, but in so doing we honor ourselves. From them we learn a lesson of sacrifice and devotion and of accountability to God and honor. We have an inspiration for the future today — our character is strengthened — this day speaks of a better and greater devotion to our country and to all that our flag represents."

After the several ceremonies in the Elm Hill Cemetery, the parade re-formed and started the march back to town, where it broke up. The firing squad of the American Legion fired three salutes, and a bugler sounded the "Last Post" at the cemetery entrance as they departed. This, they said, was a "general salute for all the dead in the cemetery."

Here we see people who are Protestant, Catholic, Jewish, and Greek Orthodox involved in a common ritual in a graveyard with their common dead. Their sense of separateness was present and expressed in the different ceremonies, but the parade and the unity gained by doing everything at one time emphasized the oneness of the total group. Each ritual also stressed the fact that the war was an experience where everyone sacrificed and some died, not as members of a separate group, but as citizens of a whole community.

LINCOLN — AN AMERICAN COLLECTIVE REPRESENTATION MADE BY AND FOR THE PEOPLE

Throughout the Memorial Day ceremony there were continual references to Lincoln and his Gettysburg Address. The symbol of Lincoln obviously was of deep significance in the various rituals and to the participants. He loomed over the memorial rituals like some great demigod over the rites of classical antiquity. What is the meaning of the myth of Lincoln to Americans? Why does his life and death as conceived in the myth of Lincoln play such a prominent part in Memorial Day?

Some of the answers are obvious. He was a great war president. He was the President of the United States and was assassinated during the Civil War. Memorial Day grew out of this war. A number of other facts about his life might be added; but for our present purposes the meaning of Lincoln the myth is more important to understand than the objective facts of his life-career.

Lincoln, product of the American prairies, sacred symbol of idealism in the United States, myth more real than the man himself, symbol and fact, was formed in the flow of events which composed the changing cultures of the Middle West. He is the symbolic culmination of America. To understand him is to know much of what America means.

In 1858, when Lincoln ran against Stephen Douglas for the United States Senate, he was Abraham Lincoln, the successful lawyer, the railroad attorney, who was noted throughout the state of Illinois as a man above common ability and of more than common importance. He was a former congressman. He was earning a substantial income. He had married a daughter of the superior classes from Kentucky. His friends were W. D. Green, the president of a railway, a man of wealth; David Davis, a representative of wealthy eastern investors in western property, who was on his way to becoming a millionaire; Jesse Fell, railway promoter; and other men of prominence and prestige in the state. Lincoln dressed like them; he had unlearned many of the habits acquired in childhood from his lowly placed parents and had learned most of the ways of those highly placed men who were now his friends. After the Lincoln-Douglas debates his place as a man of prestige and power was as high as anyone's in the whole state.

Yet in 1860, when he was nominated on the Republican ticket for the presidency of the United States, he suddenly became "Abe Lincoln, the rail splitter," "the rude man from the prairie and the river-bottoms." To this was soon added "Honest Abe," and finally, in death, "the martyred leader" who gave his life that "a nation dedicated to the proposition that all men are created equal" might long endure.

What can be the meaning of this strange transformation?

When Richard Oglesby arrived in the Republican convention in 1860, he cast about for a slogan that would bring his friend, Lincoln, favorable recognition from the shrewd politicians of New York, Pennsylvania, and Ohio. He heard from Jim Hanks, who had known Lincoln as a boy, that Lincoln had once split fence rails. Dick Oglesby, knowing what appeals are most potent in getting the support of the politicians and in bringing out a favorable vote, dubbed Lincoln "the rail splitter." Fence rails were prominently displayed at the convention, to symbolize Lincoln's lowly beginnings. Politicians, remembering the great popular appeal of "Old Hickory," "Tippecanoe and Tyler too," and "The Log Cabin and Cider Jug" of former elections, realized that this slogan would be enormously effective in a national election. Lincoln, the rail splitter, was reborn in Chicago in 1860; and the Lincoln who had become the successful lawyer, intimate of wealthy men, husband of a well-born wife, and man of status was conveniently forgotten.

Three dominant symbolic themes compose the Lincoln image. The first — the theme of the common man — was fashioned in a form pre-established by the equalitarian ideals of a new democracy; to common men there could be no argument about what kind of man a rail splitter is.

"From log cabin to the White House" succinctly symbolizes the second theme of the trilogy which composes Lincoln, the most powerful of American collective representations. This phrase epitomizes the American success story, the rags-to-riches motif, and the ideals of the ambitious. As the equal of all men, Lincoln was the representative of the Common Man, as both their spokesman and their kind; and, as the man who had gone "from the log cabin to the White House," he became the superior man, the one who had not inherited but had earned that superior status and thereby proved to everyone that all men could do as he had. Lincoln thereby symbolized the two great collective but opposed ideals of American democracy.

When Lincoln was assassinated, a third powerful theme of our Christian society was added to the symbol being created by Americans to strengthen and adorn the keystone of their national symbol structure. Lincoln's life lay sacrificed on the altar of unity, climaxing a deadly war which proved by its successful termination that the country was one and that all men are created equal. From the day of his death, thousands of sermons and speeches have demonstrated that Lincoln, like Christ, died that all men might live and be as one in the sight of God and man. Christ died that this might be true forever beyond the earth; Lincoln sacrificed his life that this might be true forever on this earth.

When Lincoln died, the imaginations of the people of the eastern seaboard cherished him as the man of the new West and translated him into their hopes for tomorrow, for to them the West was tomorrow. The defeated people of the South, during and after the reconstruction period, fitted him into their dark reveries of what might have been, had this man lived who loved all men. In their bright fantasies, the people of the West, young and believing only in the tomorrow they meant to create, knew Lincoln for what they wanted themselves to be. Lincoln, symbol of equalitarianism, of the social striving of men who live in a social hierarchy, the human leader sacrificed for all men, expresses all the basic values and beliefs of the Middle West and of the United States of America.

Lincoln, the superior man, above all men, yet equal to each, is a mystery beyond the logic of individual calculators. He belongs to the culture and to the social logics of the people for whom contradiction is unimportant and for whom the ultimate tests of truth are in the social structure in which, and for which, they live. Through the passing generations of our Christian culture the Man of the Prairies, formed in the mold of the God-man of Galilee and apotheosized into the man-god of the American people, each year less profane and more sacred, moves securely toward identification with deity and ultimate godhead. In him Americans realize themselves.

THE EFFECT OF WAR ON THE COMMUNITY

A problem of even greater difficulty confronts us on why war provides such an effective context for the creation of powerful national symbols, such as Lincoln, Washington, or Memorial Day. Durkheim gives us an important theoretical lead. He believed that the members of the group felt and became aware of their own group identity when they gathered periodically during times of plenty. For his test case, the Australian aborigines, a hunting and gathering tribe, this was the season when food was plentiful. It was then when social interaction was most intense and the feelings most stimulated.

In modern society interaction, social solidarity, and intensity of feelings ordinarily are greatest in times of war. It would seem likely that such periods might well produce new sacred forms, built, of course, on the foundations of old beliefs. Let us examine the life of American communities in wartime as a possible matrix for such developments.

The most casual survey supplies ample evidence that the effects of war are most varied and diverse as they are reflected in the life of American towns. The immediate effect of war is very great on some towns and very minor on others. During its existence it strengthens the social structure of some and greatly weakens the social systems of others. In some communities it appears to introduce very little that is new, while in others the citizens are compelled by force of circumstances to incorporate whole new experiences into their lives and into the social systems which control them.

In some communities during the Second World War there was no decided increase or decrease in the population, and war did not change the ordinary occupations of their people. Their citizens made but minor adjustments in their daily lives; no basic changes occurred in their institutions. For example, there were many small market towns servicing rural areas about them where the round of events substantially repeated what had occurred in all previous years from the time the towns grew to early maturity. A few of their boys were drafted, possibly the market crops were more remunerative, and it may be that the weekly paper had a few more war' stories. Changes there were, but they were few and minor in their effect on the basic social system.

At the other extreme, most drastic and spectacular changes occurred in the Second World War. Small towns that had formerly existed disappeared entirely, and their former localities were occupied by industrial cities born during the war and fathered by it. Sleepy rural villages were supplanted by huge industrial populations recruited from every corner of America. Towns of a few hundred people, traditionally quiet and well composed, suddenly expanded into brawling young cities with no past and no future. Market towns became industrial areas. The wives and mothers in these towns left their homes and joined the newcomers on the assembly line. The old people went into industry to take jobs they had to learn like the youngest boy working beside them. This and that boy and some of their friends left high school because they received tacit encouragement from their elders and the school authorities to go to work to help in the war effort. In some communities the whole system of control that had formerly prevailed ceased to function or was superseded by outside authority. The influx of population was so great that the schools could teach but a small portion of the children. The police force was inadequate. The usual recreational life disappeared, to be supplanted by the "taxi dance hall," "juke joint," "beer hall," and "gambling dive." Institutions such as the church and lodge almost ceased to function. In some towns one could drive through miles of trailer camps and small houses pressed against one another, all recently assembled, where the inhabitants lived in squalid anonymity with, but not of, the thousands around them. They were an aggregate of individuals concentrated in one area, but they were not a community.

We have described only the two extremes of the immediate influence of war on the community. Soon, however, those communities which had been little affected by the war felt some of its effects, and those which had been disorganized developed habits of life which conformed to the ordinary pattern of American town life. The two extremes soon approached the average.

But wars influence the average town quite differently. Changes take place, the institutional life is modified, new experiences are felt by the people, and the townsmen repeatedly modify their behavior to adapt to new circumstances brought them by new events. These modifications do not cause social breakdown. The contrary is true. The war activities strengthen the integration of many small communities. The people are more systematically organized into groups where everyone is involved and in which there is an intense awareness of oneness. The town's unity and feeling of autonomy are strengthened by competition in war activities with neighboring communities.

It is in time of war that the average American living in small cities and towns gets his deepest satisfactions as a member of his society. Despite the pessimistic events of 1917, the year when the United States entered the First World War, the people derived deep satisfaction from it, just as they did from the last war. It is a mistake to believe that the American people, particularly the small-towners, hate war to the extent that they derive no satisfaction from it. Verbally and superficially they disapprove of war, but at best this is only partly revealed in their deeper feelings. In simpler terms, their observed behavior reveals that most of them had more real satisfaction out of the Second World War, just as they did in the previous one, than they had had in any other period of their lives. The various men's and women's organizations, instead of inventing things to do to keep busy, could choose among activities which they knew were vital and significant to them and to others.

The small-towner then had a sense of significance about himself, about those around him, and about the events which occurred, in a way that he had never felt before. The young man who quit high school during the depression to lounge on the street corner and who was known to be of no consequence to himself or to anyone else in the community became a seasoned veteran, fighting somewhere in the South Pacific — a man obviously with the qualities of a hero (it was believed), willing to give up his life for his country, since he was in its military forces. He and everyone else were playing, and they knew they were playing, a vital and significant role in the present crisis. Everyone was in it. There was a feeling of unconscious well-being, because everyone was doing something to help in the common desperate enterprise in a co-operative rather than in a private spirit. This feeling is often the unconscious equivalent of what people mean when they gather to celebrate and sing "Hail, hail, the gang's all here." It also has something of the deep significance that enters into people's lives only in moments of tragedy.

The strong belief that everyone must sacrifice to win a war greatly strengthens people's sense of their importance. Everyone gives up something for the common good — money, food, tires, scrap, automobiles, or blood for blood banks. All of it is contributed under the basic ideology of common sacrifice for the good of the country. These simple acts of giving by all individuals in the town, by all families, associations, schools, churches, and factories, are given strong additional emotional support by the common knowledge that some of the local young men are representing the town in the military forces of the country. It is known that some of them may be killed while serving their country. They are sacrificing their lives, it is believed, that their country may live. Therefore, all acts of individual giving to help win the war, no matter how small, are made socially significant and add to the strength of the social structure by being treated as sacrifices. The collective effect of these small renunciations, it is believed, is to lessen the number of those who must die on the altars of their country.

Another very strong integrative factor contributed by a war that strengthens the social structure of the small town and city is that petty internal antagonisms are drained out of the group onto the common enemy. The local antagonisms which customarily divide and separate people are largely suppressed. The feelings and psychic energies involved, normally expended in local feuds, are vented on the hated symbols of the enemy. Local groups which may have been excluded from participation in community affairs are given an honored place in the war effort, and the symbols of unity are stressed rather than the separating differences. The religious groups and the churches tend to emphasize the oneness of the common war effort rather than allow their differing theologies and competitive financing to keep them in opposing groups. The strongest pressure to compose their differences is placed against management and labor. (The small number of strikes is eloquent proof of the effectiveness of such pressure.) A common hate of a common enemy, when organized in community activities to express this basic emotion, provides the most powerful mechanism to energize the lives of the towns and to strengthen their feelings of unity. Those who believe that a war's hatreds can bring only evil to psychic life might well ponder the therapeutic and satisfying effects on the minds of people who turn their once private hatreds into social ones and join their townsmen and countrymen in the feeling of sharing this basic emotion in common symbols. Enemies as well as friends should be well chosen, for they must serve as objects of the expression of two emotions basic to man and his social system — hatred and love.

The American Legion and other patriotic organizations give form to the effort to capture the feelings of well-being when the society was most integrated and feelings of unity were most intense. The membership comes from every class, creed, and nationality, for the soldiers came from all of them.

Only a very few associations are sufficiently large and democratic in action to include in their membership men or women from all class levels, all religious faiths, and most, if not all, ethnic groups. Their number could be easily counted on the fingers of one hand. Most prominent among them are the patriotic associations, all of them structural developments from wars which involved the United States. The American Legion is a typical example of the patriotic type. Less than 6 per cent of several hundred associations which have been studied include members from all social classes. Of the remaining 94 per cent, approximately half have representatives from only three classes, or less than three, out of the six discussed in Chapter III. Although the associations which include members from all levels of the community are surprisingly few, those which stress in action as well as in words such other principles of democracy as the equality of races, nationalities, and religions are even fewer. Only 5 per cent of the associations are composed of members from the four principal religious faiths in America — Protestant, Catholic, Jewish, and Greek Orthodox — and most of their members come from the lower ranks of the society.

Lincoln and Washington and lesser ritual figures (and ceremonies such as Memorial Day) are the symbolic equivalent of such social institutions as the patriotic societies. They express the same values, satisfy the same social needs, and perform similar functions. All increase the social solidarity of a complex and heterogeneous society.

How such ceremonies function in the community

Memorial Day and similar ceremonies are one of the several forms of collective representations which Durkheim so brilliantly defined and interpreted in *The Elementary Forms of the Religious Life.* He said: "Religious representations are collective representations which express collective realities." Religious collective representations are symbol systems which are composed of beliefs and rites which relate men to sacred beings. Beliefs are "states of opinion and consist in representations"; rites are "determined modes of action" which are expressions of, and refer to, religious belief. They are *visible* signs (symbols) of the invisible belief. The visible rite of baptism, for example, may express invisible beliefs about cleansing the newborn infant of sin and relating him to the Christian community.

Ceremonies, periodically held, serve to impress on men their social nature and make them aware of something beyond themselves which they feel and believe to be sacred. This intense feeling of belonging to something larger and more powerful than themselves and of having part of this within them as part of them is symbolized by the belief in sacred beings, which is given a visual symbol by use of designs which are the emblems of the sacred entities, e.g., the Cross of the Christian churches.

That which is beyond, yet part of, a person is no more than the awareness on the part of individuals and the collectivity of individuals of their participation in a social group. *The religious symbols, as well as the secular ones, must express the nature of the social structure of the group of which they are a part and which they represent.* The beliefs in the gods and the symbolic rites which celebrate their divinity are no more than men collectively worshiping their own images — their own, since they were made by themselves and fashioned from their experiences among themselves.

We said earlier that the Memorial Day rites of American towns are sacred collective representations and a modern cult of the dead. They are a cult because they consist of a system of sacred beliefs and dramatic rituals held by a group of people who, when they congregate, represent the whole community. They are sacred because they ritually relate the living to sacred things. They are a cult because the members have not been formally organized into an institutionalized church with a defined theology but depend on informal organization to bring into order their sacred activities. They are called a "cult" here, because this term most accurately places them in a class of social phenomena which can be clearly identified in the sacred behavior of non-European societies.

The cult system of sacred belief puts into the organized form of concepts those sentiments about death which are common to everyone in the community. These sentiments are composed of fears of death, which conflict with the social reassurances that our culture provides us to combat such anxieties. These assurances, usually acquired in childhood and thereby carrying some of the authority of the adults who provided them, are a composite of theology and folk belief. The deep anxieties to which we refer include anticipation of our deaths, of the deaths or possible deaths of loved ones, and, less powerfully, of the deaths or possible deaths of those we know and of men in general.

Each man's church provides him and those of his faith with a set of beliefs and a way of acting to face these problems; but his church and those of other men do not equip him with a common set of social beliefs and rituals which permit him to unite with all his fellows to confront this common and most feared of all his enemies. The Memorial Day rite and other subsidiary rituals connected with it form a cult which partially satisfies this need for common action on a common problem. It dramatically expresses the sentiments of unity of all the living among themselves, of all the living to all the dead, and of all the living and dead as a group to the gods. The gods — Catholic, Protestant, and Jewish — lose their sectarian definitions, limitations, and foreignness among themselves and become objects of worship for the whole group and the protectors of everyone.

The unifying and integrating symbols of this cult are the dead. The graves of the dead are the most powerful of the visible emblems which unify all the activities of the separate groups of the community. The cemetery and its graves become the objects of sacred rituals which permit opposing organizations, often in conflict, to subordinate their ordinary opposition and to cooperate in expressing jointly the larger unity of the total community through the use of common rites for their collective dead. The rites show extraordinary respect for all the dead, but they pay particular honor to those who were killed in battle "fighting for their country." The death of a soldier in battle is believed to be a "voluntary sacrifice" by him on the altar of his country. To be understood, this belief in the sacrifice of a man's life for his country must be judged first with our general scientific knowledge of the nature of all forms of sacrifice. It must then be subjected to the principles which explain human sacrifice whenever and wherever found. More particularly, this belief must be examined with the realization that these sacrifices occur in a society whose diety was a man who sacrificed his life for all men.

The principle of the gift is involved. In simple terms, when something valuable is given, an equally valuable thing must be returned. The speaker who quoted Scripture in his Memorial Day speech, "Whosoever shall save his life shall lose it and whosoever shall lose his life in My name shall save it," almost explicitly stated the feelings and principles involved. Finally, as we interpret it, the belief in "the sacrifice of American citizens killed in battle" is a social logic which states in ultimate terms the subordinate relation of the citizen to his country and its collective moral principles.

This discussion has shown that the Memorial Day ceremony consists of a series of separate rituals performed by autonomous groups which culminate in a procession of *all of them as one group* to the consecrated area set aside by the living for their dead. In such a place the dead are classed as individuals, for their graves are separate; as members of separate social situations, for they are found in family plots and formal ritual respect is paid them by church and association; and as a collectivity, since they are thought of as "our dead" in most of the ceremonies. The fences surrounding the cemetery place all the dead together and separate all the living from them.

The Memorial Day rite is a cult of the dead, but not just of the dead as such, since by symbolically elaborating sacrifice of human life for the country through, or identifying it with, the Christian church's sacred sacrifice of their god, the deaths of such men also become powerful sacred symbols which organize, direct, and constantly revive the collective ideals of the community and the nation.

REVIEW QUESTIONS

1. According to Warner, what is the symbolic function of the Memorial Day ceremony?

2. Why is Lincoln an important symbol for Memorial Day and other American national holidays?

3. What is the impact of the First and Second World Wars on American national life? What is different about the social impact of these wars and that of the Korean and Vietnam wars? Why?

4. Has there been a recent change in the way Americans perceive the Vietnam War that enables the conflict to symbolize national unity? If so, what is it and what is its effect?

5. What do the dead symbolize in the Memorial Day ceremony?

30

Religion and culture: God's saviours in the Sierra Madre

WILLIAM L. MERRILL

One of the most important functions of religion is to reconcile life's contradictions. Life and death, good and evil, good fortune and adversity, all constitute paradoxes that people seek to explain, and it is often religion that deals with these basic oppositions. Yet the ways in which religion structures the answers to these questions vary markedly from one society to another, reflecting adaptive concerns and other cultural assumptions about life. Religious beliefs that work well for one society may seem incomprehensible to members of another. In this article by William Merrill, we see that Catholic beliefs about God and Christ, introduced to the Rarámuri Indians of Mexico by Jesuit missionaries, have been transformed to fit traditional religious beliefs and a world view that predate contact with the West. The Rarámuri have transformed the Christian definitions of God and the Devil, and especially the events that surround Easter, to fit their own concerns for balance, for a continued harmony between people and their social and natural world.

In 1607 the Catalan Jesuit Juan Fonte intervened in a conflict involving members of two Indian groups, the Tarahumaras and the Tepehuanes, who lived in the rugged Sierra Madre of northern New Spain, where the Mexican states of Chihuahua and Durango meet today. These Indians had previously remained beyond the influence of the Jesuits, except for missions established in the previous decade among the more

Originally published as "God's Saviours in the Sierra Madre." With permission from *Natural History*, Vol. 93, No. 3; Copyright the American Museum of Natural History, 1983.

southerly Tepehuanes. For the next nine years, Fonte devoted himself in converting them to Christianity, until the Tepehuanes revolted and killed him and five of his fellow missionaries. Almost immediately, other Jesuits arrived to replace the martyrs, and a vigorous mission system gradually spread throughout the region.

From the outset, converting the Tarahumaras required some modification of the strict orthodox line. The early missionaries apparently took Catholic doctrine and ritual, combined them with European folk beliefs and dances of the day, added their own innovations, adapted the whole to what they concluded the Tarahumaras would understand and accept, and presented it to them as the word and will of God. For their part, the Tarahumaras interpreted this complex of beliefs and actions in terms of their own ideas, adopting and modifying portions of it as they saw fit. In 1767 Charles III of Spain, distrustful of them, expelled the Jesuits from his New World domains. The Franciscans inherited the Tarahumara mission system, but financial difficulties and the disruptions of war and revolution led to its decline and abandonment by the mid-nineteenth century. Responsibility for their religious affairs reverted entirely to the Tarahumaras, who then developed, in their own fashion, the beliefs and rituals inherited from the mission period.

In 1900 the Jesuits reestablished the mission system, but in the years since, they have not attempted to force orthodoxy upon the Tarahumaras. The priests are peripheral to the Indians' religious life, performing baptisms and an occasional mass but little else, and few actually live in Tarahumara communities. Today the priests actively support the Tarahumaras in the practice of their own brand of Catholicism because they consider it a key element of Tarahumara cultural identity, which they hope to preserve. There is considerable pressure on the Tarahumaras to adopt the culture of the Mexicans who have settled in their area and who now number about 200,000, four times the Indian population. The Tarahumaras have maintained control of their religion, however. The settlers — joined in recent years by tourists from abroad — participate almost exclusively as onlookers at the Indians' elaborate holy day ceremonies, particularly those of Christmas and Easter.

The people whom outsiders have for centuries called Tarahumaras refer to themselves as Rarámuri, a word that means, on increasingly specific levels, human beings in distinction to nonhumans, Indians as opposed to non-Indians, the Rarámuri proper rather than some other Indian group, and finally, Rarámuri men in contrast to Rarámuri women. The Rarámuri version of the origin of their religion differs radically from the one just outlined. They maintain that almost everything they have and do, say and believe, was communicated by God to their ancestors soon after this world began. God, they say, is their father and they associate him with the sun. His wife, their mother, is affiliated with the moon and identified as the Virgin Mary. God's elder brother, and thus the Rarámuri's uncle, is the Devil. The Devil is the father of all non-Indians, whom the Rarámuri call *chabóchi*, "whiskered ones," an apt label since Rarámuri men have little facial hair. The Devil and his wife care for the *chabóchi* just as God and his wife care for the Rarámuri. At death, the souls of the Rarámuri ascend to heaven while those of the *chabóchi* join their parents on the bottom-most level of the universe, three levels below the earth.

The Rarámuri believe that people who commit misdeeds during their lives will be punished when they die, but they worry very little about their fate in the afterlife. They are far more concerned with the here and now and consider that their well-being depends almost entirely upon their ability to maintain proper relations with the other beings in their universe, particularly God and the Devil. God, as befits a parent, is benevolently inclined toward the Rarámuri, but he will withhold his beneficence if they fail to reciprocate his attentions adequately. The Devil's tendencies are just the opposite: he will send illness and misfortune to torment the Rarámuri unless they give him food.

The nineteenth-century Norwegian explorer and anthropologist Carl Lumholtz wrote of the Rarámuri, "The only wrong toward the gods of which he may consider himself guilty is that he does not dance enough." By "dance" Lumholtz meant that whole complex of dancing, chanting, feasting, and offerings that constitutes a Rarámuri religious fiesta. It is primarily through these fiestas that the Rarámuri balance accounts with God, who is pleased by the beauty of their performances and appreciates the offerings of food and maize beer they send to him. Typically they also bury bits of food during these fiestas to placate the Devil and deflect his malevolence.

Any Rarámuri with the resources and inclination can stage a fiesta any time of the year. People sometimes sponsor fiestas because God instructs them in their dreams to do so or because they feel in special need of his protection. They also hold them to send food, tools, clothing, and other goods to recently deceased relatives; to compensate Rarámuri doctors for curing the living; or to petition God to end a drought. There are also certain times of the year when fiestas or, at least, special rituals are required, particularly at points in the life cycle of the maize upon which the Rarámuri rely for their existence and on or near the more prominent holy days in the Catholic ritual calendar.

The fiestas associated with the maize crop take place in the hamlets where the Rarámuri live rather than at the churches around which the early missionaries had intended for them to settle. When the maize is a month or two old, neighboring households jointly sponsor a fiesta, during which a Rarámuri doctor and several assistants pass through the fields curing the maize. The doctor waves a knife and wooden cross to prevent hail from destroying the crop, while his assistants sprinkle a variety of medicines to protect the plants from pests and to enhance their growth. Periodically, the doctor stops to deliver a speech encouraging the maize to grow well and to have strength because the rains will soon commence. Later, in August, when the green ears of maize are ready to be eaten, a second fiesta is staged to offer the first fruits of the year to God, for he provided the Rarámuri with their first domesticated plants.

Despite these flurries of ritual activity during the maize-growing season, the major ceremonial activity does not get under way until the end of harvest. The most elaborate ritual events between harvest and planting are the Catholic holy day ceremonies, which begin in early December and follow one another in quick succession: Immaculate Conception (December 8), then Virgin of Guadalupe Day (December 12), Christmas Eve, and Epiphany (January 6), leading up to Candlemas (February 2), which marks for the Rarámuri the beginning of the Easter season (they do not observe Lent). The predominant theme of this winter round of celebration is the perpetuation of proper relations with God by recognizing and reciprocating his blessings. Although individual households may sponsor fiestas at their homes in conjunction with these holy days, the principal ritual activities on most take place at the thirty or so churches scattered across the 20,000 square miles of Rarámuri country.

Each fiesta is sponsored by one or more individuals who, at the conclusion of the same fiesta the year before, volunteered or were asked by others in the community to provide the food and maize beer. Together with the community's political and religious leaders, these fiesta sponsors direct the events. Men, women, and children, sometimes in the hundreds, converge on the local church from hamlets as much as fifteen miles away. Most of these people help by preparing or offering food, performing the often strenuous dances and rituals that are required, or providing encouragement and moral support to the major participants. Typically, a fiesta begins on the eve of the holy day in question and lasts all night long. If a Catholic priest arrives, mass is celebrated once or twice; if not, Rarámuri ritualists recite standard prayers. In most cases, large quantities of food and maize beer are distributed and consumed after first being offered to God.

The Rarámuri regard these celebrations as opportunities for socializing and having a good time. They joke with one another and often parody the leading ritual performers, but their frivolity does not detract from the importance they ascribe to the undertaking. They expect their efforts and even their jokes to please and satisfy God so that he will give them long lives, abundant crops, and healthy children. They also hope that their activities will convince him to postpone replacing the present world with a new one, an event that many Rarámuri, influenced by some of their Mexican neighbors, anticipate will come in the year 2000.

At this time of year, between February 2 and Easter, the theme of Rarámuri ritual begins to shift from an emphasis on the relationship between the Rarámuri and God to a concern with the relationship between God and the Devil. God and the Devil are brothers but, although they occasionally interact on a friendly basis, the Devil usually is bent on God's destruction. Most of the time God fends the Devil off, but each year the Devil succeeds by trick or force in rendering God dangerously vulnerable. Invariably this occurs immediately prior to Holy Week. From the Rarámuri point of view, their elaborate Easter ceremonies are intended to protect and strengthen God so that he can recover and prevent the Devil from destroying the world. (The description that follows applies specifically to the community of Basíhuare, Chihuahua, where, more than in some other communities, the ceremonies deviate considerably from orthodox Catholicism. There is substantial regional variation in Rarámuri religion, owing to the different impact of Catholic missionaries in different areas and the rugged terrain, which has discouraged interaction among Rarámuri of separate regions.)

Soon after February 2, the men in Basíhuare assemble at the local church to appoint four of their number to the office of Pharisee. Each of the new Pharisees is paired with one of the four community officials known as Captains, who serve year-round as keepers of the peace and messengers for the top community officials. From the day of their selection until Easter Day, when their term of office ends, the Pharisees share police and messenger duties with the Captains and join with them as the principal organizers and performers of the Holy Week pageantry. The Pharisees, regarded as the Devil's allies, carry wooden swords painted white with ocher designs; the Captains, the allies of God, bear quivers made of coatis, the entrails replaced by bows and arrows.

In the weeks leading up to Easter, most men and older boys agree to assist either the Pharisees or the Captains during Holy Week. The reasons they join one group or the other are usually personal. For example, a man may choose to be a Pharisee this year because last year he was a Soldier, as the people who help the Captains are called. Or he may prefer the ceremonial roles or accouterments of one side to those of the other. Or he may follow the lead of friends or relatives. The usual outcome is a more or less equal division of the male community between the two groups.

The central theme of the Rarámuri's Holy Week—the conflict between God and the Devil and the Rarámuri's role as God's protector—is first expressed in a major way during the fiesta held in conjunction with Palm Sunday. A Palm Sunday ceremony I attended in Basíhuare gives some idea of the activities that will be taking place this year beginning on March 26. The preparations for the fiesta began at dusk on Saturday as, near the church, a bull was butchered by the men and its flesh, bones, and blood set to boiling by the women. Close by, several men removed stones and trash from a plot of ground to create what the Rarámuri call an *awírachi*, meaning "dance space" or "patio." Other men brought a bench about ten feet long from inside the church and placed it along the east side of the patio to hold the food that was to be offered to God. Behind it three crosses were erected and draped with necklaces, some of which bore small wooden crosses or metal crucifixes.

About 10:30 P.M., an old Rarámuri man wrapped in a hand-woven wool blanket stood at the western edge of the patio and began shaking a rattle and intoning the wordless phrases of the *tutubúri,* an indigenous rite thanking God for caring and providing for the Rarámuri and asking that he continue to bless them. Soon after the *tutubúri* got under way, a second, rather different kind of dance began on the opposite side of the patio. Known as the *matachín,* a term possibly of Arabic origin, this dance presumably derives from one or more Renaissance European folk dances, but no one knows exactly when or in what form Catholic missionaries introduced it to the Rarámuri. The *matachín* dancers wear long capes and mirrored crowns and dance in two lines, whirling and crossing to the accompaniment of violins and guitars in a manner reminiscent of the Virginia reel. The *matachín* dance is said to please God because it is so beautiful. The same is true of the *tutubúri,* but, unlike the *matachín,* it is never performed within the church walls.

In the intervals between *matachín* and *tutubúri* performances, two troops of mostly young men and boys, designated as Pharisees and

Soldiers, enacted the Pharisee dance, characterized by high, skipping steps executed in sinuous lines to the pounding of drums and the melody of sweet-sounding reed whistles. Some Soldiers carried bayonet-tipped staves while the Pharisees, who earlier had smeared their bodies with white earth, dragged wooden swords at their sides. The leading Pharisees donned twilled hats adorned with turkey feathers; the Rarámuri point out that the Pharisee dance bears certain similarities to the mating ritual of the turkey gobbler, but they are uncertain if the relationship is derivative or only coincidental.

About midnight, a Jesuit priest, who had arrived especially for the occasion, celebrated mass in Rarámuri and Spanish. The men knelt on the left side of the church, the women and small children on the right, and a few Mexicans stood at the rear. No Rarámuri partook of Holy Communion—in Basíhuare, they seldom do—but before and after the service, the *matachín* was danced in front of the altar.

Soon after sunrise, the first phase of the fiesta concluded. Earthen bowls of beef stew, together with stacks of tortillas and tamales and bundles of ground, parched maize, were taken to the patio and placed on the bench in front of the crosses. Seven men lifted the food to the cardinal directions, allowing the aroma and steam from the food to waft heavenward to be consumed by God. In this way, the Rarámuri acknowledged their debt to him and compensated for the sustenance he had provided them. The women then distributed the food among the people present so that all would be strengthened for the remaining activities and the journey home.

At mid-morning, one of the Rarámuri officials called *méstro*, who recite Catholic prayers and care for the accouterments of the church, rang the church bell three times. As they had done for as many years as anyone can remember, the Soldiers and Pharisees, working on opposite sides of the churchyard, began setting up wooden crosses at appropriate distances, marking the stations of the cross. Then all filed into the church for mass. At the conclusion of the service, the priest distributed palm leaves among the members of the congregation, who followed him in a procession around the churchyard, commemorating, in accordance with Catholic doctrine, Christ's entry into Jerusalem, when palm branches were strewn before him.

The Rarámuri attribute somewhat different significance to the palm. After bearing the fronds like scepters in the procession, they carry them home, for the leaves can be burned to prevent hail from destroying a crop or decocted and drunk to cure chest pains. They say the palm owes its special qualities to an event that occurred in the distant past. God, God's wife, and the Devil had been drinking maize beer for several hours when God fell asleep and the Devil succeeded in seducing God's wife, largely through his accomplished guitar playing. God awoke, catching them *in flagrante delicto*, and a fight ensued. The Devil pulled a knife and God fled, with the Devil in close pursuit. God would surely have been slain had a palm not offered its thick leaves as a hiding place. This event sealed an enduring friendship between God and the palm and established the palm's usefulness to the Rarámuri; however, it also determined that humans would fight and commit adultery in imitation of their deities.

Drums and reed whistles alternated with liturgy as the Palm Sunday procession passed through the various stations of the cross. At circuit's end, the priest retired to the house in which he stays during his visits to Basíhuare. The others assembled facing the front of the church, where their community leaders stood, grasping the wooden canes that signify their authority. The principal Rarámuri official called before him several men known to be accomplished dreamers and requested that they relate what their recent dreams had revealed about the coming year and especially the impending Holy Week. The dreamers reported that, as in years past at this time, God was in a weak and vulnerable state, this year because the Devil forced him to drink a great deal of maize beer and he had not yet recovered. The Rarámuri people must protect God and his wife until he was well again, they said, or the Devil would destroy them and the world. The official acknowledged the dreamers' advice and in a loud voice urged everyone to return to the church in three days for the Easter ceremonies to care for their parents, God and God's wife.

By mid-morning on Holy Wednesday, the Captains, Pharisees, and a few of their helpers were busy at work in the churchyard, making preparations for the Easter ceremonies. With saplings, leaves, and fibers gathered from nearby hills and canyons, they constructed archways, crosses, wreaths, and rosettes, positioning them in and around the church to mark the processional route, on two adjacent hilltops, and at the cemetery. A woman swept the church with a bundle of long grass stems while three men attended to the altar and its adornments: four candlesticks, two crosses, and a statue and portrait of the Virgin Mary. Another man cleared stones, branches, and trash from the processional path encircling the church.

The principal community officials and their families set themselves up in nearby huts and rockshelters, all of which are abandoned except on such ritual occasions. There they cleared dance patios, erected arches and crosses, and prepared the food and maize beer they would be obliged to serve in the days ahead. Like the other Rarámuri who were going to participate in the ceremony, they made sure that the clothes they would be wearing were either new or sparkling clean, as is expected during Holy Week.

The Rarámuri call Holy Week *Norírawachi,* meaning "when we walk in circles," because they spend much of Maundy Thursday, Good Friday, and Holy Saturday morning circumscribing the church in formal procession. The point of the procession is to protect the church, and, by extension, God and God's wife. The fate of the universe rests on the Rarámuri's shoulders during this period, for they must prevent the Devil from vanquishing God and destroying the world. Their every action takes on cosmic significance. They must fast until past noon on Maundy Thursday and Good Friday because to eat would bloat God's stomach. Until Friday afternoon, fighting or chopping wood would bruise or cut God, so they must avoid both. They must dance and offer food to strengthen God, and they must guard the church and its paraphernalia, particularly the reproduction, hanging above the altar, of the miraculous portrait of the Virgin of Guadalupe, who is God's wife and their mother. Four Soldiers with bayonet-bearing staves are posted in front of the altar inside the church while a drum and whistle play behind them. Four Pharisees, wooden swords in hand, keep watch on the church steps. Replacements arrive every hour or so, and the guard is maintained much of Thursday and Friday.

Despite their efforts in guarding the church, the Pharisees are cast as the Devil's allies and as the opponents of the Soldiers, who are allied with God. The Pharisees reveal their association with the Devil most dramatically on Good Friday afternoon, when they appear with three figures made of wood and long grasses representing Judas, Judas's wife, and their dog. The Rarámuri say Judas is one of the Devil's relatives, and they call him Grandfather and his wife Grandmother. They also assign personal names to them each year: one recent Easter in Basíhuare, Judas was known as Ramón, his wife was María, and the dog, Monje, or Monk. Judas and his wife wear elements of Mexican-style clothing, as befits the Devil's kin, and display their oversized genitalia prominently. The Pharisees parade the figures around the church and dance before them, then turn them over to the Soldiers who do the same. The Pharisees then hide the figures away for the night.

In Basíhuare, as in many other Rarámuri communities, the Easter ceremonies conclude on Holy Saturday, not Easter Sunday. In the morning, the Soldiers and Pharisees engage in wrestling matches, battling symbolically for control of Judas. Regardless of the outcome, the Soldiers take possession, shooting arrows into the three figures and setting them afire. Then all remaining Easter paraphernalia is dismantled or destroyed. Such destruction is necessary, the Rarámuri say, to avert strong winds in the coming months. For the same reason, they place food and maize beer at ceremonial arches on two hilltops near the church, offerings to engender the good will of the Devil and the Wind, which they personify. By noon the church and its yard lie silent, deserted in favor of the many maize beer drinking parties being held in the surrounding countryside.

The Catholic missionaries who introduced Easter ceremonies to the Rarámuri presumably intended them to be reenactments of Christ's crucifixion and resurrection and dramatizations of the conflict between good and evil. The priests themselves probably adapted their teachings somewhat to what they knew of Rarámuri religion, but their original messages have been radically transformed by the Rarámuri to conform more closely to indigenous rituals, beliefs, and values. The Christian Trinity of Father, Son, and Holy Spirit has become in Rarámuri Catholicism a Duality of Father and Mother associated with the sun and moon, respectively. The Holy Spirit is never mentioned, and the events of Christ's life of which the Rarámuri are aware are attributed to God the Father. Because God created their ancestors, the Rarámuri regard themselves as his children, but they also maintain that God and his wife have many natural offspring who live with them in heaven. They apply the term "Jesus Christ" to all the males among these children and "Saint" to all the females, identifying the robes of saints (even male ones) as dresses.

The idea that Christ died on the cross to redeem the sins of humankind makes little sense to the Rarámuri. Ethnic affiliation rather than acceptance or rejection of Christ as Saviour determines a person's fate in the afterlife: the Rarámuri ascend to heaven after death to be with their parents, God and his wife, while the *chabóchi* (non-Indians) join the Devil and his wife below. According to the Rarámuri, *chabóchi* people want to live out eternity in the Devil's realm because it is a pleasant place to live, and the Devil and his wife are their parents. On the other hand, the souls of people who commit serious crimes such as murder or grand theft are completely destroyed soon after death. There is punishment for ill deeds in the Rarámuri cosmos, but no eternal damnation with its concomitant suffering.

To some degree God and the Devil personify good and evil for the Rarámuri, but in a much less absolute way than in Christian theology. Both God and the Devil can help or harm the Rarámuri depending on how the Rarámuri act toward them. The Rarámuri endeavor to perpetuate good relations with God and to placate the Devil by performing fiestas and making food offerings to them. By so doing they repay God for caring and providing for them and encourage the Devil to refrain from attacking them. If they fail in these obligations and overtures, God and the Devil will turn against them.

The basic purpose of their fiestas and offerings and of so much else the Rarámuri do, both in and outside their rituals, is to maintain balance in the world. This orientation, which almost certainly existed among the Rarámuri before Western contact, seems to have had a substantial impact on how they interpreted and adapted the Easter ceremonies that the missionaries taught them. Implicit throughout the Easter proceedings are expressions of the complementarity and mutual obligations that exist among various segments of Rarámuri society, between males and females, for example, or community officials and the people they lead and represent. While the most obvious message in the Easter celebration is the confrontation between God and the Devil, the Rarámuri have not followed the more orthodox Christian line of desiring the complete destruction of the Devil and his influence. Instead, their goal is to produce good relations between the Devil and themselves and to restore the balance between God and the Devil that existed before God fell victim to the Devil's machinations.

REVIEW QUESTIONS

1. Why do you think it might have been difficult for the Rarámuri to adopt Catholicism?

2. What major changes did the Rarámuri Indians make in the teachings of the Catholic missionaries?

3. In the Rarámuri view, what is the purpose of the Easter ceremony? How is the ceremony organized to achieve this end?

4. What core value organizes Rarámuri religion? How is this value reflected in the Easter ceremony?

X

Culture change and applied anthropology

Nowhere in the world do human affairs remain precisely constant from year to year. New ways of doing things mark the history of even the most stable groups. Change occurs when an Australian aboriginal dreams about a new myth and teaches it to the members of his band; when a loader in a restaurant kitchen invents a way to stack plates more quickly in the dishwasher; or when a New Guinea big-man cites the traditional beliefs about ghosts to justify the existence of a new political office devised by a colonial government. Wherever people interpret their natural and social worlds in a new way, cultural change has occurred. Broad or narrow, leisurely or rapid, such change is part of life in every society.

Culture change can originate from two sources, innovation and borrowing. *Innovation* is the invention of qualitatively new forms. It involves the recombination of what people already know into something different. For example, Canadian Joseph-Armand Bombardier became an innovator when he mated tracks, designed to propel earthmoving equipment, to a small bus that originally ran on tires, producing the first snowmobile in the 1950s. Later the Skolt Lapps of Finland joined him as innovators when they adapted his now smaller, more refined, snowmobile for herding reindeer in 1961. The Lapp innovation was not the vehicle itself. That was borrowed. What was new was the use of the vehicle in herding, something usually done by men on skis.

Innovations are more likely to occur and be adopted during stressful times when traditional culture no longer works well. Bombardier, for example, began work on his snowmobile after he was unable to reach medical help in time to save the life of his critically ill son during a Canadian winter storm. Frustrated by the slowness of his horse and sleigh, he set out to create a faster vehicle.

The other basis of culture change is *borrowing*. Borrowing, or *diffusion* as it is sometimes called, refers to the adoption of something new from another group. Tobacco, for example, was first domesticated and grown in the New World but quickly diffused to Europe and Asia after 1492. Such items as the umbrella, pajamas, Arabic numerals, and perhaps even the technology to make steel came to Europe from India. Ideologies and religions may diffuse from one society to another.

An extreme diffusionist view has been used to explain most human achievements. For example, author Erik Von Däniken argues that features of ancient New World civilizations were brought by space invaders. Englishman G. Elliot Smith claimed that Mayan and Aztec culture diffused from Egypt. Thor Heyerdahl sailed a reed boat, the Ra II, from Africa to South America to prove that an Egyptian cultural origin was possible for New World civilization.

Whether something is an innovation or borrowed, it must pass through a process of *social acceptance* before it can become part of a culture. Indeed many, if not most, novel ideas and things remain unattractive and relegated to obscurity. To achieve social acceptance, an innovation must become known to members of a society, be accepted as valid, and fit into a system of cultural knowledge revised to accept it.

Several principles facilitate social acceptance. If a change wins the support of a person in authority, it may gain the approval of others. Timing is also important. It would make little sense for a Lapp to attempt the introduction of snowmobiles when there was no snow or when the men who do the reindeer herding were scattered over their vast grazing territory. Other factors also affect social acceptance. Changes have a greater chance of acceptance if they meet a felt need, if they appeal to people's prestige (in societies where prestige is important), and if they provide some continuity with traditional customs.

Change may take place under a variety of conditions, from the apparently dull day-to-day routine of a stable society to the frantic climate of a revolution. One situation that has occupied many anthropologists interested in change is *cultural contact*, particularly situations of contact where one society politically dominates another. World history is replete with examples of such domination, which vary in outcome from annihilation, in the case of the Tasmanians and hundreds of tribes in North and South America, Africa, Asia, and even ancient Europe, to the political rule that indentured countless millions of people to colonial powers.

The study of change caused by these conditions is called acculturation. *Acculturation* is the process of change that results from cultural contact. Acculturative change may affect dominant societies as well as subordinate ones. After their ascendance in India, for example, the British came to wear *khaki* clothes, live in *bungalows*, and trek through *jungles*—all Indian concepts.

But those who are subordinated experience the most far-reaching changes in their way of life. From politically independent, self-sufficient people, they usually become subordinate and dependent. Sweeping changes in social structure and values may occur with resultant social disorganization. The article by Lauriston Sharp in this section illustrates the destructive impact of a simple steel axe on the cultural and social fabric of the Yir Yoront, an Australian tribe. The selection by Peter Worsley details the reaction of Papuan and Melanesian groups to the stresses brought about by colonial domination.

Although the age of colonial empires is largely over, stress caused by factors outside the control of particular societies is not. Efficient transportation and travel bring in ideas foreign to local cultures. So does literacy and the written dissemination of new ideas. Perhaps the most powerful external force is the world market. Market demand for green sea turtles disrupted the lives of Miskito Indians as we saw in Part VI of this book. In many parts of the world, cash crops have replaced local subsistence farming. Changes in land tenure, family organization, religion, economic relations, and political structure have often been the result. A further example is Jack Weatherford's article, which details the effects of the cocaine market on local communities in Bolivia.

Anthropologists may themselves become agents of change, applying their work to practical problems. *Applied anthropology*, as opposed to academic anthropology, includes any use of anthropological knowledge to influence social interaction, to maintain or change social institutions, or to direct the course of cultural change. There are four basic uses of anthropology contained within the applied field: adjustment anthropology, administrative anthropology, advocate anthropology, and action anthropology.

Adjustment anthropology uses anthropological knowledge to make social interaction more predictable among people who operate with different cultural codes. For example, take the anthropologists who consult with companies and government agencies about intercultural communication. It is often their job to train Americans to interpret the cultural rules that govern interaction in another society. For a business person who will work in Latin America, the anthropologist may point out the appropriate culturally defined speaking distances, ways to sit, definitions of time, topics of conversations, times for business talk, and so on. All of these activities would be classified as adjustment anthropology.

Administrative anthropology uses anthropological knowledge for planned change by those who are external to the local cultural group. It is the use of anthropological knowledge by a person with the power to make decisions. If an anthropologist provides knowledge about the culture of constituents to a mayor, he or she is engaged in administrative anthropology. So would advisers to chief administrators of U.S. trust territories such as once existed in places like the Marshall Islands. Alan Holmberg's article on the Cornell Project in Vicos, Peru, details a case of administrative anthropology, for Holmberg not only gathered anthropological data about the people of Vicos, he assumed the power of decision making, formulated a plan for change, and put it into effect. He also practiced action anthropology and advocate anthropology.

Action anthropology uses anthropological knowledge for planned change by the local cultural group. The anthropologist acts as a catalyst, providing information but avoiding decision making, which remains in the hands of the people affected by decisions.

Advocate anthropology uses anthropological knowledge by the anthropologist to increase the power of self-determination for a particular cultural group. Instead of focusing on the process of innovation, the anthropologist centers attention on discovering the sources of power and how a group can gain access to them. James Spradley took such action when he studied tramps. He discovered that police and courts systematically deprived tramps of their power to control their lives and of the rights accorded normal citizens. By releasing his findings to the Seattle newspapers, he helped tramps gain additional power and weakened the control of Seattle authorities.

Whether they are doing administrative, advocate, adjustment, or action anthropology, anthropologists will take, at least in part, a qualitative approach. They will do ethnography, discover the cultural knowledge of informants, and apply this information in the ways discussed above. In contrast to the quantitative data so often prized by other social scientists, they will use the insider's viewpoint to discover problems, advise, and generate policy.

KEY TERMS

innovation	applied anthropology
borrowing	adjustment anthropology
diffusion	administrative anthropology
social acceptance	action anthropology
cultural contact	advocate anthropology
acculturation	

31

Steel axes for stone-age Australians

LAURISTON SHARP

Technology and social structure are closely linked in every society. In this article, Lauriston Sharp shows how the introduction of an apparently insignificant, hatchet-sized steel axe to Australian aborigines can alter the relationship among family members, change patterns of economic exchange, and threaten the very meaning of life itself.

I.

Like other Australian aboriginals, the Yir Yoront group which lives at the mouth of the Coleman River on the west coast of Cape York Peninsula originally had no knowledge of metals. Technologically their culture was of the old stone age or paleolithic type. They supported themselves by hunting and fishing, and obtained vegetables and other materials from the bush by simple gathering techniques. Their only domesticated animal was the dog; they had no cultivated plants of any kind. Unlike some other aboriginal groups, however, the Yir Yoront did have polished stone axes hafted in short handles which were most important in their economy.

Towards the end of the 19th century metal tools and other European artifacts began to filter into the Yir Yoront territory. The flow increased with the gradual expansion of the white frontier outward from southern and eastern Queensland. Of all the items of western technology thus made available, the hatchet, or short handled steel axe, was the most acceptable to and the most highly valued by all aboriginals.

In the mid 1930s an American anthropologist lived alone in the bush among the Yir Yoront for 13 months without seeing another white man. The Yir Yoront were thus still relatively isolated and continued to live an essentially independent economic existence, supporting themselves entirely by means of their old stone age techniques. Yet their polished stone axes were disappearing fast and being replaced by steel axes which came to them in considerable numbers, directly or indirectly, from various European sources to the south.

What changes in the life of the Yir Yoront still living under aboriginal conditions in the Australian bush could be expected as a result of their increasing possession and use of the steel axe?

II. THE COURSE OF EVENTS

Events leading up to the introduction of the steel axe among the Yir Yoront begin with the advent of the second known group of Europeans to reach the shores of the Australian continent. In 1623 a Dutch expedition landed on the coast where the Yir Yoront now live.[1] In 1935 the Yir Yoront were still using the few cultural items recorded in the Dutch log for the aboriginals they encountered. To this cultural inventory the Dutch added beads and pieces of iron which they offered in an effort to attract the frightened "Indians." Among these natives metal and beads have disappeared, together with any memory of this first encounter with whites.

The next recorded contact in this area was in 1864. Here there is more positive assurance that the natives concerned were the immediate ancestors of the Yir Yoront community. These aboriginals had the temerity to attack a party of cattle men who were driving a small herd from southern Queensland through the length of the then unknown Cape York Peninsula to a newly established government station at the northern tip.[2] Known as the "Battle of the Mitchell River," this was one of the rare instances in which Australian aboriginals stood up to European gunfire for any length of time. A diary kept by the cattle men records that:

> . . . 10 carbines poured volley after volley into them from all directions, killing and wounding with every shot with very little return, nearly all their spears having already been expended. . . . About 30 being killed, the leader thought it prudent to hold his hand, and let the rest escape. Many more must have been wounded and probably drowned, for 59 rounds were counted as discharged.

[1] An account of this expedition from Amboina is given in R. Logan Jack, *Northmost Australia* (2 vols.), London, 1921, vol. 1, pp. 18–57.

[2] R. Logan Jack, *op. cit.*, pp. 298–335.

The European party was in the Yir Yoront area for three days; they then disappeared over the horizon to the north and never returned. In the almost three-year long anthropological investigation conducted some 70 years later — in all the material of hundreds of free association interviews, in texts of hundreds of dreams and myths, in genealogies, and eventually in hundreds of answers to direct and indirect questioning on just this particular matter — there was nothing that could be interpreted as a reference to this shocking contact with Europeans.

The aboriginal accounts of their first remembered contact with whites begin in about 1900 with references to persons known to have had sporadic but lethal encounters with them. From that time on whites continued to remain on the southern periphery of Yir Yoront territory. With the establishment of cattle stations (ranches) to the south, cattle men made occasional excursions among the "wild black-fellows" in order to inspect the country and abduct natives to be trained as cattle boys and "house girls." At least one such expedition reached the Coleman River where a number of Yir Yoront men and women were shot for no apparent reason.

About this time the government was persuaded to sponsor the establishment of three mission stations along the 700-mile western coast of the Peninsula in an attempt to help regulate the treatment of natives. To further this purpose a strip of coastal territory was set aside as an aboriginal reserve and closed to further white settlement.

In 1915, an Anglican mission station was established near the mouth of the Mitchell River, about a three-day march from the heart of the Yir Yoront country. Some Yir Yoront refused to have anything to do with the mission, others visited it occasionally while only a few eventually settled more or less permanently in one of the three "villages" established at the mission.

Thus the majority of the Yir Yoront continued to live their old self-supporting life in the bush, protected until 1942 by the government reserve and the intervening mission from the cruder realities of the encroaching new order from the south. To the east was poor, uninhabited country. To the north were other bush tribes extending on along the coast to the distant Archer River Presbyterian mission with which the Yir Yoront had no contact. Westward was the shallow Gulf of Carpentaria on which the natives saw only a mission lugger making its infrequent dry season trips to the Mitchell River. In this protected environment for over a generation the Yir Yoront were able to recuperate from shocks received at the hands of civilized society. During the 1930s their raiding and fighting, their trading and stealing of women, their evisceration and two- or three-year care of their dead, and their totemic ceremonies continued, apparently uninhibited by western influence. In 1931 they killed a European who wandered into their territory from the east, but the investigating police never approached the group whose members were responsible for the act.

As a direct result of the work of the Mitchell River mission, all Yir Yoront received a great many more western artifacts of all kinds than ever before. As part of their plan for raising native living standards, the missionaries made it possible for aboriginals living at the mission to earn some western goods, many of which were then given or traded to natives still living under bush conditions; they also handed out certain useful articles gratis to both mission and bush aboriginals. They prevented guns, liquor, and damaging narcotics, as well as decimating diseases, from reaching the tribes of this area, while encouraging the introduction of goods they considered "improving." As has been noted, no item of western technology available, with the possible exception of trade tobacco, was in greater demand among all groups of aboriginals than the short handled steel axe. The mission always kept a good supply of these axes in stock; at Christmas parties or other mission festivals they were given away to mission or visiting aboriginals indiscriminately and in considerable numbers. In addition, some steel axes as well as other European goods were still traded in to the Yir Yoront by natives in contact with cattle stations in the south. Indeed, steel axes had probably come to the Yir Yoront through established lines of aboriginal trade long before any regular contact with whites had occurred.

III. RELEVANT FACTORS

If we concentrate our attention on Yir Yoront behavior centering about the original stone axe (rather than on the axe—the object— itself) as a cultural trait or item of cultural equipment, we should get some conception of the role this implement played in aboriginal culture. This, in turn, should enable us to foresee with considerable accuracy some of the results stemming from the displacement of the stone age by the steel axe.

The production of a stone axe required a number of simple technological skills. With the various details of the axe well in mind, adult men could set about producing it (a task not considered appropriate for women or children). First of all a man had to know the location and properties of several natural resources found in his immediate environment: pliable wood for a handle, which could be doubled or bent over the axe head and bound tightly; bark, which could be rolled into cord for the binding; and gum, to fix the stone head in the haft. These materials had to be correctly gathered, stored, prepared, cut to size and applied or manipulated. They were in plentiful supply, and could be taken from anyone's property without special permission. Postponing consideration of the stone head, the axe could be made by any normal man who had a simple knowledge of nature and of the technological skills involved, together with fire (for heating the gum), and a few simple cutting tools—perhaps the sharp shells of plentiful bivalves.

The use of the stone axe as a piece of capital equipment used in producing other goods indicates its very great importance to the subsistence economy of the aboriginal. Anyone—man, woman, or child—could use the axe; indeed, it was used primarily by women, for theirs was the task of obtaining sufficient wood to keep the family campfire burning all day, for cooking, or other purposes, and all night against mosquitoes and cold (for in July, winter temperature might drop below 40 degrees). In a normal lifetime a woman would use the axe to cut or knock down literally tons of firewood. The axe was also used to make other tools or weapons, and a variety of material equipment required by the aboriginal in his daily life. The stone axe was essential in the construction of the wet season domed huts which keep out some rain and some insects; of platforms which provide dry storage; of shelters which give shade in the dry summer when days are bright and hot. In hunting and fishing and in gathering vegetable or animal food the axe was also a necessary tool, and in this tropical culture, where preservatives or other means of storage are lacking, the natives spend more time obtaining food than in any other occupation—except sleeping. In only two instances was the use of the stone axe strictly limited to adult men: for gathering wild honey, the most prized food known to the Yir Yoront; and for making the secret paraphernalia for ceremonies. From this brief listing of some of the activities involving the use of the axe, it is easy to understand why there was at least one stone axe in every camp, in every hunting or fighting party, and in every group out on a "walk about" in the bush.

The stone axe was also prominent in interpersonal relations. Yir Yoront men were dependent upon interpersonal relations for their stone axe heads, since the flat, geologically recent, alluvial country over which they range provides no suitable stone for this purpose. The stone they used came from quarries 400 miles to the south, reaching the Yir Yoront through long lines of male trading partners. Some of these chains terminated with the Yir Yoront men, others extended on farther north to other groups, using Yir Yoront men as links. Almost every older adult man had one or more regular trading partners, some to the north and some to the south. He provided his partner or partners in the south with surplus spears, particularly fighting spears tipped with the barbed spines of sting ray which snap into vicious fragments when they penetrate human flesh. For a dozen such spears, some of which he may have obtained from a partner to the north, he would receive one stone axe head. Studies have shown that the sting ray barb spears increased in value as they move south and farther from the sea. One hundred and fifty miles south of Yir Yoront one such spear may be exchanged for one stone axe head. Although actual investigations could not be made, it was presumed that farther south, nearer the quarries, one sting ray barb spear would bring several stone axe heads. Apparently people who acted as links in the middle of the chain and who made neither spears nor axe heads would receive a certain number of each as a middleman's profit.

Thus trading relations, which may extend the individual's personal relationships beyond that of his own group, were associated with spears and axes, two of the most important items in a man's equipment. Finally, most of the exchanges took place during the dry season, at the time of the great aboriginal celebrations centering about initiation rites or other totemic ceremonials which attracted hundreds and were the occasion for much exciting activity in addition to trading.

Returning to the Yir Yoront, we find that adult men kept their axes in camp with their other equipment, or carried them when travelling. Thus a woman or child who wanted to use an axe—as might frequently happen during the day—had to get one from a man, use it promptly, and return it in good condition. While a man might speak of "my axe," a woman or child could not.

This necessary and constant borrowing of axes from older men by women and children was in accordance with regular patterns of kinship behavior. A woman would expect to use her husband's axe unless he himself was using it; if unmarried, or if her husband was absent, a woman would go first to her older brother or to her father. Only in extraordinary circumstances would she seek a stone axe from other male kin. A girl, a boy, or a young man would look to a father or an older brother to provide an axe for their use. Older men, too, would follow similar rules if they had to borrow an axe.

It will be noted that all of these social relationships in which the stone axe had a place are pair relationships and that the use of the axe helped to define and maintain their character and the roles of the two individual participants. Every active relationship among the Yir Yoront involved a definite and accepted status of superordination or subordination. A person could have no dealings with another on exactly equal terms. The nearest approach to equality was between brothers, although the older was always superordinate to the younger. Since the exchange of goods in a trading relationship involved a mutual reciprocity, trading partners usually stood in a brotherly type of relationship, although one was always classified as older than the other and would have some advantage in case of dispute. It can be seen that repeated and widespread conduct centering around the use of the axe helped to generalize and standardize these sex, age, and kinship roles both in their normal benevolent and exceptional malevolent aspects.

The status of any individual Yir Yoront was determined not only by sex, age, and extended kin relationships, but also by membership in one of two dozen patrilineal totemic clans into which the entire community was divided.[3] Each clan had literally hundreds of totems, from one or two of which the clan derived its name, and the clan members their personal names. These totems included natural species or phenomena such as the sun, stars, and daybreak, as well as cultural "species": imagined ghosts, rainbow serpents, heroic ancestors; such eternal cultural verities as fires, spears, huts; and such human activities, conditions, or attributes as eating, vomiting, swimming, fighting, babies and corpses, milk and blood, lips and loins. While individual members of such totemic classes or species might disappear or be destroyed, the class itself was obviously ever-present and indestructible. The totems, therefore, lent permanence and stability to the clans, to the groupings of human individuals who generation after generation were each associated with a set of totems which distinguished one clan from another.

The stone axe was one of the most important of the many totems of the Sunlit Cloud Iguana clan. The names of many members of this clan referred to the axe itself, to activities in which the axe played a vital part, or to the clan's mythical ancestors with whom the axe was prominently associated. When it was necessary to represent the stone axe in totemic ceremonies, only men of this clan exhibited it or pantomimed its use. In secular life, the axe could be made by any man and used by all; but in the sacred realm of the totems it belonged exclusively to the Sunlit Cloud Iguana people.

Supporting those aspects of cultural behavior which we have called technology and conduct, is a third area of culture which includes

[3]The best, although highly concentrated, summaries of totemism among the Yir Yoront and the other tribes of north Queensland will be found in R. Lauriston Sharp, "Tribes and Totemism in Northeast Australia," *Oceania*, Vol. 8, 1939, pp. 254–275 and 439–461 (especially pp. 268–275); also "Notes on Northeast Australian Totemism," in *Papers of the Peabody Museum of American Archaeology and Ethnology*, Vol. 20, *Studies in the Anthropology of Oceania and Asia*, Cambridge, 1943, pp. 66–71.

ideas, sentiments, and values. These are most difficult to deal with, for they are latent and covert, and even unconscious, and must be deduced from overt actions and language or other communicating behavior. In this aspect of the culture lies the significance of the stone axe to the Yir Yoront and to their cultural way of life.

The stone axe was an important symbol of masculinity among the Yir Yoront (just as pants or pipes are to us). By a complicated set of ideas the axe was defined as "belonging" to males, and everyone in the society (except untrained infants) accepted these ideas. Similarly spears, spear throwers, and fire-making sticks were owned only by men and were also symbols of masculinity. But the masculine values represented by the stone axe were constantly being impressed on all members of society by the fact that females borrowed axes but not other masculine artifacts. Thus the axe stood for an important theme of Yir Yoront culture: the superiority and rightful dominance of the male, and the greater value of his concerns and of all things associated with him. As the axe also had to be borrowed by the younger people it represented the prestige of age, another important theme running through Yir Yoront behavior.

To understand the Yir Yoront culture it is necessary to be aware of a system of ideas which may be called their totemic ideology. A fundamental belief of the aboriginal divided time into two great epochs: (1) a distant and sacred period at the beginning of the world when the earth was peopled by mildly marvelous ancestral beings or culture heroes who are in a special sense the forebears of the clans; and (2) a period when the old was succeeded by a new order which includes the present. Originally there was no anticipation of another era supplanting the present. The future would simply be an eternal continuation and reproduction of the present which itself had remained unchanged since the epochal revolution of ancestral times.

The important thing to note is that the aboriginal believed that the present world, as a natural and cultural environment, was and should be simply a detailed reproduction of the world of the ancestors. He believed that the entire universe "is now as it was in the beginning" when it was established and left by the ancestors. The ordinary cultural life of the ancestors became the daily life of the Yir Yoront camps, and the extraordinary life of the ancestors remained extant in the recurring symbolic pantomimes and paraphernalia found only in the most sacred atmosphere of the totemic rites.

Such beliefs, accordingly, opened the way for ideas of what *should be* (because it supposedly *was*) to influence or help determine what actually *is*. A man called Dog-chases-iguana-up-a-tree-and-barks-at-him-all-night had that and other names because he believed his ancestral alter ego had also had them; he was a member of the Sunlit Cloud Iguana clan because his ancestor was; he was associated with particular countries and totems of this same ancestor; during an initiation he played the role of a dog and symbolically attacked and killed certain members of other clans because his ancestor (conveniently either anthropomorphic or kynomorphic) really did the same to the ancestral alter egos of these men; and he would avoid his mother-in-law, joke with a mother's distant brother, and make spears in a certain way because his and other people's ancestors did these things. His behavior in these specific ways was outlined, and to that extent determined for him, by a set of ideas concerning the past and the relation of the present to the past.

But when we are informed that Dog-chases-etc. had two wives from the Spear Black Duck clan and one from the Native Companion clan, one of them being blind, that he had four children with such and such names, that he had a broken wrist and was left handed, all because his ancestor had exactly these same attributes, then we know (though he apparently didn't) that the present has influenced the past, that the mythical world has been somewhat adjusted to meet the exigencies and accidents of the inescapably real present.

There was thus in Yir Yoront ideology a nice balance in which the mythical was adjusted in part to the real world, the real world in part to the ideal pre-existing mythical world, the adjustments occurring to maintain a fundamental tenet of native faith that the present must be a mirror of the past. Thus the stone axe in all its aspects, uses, and associations was integrated into the context of Yir Yoront technology and conduct because a myth, a set of ideas, had put it there.

IV. THE OUTCOME

The introduction of the steel axe indiscriminately and in large numbers into the Yir Yoront technology occurred simultaneously with many other changes. It is therefore impossible to separate all the results of this single innovation. Nevertheless, a number of specific effects of the change from stone to steel axes may be noted, and the steel axe may be used as an epitome of the increasing quantity of European goods and implements received by the aboriginals and of their general influence on the native culture. The use of the steel axe to illustrate such influences would seem to be justified. It was one of the first European artifacts to be adopted for regular use by the Yir Yoront, and whether made of stone or steel, the axe was clearly one of the most important items of cultural equipment they possessed.

The shift from stone to steel axes provided no major technological difficulties. While the aboriginals themselves could not manufacture steel axe heads, a steady supply from outside continued; broken wooden handles could easily be replaced from bush timbers with aboriginal tools. Among the Yir Yoront the new axe was never used to the extent it was on mission or cattle stations (for carpentry work, pounding tent pegs, as a hammer, and so on); indeed, it had so few more uses than the stone axe that its practical effect on the native standard of living was negligible. It did some jobs better, and could be used longer without breakage. These factors were sufficient to make it of value to the native. The white man believed that a shift from steel to stone axe on his part would be a definite regression. He was convinced that his axe was much more efficient, that its use would save time, and that it therefore represented technical "progress" towards goals which he had set up for the native. But this assumption was hardly borne out in aboriginal practice. Any leisure time the Yir Yoront might gain by using steel axes or other western tools was not invested in "improving the conditions of life," nor, certainly, in developing aesthetic activities, but in sleep — an art they had mastered thoroughly.

Previously, a man in need of an axe would acquire a stone axe head through regular trading partners from whom he knew what to expect, and was then dependent solely upon a known and adequate natural environment, and his own skills or easily acquired techniques. A man wanting a steel axe, however, was in no such self-reliant position. If he attended a mission festival when steel axes were handed out as gifts, he might receive one either by chance or by happening to impress upon the mission staff that he was one of the "better" bush aboriginals (the missionaries' definition of "better" being quite different from that of his bush fellows). Or, again almost by pure chance, he might get some brief job in connection with the mission which would enable him to earn a steel axe. In either case, for older men a preference for the steel axe helped change the situation from one of self-reliance to one of dependence, and a shift in behavior from well-structured or defined situations in technology or conduct to ill-defined situations in conduct alone. Among the men, the older ones whose earlier experience or knowledge of the white man's harshness made them suspicious were particularly careful to avoid having relations with the mission, and thus excluded themselves from acquiring steel axes from that source.

In other aspects of conduct or social relations, the steel axe was even more significantly at the root of psychological stress among the Yir Yoront. This was the result of new factors which the missionary considered beneficial: the simple numerical increase in axes per capita as a result of mission distribution, and distribution directly to younger men, women, and even children. By winning the favor of the mission staff, a woman might be given a steel axe which was clearly intended to be hers, thus creating a situation quite different from the previous custom which necessitated her borrowing an axe from a male relative. As a result a woman would refer to the axe as "mine," a possessive form she was never able to use of the stone axe. In the same fashion, young men or even boys also obtained steel axes directly from the mission, with the result that older men no longer had a complete monopoly of all the axes in the bush community. All this led to a revolutionary confusion of sex, age, and kinship roles, with a major gain in independence and loss of subordination on the part of those who now owned steel axes when they had previously been unable to possess stone axes.

The trading partner relationship was also affected by the new situation. A Yir Yoront might have a trading partner in a tribe to the south whom he defined as a younger brother and over whom he would therefore have some authority. But if the partner were in contact with the mission or had other access to steel axes, his subordination obviously decreased. Among other things, this took some of the excitement away from the dry season fiesta-like tribal gatherings centering around initiations. These had traditionally been the climactic annual occasions for exchanges between trading partners, when a man might seek to acquire a whole year's supply of stone axe heads. Now he might find himself prostituting his wife to almost total strangers in return for steel axes or other white man's goods. With trading partnerships weakened, there was less reason to attend the ceremonies, and less fun for those who did.

Not only did an increase in steel axes and their distribution to women change the character of the relations between individuals (the paired relationships that have been noted), but a previously rare type of relationship was created in the Yir Yoront's conduct towards whites. In the aboriginal society there were few occasions outside of the immediate family when an individual would initiate action to several other people at once. In any average group, in accordance with the kinship system, while a person might be superordinate to several people to whom he could suggest or command action, he was also subordinate to several others with whom such behavior would be tabu. There was thus no overall chieftainship or authoritarian leadership of any kind. Such complicated operations as grass-burning animal drives or totemic ceremonies could be carried out smoothly because each person was aware of his role.

On both mission and cattle stations, however, the whites imposed their conception of leadership roles upon the aboriginals, consisting of one person in a controlling relationship with a subordinate group. Aboriginals called together to receive gifts, including axes, at a mission Christmas party found themselves facing one or two whites who sought to control their behavior for the occasion, who disregarded the age, sex, and kinship variables of which the aboriginals were so conscious, and who considered them all at one subordinate level. The white also sought to impose similar patterns on work parties. (However, if he placed an aboriginal in charge of a mixed group of post-hole diggers, for example, half of the group, those subordinate to the "boss," would work while the other half, who were superordinate to him, would sleep.) For the aboriginal, the steel axe and other European goods came to symbolize this new and uncomfortable form of social organization, the leader-group relationship.

The most disturbing effects of the steel axe, operating in conjunction with other elements also being introduced from the white man's several sub-cultures, developed in the realm of traditional ideas, sentiments, and values. These were undermined at a rapidly mounting rate, with no new conceptions being defined to replace them. The result was the erection of a mental and moral void which foreshadowed the collapse and destruction of all Yir Yoront culture, if not, indeed, the extinction of the biological group itself.

From what has been said it should be clear how changes in overt behavior, in technology and conduct, weakened the values inherent in a reliance on nature, in the prestige of masculinity and of age, and in the various kinship relations. A scene was set in which a wife, or a young son whose initiation may not yet have been completed, need no longer defer to the husband or father who, in turn, became confused and insecure as he was forced to borrow a steel axe from them. For the woman and boy the steel axe helped establish a new degree of freedom which they accepted readily as an escape from the unconscious stress of the old patterns — but they, too, were left confused and insecure. Ownership became less well defined with the result that stealing and trespassing were introduced into technology and conduct. Some of the excitement surrounding the great ceremonies evaporated and they lost their previous gaiety and interest. Indeed, life itself became less interesting, although this did not lead the Yir Yoront to discover suicide, a concept foreign to them.

The whole process may be most specifically illustrated in terms of totemic system, which also illustrates the significant role played by a system of ideas, in this case a totemic ideology, in the breakdown of a culture.

In the first place, under pre-European aboriginal conditions where the native culture has become adjusted to a relatively stable environment, few, if any, unheard of or catastrophic crises can occur. It is clear, therefore, that the totemic system serves very effectively in inhibiting radical cultural changes. The closed system of totemic ideas, explaining and categorizing a well-known universe as it was fixed at the beginning of time, presents a considerable obstacle to the adoption of new or the dropping of old culture traits. The obstacle is not insurmountable and the system allows for the minor variations which occur in the norms of daily life. But the inception of major changes cannot easily take place.

Among the bush Yir Yoront, the only means of water transport is a light wood log to which they cling in their constant swimming of rivers, salt creeks, and tidal inlets. These natives know that tribes 45 miles further north have a bark canoe. They know these northern tribes can thus fish from midstream or out at sea, instead of clinging to the river banks and beaches, that they can cross coastal waters infested with crocodiles, sharks, sting rays, and Portuguese men-of-war without danger. They know the materials of which the canoe is made exist in their own environment. But they also know, as they say, that they do not have canoes because their own mythical ancestors did not have them. They assume that the canoe was part of the ancestral universe of the northern tribes. For them, then, the adoption of the canoe would not be simply a matter of learning a number of new behavioral skills for its manufacture and use. The adoption would require a much more difficult procedure; the acceptance by the entire society of a myth, either locally developed or borrowed, to explain the presence of the canoe, to associate it with some one or more of the several hundred mythical ancestors (and how decide which?), and thus establish it as an accepted totem of one of the clans ready to be used by the whole community. The Yir Yoront have not made this adjustment, and in this case we can only say that for the time being at least, ideas have won out over very real pressures for technological change. In the elaborateness and explicitness of the totemic ideologies we seem to have one explanation for the notorious stability of Australian cultures under aboriginal conditions, an explanation which gives due weight to the importance of ideas in determining human behavior.

At a later stage of the contact situation, as has been indicated, phenomena unaccounted for by the totemic ideological system begin to appear with regularity and frequency and remain within the range of native experience. Accordingly, they cannot be ignored (as the "Battle of the Mitchell" was apparently ignored), and there is an attempt to assimilate them and account for them along the lines of principles inherent in the ideology. The bush Yir Yoront of the mid-thirties represent this stage of the acculturation process. Still trying to maintain their aboriginal definition of the situation, they accept European artifacts and behavior patterns, but fit them into their totemic system, assigning them to various clans on a par with original totems. There is an attempt to have the myth-making process keep up with these cultural changes so that the idea system can continue to support the rest of the culture. But analysis of overt behavior, of dreams, and of some of the new myths indicates that this arrangement is not entirely satisfactory, that the native clings to his totemic system with intellectual loyalty (lacking any substitute ideology), but that associated sentiments and values are weakened. His attitude towards his own and towards European culture are found to be highly ambivalent.

All ghosts are totems of the Head-to-the-East Corpse clan, are thought of as white, and are of course closely associated with death. The white man, too, is closely associated with death, and he and all things pertaining to him are naturally assigned to the Corpse clan as totems. The steel axe, as a totem, was thus associated with the Corpse clan. But as an "axe," clearly linked with the stone axe, it is a totem of the Sunlit Cloud Iguana clan. Moreover, the steel axe, like most European goods, has no distinctive origin myth, nor are mythical ancestors associated with it. Can anyone, sitting in the shade of a *ti* tree one afternoon, create a myth to resolve this confusion? No one has, and the horrid suspicion arises as to the authenticity of the origin myths, which failed to take into account this vast new universe of the white man. The steel axe, shifting hopelessly between one clan and the other, is not only replacing the stone axe physically, but is hacking at the supports of the entire cultural system.

The aboriginals to the south of the Yir Yoront have clearly passed beyond this stage. They are engulfed by European culture, either by the mission or cattle station sub-cultures or, for some natives, by a baffling, paradoxical combination of both incongruent varieties. The totemic ideology can no longer support the inrushing mass of foreign culture traits, and the myth-making process in its native form breaks down completely. Both intellectually and emotionally a saturation point is reached so that the myriad new traits which can neither be ignored nor any longer assimilated simply force the aboriginal to abandon his totemic system. With the collapse of this system of ideas, which is so closely related to so many other aspects of the native culture, there follows an appallingly sudden and complete cultural disintegration, and a demoralization of the individual such as has seldom been recorded elsewhere. Without the support of a system of ideas well devised to provide cultural stability in a stable environment, but admittedly too rigid for the new realities pressing .in from outside, native behavior and native sentiments and values are simply dead. Apathy reigns. The aboriginal has passed beyond the realm of any outsider who might wish to do him well or ill.

Returning from the broken natives huddled on cattle stations or on the fringes of frontier towns to the ambivalent but still lively aboriginals settled on the Mitchell River mission, we note one further devious result of the introduction of European artifacts. During a wet season stay at the mission, the anthropologist discovered that his supply of tooth paste was being depleted at an alarming rate. Investigation showed that it was being taken by old men for use in a new tooth paste cult. Old materials of magic having failed, new materials were being tried out in a malevolent magic directed towards the mission staff and some of the younger aboriginal men. Old males, largely ignored by the missionaries, were seeking to regain some of their lost power and prestige. This mild aggression proved hardly effective, but perhaps only because confidence in any kind of magic on the mission was by this time at a low ebb.

For the Yir Yoront still in the bush, a time could be predicted when personal deprivation and frustration in a confused culture would produce an overload of anxiety. The mythical past of the totemic ancestors would disappear as a guarantee of a present of which the future was supposed to be a stable continuation. Without the past, the present could be meaningless and the future unstructured and uncertain. Insecurities would be inevitable. Reaction to this stress might be some form of symbolic aggression, or withdrawal and apathy, or some more realistic approach. In such a situation the missionary with understanding of the processes going on about him would find his opportunity to introduce his forms of religion and to help create a new cultural universe.

REVIEW QUESTIONS

1. What part did traditional stone axes play in the social integration of Yir Yoront society?

2. How could a simple tool such as a small steel axe disrupt Yir Yoront social organization?

3. How did the way the missionaries gave out steel axes contribute to Yir Yoront social disorganization?

4. Can the model of change be applied to other cases? What are some examples?

32

Cargo cults

PETER M. WORSLEY

*When one cultural group becomes dominated by another, its original
meaning system may seem thin, ineffective, and contradictory. The
resulting state of deprivation often causes members to rebuild their
culture along more satisfying lines. In this article Peter Worsley describes such a movement among the peoples of New Guinea and adjacent islands, an area where Western influence has caused cultural
disorientation and where cargo cults have provided the basis for
reorganization.*

Patrols of the Australian Government venturing into the "uncontrolled" central highlands of New Guinea in 1946 found the primitive
people there swept up in a wave of religious excitement. Prophecy was
being fulfilled: The arrival of the Whites was the sign that the end of
the world was at hand. The natives proceeded to butcher all of their
pigs — animals that were not only a principal source of subsistence but
also symbols of social status and ritual preeminence in their culture.
They killed these valued animals in expression of the belief that after
three days of darkness "Great Pigs" would appear from the sky. Food,
firewood, and other necessities had to be stockpiled to see the people
through to the arrival of the Great Pigs. Mock wireless antennae of
bamboo and rope had been erected to receive in advance the news of
the millennium. Many believed that with the great event they would
exchange their black skins for white ones.

This bizarre episode is by no means the single event of its kind in

From "Cargo Cults," by Peter M. Worsley, *Scientific American* 200 (May 1959): 117–128.
Reprinted with permission of W. H. Freeman and Company. Copyright © 1959 by
Scientific American, Inc. All rights reserved. Illustrations are omitted.

the murky history of the collision of European civilization with the indigenous cultures of the southwest Pacific. For more than one hundred years traders and missionaries have been reporting similar disturbances among the people of Melanesia, the group of Negro-inhabited islands (including New Guinea, Fiji, the Solomons, and the New Hebrides) lying between Australia and the open Pacific Ocean. Though their technologies were based largely upon stone and wood, these peoples had highly developed cultures, as measured by the standards of maritime and agricultural ingenuity, the complexity of their varied social organizations, and the elaboration of religious belief and ritual. They were nonetheless ill prepared for the shock of the encounter with the Whites, a people so radically different from themselves and so infinitely more powerful. The sudden transition from the society of the ceremonial stone ax to the society of sailing ships and now of airplanes has not been easy to make.

After four centuries of Western expansion, the densely populated central highlands of New Guinea remain one of the few regions where the people still carry on their primitive existence in complete independence of the world outside. Yet as the agents of the Australian Government penetrate into ever more remote mountain valleys, they find these backwaters of antiquity already deeply disturbed by contact with the ideas and artifacts of European civilization. For "cargo"—Pidgin English for trade goods—has long flowed along the indigenous channels of communication from the seacoast into the wilderness. With it has traveled the frightening knowledge of the white man's magical power. No small element in the white man's magic is the hopeful message sent abroad by his missionaries: the news that a Messiah will come and that the present order of Creation will end.

The people of the central highlands of New Guinea are only the latest to be gripped in the recurrent religious frenzy of the "cargo cults." However variously embellished with details from native myth and Christian belief, these cults all advance the same central theme: the world is about to end in a terrible cataclysm. Thereafter God, the ancestors, or some local culture hero will appear and inaugurate a blissful paradise on earth. Death, old age, illness, and evil will be unknown. The riches of the white man will accrue to the Melanesians.

Although the news of such a movement in one area has doubtless often inspired similar movements in other areas, the evidence indicates that these cults have arisen independently in many places as parallel responses to the same enormous social stress and strain. Among the movements best known to students of Melanesia are the "Taro Cult" of

New Guinea, the "Vailala Madness" of Papua, the "Naked Cult" of Espiritu Santo, the "John Frum Movement" of the New Hebrides, and the "Tuka Cult" of the Fiji Islands.

At times the cults have been so well organized and fanatically persistent that they have brought the work of government to a standstill. The outbreaks have often taken the authorities completely by surprise and have confronted them with mass opposition of an alarming kind. In the 1930's, for example, villagers in the vicinity of Wewak, New Guinea, were stirred by a succession of "Black King" movements. The prophets announced that the Europeans would soon leave the island, abandoning their property to the natives, and urged their followers to cease paying taxes, since the government station was about to disappear into the sea in a great earthquake. To the tiny community of Whites in charge of the region, such talk was dangerous. The authorities jailed four of the prophets and exiled three others. In yet another movement, that sprang up in declared opposition to the local Christian mission, the cult leader took Satan as his god.

Troops on both sides in World War II found their arrival in Melanesia heralded as a sign of the Apocalypse. The G.I.'s who landed in the New Hebrides, moving up for the bloody fighting on Guadalcanal, found the natives furiously at work preparing airfields, roads, and docks for the magic ships and planes that they believed were coming from "Rusefel" (Roosevelt), the friendly king of America.

The Japanese also encountered millenarian visionaries during their southward march to Guadalcanal. Indeed, one of the strangest minor military actions of World War II occurred in Dutch New Guinea, when Japanese forces had to be turned against the local Papuan inhabitants of the Geelvink Bay region. The Japanese had at first been received with great joy, not because their "Greater East Asia Co-Prosperity Sphere" propaganda had made any great impact upon the Papuans, but because the natives regarded them as harbingers of the new world that was dawning, the flight of the Dutch having already given the first sign. Mansren, creator of the islands and their peoples, would now return, bringing with him the ancestral dead. All this had been known, the cult leaders declared, to the crafty Dutch, who had torn out the first page of the Bible where these truths were inscribed. When Mansren returned, the existing world order would be entirely overturned. White men would turn black like Papuans, Papuans would become Whites; root crops would grow in trees, and coconuts and fruits would grow like tubers. Some of the islanders now began to draw together into large "towns"; others took Biblical names such as "Jericho" and "Galilee" for their villages. Soon they adopted military uniforms and began drilling. The Japanese, by now highly unpopular, tried to disarm and disperse the Papuans; resistance inevitably developed. The climax of this tragedy came when several canoe-loads of fanatics sailed out to attack Japanese warships, believing themselves to be invulnerable by virtue of the holy water with which they had sprinkled themselves. But the bullets of the Japanese did not turn to water, and the attackers were mowed down by machine-gun fire.

Behind this incident lay a long history. As long ago as 1857 missionaries in the Geelvink Bay region had made note of the story of Mansren. It is typical of many Melanesian myths that became confounded with Christian doctrine to form the ideological basis of the movements. The legend tells how long ago there lived an old man named Manamakeri ("he who itches"), whose body was covered with sores. Manamakeri was extremely fond of palm wine, and used to climb a huge tree every day to tap the liquid from the flowers. He soon found that someone was getting there before him and removing the liquid. Eventually he trapped the thief, who turned out to be none other than the Morning Star. In return for his freedom, the Star gave the old man a wand that would produce as much fish as he liked, a magic tree, and a magic staff. If he drew in the sand and stamped his foot, the drawing would become real. Manamakeri, aged as he was, now magically impregnated a young maiden; the child of this union was a miracle-child who spoke as soon as he was born. But the maiden's parents were horrified, and banished her, the child, and the old man. The trio sailed off in a canoe created by Mansren ("The Lord"), as the old man now became known. On this journey Mansren rejuvenated himself by stepping into a fire and flaking off his scaly skin, which changed into valuables. He then sailed around Geelvink Bay, creating islands where he stopped, and peopling them with the ancestors of the present-day Papuans.

The Mansren myth is plainly a creation myth full of symbolic ideas relating to fertility and rebirth. Comparative evidence — especially the shedding of his scaly skin — confirms the suspicion that the old man is, in fact, the Snake in another guise. Psychoanalytic writers argue that the snake occupies such a prominent part in mythology the world over because it stands for the penis, another fertility symbol. This may be so, but its symbolic significance is surely more complex than this. It is the "rebirth" of the hero, whether Mansren or the Snake, that exercises such universal fascination over men's minds.

The nineteenth-century missionaries thought that the Mansren story would make the introduction of Christianity easier, since the concept of "resurrection," not to mention that of the "virgin birth" and the "second coming," was already there. By 1867, however, the first cult organized around the Mansren legend was reported.

Though such myths were widespread in Melanesia, and may have sparked occasional movements even in the pre-White era, they took on a new significance in the late nineteenth century, once the European powers had finished parceling out the Melanesian region among themselves. In many coastal areas the long history of "black-birding" — the seizure of islanders for work on the plantations of Australia and Fiji — had built up a reservoir of hostility to Europeans. In other areas, however, the arrival of the Whites was accepted, even welcomed, for it meant access to bully beef and cigarettes, shirts and paraffin lamps, whisky and bicycles. It also meant access to the knowledge behind these material goods, for the Europeans brought missions and schools as well as cargo.

Practically the only teaching the natives received about European life came from the missions, which emphasized the central significance of religion in European society. The Melanesians already believed that man's activities — whether gardening, sailing canoes, or bearing children — needed magical assistance. Ritual without human effort was not enough. But neither was human effort on its own. This outlook was reinforced by mission teaching.

The initial enthusiasm for European rule, however, was speedily dispelled. The rapid growth of the plantation economy removed the bulk of the able-bodied men from the villages, leaving women, children, and old men to carry on as best they could. The splendid vision of the equality of all Christians began to seem a pious deception in face of the realities of the color bar, the multiplicity of rival Christian missions and the open irreligion of many Whites.

For a long time the natives accepted the European mission as the means by which the "cargo" would eventually be made available to them. But they found that acceptance of Christianity did not bring the cargo any nearer. They grew disillusioned. The story now began to be put about that it was not the Whites who made the cargo, but the dead ancestors. To people completely ignorant of factory production, this made good sense. White men did not work; they merely wrote secret signs on scraps of paper, for which they were given shiploads of goods. On the other hand, the Melanesians labored week after week for pitiful wages. Plainly the goods must be made for Melanesians somewhere, perhaps in the Land of the Dead. The Whites, who possessed the secret of the cargo, were intercepting it and keeping it from the hands of the islanders, to whom it was really consigned. In the

Madang district of New Guinea, after some forty years' experience of the missions, the natives went in a body one day with a petition demanding that the cargo secret should now be revealed to them, for they had been very patient.

So strong is this belief in the existence of a "secret" that the cargo cults generally contain some ritual in imitation of the mysterious European customs which are held to be the clue to the white man's extraordinary power over goods and men. The believers sit around tables with bottles of flowers in front of them, dressed in European clothes, waiting for the cargo ship or airplane to materialize; other cultists feature magic pieces of paper and cabalistic writing. Many of them deliberately turn their backs on the past by destroying secret ritual objects, or exposing them to the gaze of uninitiated youths and women, for whom formerly even a glimpse of the sacred objects would have meant the severest penalties, even death. The belief that they were the chosen people is further reinforced by their reading of the Bible, for the lives and customs of the people in the Old Testament resemble their own lives rather than those of the Europeans. In the New Testament they find the Apocalypse, with its prophecies of destruction and resurrection, particularly attractive.

Missions that stress the imminence of the Second Coming, like those of the Seventh Day Adventists, are often accused of stimulating millenarian cults among the islanders. In reality, however, the Melanesians themselves rework the doctrines the missionaries teach them, selecting from the Bible what they themselves find particularly congenial in it. Such movements have occurred in areas where missions of quite different types have been dominant, from Roman Catholic to Seventh Day Adventist. The reasons for the emergence of these cults, of course, lie far deeper in the life-experience of the people.

The economy of most of the islands is very backward. Native agriculture produces little for the world market, and even the European plantations and mines export only a few primary products and raw materials: copra, rubber, gold. Melanesians are quite unable to understand why copra, for example, fetches thirty pounds sterling per ton one month and but five pounds a few months later. With no notion of the workings of world-commodity markets, the natives see only the sudden closing of plantations, reduced wages and unemployment, and are inclined to attribute their insecurity to the whim or evil in the nature of individual planters.

Such shocks have not been confined to the economic order. Governments, too, have come and gone, especially during the two world

wars: German, Dutch, British, and French administrations melted overnight. Then came the Japanese, only to be ousted in turn largely by the
previously unknown Americans. And among these Americans the
Melanesians saw Negroes like themselves, living lives of luxury on
equal terms with white G.I.'s. The sight of these Negroes seemed like a
fulfillment of the old prophecies to many cargo cult leaders. Nor must
we forget the sheer scale of this invasion. Around a million U.S. troops
passed through the Admiralty Islands, completely swamping the inhabitants. It was a world of meaningless and chaotic changes, in which
anything was possible. New ideas were imported and given local
twists. Thus in the Loyalty Islands people expected the French Communist Party to bring the millennium. There is no real evidence, however, of any Communist influence in these movements, despite the
rather hysterical belief among Solomon Island planters that the name
of the local "Masinga Rule" movement was derived from the word
"Marxian"! In reality the name comes from a Solomon Island tongue,
and means "brotherhood."

Europeans who have witnessed outbreaks inspired by the cargo
cults are usually at a loss to understand what they behold. The islanders throw away their money, break their most sacred taboos, abandon their gardens, and destroy their precious livestock; they indulge in
sexual license or, alternatively, rigidly separate men from women in
huge communal establishments. Sometimes they spend days sitting
gazing at the horizon for a glimpse of the long-awaited ship or airplane; sometimes they dance, pray, and sing in mass congregations,
becoming possessed and "speaking with tongues."

Observers have not hesitated to use such words as "madness,"
"mania," and "irrationality" to characterize the cults. But the cults
reflect quite logical and rational attempts to make sense out of a social
order that appears senseless and chaotic. Given the ignorance of the
Melanesians about the wider European society, its economic organization and its highly developed technology, their reactions form a consistent and understandable pattern. They wrap up all their yearning and
hope in an amalgam that combines the best counsel they can find in
Christianity and their native belief. If the world is soon to end, gardening or fishing is unnecessary; everything will be provided. If the Melanesians are to be part of a much wider order, the taboos that prescribe
their social conduct must now be lifted or broken in a newly prescribed
way.

Of course the cargo never comes. The cults nonetheless live on. If
the millennium does not arrive on schedule, then perhaps there is
some failure in the magic, some error in the ritual. New breakaway

groups organize around "purer" faith and ritual. The cult rarely disappears, so long as the social situation which brings it into being persists.

At this point it should be observed that cults of this general kind are not peculiar to Melanesia. Men who feel themselves oppressed and deceived have always been ready to pour their hopes and fears, their aspirations and frustrations, into dreams of a millennium to come or of a golden age to return. All parts of the world have had their counterparts of the cargo cults, from the American Indian ghost dance to the Communist-millenarist "reign of the saints" in Münster during the Reformation, from medieval European apocalyptic cults to African "witch-finding" movements and Chinese Buddhist heresies. In some situations men have been content to wait and pray; in others they have sought to hasten the day by using their strong right arms to do the Lord's work. And always the cults serve to bring together scattered groups, notably the peasants and urban plebeians of agrarian societies and the peoples of "stateless" societies where the cult unites separate (and often hostile) villages, clans, and tribes into a wider religio-political unity.

Once the people begin to develop secular political organizations, however, the sects tend to lose their importance as vehicles of protest. They begin to relegate the Second Coming to the distant future or to the next world. In Melanesia ordinary political bodies, trade unions and native councils are becoming the normal media through which the islanders express their aspirations. In recent years continued economic prosperity and political stability have taken some of the edge off their despair. It now seems unlikely that any major movement along cargo-cult lines will recur in areas where the transition to secular politics has been made, even if the insecurity of prewar times returned. I would predict that the embryonic nationalism represented by cargo cults is likely in future to take forms familiar in the history of other countries that have moved from subsistence agriculture to participation in the world economy.

REVIEW QUESTIONS

1. What do the Melanesians mean by cargo, and why is it so important to them?

2. What are the main features of cargo cults? What is their purpose?

3. Why have so many cargo cults, each remarkably similar to the others, appeared in so many different places in Melanesia?

4. How do cargo cults contribute to culture change in Melanesia?

33

Cocaine and the economic deterioration of Bolivia

JACK McIVER WEATHERFORD

The demands of the world market have eroded local subsistence econo-
mies for centuries. Lands, once farmed by individual families to meet
their own needs, now grow sugarcane, cotton, grain, or vegetables
for market. Deprived of their access to land, householders must work
as day laborers or migrate to cities to find jobs. Villages are denuded
of the men who have gone elsewhere for work, leaving women to farm
and manage the family. The rhythm and structure of daily village life
is altered dramatically. In this article, Jack McIver Weatherford de-
scribes the impact of a new world market for cocaine on the structure
and lives of rural Bolivians. Fed by an insatiable demand in Europe
and the United States, the Bolivian cocaine trade has drawn males
from the countryside, disrupted communications, destroyed families,
unbalanced the local diet, and upset traditional social organization.

"They say you Americans can do anything. So, why can't you make your own cocaine and let our children come home from the coca plantations in the Chapare?" The Indian woman asked the question with confused resignation. In the silence that followed, I could hear only the rats scurrying around in the thatched roof. We continued shelling corn in the dark. The large house around us had once been home to an extended clan but was now nearly empty.

There was no answer to give her. Yet it was becoming increas-

This article was written especially for this book. Copyright © 1986 by Jack McIver Weatherford.

ingly obvious that the traditional Andean system of production and distribution built over thousands of years was now crumbling. Accompanying the destruction of the economic system was a marked distortion of the social and cultural patterns of the Quechua Indians. Since early in Inca history, the village of Pocona where I was working had been a trading village connecting the highlands which produced potatoes, with the lowlands, which produced coca, a mildly narcotic plant used by the Incas. Over the past decade, however, new market demands from Europe and the United States have warped this system. Now the commodity is cocaine rather than the coca leaves, and the trade route bypasses the village of Pocona.

Bolivian subsistence patterns range from hunting and gathering in the jungle to intensive farming in the highlands, and since Inca times many parts of the country have depended heavily on mining. In the 1980s all of these patterns have been disrupted by the Western fad for one particular drug. Adoption of cocaine as the "drug of choice" by the urban elite of Europe and America has opened up new jungle lands and brought new Indian groups into Western economic systems. At the same time the cocaine trade has cut off many communities such as Pocona from their traditional role in the national economy. Denied participation in the legal economy, they have been driven back into a world of barter and renewed isolation.

The vagaries of Western consumerism produce extensive and profound effects on Third World countries. It makes little difference whether the demand is for legitimate products such as coffee, tungsten, rubber, and furs marketed through legal corporations or for illegal commodities such as opium, marijuana, cocaine, and heroin handled through criminal corporations. The same economic principles that govern the open, legal market also govern the clandestine, illegal markets, and the effects of both are frequently brutal.

Before coming to this Bolivian village, I assumed that if Americans and Europeans wanted to waste their money on cocaine, it was probably good that some of the poor countries such as Bolivia profit from it. In Cochabamba, the city in the heart of the cocaine-producing area, I had seen the benefits of this trade among the *narco chic* who lived in a new suburb of houses styled to look like Swiss chalets, Spanish *haciendas,* and English country homes. All these homes were surrounded by large wrought-iron fences, walls with broken glass set in the tops, and with large dogs that barked loudly and frequently. Such homes cost up to a hundred thousand dollars, an astronomical sum for Bolivia. I had also seen the narco elite of Cochabamba wearing gold chains and the latest Miami fashions and driving Nissans, Audis, Ford Broncos, an occasional

BMW, or even a Mercedes through the muddy streets of the city. Some of their children attended the expensive English-speaking school; much of Cochabamba's meager nightlife catered to the elite. But as affluent as they may be in Bolivia, this elite would probably not earn as much as working-class families in such cities as Detroit, Frankfurt, or Tokyo.

Traveling outside of Cochabamba for six hours on the back of a truck, fording the same river three times, and following a rugged path for the last 25 kilometers, I reached Pocona and saw a different face of the cocaine trade. Located in a valley a mile and a half above sea level, Pocona is much too high to grow the coca bush. Coca grows best below 6 thousand feet, in the lush area called the Chapare where the eastern Andes meet the western edge of the Amazon basin and rain forest.

Like the woman with whom I was shelling corn, most of the people of Pocona are older, and community life is dominated by women together with their children who are still too young to leave. This particular woman had already lost both of her sons to the Chapare. She did not know it at the time, but within a few months, she was to lose her husband to the same work as well. With so few men, the women are left alone to plant, work, and harvest the fields of potatoes, corn, and fava beans, but with most of the work force missing, the productivity of Pocona has declined substantially.

In what was once a moderately fertile valley, hunger is now a part of life. The daily diet consists almost exclusively of bread, potato soup, boiled potatoes, corn, and tea. The majority of their daily calories comes from the potatoes and from the sugar that they put in their tea. They have virtually no meat or dairy products and very few fresh vegetables. These products are now sent to the Chapare to feed the workers in the coca fields, and the people of Pocona cannot compete against them. The crops that the people of Pocona produce are now difficult to sell because truck drivers find it much more profitable to take goods in and out of the Chapare rather than face the long and unprofitable trip to reach such remote villages as Pocona.

Despite all the hardships caused by so many people being away from the village, one might assume that more cash should be flowing into Pocona from the Chapare, where young men easily earn three dollars a day — three times the average daily wage of porters or laborers in Cochabamba. But this assumption was contradicted by the evidence of Pocona. As one widowed Indian mother of four explained, the first time her sixteen-year-old son came home, he brought bags of food, presents, and money for her and the younger children. She was very glad that he was working in the Chapare. On the second visit home he brought only a plastic bag of white powder for himself, and instead of bringing food, he took away as much as he could carry on the two-day trip back into the Chapare.

The third time, he told his mother that he could not find enough work in the Chapare. As a way to earn more money he made his mother bake as much bread as she could, and he took Mariana, his ten-year-old sister, with him to sell the bread to the workers in the Chapare. According to the mother, he beat the little girl and abused her repeatedly. Moreover, the money she made disappeared. On one of Mariana's trips home to get more bread, the mother had no more wheat or corn flour to supply her son. So, she sent Mariana away to Cochabamba to work as a maid. The enraged son found where Mariana was working and went to the home to demand that she be returned to him. When the family refused, he tried but failed to have her wages paid to him rather than to his mother. Mariana was separated from her family and community, but at least she was not going to be one more of the prostitutes in the Chapare, and for her mother that was more important.

The standard of living in Pocona was never very high, but with the advent of the cocaine boom in Bolivia, the standard has declined. Ten years ago, Pocona's gasoline-powered generator furnished the homes with a few hours of electric light each night. The electricity also allowed a few families to purchase radios, and occasionally someone brought in a movie projector to show a film in a large adobe building on the main square. For the past two years, the people of Pocona have not been able to buy gasoline for their generator. This left the village not only without electricity but without entertainment and radio or film contact with the outside world. A few boys have bought portable radios with their earnings from the Chapare, but their families were unable to replace the batteries. Nights in Pocona are now both dark and silent.

In recent years the national economy of Bolivia has been virtually destroyed, and peasants in communities such as Pocona are reverting to barter as the only means of exchange. The value of the peso may rise or fall by as much as 30 percent in a day; the peasants cannot take a chance on trading their crops for money that may be worth nothing in a week. Cocaine alone has not been responsible for the destruction of the Bolivian economy, but it has been a major contributor. It is not mere coincidence that the world's largest producer of coca is also the country with the world's worst inflation.

During part of 1986, inflation in Bolivia varied at a rate between 2,000 and 13,000 percent, if calculated on a yearly basis. Prices in the cities changed by the hour, and on some days the dollar would rise at the rate of more than 1 percent per hour. A piece of bread cost 150,000 pesos, and an American dollar bought between two and three million pesos on the black market. Large items such as airplane tickets were calculated in the billions of pesos, and on one occasion I helped a man carry a large box of money to pay for such a ticket. It took two professional counters half an hour to count the bills. Workers were paid in stacks of bills that were often half a meter high. Because Bolivia is too undeveloped to print its money, the importation of its own bills printed in West Germany and Brazil was one of the leading imports in the mid-1980s.

Ironically, by no longer being able to participate fully in the money economy, the villagers of Pocona who have chewed coca leaves for centuries now find it difficult to afford the leaves. The narcotics industry pays such a high price that the people of Pocona can afford only the rejected trash from the cocaine industry. Whether chewed or made into a tea, the coca produces a mild lift somewhat like a cup of coffee but without the jagged come down that follows a coffee high. Coca also reduces hunger, thirst, headaches, stomach pains, and the type of altitude sickness known as *sorroche*.

Were this all, coca use might be viewed as merely a bad habit somewhat like drinking coffee, smoking cigarettes, or overindulging in chocolates, but unlike these practices coca actually has a number of marked health benefits. The coca leaf is very high in calcium. In a population with widespread lactose intolerance and in a country without a national system of milk distribution, this calcium source is very important. The calcium also severely reduces cavities in a population with virtually no dental services outside the city. Coca also contains large amounts of vitamins A, C, and D, which are often lacking in the starchy diet of the mountain peasants.

Without coca, and with an excess of corn that they cannot get to market, the people of Pocona now make more *chicha*, a form of home-fermented corn beer that tastes somewhat like the silage that American dairymen feed their cows. It is ironic that as an affluent generation of Americans are decreasing their consumption of alcohol in favor of drugs such as cocaine, the people of Pocona are drinking more alcohol to replace their traditional coca. *Chicha*, like most beers, is more nutritious than other kinds of distilled spirits but lacks the health benefits of the coca leaves. It also produces intoxication, something that no amount of coca leaves can do. Coca chewing is such a slow process and produces such a mild effect that a user would have to chew a bushel of leaves to equal the impact of one mixed drink or one snort of cocaine.

In many ways, the problems and complaints of Pocona echo those of any Third World country with a cash crop, particularly those caught in the boom-and-bust cycle characteristic of capitalist systems. Whether it is the sisal boom of the Yucatan, the banana boom of Central America, the rubber boom of Brazil, or the cocaine boom in Bolivia, the same pattern develops. Rural villages are depleted of their work forces. Family and traditional cultural patterns disintegrate. And the people are no longer able to afford certain local products that suddenly become valued in the West. This is what happened to Pocona.

Frequently, the part of a country that produces the boom crop benefits greatly, while other areas suffer greatly. If this were true in Bolivia, benefits accruing in the coca-producing area of the Chapare would outweigh the adjustment problems of such villages as Pocona. As it turns out, however, the Chapare has been even more adversely affected.

Most of the young men who go to the Chapare do not actually work in the coca fields. The coca bush originated in this area and does not require extensive care. One hectare can easily produce 800 kilograms of coca leaves in a year, but not much labor is needed to pick them. After harvesting, the leaves are dried in the sun for three to four days. Most of these tasks can easily be done by the farmer and his family. Wherever one goes in the Chapare one sees coca leaves spread out on large drying cloths. Old people or young children walk up and down these cloths, turning the drying leaves with their whisk brooms.

The need for labor, especially the labor of strong young men, comes in the first stage of cocaine production, in the reduction of large piles of leaves into a small quantity of *pasta*, or coca paste from which the active ingredient, cocaine, can then be refined. Three to five hundred kilograms of leaves must be used to make one kilogram of pure cocaine. The leaves are made into *pasta* by soaking them in vats of kerosene and by applying salt, acetone, and sulfuric acid. To make the chemical reaction occur, someone must trample on the leaves for several days — a process very much like tromping on grapes to make wine, only longer. Because the corrosive mixture dissolves shoes or boots, the young men walk barefooted. These men are called *pistacocas* and usually work in the cool of the night, pounding the green slime with their feet. Each night the chemicals eat away more skin and very quickly open ulcers erupt. Some young men in the Chapare now have feet that are so diseased that they are incapable of standing, much less walking. So, instead, they use their hands to mix the *pasta*, but their hands are eaten away even faster than their feet. Thousands and possibly tens of thousands of young Bolivian men now look like lepers with permanently disfigured hands and feet. It is unlikely that any could return to Pocona and make a decent farmer.

Because this work is painful, the *pistacocas* smoke addictive cigarettes coated with *pasta*. This alleviates their pain and allows them to continue walking the coca throughout the night. The *pasta* is contaminated with chemical residues, and smoking it warps their minds as quickly as the acids eat their hands and feet. Like Mariana's brother, the users become irrational, easily angered, and frequently violent.

Once the boys are no longer able to mix coca because of their mental or their physical condition, they usually become unemployed. If their wounds heal, they may be able to work as loaders or haulers, carrying the cocaine or transporting the controlled chemicals used to process it. By and large, however, women and very small children, called *hormigas* (ants), are better at this work. Some of the young men then return home to their villages; others wander to Cochabamba, where they might live on the streets or try to earn money buying and selling dollars on the black market.

The cocaine manufacturers not only supply their workers with food and drugs, they keep them sexually supplied with young girls who serve as prostitutes as well. Bolivian health officials estimate that nearly half of the people living in the Chapare today have venereal disease. As the boys and girls working there return to their villages, they take these diseases with them. Increasing numbers of children born to infected mothers now have bodies covered in syphilitic sores. In 1985, a worse disease hit with the first case of AIDS. Soon after the victim died, a second victim was diagnosed.

In an effort to control its own drug problem, the United States is putting pressure on Bolivia to eradicate coca production in the Andean countries. The army invaded the Chapare during January of 1986, but after nearly three weeks of being surrounded by the workers in the narcotics industry and cut off from their supply bases, the army surrendered. In a nation the size of Texas and California combined but with a population approximately of the city of Chicago, it is difficult for the government to control its own territory. Neither the Incas nor the Spanish conquistadores were ever able to conquer and administer the jungles of Bolivia, where there are still nomadic bands of Indians who have retreated deep into the jungle to escape Western encroachment. The army of the poorest government in South America is no better able to control this country than its predecessors. The government runs the cities, but the countryside and the jungles operate under their own laws.

One of the most significant effects of the coca trade and of the campaigns to eradicate it has come on the most remote Indians of the jungle area. As the campaign against drugs has pushed production into more inaccessible places and as the world demand has promoted greater cultivation of coca, the coca growers are moving into previously unexplored areas. A coca plantation has been opened along the Chimore river less than an hour's walk from one of the few surviving bands of Yuqui Indians. The Yuquis, famous for their 8-foot-long bows and their 6-foot arrows, are now hovering on the brink of extinction. In the past year, the three bands of a few hundred Yuquis have lost eleven members in skirmishes with outsiders. In turn, they killed several outsiders this year and even shot the missionary who is their main champion against outside invaders.

According to the reports of missionaries, other Indian bands have been enlisted as workers in the cocaine production and trafficking, making virtual slaves out of them. A Bolivian medical doctor explained to me that the Indians are fed the cocaine in their food as a way of keeping them working and preventing their escape. Through cocaine, the drug traffickers may be able to conquer and control these last remnants of the great Indian nations of the Americas. If so, they will accomplish what many have failed to do in the five-hundred-year campaign of Europeans to conquer the free Indians.

The fate of the Indians driven out of their homelands is shown in the case of Juan, a thirteen-year-old Indian boy from the Chimore river where the Yuquis live. I found him one night in a soup kitchen for street children operated in the corner of a potato warehouse by the Maryknoll priests. Juan wore a bright orange undershirt that proclaimed in bold letters Fairfax District Public Schools. I sat with him at the table coated in potato dust while he ate his soup with his fellow street children, some of whom were as young as four years old. He told me what he could remember of his life on the Chimore; he did not know to which tribe he was born or what language he had spoken with his mother. It was difficult for Juan to talk about his Indian past in a country where it is a grave insult to be called an Indian. Rather than talk about the Chimore or the Chapare, he wanted to ask me questions because I was the first American he had ever met. Was I stronger than everyone else because he had heard that Americans were the strongest people in the world? Did we really have wolves and bears in North America, and was I afraid of them? Had I been to the Chapare? Did I use cocaine?

In between his questions, I found out that Juan had come to Cochabamba several years ago with his mother. The two had fled the Chapare, but he did not know why. Once in the city they lived on the streets for a few years until his mother died, and he had been living alone ever since. He had become a *polilla* (moth), as they call such street boys. To earn money he washed cars and he sold cigarettes laced with *pasta*. When he tired of talking about himself and asking about the animals of North America, he and his two friends made plans to go out to one of the nearby *pasta* villages the next day.

Both the Chapare (which supplied the land for growing coca) and highland villages such as Pocona (which supplied the labor) were suffering from the cocaine boom. Where then is the profit? The only other sites in Bolivia are the newly developing manufacturing towns where cocaine is refined. Whereas in the past most of this refining took place in Colombia, both the manufacturers and the traffickers find it easier and cheaper to have the work done in Bolivia, closer to the source of coca leaves and closer to much cheaper sources of labor. The strength of the Colombian government and its closeness to the United States also make the drug trafficking more difficult there than in Bolivia, with its weak, unstable government in La Paz.

Toco is one of the villages that has turned into a processing point for cocaine town. Located at about the same altitude as Pocona but only a half-day by truck from the Chapare, Toco cannot grow coca, but the village is close enough to the source to become a major producer of the pasta. Traffickers bring in large shipments of coca leaves and work them in backyard "kitchens." Not only does Toco still have its young men at home and still have food and electricity, but it has work for a few hundred young men from other villages.

Unlike Pocona, for which there are only a few trucks each week, trucks flow in and out of Toco every day. Emblazoned with names such as Rambo, El Padrino (The Godfather), and Charles Bronson rather than the traditional truck names of San José, Virgen de Copacabana, or Flor de Urkupina, these are the newest and finest trucks found in Bolivia. Going in with a Bolivian physician and another anthropologist from the United States, I easily got a ride, along with a dozen Indians on a truck, which was hauling old car batteries splattered with what appeared to be vomit.

A few kilometers outside of Toco we were stopped by a large crowd of Indian peasants. Several dozen women sat around on the ground and in the road spinning yarn and knitting. Most of the women had babies tied to their shoulders in the brightly colored *awayu* cloth, which the women use to carry everything from potatoes to lambs. Men stood around with farm tools, which they now used to block the roads. The men brandished their machetes and rakes at us, accusing us all of being smugglers and *pistacocas*. Like the Indians on the truck with us, the three of us stood silently and expressionless in the melee.

The hostile peasants were staging an ad hoc strike against the coca trade. They had just had their own fields of potatoes washed away in a flash flood. Now without food and without money to re-plant, they were demanding that someone help them or they would disrupt all traffic to and from Toco. Shouting at us, several of them climbed on board the truck. Moving among the nervous passengers, they checked for a shipment of coca leaves, kerosene, acid, or anything else that might be a part of the coca trade. Having found nothing, they reluctantly let us pass with stern warnings not to return with cocaine or *pasta*. A few weeks after our encounter with the strikers, their strike ended and most of the men went off to look for work in the Chapare and in Toco; without a crop, the cocaine traffic was their only hope of food for the year.

On our arrival in Toco we found out that the batteries loaded with us in the back of the truck had been hollowed out and filled with acid to be used in making *pasta*. *Chicha* vomit had been smeared around to discourage anyone from checking them. After removal of the acid, the same batteries were then filled with plastic bags of cocaine to be smug-gled out of Toco and into the town of Cliza and on to Cochabamba and the outside world.

Toco is an expanding village with new cement-block buildings going up on the edge of town and a variety of large plumbing pipes, tanks, and drains being installed. It also has a large number of motor-cycles and cars. By Bolivian standards it is a rich village, but it is still poorer than the average village in Mexico or Brazil. Soon after our arrival in Toco, we were followed by a handful of men wanting to sell us *pasta*, and within a few minutes the few had grown to nearly fifty young men anxious to assist us. Most of them were on foot, but some of them circled us in motorcycles, and many of them were armed with guns and machetes. They became suspicious and then openly hostile when we convinced them that we did not want to buy *pasta*. To escape them we took refuge in the home of an Indian family and waited for the mob to disperse.

When we tried to leave the village a few hours later, we were trapped by a truckload of young men who did not release us until they had checked with everyone we had met with in the village. They wondered why we were there if not to buy *pasta*. We were rescued by the doctor who accompanied us; she happened to be the niece of a popular Quechua writer. Evoking the memory of her uncle who had done so much for the Quechua people, she convinced the villagers of

Toco that we were Bolivian doctors who worked with her in Cocha-bamba, and that we were not foreigners coming to buy *pasta* or to spy on them. An old veteran who claimed that he had served in the Chaco War with her uncle vouched for us, but in return for having saved us he then wanted us to buy *pasta* from him.

The wealth generated by the coca trade from Bolivia is easy to see. It is in the European cars cruising the streets of Cochabamba and Santa Cruz, and in the nice houses in the suburbs. It is in the motorcy-cles and jeeps in Toco, Cliza, and Trinidad. The poverty is difficult to see because it is in the remote villages like Pocona, among the impov-erished miners in the village Porco, and intertwined in the lives of peasants throughout the highland districts of Potosi and Oruro. But it is in these communities such as Pocona that 70 percent of the popula-tion of Bolivia lives. For every modern home built with cocaine money in Cochabamba, a tin mine lies abandoned in Potosi that lost many of its miners when the world price for tin fell and they had to go to the Chapare for food. For every new car in Santa Cruz or every new motorcycle in Toco, a whole village is going hungry in the mountains.

The money for coca does not go to the Bolivians. It goes to the criminal organizations that smuggle the drugs out of the country and into the United States and Europe. A gram of pure cocaine on the streets of Cochabamba costs five dollars; the same gram on the streets of New York, Paris, or Berlin costs over a hundred dollars. The price increase occurs outside Bolivia.

The financial differential is evident in the case of the American housewife and mother sentenced to the Cochabamba prison after being caught with six and a half kilograms of cocaine at the airport. Like all the other women in the prison, she now earns money washing laundry by hand at a cold-water tap in the middle of the prison yard. She receives the equivalent of twenty cents for each pair of pants she washes, dries, and irons. In Bolivian prisons, the prisoner has to fur-nish his or her own food, clothes, medical attention, and even her own furniture.

She was paid five thousand dollars to smuggle the cocaine out of Bolivia to the Caribbean. Presumably someone else was then to be paid even more to smuggle it into the United States or Europe. The money that the American housewife received to smuggle the cocaine out of the country would pay the salary of eighty *pistacocas* for a month. It would also pay the monthly wages of 250 Bolivian schoolteachers, who earn the equivalent of twenty U.S. dollars per month in pay. Even though her price seemed high by Bolivian standards, it is a small part of the final money generated by the drugs. When cut and sold on the streets of the United States, her shipment of cocaine would probably bring in five to seven million dollars. Of that amount, however, only about five hundred dollars goes to the Bolivian farmer.

The peasant in the Chapare growing the coca earns three times as much for a field of coca as he would for a field of papayas. But he is only the first in a long line of people and transactions that brings the final product of cocaine to the streets of the West. At the end of the line, cocaine sells for four to five times its weight in gold.

The United States government made all aid programs and loans to Bolivia dependent on the country's efforts to destroy coca. This produces programs in which Bolivian troops go into the most accessible areas and uproot a few fields of aging or diseased coca plants. Visiting drug-enforcement agents from the United States together with American congressmen applaud, make their reports on the escalating war against drugs, and then retire to a city hotel where they drink hot cups of coca tea and cocktails.

These programs hurt primarily the poor farmer who tries to make a slightly better living by growing coca rather than papayas. The raids on the fields and cocaine factories usually lead to the imprisonment of ulcerated *pistacocas* and women and children *hormigas* from villages throughout Bolivia. Local authorities present the burned fields and full prisons to Washington visitors as proof that the Bolivian government has taken a hard stance against drug trafficking.

International crime figures with bank accounts in New York and Zurich get the money. Bolivia ends up with hunger in its villages, young men with their hands and feet permanently maimed, higher rates of venereal disease, chronic food shortages, less kerosene, higher school dropout rates, increased drug addiction, and a worthless peso.

REVIEW QUESTIONS

1. List and describe the major effects of the cocaine trade on rural Bolivian life.

2. Why has the production of coca and the manufacture of cocaine created a health hazard in Bolivia?

3. Why has the cocaine trade benefited the Bolivian economy so little?

4. How has the cocaine trade disrupted village social organization in Bolivia?

34

Change and development in Vicos

ALAN R. HOLMBERG

*In the 1950s, Alan Homberg and a group of professional anthropolo-
gists from Cornell University began the Vicos Project, one of the
most ambitious attempts to apply anthropology the discipline has ever
seen. Renting a Peruvian hacienda that was organized like a feudal
fief, they systematically set about its transformation into an inhabi-
tant-owned, productive, democratic cooperative. In the end, the experiment achieved the goals set for it despite growing resistance from
Peruvian landowners and officials. Its story continues to unfold today as its example spreads to other communities.*

More than fifty percent of the world's population is peasantry, the
large majority of whom are living in the so-called underdeveloped
countries or newly emerging nations under natural conditions and social structures that have denied them effective participation in the modernization process. In the context of a modern state, this peasantry
plays little or no role in the decision-making process; its members
enjoy little access to wealth; they live under conditions of social disrespect; a large majority of them are illiterate, unenlightened, and lacking
in modern skills; many are victims of ill health and disease. Characteristic of this sector of the world's population is a deep devotion to
magico-religious practice as a means of mitigating the castigations of a
harsh and cruel world over which it has little or no control. Such, in
fact, were the conditions of life on the *Hacienda Vicos*, a community
which is the subject of this paper and those to follow.

Alan Holmberg. Originally published as "The Changing Values and Institutions of Vicos
in the Context of National Development," in the *American Behavioral Scientist*, March,
1965, pp. 3–8. Copyright © 1965 by Sage Publications, Inc. Reprinted by permission of
Sage Publications, Inc.

Operating on the assumption that these conditions of human in-dignity are not only anachronistic in the modern world but are also a great threat to public and civic order everywhere, Cornell University, in 1952—in collaboration with the Peruvian Indianist Institute—em-barked on an experimental program of induced technical and social change which was focused on the problem of transforming one of Peru's most unproductive, highly dependent manor systems into a productive, independent, self-governing community adapted to the re-ality of the modern Peruvian state.

Up until January, 1952, Vicos was a manor or large estate, situ-ated in a relatively small intermontane valley of Peru, about 250 miles north of the capital city of Lima. Ranging in altitude from about 9,000 to 20,000 feet, Vicos embraced an area of about 40,000 acres and had an enumerated population of 1,703 monolingual Quechua-speaking Indi-ans who had been bound to the land as serfs or peons since early colonial times.

Vicos was a public manor, a type not uncommon in Peru. Title to such properties is frequently held by Public Benefit or Charity Societies which rent them out to the highest bidder at public auction for periods ranging from 5 to 10 years. Each such manor has particular lands, usually the most fertile bottom lands, reserved for commercial exploita-tion by the successful renter who utilizes, virtually free of charge for several days of each week, the serf-bound labor force, usually one adult member of every family, to cultivate his crops. The rent from the property paid to the Public Benefit Society is supposed to be used for charitable purposes, such as the support of hospitals and other welfare activities, although this is not always the case. Under the contractual arrangements between the renter and the Public Benefit Society (and sometimes the indigenous population) the former is legally but not always functionally bound to supply, in return for the labor tax paid by his serfs, plots of land (usually upland) of sufficient size to support the family of each inscribed peon.

Manors like Vicos are socially organized along similar lines. At the head of the hierarchy stands the renter or *patron*, frequently absen-tee, who is always an outsider and non-Indian or Mestizo. He is the maximum authority within the system and all power to indulge or deprive is concentrated in his hands. Under his direction, if absentee, is an administrator, also an outsider and Mestizo, who is responsible to the renter for conducting and managing the day-to-day agricultural or grazing operations of the property. Depending on the size of the manor, the administrator may employ from one to several Mestizo foremen who are responsible for the supervision of the labor force.

They report directly to the administrator on such matters as the number of absentee members of the labor force, and the condition of the crops regarding such factors as irrigation, fertilization and harvest.

Below and apart from this small non-Indian power elite stands the Indian society of peons, the members of which are bound to a soil they do not own and on which they have little security of tenure. The direct link between the labor force and the administration is generally through a number of Indian straw bosses, appointed by the *patron* and responsible for the direct supervision of the labor force in the fields. Each straw boss or *Mayoral*, as he was known at Vicos, had under his direction a certain number of *peones* from a particular geographic area of the manor. In 1952 there were eight straw bosses at Vicos, with a total labor force of about 380 men. In addition to the labor tax paid by the Indian community, its members were obligated to supply other free services to the manor such as those of cooks, grooms, swineherds, watchmen, and servants. The whole system is maintained by the application of sanctions ranging from brute force to the impounding of peon property.

In matters not associated directly with manor operations, the Indian community of Vicos was organized along separate and traditional lines. The principal indigenous decision-making body consisted of a politico-religious hierarchy of some seventeen officials known as *Varas* or *Varayoc*, so named from the custom of carrying a wooden staff as a badge of office. The major functions of this body included the settling of disputes over land and animals in the Indian community, the supervision of public works such as the repair of bridges and the community church, the regulation of marriage patterns, and the celebration of religious festivals. The leading official in this hierarchy was the *Alcalde* or mayor who assumed office, after many years of service to the community, by a kind of elective system and who occupied it for only one year. The *Varayoc* were the principal representatives of the Indian community to the outside world.

In 1952 all Vicosinos were virtual subsistence farmers, occupying plots of land ranging in size from less than one-half to about five acres. The principal crops raised were maize, potatoes and other Andean root crops, wheat, barley, rye, broad beans, and quinoa. In addition, most families grazed some livestock (cattle, sheep, goats, and swine) and all families raised small animals like guinea pigs and chickens as a way of supplementing their diets and their incomes. After thousands of years of use and inadequate care, however, the land had lost its fertility, seeds had degenerated, and the principal crops and animals were stunted and diseased. Per capita output was thus at a very low level, although the exact figure is not known.

Most were victims of a host of endemic diseases. Studies in parasitology demonstrated that 80 percent of the population was infected with harmful parasites, and epidemics of such diseases as measles and whooping cough had been frequent over the years. There were, to be sure, native curers employing magico-religious practices and ineffectual herbal remedies to cope with these well-being problems but it can be said that the community had little or no access to modern medicine. The goal of the traditional Vicosino was simply to survive as long as he possibly could, knowing full well that he might be a victim of fate at any moment.

The principal avenue for gaining respect in traditional Vicos society was to grow old and to participate in the politico-religious hierarchy, the top positions of which could be occupied only after many years of faithful service to the community. Wealth was also a source of gaining prestige and recognition but it could not be amassed in any quantity, by native standards, until one's elders had died or until an individual himself had lived frugally and worked very hard for many years. In other words, the principal role to which high rank was attached was that of a hard working, muscle-bound virtual subsistence farmer who placed little or no value on other occupations or skills. Consequently there was just no place for a rebellious or symbolically creative individual in traditional Vicos society. The manor system was, of course, in large part responsible for this. It needed few skills beyond brawn and enlightenment could not be tolerated, because the more informed the population, the more it might become a threat to the traditional manor system. Records show that all protest movements at Vicos had been pretty much squelched by a coalition of the landlords, the clergy, and the police. As a result, over a period of several hundred years the community had remained in static equilibrium and was completely out of step with anything that was occurring in the modern world. The rule at Vicos was conformity to the status quo. It pervaded all institutions and dominated the social process. The peon was subservient to the overlord; the child, to the parents; and both were beaten into submission. Even the supernatural forces were punishing, and the burdens one bore were suffered as naturally ordained by powers beyond one's control.

INTERVENTION FROM WITHOUT

The Cornell Peru Project intervened in this context in 1952 in the role of *patron*. Through a partly fortuitous circumstance — the industrial firm which was renting Vicos on a ten year lease that still had five years to run went bankrupt — we were able to sublease the property and its serfs for a five year period. For a couple of years prior to this time, however, the Peruvian anthropologist, Dr. Mario Vazquez, had conducted a very detailed study of this manor as a social system, as part of a larger comparative study of modernization of peasant societies that the Department of Anthropology at Cornell was conducting in several areas of the world. Thus when the opportunity to rent the *hacienda* arose, we seized upon it to conduct our own experiment in modernization. In its negotiations prior to renting the *hacienda*, Cornell received full support of the Peruvian Government through its Institute of Indigenous Affairs, a semiautonomous agency of the Ministry of Labor and Indigenous Affairs. In December, 1951, a formal Memorandum of Agreement was drawn up between Cornell and the Institute of Indigenous Affairs, and the Cornell Peru Project became a reality at Vicos on January 1, 1952.

Several months prior to assuming the responsibilities of the power role at Vicos, a plan of operations was drawn up which was focused on the promotion of human dignity rather than indignity and the formation of institutions at Vicos which would allow for a wide rather than a narrow shaping and sharing of values for all the participants in the social process. The principal goals of this plan thus became the devolution of power to the community, the production and broad sharing of greater wealth, the introduction and diffusion of new and modern skills, the promotion of health and well being, the enlargement of the status and role structure, and the formation of a modern system of enlightenment through schools and other media. It was hoped that by focusing on institutions specialized to these values as independent variables this would also have some modernizing effect on the more dependent variables, namely, the institutions specialized to affection (family and kinship) and rectitude (religion and ethics), which are sensitive areas of culture in which it is generally more hazardous to intervene directly.

In designing our program and a method of strategic intervention, we were very much aware of two, among many, guiding principles stemming from anthropological research: First, innovations are most likely to be accepted in those aspects of culture in which people themselves feel the greatest deprivations; and second, an integrated or contextual approach to value-institutional development is usually more lasting and less conflict-producing than a piecemeal one. Consequently, we established our operational priorities on the basis of the first principle but tried to optimize change in all areas at the same time, realizing, of course, that with scarce resources, all values could not be maximized concurrently. Perhaps, a few examples will best illustrate our use of the method of strategic intervention.

Our first entry into more than a research role at Vicos coincided with a failure of the potato harvest of both the *patron* and the serf community due to a blight which had attacked the crop. The poor of the community were literally starving, and even the rich were feeling the pinch. Complaints about the theft of animals and food were rife. At the same time, previous study of the manor had enlightened us about the major gripes of the serfs against the traditional system. These turned out not to be such things as the major commitment of each head of household to contribute one peon to the labor force for three days of each week, but the obligation of the Indian households to supply the extra, free services to the manor previously mentioned. Since we were in a position of power, it was relatively easy to abolish these services. A decision was made to do so, and volunteers were hired to perform these jobs for pay. Thus an immediate positive reinforcement was supplied to the community in our power relationship with it.

An added incentive to collaborate with the new administration resulted from the fact that we as *patrones* reimbursed the serfs for labor which they had performed under the previous administration but for which they had not been paid for approximately three years. Under the traditional system each peon was entitled to about three cents per week for the work performed under the labor tax. In some Peruvian manors this is paid in the form of coca leaves, which most adult males chew, but at Vicos it was supposed to have been paid in cash. By deducting the back pay from the cost of the transfer of the manor to our control, we fulfilled earlier commitments, with the money of the previous administration, and received the credit for it. Through such small but immediately reinforcing interventions, a solid base for positive relations with members of the community was first established. In this regard, of course, we were greatly aided by Dr. Vazquez, who had previously spent almost two years in the community, living with an Indian family, and who personally knew, and was trusted by almost every one of its members.

INCREASING AGRICULTURAL PRODUCTIVITY

As mentioned above, one of the most immediate and urgent tasks at Vicos was to do something about its failing economy which, in reality, meant increasing its agricultural productivity. Manors like Vicos are never productive because the renter during his period of tenure puts as little as possible into the operation and exploits the property for as much as he possibly can. The serfs, on the other hand, make no improvements on their lands, or other capital investments, because they, too, have no security of tenure. As a consequence, most such manors are in a very bad state of repair.

Since the Cornell Peru Project possessed funds only for research and not for capital development, the wealth base had to be enlarged by other capital means. It was decided, in consultation with Indian leaders, who were early informed about the goals of the Project, that no major changes would be initiated immediately in the day-to-day operations of the manor. We even retained the former Mestizo administrator, a close friend of the Project Director and Field Director, who agreed to reorient his goals to those of the Project.

The principal resources available to the Project were the labor of the Indian community and the lands which had been formerly farmed by the overlord. By employing this labor to farm these lands by modern methods (the introduction of fertilizer, good seed, pesticides, proper row spacing, etc.), and by growing marketable food crops, capital was accumulated for enlarging the wealth base. Returns from these lands, instead of being removed from the community, as was the case under the traditional system, were plowed back into the experiment to foment further progress towards our goals. Profits from the Project's share of the land were not only employed further to improve agricultural productivity but also to construct health and educational facilities, to develop a wider range of skills among the Indian population, and to reconstruct what had been a completely abandoned administrative center of operations. At the same time, new techniques of potato production and other food crops, first demonstrated on Project lands, were introduced to the Indian households which, within a couple of years, gave a sharp boost to the Indian economy. In short, by 1957 when Cornell's lease on the land expired, a fairly solid economic underpinning for the whole operation had been established, and the goal of considerably enlarging the wealth base had been accomplished.

Devolution of power

From the very first day of operations, we initiated the process of power devolution. It was decided that it would be impossible to work with the traditional *Varas* as a leadership group, because they were so occupied during their terms of office with religious matters that they would have no time to spend on secular affairs. On the other hand, the former straw bosses, all old and respected men, had had a great deal of direct experience in conducting the affairs of the manor for the *patron*. It was decided not to bypass this group even though we knew that its members had enjoyed the greatest indulgences under the traditional system and, being old, would be less likely to be innovative than younger men. Under prevailing conditions, however, this seemed to be the best alternative to pursue. As it turned out, it proved to be an effective transitional expedient. Gradually, as success was achieved in the economic field, it became possible to replace (by appointment) the retiring members of this body with younger men more committed to the goals of modernization. For instance, men finishing their military service, an obligation we encouraged them to fulfill, returned home with at least an exposure to other values and institutions in Peruvian society. In pre-Cornell days such returning veterans were forced back in the traditional mold within a few days time, with no opportunity to give expression to any newly found values they may have acquired. Insofar as possible, we tried to incorporate people of this kind into decision-making bodies and tried to provide them opportunities to practice whatever new skills they had acquired. In the first five years of the Project, not only did age composition of the governing body completely change, but decision-making and other skills had developed to a point where responsibility for running the affairs of the community was largely in indigenous hands. A complete transfer of power took place in 1957, when a council of 10 delegates, and an equal number of subdelegates, was elected to assume responsibility for community affairs. This council, elected annually, has performed this function ever since.

In the area of well-being it was much more difficult to devise a strategy of intervention that would show immediate and dramatic pay-off. This is a value area, to be sure, in which great deprivation was felt at Vicos, but it is also one in which the cooperation of all participants in the community was necessary in order to make any appreciable impact on it. The major well-being problems at Vicos, even today, stem from public health conditions. All individuals are deeply concerned about their personal well-being but are unwilling to forego other value indulgences to make this a reality for the community as a whole. Nor were the resources available to do so at the time the Project began.

A variety of attempts was made to tackle the most urgent health problems. In collaboration with the Peruvian Ministry of Health and Social Welfare, a mobile clinic was started at Vicos, which made at least one visit to the community each week. Support for this effort came from the community itself in the form of the construction of a small sanitary post at which the sick could be treated. It was hoped to staff this clinic through the Public Health services of Peru, but all attempts to do so were frustrated by lack of budget and responsibly trained personnel. In Peru, such services seldom extend into rural areas because the preferred values of the medical profession are, as almost everywhere, associated with city life. Consequently, no major public health effort was launched and the community's state of well-being has shown little net gain. What gains have been made stem principally from improved nutrition, but as enlightenment about the germ theory of disease diffuses and the results of modern medicine are clearly demonstrated, through the application of public health measures that take native beliefs into account, we expect a sharp rise in the well-being status of the community to follow.

Optimizing goals

Strategies for optimizing Project goals for the respect, affection, and rectitude values, first rested heavily on the examples set by Project personnel. From the very beginning, for example, an equality of salutation was introduced in all dealings with the Vicosinos; they were invited to sit down at the tables with us; there was no segregation allowed at public affairs; Project personnel lived in Indian houses. At the same time, we attempted to protect the constitutional rights of Vicosinos, which had been previously flagrantly violated by the Mestizo world. Abuses by Mestizo authorities and army recruiters were no longer tolerated. The draft status of all Vicosinos was regularized; they were encouraged to fulfill their legal obligations to the nation. While not directly intervening in the family, or tampering with religious practice, the indirect effect of optimizing other values on the respect position of the community soon became evident. As Vicosinos mastered modern techniques of potato production, for example, they were approached by their Mestizo compatriots in the surrounding area, seeking advice as to how to improve their crops.

Even the rectitude patterns at Vicos began to change. When we first took control of the manor, rates of theft were extremely high. Every peon farmer, as his crops were maturing, had to keep watchmen in his fields at night. As the Indian economy rose and starvation was eliminated, this practice disappeared completely. Even the parish priest became an enthusiastic supporter of the Project. His services were more in demand, to say nothing of their being much better paid.

A strategy of promoting enlightenment at Vicos was initiated through the adaptation of a traditional manor institution to goals and values of the Project. In most Andean manors run along the lines of Vicos, the peons, after completing their three days labor, must report to the manor house where they receive their work orders for the following week. This session of all peons, straw bosses, and the *patron* is known as the *mando*. We devised a strategy of meeting the day before the *mando* with the *mayorales* or decision-making body and utilizing the *mando* to communicate and discuss the decisions taken. Since heads of all households were present, the *mando* provided an excellent forum for the communication of news, the discussion of plans, progress towards goals, etc.

A long-run strategy of enlightenment rested on the founding of an educational institution at Vicos that could provide continuity for Project goals, training of leadership dedicated to the process of modernization, and the formation of a wide range of skills. Through collaboration with the Peruvian Ministry of Education and the Vicos community itself, this became a possibility. Within the period of Cornell's tenure, levels of enlightenment and skill rose sharply and their effects have been substantial throughout the society.

TRANSFER OF TITLE

In 1957, at the time Cornell's lease in Vicos expired, the Project made a recommendation to the Peruvian Government, through its Institute of Indigenous Affairs, to expropriate the property from the holders of the title, the Public Benefit Society of Huaraz, in favor of its indigenous inhabitants. By this time we felt that a fairly solid value institutional base, with the goals of modernization that we had originally formulated, had been established in the community. The Peruvian Government acted upon the recommendation and issued a decree of expropriation.

It was at this point that the experiment became especially significant, both in the local area and throughout the nation, for national development. Prior to this time, although considerable favorable national publicity had been given to the Project, little attention had been paid to it by the local power elite, except in terms of thinking that the benefits of the developments that had taken place would eventually revert to the title holders. It was inconceivable in the local area that such a property might be sold back to its indigenous inhabitants. Consequently, local power elites immediately threw every possible legal block in the way of the title reverting to the Indian community. They set a price on the property that would have been impossible for the Indian community ever to pay; members of the Project were charged with being agents of the communist world; the Vicosinos were accused of being pawns of American capitalism; Peruvian workers in the field were regarded as spies of the American government. Even such a "progressive" organization as the Rotary Club of Huaraz roundly denounced the Project, accusing its field director of being an agent of communism.

Fortunately, the Project had strong support in the intellectual community of the capital and among many of Peru's agencies of government. The codirector of the Project and President of the Indigenous Institute of Peru (also an internationally recognized scholar in high altitude biology), Dr. Carlos Monge M., was tireless in his effort to see justice done to the Vicosinos. But even his efforts did not bear fruit until almost five years had passed. The reason for this was that not only were the legal blocks of the resistance formidable, but the central government of Peru at this time was an elite government, which, while giving great lip service to the cause of the Vicosinos, was reluctant to take action in their favor. It is a matter of record that many high officials of government were themselves *hacendados*, hesitant to alter the status quo. Consequently, they were able to delay final settlement.

Meanwhile the Vicosinos, now renting the manor directly, were reluctant to develop Vicos because of the danger of their not being able to enjoy the fruits of their labor. While agricultural production rose through the stimulation of a loan from the Agricultural Bank of Peru, other capital investments were not made because of the fear that the price of the property would rise with every investment made. Finally, through pressure exerted by the President of the Institute of Indigenous Affairs and U.S. government officials in Peru, an agreement was reached between the Public Benefit Society and the Vicos community for the direct sale of the property to the Vicosinos at a price and on terms that they could realistically pay. Thus, after a five year wait following the devolution of power, the community actually became independent in July, 1962. Since that time Cornell has played largely a research, advisory, and consultant role, although the Peruvian National Plan of Integration of the Indigenous Populations has had an official government program of development at Vicos since Cornell relinquished control in 1957.

RESULTS

What can be said in a general way about results of the Vicos experience so far? In the first place, if one criterion of a modern democratic society is a parity of power and other values among individuals, then vast gains have been made at Vicos during the past decade. Starting from the base of a highly restrictive social system in which almost all power and other value positions were ascribed and very narrowly shared, the Vicosinos have gradually changed that social system for a much more open one in which all value positions can be more widely shared and they can be attained through achievement. This in itself is no mean accomplishment, particularly since it was done by peaceful and persuasive means.

In the second place, the position of the Vicos community itself, vis-a-vis the immediately surrounding area and the nation as a whole, has undergone a profound change. Starting at the bottom of the heap, and employing a strategy of wealth production for the market place and enlightenment for its people, the community of Vicos has climbed to a position of power and respect that can no longer be ignored by the Mestizo world. This is clearly indexed by the large number of equality relationships which now exist at Vicos (and in intercommunity relationships between Vicos and the world outside), where none existed before.

Finally, of what significance is Vicos in the context of national development? Peru is a country with a high degree of unevenness in its development. The highly productive agricultural coast, with off-shore fishing grounds that are among the richest in the world, is moving ahead at a modern and rapid pace. In contrast, the overpopulated sierra, containing major concentrations of indigenous populations, many of whom live under a medieval type agricultural organization, such as exists at Vicos, is lagging far behind. The major lesson of Vicos, for Peru as a whole, is that its serf and suppressed peasant populations, once freed and given encouragement, technical assistance and learning, can pull themselves up by their own bootstraps and become productive citizens of the nation. It is encouraging to see that the present Peruvian Government is taking steps in the right direction. Its programs of land reform and Cooperation Popular may go a long way towards a more peaceful and rapid development of the country as a whole.

REVIEW QUESTIONS

1. How was the Indian *hacienda* described in this article originally organized? Why did *hacienda* organization inhibit economic production and lead to low self-esteem among the Indians?

2. What were the goals of the Cornell Vicos Project? How were they implemented?

3. What obstacles did the Vicos Project face when it attempted to transfer the *hacienda's* title to its inhabitants? How were these obstacles overcome?

4. Many people have raised ethical questions about development projects like this. What do you think are some of the ethical questions concerning the anthropologist's actions in Vicos? How do you think Holmberg would defend the project?

To the Student:

To make *Conformity and Conflict* a better book in its next edition, we need to know what you think of the book as it is now. Please help us by filling out this questionnaire and returning it to: *Conformity and Conflict*, Little, Brown and Co., College Division, 34 Beacon Street, Boston, Mass. 02106.

School: _____ Course title: _____

Instructor's name: _____

Please give us your reactions to the selections:

		Keep	Drop	Didn't Read
1.	Spradley, Ethnography and culture	____	____	____
2.	Lee, Eating Christmas in the Kalahari	____	____	____
3.	Bohannan, Shakespeare in the bush	____	____	____
4.	Kurin, Acceptance in the field: Doctor, lawyer, Indian chief	____	____	____
5.	Spradley and Mann, The ethnography of speaking: How to ask for a drink at Brady's	____	____	____
6.	Hall and Hall, The sounds of silence	____	____	____
7.	Turner, Cosmetics: The language of bodily adornment	____	____	____
8.	Fernea and Fernea, Behind the veil	____	____	____
9.	Meigs, Blood kin and food kin	____	____	____
10.	Cohen, Marriage, alliance, and the incest taboo	____	____	____
11.	Scott, Sororities and the husband game	____	____	____
12.	Wolf, Uterine families and the women's community	____	____	____
13.	Friedl, Society and sex roles	____	____	____
14.	Stein, Male and female: The doctor-nurse game	____	____	____
15.	Gregor, Men's clubs: No girls allowed	____	____	____
16.	Benderly, Rape-free or rape-prone	____	____	____
17.	Lee, The hunters: Scarce resources in the Kalahari	____	____	____
18.	Harris, India's sacred cows	____	____	____
19.	Freed and Freed, Population control: One son is no sons	____	____	____

20. Bohannan, The impact of money on an African subsistence economy   _____ _____ _____
21. Liebow, Men and jobs   _____ _____ _____
22. Nietschmann, Subsistence and market: When the turtle collapses   _____ _____ _____
23. Spradley and McCurdy, Law and order   _____ _____ _____
24. Chagnon, Yanomamö: The fierce people   _____ _____ _____
25. Sahlins, Poor man, rich man, big-man, chief   _____ _____ _____
26. Weatherford, Big-men on capitol hill   _____ _____ _____
27. Newman, When technology fails: Magic and religion in New Guinea   _____ _____ _____
28. Gmelch, Baseball magic   _____ _____ _____
29. Warner, An American sacred ceremony   _____ _____ _____
30. Merrill, Religion and culture: God's saviours in the Sierra Madre   _____ _____ _____
31. Sharp, Steel axes for stone-age Australians   _____ _____ _____
32. Worsley, Cargo cults   _____ _____ _____
33. Weatherford, Cocaine and the economic deterioration of Bolivia   _____ _____ _____
34. Holmberg, Change and development in Vicos   _____ _____ _____

II. Was the general introduction (Chapter I) helpful? _____
How might it be improved?

_____

III. Were the chapter and article introductions helpful? _____
How might they be improved?

_____

IV. Please add any comments or suggestions. _____

_____

_____

_____

May we quote you in our promotional efforts for this book? __ Yes __ No

_____   _____

      Date   Signature

_____

                 Mailing address

LOOK FOR BARCODE
←——————————————